International Social Work

International Social Work

PROFESSIONAL ACTION IN AN INTERDEPENDENT WORLD

Lynne M. Healy

University of Connecticut School of Social Work

New York   Oxford

OXFORD UNIVERSITY PRESS

2001

Oxford University Press

Oxford   New York
Athens   Auckland   Bangkok   Bogotá   Buenos Aires   Calcutta
Cape Town   Chennai   Dar es Salaam   Delhi   Florence   Hong Kong   Istanbul
Karachi   Kuala Lumpur   Madrid   Melbourne   Mexico City   Mumbai
Nairobi   Paris   São Paulo   Shanghai   Singapore   Taipei   Tokyo   Toronto   Warsaw

and associated companies in
Berlin   Ibadan

Published by Oxford University Press, Inc.
198 Madison Avenue, New York, New York 10016
http://www.oup-usa.org

Library of Congress Cataloging-in-Publication Data
Healy, Lynne M.
      International social work : professional action in an interdependent world /
Lynne M. Healy.
         p.   cm.
      Includes bibliographical references and index.
      ISBN-13 978-0-19-512445-3; 978-0-19-512446-0 (pbk.)
      ISBN 0-19-512445-6; 0-19-512446-4 (pbk.)
         1. Social work—International cooperation.   2. Social workers—Vocational
guidance.   I. Title.
HV40.35 .H43 2001
361.3'2—dc21   00-058875

Printing (last digit): 9 8 7 6 5 4

Printed in the United States of America
on acid-free paper

Dedicated to my husband, Henry,
and son, Michael,
for their love and support

Contents

Foreword

In this impressive volume, Lynne Healy presents to all concerned with the well-being of the people of the world the challenge of global interdependence and how to meet it. Social workers, wherever they may be located, should benefit from its comprehensive coverage of international social work, but for the profession in the United States, it will have special value. Its publication could not have come at a better time.

For almost a century, social work in the United States has recorded an off and on engagement with international movements and professional activities. In the last years of the old century, after a long period of domestic preoccupation, the profession has begun to recognize the impact of globalization on almost every problem with which the profession is concerned. To such universal everyday problems affecting the status of women, aging populations, family breakdown, drug addiction, and child abuse and neglect, massive new problems have emerged. Explosions of civil strife and ethnic cleansing have focused attention on the children of war and intensified problems relating to refugees, resettlement, and immigration. The world-wide spread of AIDS has created a new category of abandoned and orphaned children. Problems such as these demand the attention of social work educators and practitioners, together with every professional group working toward their solution.

For social work, the place to start is in preparation for the profession. As Dr. Healy makes clear, it is hard to imagine a social work career in the 21st century that does not involve practice or problem situations with a global dimension. Students preparing for practice in the new century must acquire knowledge and understanding beyond what is currently required. Neglect of international content in the social work curriculum, at least in the United States, is perhaps due not so much to lack of interest on the part of faculty members, but rather to lack of knowledge, particularly knowledge drawn from firsthand experience in other lands. This has not always been the case. In fact, the importance of international communication is seen as far back as the early years of the 20th century when the first schools of social work made their appearance.

The historical record of the profession contains many descriptions of the way in which both the problems and remedial programs associated with poverty devised in Britain traveled across the Atlantic. Stephen Gurteen spent a summer in London observing the work of the Charity Organization

Society, adapted what he saw to the needs of Buffalo, New York, and founded a nationwide movement. Mary Richmond visited London and looked to Britain's friendly visiting for guidance on what became American social casework. After an eye-opening visit to Toynbee Hall in London, Jane Addams established Hull House in Chicago. Edith Abbott studied at the London School of Economics and, for decades, every issue of the *Social Service Review* contained significant material on social movements and professional developments in other countries.

Organizations, as well as individuals, fostered international exchange of ideas and experience. An International Conference of Charities, Correction and Philanthropy held in Chicago in 1893 at the time of the World's Fair brought together a goodly number of charity workers and philanthropists from a variety of countries to remodel charity work as scientific philanthropy. Although the need to replicate this gathering was often discussed in charity circles, it was not until 1928 that some 3,000 delegates from 42 countries met in Paris to search again for a new and improved approach to humanitarian work. It was at that meeting, under the leadership of Dr. René Sand of Belgium, that two significant nongovernmental organizations were founded: the International Conference of Social Work (later the International Council on Social Welfare) and the International Committee of Schools of Social Work (later International Association of Schools of Social Work). The attention paid to the enduring influence of pioneers like Dr. Sand and the international professional social work organizations on the development of international ties and cooperation is one of the most attractive features of this volume.

In the years between the two World Wars, serious involvement of American social work educators and practitioners in international activities practically disappeared. That changed dramatically with the outbreak of World War II. In 1945, Gordon Hamilton, better known in the United States and abroad as a theorist and teacher of casework, underlined the importance of a world view in social work education. She wrote: "An international or world view should be the natural heritage of students of social work . . . courses which promote international and interracial understanding are as significant for social welfare as those that teach standard of living, social security, personality, and family relationships" (Hamilton, 1945, pp. 142–143). She was not alone in the call for international involvement.

With the advent of the United Nations in 1945, the entire profession, as represented by the national employing agencies, the professional associations of social workers, and schools of social work, recognized the need for American social workers to contribute to humanitarian efforts to deal with the massive social problems caused by World War II and its aftermath. The time was ripe for an international awakening. Educational exchange and advisory services, originally authorized by the U.S. Congress in 1939 to foster good neighbor relations with Latin America, had already involved schools of social work and individual faculty members in consultation assignments and work with colleagues from other countries. Many educators and practitioners had also served in the relief and welfare activities of UNRRA, which operated in the war zones prior to the establishment of the United Nations. All the major voluntary social work organizations together with key governmental agencies came together to work with the United Nations and to promote continuing international cooperation in the field of social welfare through a permanent Committee on International Organization for Social Work. This Committee continued to operate for many years within the National Social Welfare Assembly.

The United Nations undoubtedly exerted the major energizing influence on social work to embrace international activities and was largely responsible for the rapid spread of programs of social work education throughout the developing world. The Social Commission, now the Commission for Social Development, assumed responsibility for the humanitarian programs of the League of Nations together with the relief and rehabilitation activities of UNRRA, which led to a strong emphasis on social welfare programs and services. American social workers, particularly social work educators, were much in demand both for assignments in other countries as consultants and as mentors to colleagues from abroad in social welfare exchange programs. Firsthand international experience inevitably influenced the educators in their teaching when they rejoined their schools of social work. At the same time, scores of social welfare personnel, in all categories from the highest government officials to the untrained aspiring social worker, flocked to the United States for programs of observation and professional education.

Whether from granting or receiving countries, social workers who were involved at the time in international or bilateral exchange programs and advisory services remember, with wistful appreciation, the exciting and rewarding experience of sharing with colleagues from around the world. And only those who participated perhaps understand the hunger expressed for American help in reconstructing social work education in the war-torn countries and in developing services and training of personnel in the new nations.

At a later date, the result of this intensive international involvement was excoriated as social work imperialism. Instances of inappropriate imposition of educational structures and content may indeed have existed, but again, this was probably due to insufficient knowledge of other cultures and their social and economic forces rather than a determined desire to propagate American casework. This book—especially Chapter 4 on the similarities and difference in social work in the various countries, Chapter 7 on values, and Chapter 12 on exchange and on concepts for universal social work—provides the necessary knowledge for productive collegial interaction in international work.

By the end of the 1960s, domestic problems in the United States had pretty much eliminated the flourishing internationalism of the immediate post-war period. Schools of social work were preoccupied with student unrest, faculty discontent, and minority concerns. A general malaise related to the Vietnam War together with spreading anti-American sentiments abroad also dampened desire for international involvement. With the end of the Cold War and the emergence of requests from Russia and other countries in Eastern Europe for help in establishing programs of professional education, the wheel turned again.

In this new century, it is increasingly evident, as noted by Dr. Healy in her preface, that the social problems and conditions arising out of global interdependence create for the social work profession significant areas of international responsibility and demands for expanded knowledge and competencies. This, combined with the far-reaching opportunities offered by the technological revolution, makes international involvement inevitable. To remain isolated from the reality of globalization is no longer a matter of choice. Commitment and dedicated efforts are required to address the problems caused or aggravated by the dark side of globalization and to capitalize on the new opportunities we have to attack the seemingly insoluble problem of worldwide poverty.

A ringing endorsement of this challenge to the social work profession permeated the program of a World Assembly of social work educators and practitioners held in Montreal, Canada, in the summer of 2000. Globalization, with all its promise and problems, occupied center stage. Stephen Lewis of UNICEF, in describing the tragic circumstances of victims of war, ethnic violence, poverty, and AIDS, eloquently proclaimed social work the profession most needed and best suited to provide humanitarian leadership and assistance. He declared: "The world is waiting for your voice" (Lewis, 2000).

Against that background, the publication of this thoroughly researched and scholarly presentation of international social welfare and social work in its every aspect—policy, practice, history, education, ethics and values—is an event to be celebrated. Over the past five years a considerable number of books have appeared on this subject. They have dealt with particular spheres of activity, including comparative social welfare policy, comparative treatments of the profession and its practice, social work education worldwide, and social development. What has been missing and sorely needed is a comprehensive overview of international social work. This book admirably fills that gap. It should become required reading in the United States and elsewhere for social work faculty and students, for educators and practitioners, and for all professions facing the challenge of how to make the world a better place as we move forward into the new millennium and the 21st century.

Katherine A. Kendall, Ph.D., ACSW
Honorary President, IASSW

Hamilton, G. (1945). Education for social work. In Rikurtz (Ed.), *Social Work Yearbook 1945* (pp 137–145). New York: Russell Sage Foundation.
Lewis, S. (2000). Opening Ceremonies Keynote Speech, presented at the Joint Conference of the International Federation of Social Workers and the International Association of Schools of Social Work, July 29, 2000, Montreal.

Preface

As the 21st century begins, the reality of global interdependence is widely appreciated. The profession of social work, having entered its second century as an organized profession, is now a global profession. Social work practice and policy are increasingly shaped by global phenomena, and there are many opportunities for social work to make an impact on the world scene. These are exciting times for international social work. Too often, however, the profession is impeded by the lack of a global perspective. Throughout my career, I have been puzzled by the extent to which the social work profession has allowed national borders to define its arenas of concern and action. I have written this book to encourage social workers to think beyond borders and to exercise professional responsibility and action in our interdependent world. The theme of professional action is central to the book. Social work is an applied profession that uses knowledge to effect change at levels ranging from individual to institutional or even societal. Therefore, a dynamic, action-oriented conceptualization of international social work is needed. Ideally, there should be no dichotomy between the domestic and the global, as interdependence is making such distinctions irrelevant. At present, however, separate attention is needed to increase awareness of the international dimensions of social work. I apologize for the extent to which my efforts may inadvertently aggravate the dichotomy rather than move toward a seamless view of a global social work reality.

Audience and Contents

This book is intended for all social workers who want to increase their knowledge of international dimensions of social work. Graduate and undergraduate students will gain a global view of their profession. Faculty who want to develop expertise in order to include international perspectives in their own teaching should find the book a useful foundation and a base for further explorations into more specialized areas of international social work. More and more practitioners are interested in international issues. Some are interested in practicing internationally; more, however, see opportunities for understanding the international dimensions of their own practice at home and for contributing a voice to policy processes that affect international populations and other countries. I hope this book will be useful to them in preparing for these important roles.

While it is assumed that the majority of readers will be in North America, the book is intended to be relevant in other countries as well. I have tried to maintain a balance between writing for a global audience and providing sufficient anchoring in the North American practice and policy context to strengthen global professional responsibility in the United States and Canada.

The aim of this book is to provide comprehensive treatment of international social work. In the first chapter, the concept of international social work is introduced and defined. The major themes of the book, global interdependence and international professional action, are outlined. The succeeding chapters cover the history of the profession of social work as it developed around the world; selected examples of social work contributions to international practice and policy; similarities and differences in the practice of social work in different countries today; treatment of global interdependence as it affects social work issues; descriptions of the major international organizations that do work related to social welfare; value and ethical considerations; international practice and international aspects of domestic social work practice; and policy influencing at the global level. The book concludes with a discussion of educational preparation for international social work and identification of themes and challenges for the future.

While the goal of the book is comprehensive treatment of international social work, comprehensiveness, of course, could not be fully achieved. It is certainly limited by the enormity of the topic. It was not possible to address the full range of global problems and issues of interest to social work. Thus some very important issues have received scant attention and others are omitted altogether. The hope is that readers will use the information provided as a base on which to build knowledge of additional topics of interest.

Use of Examples: Countries, Cases, and Pioneers

Examples from a sample of countries are used to illustrate the text. Geographic comprehensiveness was a major challenge and could not be achieved. In selecting countries for inclusion, a number of factors have been considered. An attempt has been made to include countries from each of the world's regions, with different traditions, religions, ethnic makeup, and different experiences with the introduction and development of social work. An important consideration, however, was the author's personal connection and familiarity with the countries selected. This allowed access to rich sources of information drawn from personal interviews and, in some instances, site visits, as well as published materials. The countries highlighted are Argentina, Armenia, Denmark, Jamaica, Japan, and Mauritius. In Chapter 4, these countries will be emphasized in the discussion of ways social work is practiced today, typical social work functions, the most important problems faced, and professional organizations and education. In Chapter 2, the founding of social work in most of these countries is explained. Later, in chapters on global interdependence, policy, and values, examples from them will be woven in as appropriate.

As needed, examples and material on countries other than those named above will be included. In the chapter on the history of social work, for example, adequate treatment requires discussion of the important roles of England, Germany, and the Netherlands. Material from India and Africa will be included in the discussion on values, as the topic has been extensively discussed in the social work literature emerging from these two areas. Considerable information is also included on the United States and Canada.

Case examples are used throughout the book to illustrate the content. Most have been contributed by practitioners. By design, the cases are not presented in a uniform format and vary considerably in length. I have preserved the style of the case contributor wherever possible. Chapters 2 and 3 on the history of social work internationally are further illustrated by brief biographies of people who have played important roles in international social work. Again, the eight pioneers presented were selected from many possible candidates. Their stories illustrate the history of social work from a more personal perspective.

Terms and Acronyms

International study includes numerous acronyms that may be confusing to the reader. In addition, terms are used that may not be familiar to some social workers. In the text, full names of organizations are used at the first mention followed by acronyms in parentheses. A glossary of acronyms and terms is included at the end of the book to aid the reader, especially if chapters are read out of sequence.

Acknowledgments

Many people have assisted in the research needed to develop this book. Lara Herscovitch, previously of Save the Children, authored Chapter 8 on international relief and development practice. Her practical experiences and intellectual understanding of development add an important dimension to the book.

Special thanks are owed Katherine Kendall for her ongoing practical assistance and for the inspiration she has provided to me since we met in 1982. She read and provided helpful suggestions for refining the manuscript. Werner Boehm at Rutgers and M. C. "Terry" Hokenstad of Case Western Reserve also provided encouragement and support for my explorations of international social work early in my academic career. As I collected information for the book, Mary Catherine Jennings was generous in sharing her experiences as a social welfare attaché. Friends and colleagues around the world have been of considerable assistance in providing information about social work in their countries. Although they are too numerous to mention, special thanks are sent to John Maxwell and Sybil Francis of Jamaica, Ruth Teubal of Argentina, Inger Hjerrild of Denmark, Satinder Ragobur of Mauritius, and the late Yoko Kojima of Japan. I also thank them for the hospitality they have provided on various visits. My colleagues at the University of Connecticut, Kasumi Hirayama and Nancy Humphreys, also shared information for the country studies.

Several colleagues and students assisted me by reading and commenting on sections of the book as I wrote. I especially want to thank Barbara Pine of the University of Connecticut and Lorrie Greenhouse Gardella of Saint Joseph College, who offered many useful suggestions. Students in Professor Gardella's senior seminar and students in my class on international issues at the University of Connecticut also read and commented on draft chapters. Two University of Connecticut social work graduates deserve special mention for providing case examples that enrich the book: David Bourns, now with Save the Children, and Vichhyka Ngy, director of Asian Family Services. Both are practicing international social work. Bethany Walcott, formerly a graduate student at the University of Connecticut, assisted with library research over a two-year period. In its final stage, Frank Raymond of the University of South Carolina reviewed the manuscript and provided not only a useful critique, but also assisted me in improving the commentaries on technology.

Invaluable secretarial support has been given by Pam Harrison and Virginia Starkie. They were always there when I needed them. Pam's computer skills, talent for design, expert typing, and dedication are deeply appreciated. Frank Reeves provided expert help with diagram design and photo production. Jan Lambert, social work librarian at the Harleigh Trecker Library, assisted with reference queries and tracked down important fugitive materials. I also thank the University of Connecticut School of Social Work for its growing commitment to international social work. The school has provided opportunities for me to expand my understanding of this area through teaching and through fostering links with the University of the West Indies, the University of Mauritius, the School of Social Work in Esbjerg, Denmark, and Yerevan State University in Armenia.

Finally, I want to thank Oxford University Press and its editors for their interest in this book. Jeffrey Broesche has been a helpful and responsive editor whenever I needed assistance.

International Social Work

CHAPTER 1

INTERNATIONAL SOCIAL WORK

Why Is It Important and What Is It?

> I imagine centuries in which in the higher minds in the States a no-
> ble sense of world duty, a world consciousness, will struggle with
> mass mentality and gradually pervade it.
>
> JANE ADDAMS, 1930, P. 8, QUOTING GEORGE RUSSELL

Social workers around the world have numerous opportunities for international action:

- a social worker administering a shelter for battered women in Massachusetts is asked to admit an undocumented immigrant from El Salvador
whose husband has threatened to kill her

- social workers from Mexico and Texas meet to work out policies to deal
with parents who move their children back and forth across the border to
evade child abuse and neglect investigations

- a social worker serving in the Peace Corps helps a community in Equa-
torial Guinea determine its priorities for involvement in a rural health
project

- members of the International Federation of Social Workers (IFSW) write
letters to their governments and to Amnesty International and the United
Nations (UN) to protest jailing of their colleagues in Chile

- institutional social workers and social pedagogues from Denmark and
Germany introduce child-care institutions in New York to a professional
model of child care

- social workers in Jamaica organize a coalition on the Rights of the Child
and prepare an alternative report on their country's progress to submit to
the UN Center for Human Rights in Geneva

In each brief vignette above, social workers, individually or through their
agencies and organizations, have engaged in international action, action that
requires knowledge about international relations, about the realities of other
nations, and about the profession of social work as it is practiced throughout the world. The range of action is broad—from full-time professional over-

seas practice to domestic practice in which an occasional case with international dimensions is encountered. Still other actions call on the advocacy responsibilities of the profession and its members and are often carried out in addition to regular employment duties.

This book is based on a number of assumptions about the importance of international learning in social work and about the nature of the social work environment. Global interdependence has grown enormously over the past several decades to the point that its general acceptance has become almost a cliché. But in spite of Jane Addams's early embrace of global-mindedness (as shown by her selection of the quotation above and the subtitle for her autobiographical book, *Growing World Consciousness*) social work has not fully recognized the extent to which its practice and professional environment are shaped by interdependence, nor has the profession seized available opportunities for increasing its impact internationally. This text will provide knowledge of the international dimension of social work—both to strengthen the ability of social workers to contribute to and benefit from international developments in the profession and to improve social workers' competence in their everyday practice in the context of global interdependence. Global interdependence, therefore, is an overarching theme in the pages that follow.

Another theme is international professional action. Considerable emphasis is put on the responsibilities of the social work profession as a whole and of individual social workers for action related to international social problems and practice challenges. For many this is a new idea. What is meant by international responsibilities is explained briefly below and in depth in the chapters that follow.

GLOBAL INTERDEPENDENCE:
WHY INTERNATIONAL SOCIAL WORK?

As expressed by Walter Lorenz (1997), " 'Going beyond the national level' in social work cannot be the personal hobby of a few specialists who are dealing with migrant and refugee groups or with ethnic minorities . . . or of a few idealists who want to promote international exchanges to widen their horizon and to learn more about methods and practices in other countries. On the contrary, all social work is enmeshed in global processes of change" (p. 2). Global interdependence has created significant areas of international responsibility as well as new opportunities for social work impact by reshaping the social work environment in four important ways.

1. International social forces and events, most dramatically the movement of populations, have changed the makeup of social agency caseloads and affected domestic practice in many countries, including the United States. Competent social work practice in most countries now demands new

knowledge and competencies to cope with the social problems and conditions emerging from interdependence.

2. Social problems are now shared by both more and less economically developed countries far more often than in previous decades, making mutual work and exchange more desirable. Increasingly, it is as likely that practice innovations and potential problem solutions will be generated in places previously labeled less developed, as in the industrialized nations. This aspect of interdependence has led to a growing shared agenda for social work action. Most nations are currently struggling with homelessness and street children, growing numbers of aged, changes in family patterns leading to less available family care, unemployment and underemployment, and many other social problems.

3. The actions of one country—politically, economically, and socially—now directly and indirectly affect other countries' social and economic well-being and the overall social health of the planet. As President Clinton (1993) noted in his first inaugural address, it is difficult to identify a purely domestic problem: "There is no longer a clear division between what is foreign and what is domestic. The world economy, the world environment, the world AIDS crisis, the world arms race—they affect us all" (p. A15). Thus nations increasingly share social problems, and the actions that any nation takes can directly affect the well-being of the population of other nations. The nuclear accident at Chernobyl in the Ukraine in 1986, which spread radioactive material over much of Europe, was a dramatic, but by no means isolated, example of this fact. Logically, then, no single nation or the professional groups within it can solve these problems by acting alone.

4. Finally, there are enhanced opportunities for international sharing and exchanging made possible by rapidly advancing technological developments in areas such as communications. Computer and video linkages, for example, have dramatically changed global communications (Asamoah, Healy, & Mayadas, 1997). The dimensions of global interdependence will be explored in more depth in Chapter 5.

Appropriate goals for the social work profession and individual social workers across the globe grow out of these trends. Thus it is important that social workers be prepared to (a) address internationally related case and community problems that arise in their domestic practice, (b) contribute to mutual problem solving on global social problems, and (c) monitor the impact of their own nation's policies on other countries' and peoples' well-being. In addition, they need to develop the capacity to benefit from and contribute to international dialogue and exchange to support the achievement of the three main goals cited above (Asamoah et al., 1997). Each of these goals moves beyond awareness to professional action—professional action that will require new knowledge and attitudes.

What Every Social Worker Needs to Know

Awareness may well be the starting point for international action. Noted experts in the field of higher education have long argued that a general worldview achieved through education in the history, literature, art, religions, and cultures of the world is an essential part of being an "educated person." Successive reform efforts in higher education in the United States have sought to ensure that students receive some baseline level of world knowledge. Recognizing serious gaps in graduates' knowledge of the world, many colleges and universities have adopted requirements that students in the United States take at least one course in "non-Western" studies. In spite of these efforts, education for global awareness seems to have been less successful in the United States than in many other countries. A recent study of university professors in 14 countries (England, Russia, Germany, Japan, South Korea, Chile, Israel, Australia, Brazil, Mexico, Sweden, Hong Kong, the Netherlands, and the United States) found that "with the exception of the United States, international mindedness in the surveyed countries is quite high" (Lewis & Altbach, 1996, p. 33). More than 90% of American professors surveyed expressed no need to read books or journals published outside their own country in order to keep up in their fields—a quite astounding finding of disinterest in their professions beyond national borders, and possibly indicative of ethnocentrism.

Social work is an applied profession, and the emphasis of its baccalaureate- and master-level educational programs is on preparing students for effective practice. For this reason, the majority of social work students, practitioners, and faculty do not define acquisition of a worldview as a priority educational outcome. While it is hoped that students and practitioners will in fact gain a worldview from reading this book, its emphasis will be on the international knowledge that is specifically focused on social work and that prepares the reader for professional action. Readers will gain the following essential professional knowledge from the chapters that follow:

- familiarity with the history, scope, and functions of social work around the world, including a discussion of its similarities and differences
- knowledge of ways the profession is organized for international action through the major professional organizations
- knowledge of the major agencies involved in international social work and social welfare and their functions, including the social welfare responsibilities of the UN
- awareness of practice roles and opportunities for social work in international relief and development
- awareness of aspects of global interdependence that affect domestic social welfare issues and related knowledge to improve international aspects of domestic social work practice
- knowledge of the role of the UN in setting standards for international social welfare policy

- awareness of the impact of national policies on social welfare conditions in other countries and the reciprocal impact of other countries' policies
- appreciation of the international aspects of cultural diversity to facilitate enhanced service to international populations
- knowledge of the major sources of global and cross-national data on social work
- examination of value dilemmas in international work

Throughout the book, applicability of these knowledge areas to practice and other forms of professional action will be discussed.

WHAT IS INTERNATIONAL SOCIAL WORK?

The definition of the term *international social work* has been the subject of much debate. First, there may be confusion over the use of the terms *international, global,* and *cross-national.* Beginning with the *Random House Webster's College Dictionary* (1995) definitions, global means pertaining to or involving the whole world, while international can mean any of the following: between or among two or more nations, of or pertaining to two or more nations or their citizens, pertaining to the relations between nations, having members or activities in several nations, or transcending national boundaries or viewpoints. Stein (1990) agrees with this distinction, noting that while the terms are often used interchangeably, the more technical usage of global "signified phenomena affecting the entire planet" (p. 13). Cross-national, too, is sometimes used interchangeably with international. When it is differentiated, cross-national has a more limited meaning and is used to apply to comparisons or transactions of or between several or a limited number of nations (Estes, 1984).

Beyond these simple definitions, international social work remains a complex concept, actually comprised of a number of component concepts. It is used to refer to comparative social welfare, international practice, cross-cultural knowledge and understanding, intergovernmental work on social welfare, concern and action on global social problems, a worldwide collegiality among social workers, professional exchange activities, and a general worldview. At least one author has argued that the concept is so complex and amorphous that there may be no such thing as international social work (Akimoto, 1995). Is he correct? Or is international social work any one of the above-listed concepts, a combination of several, or perhaps an umbrella concept that can encompass all these ideas?

Evolution of the Concept

In 1956, the Council on Social Work Education (CSWE) in the United States formed a working committee to develop a definition of international social work. Committee members wrestled with the question of narrow versus

broad interpretation and examined at least six different usages of the term
international social work, "ranging from social workers working in other
countries to refugee services to common professional concerns with social
workers in other parts of the world" (Healy, 1995, p. 423). The committee
opted for a narrow definition, thus ruling out most of the aspects of international work noted above.

> It was the consensus of our sub-committee that the term 'international social
> work' should properly be confined to programs of social work of international
> scope, such as those carried on by intergovernmental agencies, chiefly those of
> the U.N.; governmental; or non-governmental agencies with international pro-
> grams. (Stein, 1957, p. 3)

Others, both earlier and more recently, have favored a broad definition.
Kimberly (1984) argued that international social work, as a relatively new
field, should be left open for broad interpretation rather than prematurely
limiting its scope. Sanders and Pederson (1984), too, used a broad definition:
"International social work means those social work activities and concerns
that transcend national and cultural boundaries" (p. xiv).

Many recent writers have assumed that international social work is a
new term and have neglected historical sources. In fact, in a paper delivered
at the First International Conference of Social Work in 1928, Jebb (1929), from
London, used the term and discussed the conditions needed for such work
to be practical. Articles entitled "International Social Work" appeared in the
Social Work Yearbook beginning in 1937. Selecting a broad view of the international field, Warren defined international social work as follows in his 1939
article in the *Social Work Yearbook*:

> International Social Work includes four main types of activities: a) international
> social case work; b) international assistance, public and private, to disaster or
> war sufferers and distressed minority groups; c) international conferences on so-
> cial work; and d) international cooperation by governments and private bodies
> through the medium of the League of Nations, the International Labour Orga-
> nization and the Health Organization of the League, in combatting disease and
> securing social and political peace and harmony throughout the world. (p. 192)

It is interesting to note that this early definition includes the exchanges of
ideas by social workers at international meetings as well as intercountry
work, intergovernmental work, and relief work.

International social case work was defined in the same article as "the application of case work methods to the problems of families and individuals
whose social adjustments require cooperative action in two or more countries" (Warren, 1939, p. 192).

In a survey of member schools of the International Association of Schools
of Social Work (IASSW) in 1989/90, educators were asked to identify the
component concepts they considered essential to the definition of international social work. Respondents from over 200 member schools from all five
regions of the world (Africa, Asia and the Pacific, Europe, North America,

and Latin America) selected the following concepts as essential, in descending order: cross-cultural understanding, comparative social policy, concern with global problems, a general worldview, knowledge of a common profession worldwide, international practice, intergovernmental social welfare, and a sense of collegiality with social workers in other countries (Healy, 1990). The number of educators selecting the concepts ranged from a high of 59% identifying cross-cultural understanding as key to only 15% selecting a sense of worldwide professional collegiality. This indicates that no concept was viewed as essential by all.

Akimoto (1995) raises challenging questions about the concept of international social work. Because most definitions of international social work include a social worker working in another country or a social work researcher collecting data in another country, he asks whether it is appropriate to call it domestic social work if a Japanese person does something in Japan while labeling the same activity international social work if it is performed in Japan by a Kenyan or an American. At the end of the book, an answer to this question will be attempted, although the issues raised by Akimoto remain thorny ones for those concerned with definition.

What is clear from a review of both recent and historical literature and research is that the concept of international social work is complex and can be defined either narrowly or broadly. It is not a new idea, having been explored in some detail for at least 60 years, yet it remains open to further work and interpretation.

Author's Definition of International Social Work

In this book, international social work is defined as international professional action and the capacity for international action by the social work profession and its members. International action has four dimensions: internationally related domestic practice and advocacy, professional exchange, international practice, and international policy development and advocacy. Each is explained below and illustrated in an accompanying case example.

Internationally Related Domestic Practice and Advocacy. The first dimension is social work competence in internationally related aspects of domestic social work practice and professional advocacy. Social workers are increasingly called on to deal with problems that have an international dimension, meaning that two or more countries are involved in some way in the case or policy issue. There are many examples of internationally related domestic practice problems, including refugee resettlement, work with other international populations, international adoption work, and social work in border areas. Although some social workers specialize in these areas, all social workers may encounter international issues in carrying out their professional responsibilities.

Case 1.1 shows an example of internationally related domestic practice. The vignette describes the adjustment issues faced by adolescent immigrants

CASE 1.1: WORKING WITH INTERNATIONAL POPULATIONS

Internationally related cases may occur in any social worker's caseload. The following example relates the comments shared in group sessions by adolescents in the Toronto school system. The teenagers involved had recently migrated to Canada from Jamaica after years of separation from their mothers, who had migrated earlier. The comments suggest the adjustment difficulties faced by these teens and their parents and the special challenges for the social workers who are attempting to help them.

Teen 1 recounts:

> My mom told me that I messed up her whole life since I came to Canada—that her husband left her, that she never has money anymore and that I eat out all her food. She went so far as to call me a fat, black, lazy-ass, good for nothing kid and threatened to send me back home. (Glasgow & Gouse-Sheese, 1995, p. 14)

Another student relayed:

> The first day after arriving in Canada I got into a big fight with my mother. I left all my clothes back home. I pictured things were cheap in Canada and my room was full of new clothes, the kind I really wanted. But, I was wrong! My mother got mad at me. She cuss and swore at me. She asked if I think money grew on trees. I wanted to say "yes" but I did not. I wondered what happened to the nice mother I met back home. From since then things got bad between us. (Glasgow & Gouse-Sheese, 1995, p. 10)

Other teens in the group told of conflicts with new stepparents and siblings they had never met, of feeling strange around their mothers because they had spent very little time with them, and of missing their caretakers in Jamaica. The social workers decided to involve these teens in a support and discussion group. The choice of intervention was important for several reasons. First, West Indians tend to be suspicious of therapeutic services and would not be likely to use individual counseling. More importantly, each of the teens felt isolated. Each entered the group feeling that he or she was the only one experiencing these problems. Thus, the groupwork approach reduced the teens' isolation, provided a safe place for them to vent—a behavior not condoned at home, and provided an avenue for facilitated problem solving through the group and its leaders.

from Jamaica as expressed to their school social worker, a group worker for the Toronto Board of Education.

In order to assist these students—who could be encountered in Miami, Florida; Hartford, Connecticut; London, England; or many other places—the social worker needs knowledge about life in Jamaica, Jamaican family patterns and parenting styles, and the migration experience of Jamaican parents and children. In such circumstances, international knowledge is necessary to provide competent social work services to cases in the domestic caseload.

A related "domestic" professional responsibility requires the capacity and willingness of the profession to develop and promulgate positions on social aspects of their own country's foreign policy and aspects of national policy that affect peoples in other countries, such as legislation on immigration. It is logical that as part of accepted advocacy responsibilities of the profession, social workers have an obligation to monitor such legislation as it is being proposed, to follow impending votes at the UN and foreign policy directives and to ensure that social work's voice is heard on relevant issues. Case 1.2 discusses an example of advocacy following World War II.

Case 1.2 demonstrates that the social workers who attended the 1947 delegate meeting of their professional organization engaged in discussions of important international issues of their day. They were sufficiently educated on the issues and on their potential impact to take a policy position for the profession and to advocate for their position with national decision makers.

Professional Exchange. The second dimension of international action is the capacity to exchange social work information and experiences internationally and to use the knowledge and experience to improve social work practice and social welfare policy at home. This includes a range of actions, such as reading foreign periodicals and books in one's field, corresponding with professionals in other countries or hosting visitors, participating in professional interchange at international meetings, and identifying and adapting social welfare innovations in other countries to one's own setting. Increasingly, professional exchange is facilitated by technological advances in computer-assisted communications and teleconferencing.

Case 1.3 describes borrowing and adapting an innovation to address extreme poverty: the well-known Grameen Bank concept.

The ability to transfer international human service innovations to one's own setting first requires knowledge of social welfare developments in other countries. Successful transfer also requires sophisticated understanding of the similarities and differences between the "exporting" and "importing" countries in order to determine needed adaptations. Indeed, "borrowers" of the Grameen concept in the United States and other industrialized countries realized that among the conditions making microlending successful in Bangladesh were "unregulated market conditions that thrive on low-skilled enterprises; absence of income maintenance programs; availability of free health care; and a lower cost of living" (Banerjee, 1998, p. 79). But other cultural and structural differences favored successful adaptation such as the relatively better social position for women and acceptance of their free movement in society. Increasingly, potential innovations can be found in industrialized and developing countries alike, making knowledge of other systems more valuable for its potential for domestic applicability.

CASE 1.2: INFLUENCING FOREIGN SOCIAL POLICY

In 1947, a number of important policy issues before the U.S. Congress were matters concerned with international social welfare. One of the most urgent was a requested appropriation for continued postwar relief. Others included matters relating to immigration—especially the relaxation of U.S. immigration limits to permit resettlement of displaced persons—and to U.S participation in the emerging international organizations being organized under the UN umbrella.

The pending appropriations bill was to approve $350 million for relief to Austria, Greece, Hungary, Italy, Poland, and China. The issue was brought to the 1947 Delegate Conference of the American Association of Social Workers (AASW), one of the predecessor organizations to the National Association of Social Workers (NASW). The delegates passed a resolution urging Congress to appropriate the money at once in order to continue to provide basic supplies of food, clothing, shelter, and medicines to Europe and China. The resolution continued:

> Be it further resolved that this and any other funds appropriated be made available to countries in proportion to their need as appraised by competent international instrumentalities such as the Technical Committee of the United Nations, and regardless of political or other considerations. (American Association of Social Workers, 1947)

The resolution indicates that social workers in 1947 advocated sound principles for foreign aid. They were concerned that need take precedence over politics and that aid be fairly distributed. "This government should spare no effort to assure fair and non-discriminatory administration not only between groups within a given country but also between one country and another" (Howard, 1947, p. 5). They also recognized the advantages of multilateral aid rather than aid given specifically from one country to another: "The U.S. government . . . should do all in its power to strengthen and make more effective all international agencies responsible for social welfare services, thus speeding the day when unilateral approaches to world needs may be abandoned in favor of world cooperation" (Howard, 1947, p.4).

The AASW resolution was sent to the secretary of state, the chair of the Foreign Relations Committee of the Senate, and the chair of the Foreign Affairs Committee of the House of Representatives.

International Practice. The third dimension of international action is the preparation of some professional social workers to contribute directly to international development work through employment or volunteer work in international development agencies. Success in this sphere depends on the extent to which international knowledge can be blended with social work

CASE 1.3: INTERNATIONAL EXCHANGE AND BORROWING

International exchange among social workers can yield many benefits. Perhaps the highest order of exchange is what is called *international technology transfer,* the identification, adaptation, and transplantation of innovations from one country to another. This case discusses transfer of innovations in microlending from Bangladesh to the United States.

Case

The Grameen Bank is world renowned for its success in encouraging small enterprise development among impoverished and powerless women in Bangladesh. Founded in 1976, the Grameen Bank introduced a "peer-lending banking approach geared to improving the human rights of mainly poor women" (Jansen & Pippard, 1998, p. 104). Through provision of very small loans without collateral and through collective "savings clubs," poor women have been able to start small businesses, gain at least minimal financial security, and, as a result, improve their status in the community.

The impact has been widespread. As Banerjee (1998) notes: "The Grameen Bank's phenomenal success with micro-lending . . . reverberates throughout much of the globe" (p. 64). A number of microenterprise projects for the poor in the United States are now being introduced using the Grameen model. Although controversial among U.S. social workers, many of whom object to encouraging people living below the poverty level to save some of their meager grants, the adaptation of an international innovation is yielding some promising results. Jansen and Pippard (1998) mention two such projects: the Women's Self Employment Project, "Full Circle Fund," in urban Chicago and the "Good Faith Fund" in rural Pine Bluff, Arkansas. Evaluations of the U.S. efforts show "not only is economic success evident but studies indicate women gained a sense of autonomy, as well as improved family relationships as part of these economic opportunities, findings not unlike those documented about women participants of the Grameen Bank" (Jansen & Pippard, 1998, p. 118).

skills. Case 1.4 briefly describes an intervention designed and carried out by an interdisciplinary team at a nongovernmental development agency with several social workers as members. The social workers in this case used their knowledge of human behavior, skill in community organizing, and practice skills in planning, management, and evaluation to contribute to the development project in war-torn Bosnia.

Thus social workers in international relief and development work utilize many of the skills learned in their professional training. They combine these with a commitment to development, knowledge of the international

CASE 1.4: INTERNATIONAL DEVELOPMENT PRACTICE WITH CHILDREN IN ESPECIALLY DIFFICULT CIRCUMSTANCES
David Bourns, 1999

An emergency education program initiated in the then war-torn country of Bosnia demonstrates the usefulness of social work skills in overseas work with international relief and development organizations. This program sought to provide support to preschool-age children who had been exposed to the violence of war and to begin to normalize their chaotic existence amid the destruction. The program, a neighborhood preschool, needed to meet local educational standards but also had to address the specific needs of war-affected children. Many skills were demanded of the international staff working on the program. They worked closely with Bosnian educators, establishing constructive cross-cultural communication in order to develop a mutually acceptable curriculum. The staff's experience with abused and traumatized children and knowledge of child development were essential to program success. Although individual counseling could not be provided within the scope of the project, staff did refer children in need of special services wherever possible.

Community involvement was key to ensuring that the program could be sustained. A safe structure had to be located, and community members had to be mobilized to help clean war debris from bombed-out buildings. Teachers had to be identified among the local population; if trained teachers were not available, then other adults who were willing to volunteer and be trained had to be found. Motivating people suffering from the effects of a protracted conflict required solid community organizing skills. The task of the international staff, as in most development projects, was to help build local capacity, not to do the job. There were also many administrative and logistical support tasks. From the delivery of material supplies to the monitoring of project funding in each location and to enhancing and monitoring the personal security of all staff working in the field, constant vigilance of well-designed administrative systems meant the difference not only between success and failure but between life and death.

context, and well-honed sensitivity and communication skills for cross-cultural work.

International Policy Development and Advocacy. Finally, the capacity of the social work profession as a worldwide movement to formulate and promulgate positions on important social issues and make a contribution to the resolution of important global problems related to its sphere of expertise is the fourth component of international professional action. Case 1.5 describes an educational activity carried out by a group under the auspices of the

CASE 1.5: INFLUENCING POLICY THROUGH DIALOGUE

Through the IASSW, social workers organized a symposium on violence against women for the nongovernmental organization (NGO) forum held in conjunction with the UN Fourth World Conference on Women held in Beijing, China, in 1995. Building on an area of social work expertise, a 4-hour workshop was organized to share knowledge about domestic violence and, more importantly, to develop action strategies for antiviolence work in participants' home settings. Social workers from 27 nations heard panel presentations and joined working discussion groups. The participants developed and adopted a resolution for presentation to the official UN delegates conference the next day. This resolution, offered by IASSW through its consultative status with the UN, contained 10 recommendations for reducing gender-based violence and enhancing personal, social, and economic development (Wetzel, 1995).

This venture incorporated key elements of mutual work on policy development. Social workers from many nations met, exchanged information, and worked together to develop policy recommendations on a key world social problem. Then they used mechanisms available through an established social work professional organization to advance the recommendations to the relevant UN policy body. While social workers have participated in other UN meetings, it was noted that this may have been the first organized social work presence at a UN conference on women.

IASSW at the UN Conference on Women in Beijing, China, in 1995. The goal of the educational effort was to influence UN policy deliberations.

This effort required more than knowledge of domestic violence in each organizer's country. Knowledge about women's status around the world, about political constraints in various countries that make some types of social action impossible, and skill in cross-cultural communication were necessary. Real change and action on global problems are possible when professionals engage in mutual work across national and cultural boundaries.

To summarize, the definition of international social work to be used in this book encompasses four areas for action: internationally informed domestic practice and related policy advocacy, participation in and utilization of international exchange, international practice, and international policy formulation and advocacy. The first two potentially involve all social workers; the third, will involve only a small percentage; and the fourth, while involving all social workers indirectly as part of the profession, may directly involve relatively few. This four-pronged definition will serve as the theme for the book—international action for the profession—along with global interdependence, which makes it timely.

TERMINOLOGY

Terminology in international social work can be confusing and, at times, controversial. Throughout the more than 40 years of the development movement, terms used to classify nations have changed several times, and there is still no agreement on optimal terms.

The terms *first world, second world,* and *third world* were common descriptors in the 1960s. Describing the mostly Western industrialized nations; the Soviet Union and its satellite nations; and the newly independent and nonaligned nations of Asia, Africa, and Latin America; respectively, these terms had some relevance during the cold war era. The term third world increasingly was viewed as a negative term, implying to some the idea of third rate or last in consideration; the actual derivation of the term is from a phrase describing the Third Estate in the French Revolution.

Developed and *developing* are the most commonly used replacement terms for first and third world, respectively. The labels *North* and *South* are also used. These terms refer loosely to geography, as generally more of the developed nations are in the Northern Hemisphere and more of the developing nations are in the Southern Hemisphere. Where used, North and South should be viewed more as political terms than geographic ones; Australia, for example, is in the North.

In this book, I will use the UN Development Program (UNDP) and UNICEF terms *industrialized* and *developing* to refer to nations where broad classifications are needed. This choice has been made for several reasons. The use of industrialized improves on developed-developing by avoiding the implication that the development process has been completed in some nations. North and South will not be used because the terms may be confusing to readers. Most importantly, using terms currently accepted by UNDP and UNICEF is in harmony with one of the purposes of the book, which is to introduce social workers to the international arena, including the work of major global organizations.

COUNTRIES SELECTED AS SPECIAL EXAMPLES FOR THE TEXT

Studying international social work requires examination of individual countries as well as the global picture. Although the book will refer to many different countries, in addition to the United States, six have been selected for special purposes of comparison: Argentina, Armenia, Denmark, Jamaica, Japan, and Mauritius. As explained in the preface, the countries were selected both for their diversity and because the author had access to needed data. These countries' experiences in social work will be discussed in the first section of the book to aid the reader's understanding of international social work.

The countries selected vary along many dimensions, including factors related to their state of development and their experiences in the establishment and current status of the social work profession. Table 1.1 compares the countries on a number of dimensions. Readers are encouraged to refer to the table periodically to relate social work comparisons to levels of human well-being and population characteristics of the example countries.

One way of comparing countries is to use rankings of well-being developed by the international intergovernmental agencies of the UN or the World Bank. For example, the countries selected range in their rank (of 174 countries) on the UNDP's Human Development Index (HDI)—an index of progress on human well-being—from a high of 3rd for Japan and 4th for the United States to 84th for Jamaica and 99th for Armenia (UNDP, 1998). None of the countries chosen, however, falls into the low human development group—the 48 countries with the worst performance on adult literacy, life expectancy, and per capita gross national product (GNP), which are the components of the HDI. UNICEF ranks countries by the under-5 (U-5) mortality, selecting this as a single measure of a country's progress in meeting the needs of children for survival and development. On this measure, the United States ranks 26th, with a U-5 mortality rate of 10, well behind Japan (5th) and Denmark (6th). Sweden and Finland lead all nations with a rate of 5 per 1,000. On this measure, Jamaica does almost as well as the United States, ranking 30th with its rate of 13 (UNICEF, 1997).

Population statistics give only a limited picture of national differences. National aggregate data are limited by being just that, national aggregates. They fail to express the range of experiences within a country and cannot capture important dimensions of culture and history. Within-country differences among the population in levels of well-being can be great. Denmark is characterized by fairly equitable distribution of social benefits, and only a small percentage of the population lives in poverty. In the United States, income disparity is great, as it is in Jamaica and Argentina. Thus while overall levels of health and educational attainment may be satisfactory, sectors of the population live in severe poverty.

The countries selected represent many geographic regions—Asia, South America, Africa, the Caribbean, and Europe. Each has had a unique history, which has shaped its national culture and population, including experiences with colonization, mass immigration, and struggles for independence. Jamaica was colonized by Great Britain and experienced many years of slavery and colonial rule prior to the independence movement that was finally successful in 1962. Argentina was colonized by Spain, with near annihilation of the indigenous population; independence was secured in 1816, only a generation after the United States' war for independence. Mauritius was colonized first by the French and then by the British and experienced the importation and enslavement of Africans followed by the slavery-like period of indentured servitude of peoples from India. As a result, Mauritius is a highly diverse society, ethnically, religiously, and linguistically, and diversity is a major policy issue. The United States, having experienced many

TABLE 1.1

	Population (in Millions) UNDP 1988	GNP per Capita UNICEF 1997	Infant Mortality	Under 5 Mortality	Life Expectancy	% Population over 65	% Population Under 15	% Living in Poverty UNDP 1998	Human Development Index rank	Date of National Independence	Date of 1st Social Work	S.W. Professional Organization
Argentina	34.8	$8,110	24	27	73	9.0%	31.0%	26.0%	36	1816	1936	Association of Social Workers
Armenia	3.6	$680	26	31	73	7.1%	26.4%	N/A	99	1991	1990	Armenian National Association of the Social Services, Social Work Section 1998
Denmark	5.2	$27,970	6	7	76	15.2%	17.0%	8.0%	18	N/A	1937	Association of Social Workers
Jamaica	2.5	$1,540	11	13	74	7.0%	34.0%	32.0%	84	1962	1961	Jamaica Association of Social Workers
Japan	125.1	$34,630	4	6	80	13.7%	16.0%	4.0%	8	N/A	1921	Japan Association of Social Workers 1960
Mauritius	1.1	$3,150	19	23	71	6.0%	29.0%	11.0%	61	1968	N/A	Mauritius Association of Social Workers 1964
U.S.	267.1	$25,880	8	10	76	12.6%	22.0%	14.0%	4	1776	1898	National Association of Social Workers 1955

waves of large-scale immigration from many parts of the world, also has a highly diverse population. Denmark and Japan, on the other hand, have considerable homogeneity within their populations.

Among the countries included, religious traditions vary widely, with a Hindu majority and sizable Christian and Muslim groups in Mauritius, Buddhism and Shintoism both practiced by most of the population in Japan, and large majority religions in Argentina (90% Roman Catholic) and Denmark (91% Lutheran). Although Armenia is considered 94% Armenian Orthodox, Armenia was subsumed into the Soviet Union from 1921 to 1991 and endured 70 years of religious suppression.

These brief comments on history and population diversity only suggest the richness of differences in national experiences of the countries highlighted. The important lesson is that the variety of national characteristics and histories of the countries discussed will assist in examining social work in its international context. Through gaining an understanding of social work's development, current definitions and practice, and future challenges in these national contexts, comprehension of the profession in its global reality can be approached. The next two chapters examine the history of the development of the social work profession and the history of social work in international action.

REFERENCES

Addams, J. (1930). *The second twenty years at Hull House: September 1909 to September 1929 with a record of a growing world consciousness.* New York: MacMillan.

Akimoto, T. (1995). *Towards the establishment of an international social work/welfare concept.* Unpublished paper. Japan Women's University, Kanagawa Japan.

American Association of Social Workers. (1947, May). Resolutions on international social welfare. *The Compass*, as reprinted in "From the Archives," *Journal of Progressive Human Services, 9*(1), 72–73.

Asamoah, Y.A., Healy, L.M., & Mayadas, N.S. (1997). Ending the international-domestic dichotomy: New approaches to a global curriculum for the millennium. *Journal of Social Work Education, 33*(2), 389–401.

Banerjee, M.M. (1998). Micro-enterprise development: A response to poverty. *Journal of Community Practice, 5*(1/2), 63–83.

Clinton, W.J. (1993, January 21). Inaugural address. *The New York Times*, p. A15.

Estes, R.J. (1984). Education for international social welfare research. In D.S. Sanders & P. Pederson (Eds.), *Education for international social welfare* (pp. 56–86). Manoa, Hawaii: University of Hawaii School of Social Work.

Glasgow, G.F., & Gouse-Sheese, J. (1995). Themes of rejection and abandonment in group work with Caribbean adolescents. *Social Work with Groups, 17*(4), 3–27.

Healy, L.M. (1990). [International content in social work educational programs worldwide]. Unpublished raw data.

Healy, L.M. (1995). Comparative and international overview. In T.D. Watts, D. Elliott, & N.S. Mayadas (Eds.), *International handbook on social work education* (pp. 421–439). Westport, CT: Greenwood Press.

Howard, D.S. (1947, May). Urgent international welfare measures—Our responsibility. *The Compass,* reprinted in "From the Archives," (1998). *Journal of Progressive Human Services, 9*(1), 65–72.

Jansen, G.G., & Pippard, J.L. (1998). The Grameen Bank in Bangladesh: Helping poor women with credit for self-employment. *Journal of Community Practice, 5*(1/2), 103–123.

Jebb, E. (1929). International social service. In *International Conference of Social Work* [Proceedings] (Vol. I, pp. 637–655). First Conference, Paris, July 8–13, 1928.

Kimberly, M.D. (Ed.). (1984). *Beyond national boundaries: Canadian contributions to international social work and social welfare.* Ottowa: Canadian Association of Schools of Social Work.

Lewis, L.S., & Altbach, P.G. (1996). The professoriate in international perspective. *Academe, Bulletin of the AAUP, 82*(3), 29–33.

Lorenz, W. (1997, August 24). *Social work in a changing Europe.* Paper presented to the Joint European Regional Seminar of IFSW and EASSW on Culture and Identity, Dublin, Ireland.

Sanders, D.S., & Pederson, P. (Eds.). (1984). *Education for international social welfare.* Manoa, Hawaii: University of Hawaii School of Social Work.

Stein, H. (1957, January). *An international perspective in the social work curriculum.* Paper presented at the Annual Meeting of the Council on Social Work Education, Los Angeles, CA.

Stein, H. (1990). The international and the global in education for the future. In K. Kendall (Ed.). *The international in american education:* pp. 11–16. New York: Hunter College School of Social Work.

UNICEF (1997). *The state of the world's children 1997.* New York: Oxford University Press.

UNDP (1998). *Human development report 1998.* New York: Oxford University Press.

Warren, G. (1939). International social work. In R. Kurtz (Ed.), *Social work yearbook* (pp. 192–196). New York: Russell Sage Foundation.

Wetzel, J.W. (1995). "IASSW woman's caucus in China," *IASSW Newsletter.* Issue 3, International Association of Schools of Social Work.

CHAPTER 2

THE HISTORY OF THE DEVELOPMENT
OF SOCIAL WORK

It is difficult to affix a date to the beginning of the profession of social work. Although the NASW has declared 1998 to be the 100th anniversary of the profession, it is actually the anniversary of the first social work training course in the United States, a summer school held in New York in 1898. Earlier training courses existed in England, and perhaps elsewhere, and the first true school of social work was begun in Amsterdam in 1899. In the countries in which social work has developed, helping activities began under a variety of auspices. When can these be labeled social work? Is one hallmark that they became secular rather than exclusively under the control of religious personnel? Or that they were undertaken by individuals who devoted themselves to helping as a regular activity rather than an occasional volunteer one? Van Wormer (1997), for example, reports that the first recorded employment of a social worker was the hiring of Mary Stewart, a trained Charity Organization Society (COS) worker, in 1895 by the Royal Free Hospital in London. Her task was to determine whether patients were eligible for free treatment. Another explanation is that social work became a profession when those providing such helping services began to systematize their efforts and to train others to provide services in a similar way.

Clearly, the easiest date to identify is the beginning of formalized training for social work. It can indeed be argued that this is the point at which social work becomes a profession. Earlier markers include the establishment of agencies such as settlement houses and the Young Women's Christian Association (YWCA). Founding of these agencies represented organized efforts to provide social services, often through paid staff who devoted themselves to this work as their main enterprise.

INTERNATIONAL DEVELOPMENT

In describing the origins of social work around the world, an effort will be made to discuss both services and education. It should be recognized, however, that the founding of a school of social work or even a formalized training program is much more likely to be well documented and can therefore be reported with more accuracy.

Two distinct patterns in the evolution of social work are evident. Social work schools emerged almost simultaneously in London, Amsterdam, New

York City, and Berlin around 1900 (de Jongh, 1972). For a long time it has been thought that this was a spontaneous development; new research into correspondence and papers from her day shows that Mary Richmond, a pioneer in social casework in the United States, not only read British works on the COS movement but also attended committee meetings in London at which the training course was being planned (Kendall, 2000). Formal training in the United States and Europe was organized to meet the needs of staff providing social services that had been developed to address the human needs that were by-products of the industrial revolution. Family services, settlement houses, and assistance to orphans, widows, immigrants, and young working women sprang up in response to harsh employment conditions. In contrast, de Jongh (1972) says: "I do not know of any developing country in which social work education was an original product of national development; the origins can always be traced back to strong foreign influences" (p. 23). Thus we have two patterns: Social work evolving in the United States and much of Europe as an indigenous response to the conditions of late 19th-century life, and social work being introduced into countries in Asia and Africa by American and European experts to address the problems of "underdevelopment." A third pattern, which emerged after de Jongh's work, is the introduction, or reintroduction, of modern social work in the countries of the former Soviet Union and Eastern bloc, including Russia, the nations of Eastern Europe, China, and Vietnam; this process has also involved substantial foreign influence.

Social Work Services Emerge in Europe and the United States

As summarized by Van Wormer (1997), "two social movements in social welfare that began at the end of the nineteenth century shaped the development of the profession of social work: the Charity Organization Societies (COSs) and the settlement house establishments" (p. 162). Each developed as a response to the social ills of the times, but they differed in philosophy and approach. Both institutions began in London, the Charity Organization Society in 1869 and the first settlement house, Toynbee Hall, in 1884. Within less than a decade, each was transplanted to the United States—remarkable examples of early technology transfer in the human services. The first COS in the United States began in 1877 in Buffalo and was followed by rapid development of societies in other cities. Hull House was founded in Chicago in 1889, following Jane Addams' visit to Toynbee Hall. The reform orientation of social work was strongly influenced by the settlement house movement in the United States and Europe. The COS workers, with their emphasis on the needy individual and the combination of "scientific" record-keeping and friendly visiting, were the forerunners of social caseworkers. Their demands for more formal training led to the establishment of the New York course mentioned above, in 1898.

Services developed in other parts of the world, as well, often as a result of colonial activities. Jamaica provides an interesting example:

The extent to which services established in the then British West Indies colonies were conceived as export models from the mother country is reflected in the names of the programmes established in the Region. None demonstrates this more completely than the Kingston Charity Organization Society founded in 1900 which was promoted with a view to rationalizing the delivery of private charity in the community. It did not however assume the central prominence in the development of social services and the systematizing and ultimate professionalizing of social work service delivery that was achieved by the original London Charity Organization Society of the 1850's or the transplanted varieties in Buffalo, New York, Montreal and other prominent northern American and Canadian cities. The K.C.O.S. settled into being essentially a private relief-giving agency. (Maxwell, 1993, p. 9)

Social Work Education Develops

Professional education may well be the cornerstone of the establishment of a profession. In 1899, the first school of social work was begun in Amsterdam, the Institute for Social Work Training. According to its prospectus, this was a 2-year course that aimed "at the methodical, theoretical and practical training of those who wish to dedicate themselves to certain important tasks in the field of social work" (United Nations, 1958, p. 109). Five fields of study were offered: welfare of the poor, housing management, "Toynbee work" (settlement house work), child care for orphans and deserted children, and social work in factories and workshops.

This comprehensive program followed efforts elsewhere to offer series of lectures for training of social workers. Octavia Hill was conducting training in England as early as 1873. Series of lectures followed in London throughout the 1890s. In 1895, a summer institute was sponsored in Chicago by Hull House. Then, in 1898, the New York COS began a summer school in philanthropic work after Mary Richmond had urged more organized training in a speech to the 1897 National Conference on Social Work. Seen as the beginning of professional social work education in the United States, the summer institute had become a 1-year full-time course by 1904 and eventually became the Columbia University School of Social Work (United Nations, 1958). In the previous year, 1903, the School of Sociology in London began a 2-year course of theory and practice that grew from the efforts of the COS and its "professionalizing effect." On the European continent, Alice Salomon began a training course for young women interested in doing social work in 1899 and founded the first school of social work in Germany (in Berlin) in 1908 (Wieler, 1988). Thus, as noted by de Jongh, social work education emerged almost simultaneously in Britain, the United States, and the European continent at the turn of the century, quickly progressing in each location from lectures to full-time training.

Further east in Europe, the Training School for Social Work was founded at the Free University of Poland in Warsaw in 1925 by Madame Helene Radlinska. Its 2-year program, too, was preceded by several short courses in social work (International Conference of Social Work, 1929). Madame Radlinska commented to the educators assembled in 1928 for the First International Conference of Social Work that she found it difficult to balance theory and practice. "In fact, there are very few professors who combine practical experiences with academic qualifications; therefore it is difficult to correlate the practice and theory of social work" (Radlinska, 1929, p. 92). This, indeed, has been and continues to be a challenge everywhere in the early years of developing professional education in social work.

The Spread Beyond Europe: Early Social Work and Social Work Education in Latin America, Asia, and Africa

By the 1920s, international influences had begun to play a major role in the spread of professional social work. The School of Social Work at Santiago, Chile, the first school in Latin America, was founded in 1925 by Alejandro del Rio, a physician, with assistance from another physician, René Sand of Belgium. It was founded after a visit to Europe by Dr. del Rio to examine the roles social workers played there in assisting physicians. His chance meeting with Dr. Sand on the ship led him to include a stop at the Central School of Social Studies in Brussels (Kendall, 2000). The first principal of the school in Chile was Madame Bernier from Belgium, recruited by Sand at del Rio's request. Dr. del Rio remained affiliated with the school until 1932 and continued to seek assistance from Dr. Sand, as documented in letters exchanged between the two (Kendall, 2000).

A similar pattern followed in neighboring Argentina where doctors investigated the idea of using "hygiene visitors," which they had observed in Europe. In the early 1930s, a school was founded in connection with the School of Medicine at the University of Buenos Aires to train auxiliaries for doctors. Early influences on the development of Argentine social work came from Belgium, France, and Germany and emphasized charity work and social work as auxiliary to other professions (R. Teubal, personal communication, March 13, 1997). A tradition of charity work in Argentina long preceded the establishment of the school. In 1823, for example, a women's organization called the Charity Society was established and given authority to administer institutions for children, women, and the aged. In existence until 1948, this organization has been described as "by far the most powerful charity organization in the 19th century" (Queiro-Tajalli, 1995, p. 92). Until the 1940s, Argentine social work and social work education were influenced by European ideas and by their own religious and charity traditions. From the 1940s to the 1960s, U.S. influence grew, introducing psychology and concepts of psychotherapy to Argentine social work.

The first schools in Africa began at opposite ends of the continent, in South Africa in 1924 and in Egypt in 1936. In South Africa, social work training began in order to address the problems of "poor whites"; theory for the training was borrowed from North America and Europe with little attention to adaptation (Mazibuko, McKendrick, & Patel, 1992). The 1924 course was founded at the University of Cape Town. Within a decade, it had been joined by social work programs in Pretoria and Stellenbosch; in 1938, the Joint Universities Committee on Social Studies was established to promote the study of social work in South Africa (Ntusi, 1995). While there was an opposing tradition of liberalism that advocated diversity and openness, early social work education was also linked to Broederbond, an Afrikaner advancement movement that opposed any cultural assimilation. As explained by Ntusi (1995):

> The provision of social work services to the poor whites served two purposes. It unified and strengthened the ethnic boundaries and gave rise to a certified professional elite, loyal to the government and all out to achieve the government's goal of stamping out white poverty. (p. 263)

In this tradition, Dr. Verwoerd established a department of sociology and social work at the University of Stellenbosch in 1932. The two traditions of liberalism—focusing on poverty in general—and the Afrikaner focus on services to whites—continued unchanged in South African social work education for decades.

The first school to focus on educating nonwhites for social work was the Jan H. Hofmeyr School of Social Work, founded in 1941 with assistance from the YMCA (Kendall, 2000). It was the result of the work of Hofmeyr, a South African philanthropist who believed in equal opportunity, and Ray Phillips, a Congregationalist missionary with a PhD from Yale; Phillips was committed to the "absolute equality of men and women of every race and condition," and his work in founding the school was one way to put his beliefs into action (Kendall, 2000, p. 85).

Social work education in the Middle East/North Africa was begun in Cairo in 1936, the year that Egypt gained recognition as an independent nation. According to Ragab (1995), in the early stage of development, "the American model was successfully transplanted into Egypt" (p. 281). The founders, including several foreign-born and -trained social workers, were confident that the many social problems facing the new nation could be handled with an approach to social reform based on sound theory and research. "The school was an instant success . . . as the country was teeming with idealistic, enthusiastic youth searching for a role in national reconstruction and development" (Ragab, 1995, p. 284). Social services also became more formalized and job opportunities grew as the government established the Ministry of Social Affairs and Labour in 1939 to provide public social services. Prior to 1939, social services in Egypt were entirely voluntary, organized by mosques and NGOs (Walton & El Nasr, 1988). While several other schools developed in Egypt, only in 1975 did social work education move into the university when the Higher Institute of Social Work in Cairo became a part of the new Helwan University.

A settlement house–like agency, the Nagpada Neighborhood House, was founded in 1926 in the slums of Bombay, India, by Dr. Clifford Manshardt, an American missionary. An ordained Congregational minister, Manshardt was rejected when he first applied for missionary work because church officials found him to be "commendably idealistic but religiously inadequate" (Manshardt, 1967, p. 9). Especially troubling to the church were his views on the brotherhood of man, which he saw extending to all, no matter what their faith. He was finally appointed to a social work post and told that with his unorthodox views, he could not be used in regular church work with Indian Christian families because his ideas "might disturb their faith"; in a social work role, however, the church deemed that he "could do little harm—and very likely considerable good" (Manshardt, 1967, p. 11).

From his work in the settlement, Manshardt was convinced "that the standard of social work in India could not be raised appreciably until a permanent School of Social Work was set up to engage in a continuous study of Indian Social Problems and to offer training for social work on a graduate basis" (Manshardt, 1941, p. 15). With financing from the trust of an Indian industrialist, Manshardt opened India's first professional school, the Sir Dorabji Tata Graduate School of Social Work, in Bombay in 1936. The faculty consisted of a German Jewish refugee, an American visiting professor, and two Indians, one with a background in education and theology and the other a sociologist (Desai, 1987). The school focused on urban problems and pioneered in training labor welfare officers to cope with the new factory labor force as families moved into Bombay from rural villages. Labor welfare has continued to be important in Indian social work. A second school, the Delhi School (originally located in Lucknow), came into existence in 1946 "under the auspices of the National Y.W.C.A. of India, Burma and Ceylon with substantial assistance from the Foreign Division of the Y.W.C.A. of the United States" (Yelaja, 1969, p. 365). In keeping with the pattern identified by de Jongh (1972), discussed earlier in the chapter, India is another case in which the "birth and early growth of social work and its professionalization . . . was not the product of indigenous inspiration" (Kudchodkar, 1963, p. 96). Indian social work education was heavily influenced by U.S. models for many years.

The first recognized social work service in China (as recorded in the literature) were medical social work services in a hospital social work department in Beijing, established in 1921 by American social worker Ida Pruitt. The department provided social casework services, adoption work, and rehabilitation services; it addition, in-service training was provided for social workers—probably the first social work training in China. American professors from Princeton set up a sociology department at Yanjing University (now Beijing) in 1922, a department that became the Department of Sociology and Social Services just a few years later (Leung, 1995). Social work and social work education were heavily influenced by American missionaries and related organizations such as the Young Men's Christian Association (YMCA) and YWCA; although there was some work in rural areas, the emphasis was on urban clinical practice, a model poorly matched to the pressing needs of China (Leung, 1995).

Further Developments in the 1930s. In those countries in Europe where social work education was developed after the "first wave," foreign influences also played a role. In Denmark, for example, the first school was founded in 1937 in Copenhagen by Manon Luttichau. Working with a private organization

A PIONEER IN DENMARK: MANON LUTTICHAU

Photo by Anne-Li Engström, 1988.

Manon Luttichau was the most influential individual in the founding of professional social work in Denmark. Born on April 9, 1900, a year after the first school of social work was established in Europe, she became interested in the "pre-professional" social work activities then underway in Denmark. Early work there was being done in settlement houses for young women, some of them pregnant with nowhere to go. Social work was also done as "street work"—assisting women near the train stations, for example. From 1922 to 1932, Luttichau was an assistant with one of these organizations, a private organization called Care for Danish Women (translated). During these years, she also traveled to other countries, including the United States, to gather knowledge and inspiration to establish social work as a profession in Denmark.

On April 1, 1934, she became employed at the Copenhagen Municipal Hospital as a "social worker"—a new title in Denmark that she undoubtedly brought back from her visit to the United States. In 1936, she brought together a group of physicians, lawyers, and others to plan social work education for Denmark. Beginning on January 5, 1937, the classes took place in the hospital auditorium, using donated space and 29 volunteers as teachers. This was originally called the Social School in Denmark. Luttichau was the "dean" for the first two groups of students. She also founded the National Association of Social Workers in Denmark in 1938.

A true internationalist, Luttichau believed that interchange among countries was essential to the process of developing a profession. Learning from the experience of others and exchanging ideas with social workers in other nations were things she highly valued. She herself traveled in Europe and to the United States and participated in at least one of the early international conferences on social work.

The pioneer of professional social work in Denmark, she died on her 95th birthday in 1995.

(From information supplied by Inger Hjerrild, Esbjerg School of Social Work, Esbjerg, Denmark based on her historical research)

called Care for Danish Women (Danske Kvinders Velfaerd) during the 1920s and early 1930s, Luttichau had traveled to the United States on a study tour and while there realized that social workers needed a professional education. Returning to Denmark, she wrote that while common sense is important, it is not enough to make one a social worker. She also traveled to Germany and encouraged others interested in social work to travel and learn. She was convinced that no social worker can sit in their own country to develop social work but must visit other places to exchange ideas (Inger Hjerrild, personal communication, April 17, 1997).

Efforts to Gain Recognition as a Profession

It was not easy for social work to achieve recognition as a profession. In 1915, Abraham Flexner dismayed his audience at the U.S. National Conference of Charities and Correction by stating that social work was not a profession because it did not have a body of educationally transmissible techniques and because the boundaries of social work were too broad (Popple, 1995). In about the same period of history, Alice Salomon, seeing the increased demand for social workers in Germany toward the later years of WWI, decided it would be important for schools of social work to have uniform standards. In Germany, state approval was needed to promulgate uniform standards, as such an action would have required recognition of professional status. Salomon therefore called together representatives of the schools and government representatives from the Ministries of the Interior and of Education. They gathered for a morning of discussion about the need for professional recognition and standards, but the results were not positive.

As Salomon wrote in her autobiography: "Then the head of the public health section of the Ministry, a very stiff and worthy gentleman, finally broke out: 'You talk about a number of different things, about training for health work—for educational activities—for relief—for protection of labor—and all this you call a profession of social workers. What you talk about does not exist" (n.d., p. 197). She goes on to say that a similar process and outcome occurred in France. The first five schools of social work there and the director of the Public Relief and Hygiene Board in Paris petitioned the Minister of Health asking for regulation of social work. The reply was " 'the petition deals with a profession which cannot be defined, which hardly exists in France, and the character of which makes regulations impossible' " (p. 197).

Publication of Mary Richmond's *Social Diagnosis* (1917) was heralded as an answer to Flexner, giving social work a communicable technique. There is evidence that this book made an impact in European social work training as well as an important contribution in the United States.

Gender and the Social Work Profession

Part of the difficulty in securing recognition may have been gender bias because social work was and still is considered a profession for women. Alice

Salomon, referring to the negative reactions of officials to the young social work profession, said:

> Behind this expression of hostility was the distrust of learned and progressive women. They considered our endeavors as part of the struggle ever latent between men and women, now transferred to a new sphere of life. They fought against a type of school which would prepare for a profession pre-eminently suited to women, conceived by women, and formed according to their scale of values. So far all professions—that of the nurse and the teacher included—had been shaped by men. Most educational institutions were directed by men, in conformity with men's notions of women's duties and capacities. The object of education for women had been to form men's "helpmates." Our opponents were right in guessing that we wanted more. We wanted to make women responsible for services in which human needs should be met with a woman's understanding. A man brought up in the tradition of German officialdom could not even grasp the nature of our aspirations, much less approve. (n.d., p. 198)

Early social work was indeed a female profession. As late as 1937, 83 of the 179 schools of social work in the world were for women only, just 9 were reserved for men. In some European countries, including Austria, France, Hungary, Italy, Norway, Portugal, Romania, and Switzerland, the only social work training institutions were reserved for women. In addition, many of the pioneers of social work in North America and in Europe were actively involved in the struggle for women's suffrage and broader women's rights. Rights of women within family law, for property ownership, and in the world of work-related issues, such as equal pay, were advocated by the founders of social work. The extent of the feminine character of early social work is striking.

Links With Pacifism

Links with the early women's movement also led to international collaborations on behalf of peace. Shortly after the beginning of professional social work training, professional pioneers from several countries had the opportunity to meet each other at the International Congress of Women in Berlin in 1904 and again in Canada at the 1909 Congress of the International Council of Women. Here, for example, Jane Addams met Alice Salomon and the two began a friendship "strengthened by their mutual commitment to international pacifism" (Lorenz, 1994, p. 60). The link between social work and peace was clear to Salomon who wrote: "War annihilates everything that social work tries to accomplish . . . this is the reason why social workers should be the first ones to facilitate and maintain peace-creating international relations" (Wieler, 1989, p. 19). During the first 50 years of social work, the commitment to pacifism was rudely challenged by heightened nationalism and two devastating world wars.

The Depression and Growing Nationalism

The worldwide depression occupied social workers with domestic crises in many countries during the 1930s. National response in the form of new policies and services changed the nature and activities of social work. In the United States, for example, widespread unemployment convinced most that poverty was not the result of individual inadequacies or traits but was systemic. A social worker, Harry Hopkins, was the architect of many of the New Deal policy solutions to the crisis. Although the American version of the welfare state was minimal, the changes altered the environment of social work practice and influenced future philosophical developments around the nature of human need.

In other parts of the world, especially Europe and Japan, an increase in nationalism and militarism was the response to economic hardship or national humiliation, setting in motion the forces that led to the Second World War.

The unrest of the 1930s was widely felt. Several years of labor unrest and social protests took place throughout the West Indies, for example. "The social disturbances of the late 1930s which were explosive expressions of smoldering discontent by a deprived and exploited proletariat in the Caribbean, led to investigations of the root conditions by the famous Moyne Commission of 1938" (Brown, 1991, p. 22). This commission, appointed by the British government, made recommendations for improvement of social and economic conditions in the West Indian colonies, emphasizing social welfare services as "the major means for improving the West Indian quality of life" (Brown, 1991, p. 22). Thus similar to the unrest due to the Great Depression in the United States, social welfare services, and ultimately social work, were bolstered in Jamaica and other West Indian nations.

War, however, interrupted the depression and its resultant focus on social needs.

World War II and the Nazi Period

The late 1930s and early 1940s brought calamity for the world and, at times, brought out the worst in the profession of social work. Active collaboration with the Nazi-controlled government in Germany is almost certainly the darkest episode in social work history. It should be noted that there were also many instances of positive, even heroic, efforts by European social workers during this period. As Alice Salomon, born into a Jewish family, reflects in her autobiography:

> The attitudes of my most intimate group of fellow workers, the staff of the School of Social Work and the Academy, most of whom were Protestant in predominantly Protestant Berlin, were typical of educated women. There were instances of human strength and human weakness. Some came out of the battle finer and stronger personalities, others lost whatever moral poise they had ever possessed. There were some women on our staff who would have been considered irreproachable by Nazi standards but for having worked closely with me. They tried to atone for this with redoubled fervor, saying "Heil Hitler" twice where others said it once. (n.d., p. 243)

ALICE SALOMON

Joachim Wieler, personal collection

Alice Salomon, called "the Jane Addams of Germany" by Julia Lathrop (Salomon, n.d., p. 180), was a founder of social work education in Europe and a leader in international movements for social work education, women's rights, and peace. Among her accomplishments were the founding of the first school of social work in Germany in 1908, publication of 28 books and about 250 articles and service as the first president of the International Association of Schools of Social Work (Wieler, 1988). Salomon also had many "firsts" for women, including receiving a doctorate from the University of Berlin in 1906. Just a few years after the school she founded in Berlin was named the Alice Salomon School of Social Work to honor her, she was sent into exile in 1937 by the Nazis and died, nearly forgotten and alone, in New York in 1948.

Born in 1872 into a Jewish family, she converted to Christianity in 1914 but continued to be active in Jewish social services. She developed a strong interest in the plight of women, especially in the workplace, and attacked the issue with both action and scholarship. She began a training course for young women interested in doing social work in 1899, providing opportunities for training and meaningful work for women, who were denied work in most fields. Simultaneously, she fought to gain admission to the University of Berlin (then closed to women) and was awarded the doctorate for her dissertation on "Unequal Payment of Men's and Women's Work"—a very early study of the concept of comparable worth (Wieler, 1988).

A feminist, Salomon's life "was devoted nationally and internationally, in about equal parts to social work and to extensive work with councils of women" (Kendall, 1989, p. 28). She became active in the International Council of Women, rising to a leadership position in the organization. In her autobiography, she emphasizes her commitment to peace and the increasing dissonance she felt living in a militaristic Germany from 1914

(continued)

until her exile. She became active in the international peace movement, joining with Jane Addams in working through the International League for Peace and Freedom, activities for which Addams eventually won a Nobel prize and for which Salomon was sent into exile. With World War I well under way, she was instrumental in arranging an audience for Jane Addams in Berlin in 1915 with the German chancellor as part of a delegation from a women's peace conference in The Hague, which was dispatched to the capital of each nation at war to try to talk the governments into peace. Needless to say, the mission failed. But how interesting it is to think about the courage and commitment of the women who would meet in Europe during a war and travel to hostile nations to talk about peace.

In her 60th year, Salomon was honored for her work in Germany and internationally. The school she had begun was named after her, she was given an honorary doctorate, and she received the Silver Medal for Merit to the State, bestowed unanimously by the Prussian Cabinet. Within a year, however, Hitler came to power and the society Salomon had worked to create began to crumble rapidly. She was soon identified as an enemy of the Nazis; she was Jewish under the law, and her work in peace and disarmament, women's rights, and internationalism all conflicted with Nazi doctrine. Social work as a profession had championed reforms on behalf of the disabled, including the retarded and mentally ill—populations now labeled inferior and subject to extermination.

Salomon was stripped of her honors and offices, and her name was removed from the School of Social Work. While under intense pressure and in personal danger, she conducted and published the first international survey of social work education in 1937 under a grant from the Russell Sage Foundation. When she returned to Berlin from a speaking tour in the United States, she was summoned by the Gestapo and, after hours of interrogation, given the choice of leaving Germany permanently or being put into a concentration camp. As reported by *The New York Times* on July 13, 1937, "Alice Salomon, the founder and the distinguished head of the first school of social work in Germany, the Sociale Frauenschule of Berlin, who completed a lecture tour across the American continent last winter and who has visited this country on two other occasions since the war, has now been expelled from the Reich by order of the Nazi secret police" (cited in "Alice Salomon Exiled," 1937, p. 510). After a brief stay in England, she came to the United States where she lived an increasingly lonely existence until her death in 1948. According to Wieler (1988):

> After more than three-quarters of a century of service to and with throngs of people, Alice Salomon died so alone that even the exact time, date and cause of her death were never established . . . the woman who had helped, protected, and taught countless social workers, championed the rights of women and created an international awareness and structure for social work education, went to her final rest with four people in attendance. There was no ceremony. (p. 170)

German social work educators also intensely pressured her to resign from the presidency of the International Association of Schools of Social Work, threatening that all German schools would withdraw from the Association if she did not comply (Nitzsche, 1935). Several times Salomon resigned in order to save the association; however, each time the international membership re-installed her as president.

The involvement of social workers in collaboration apparently went beyond shunning Jewish colleagues. According to Lorenz (1994):

> It is a fact that the welfare machinery of Nazi Germany, by "doing its duty" willingly or reluctantly, delivered thousands of people into the hands of the henchmen of the regime, caused untold anguish and suffering, deepened divisions at all levels of society and discredited its own humanitarian ideals. The murder of millions of Jewish citizens of Germany and its occupied countries, by which the regime is most vividly remembered, was not an isolated case of extremism disconnected from other "achievements": it is the epitome of its politics, including welfare politics. . . . Once the granting of human rights became conditional . . . , the logic of discrimination, segregation and exclusion established itself as an unimpeded force in everyday professional discourse and could eventually not stop short of extending the line to extermination. (p. 63)

Lorenz traces the evolution of acquiescence. In the 1920s, possibly due to harsh postwar conditions in Germany, "the distinction between educable and ineducable youngsters—between 'valuable and inferior' persons—was beginning to enter the language and practice of German welfare staff" (Lorenz, 1994, p. 62). This grew to support for sterilization of the mentally ill and handicapped and then to segregation and elimination of other classes of undesirable people. An early Nazi social policy measure allowed sterilization of the mentally ill, alcoholics, and the handicapped and included a mandatory reporting clause that extended to many professions—a chilling early example of the practice of mandatory reporting, now seen as a client protection. "The actual legitimation of the procedure depended essentially on experts such as doctors and social workers making the 'right diagnosis' " (Lorenz, 1994, p. 65). Social work skills and methods of assessment, diagnosis, and report writing were used to identify "unworthy life" whose existence as "parasites is medically and economically unjustified," as stated in directives from the City of Frankfort, published in 1933 (cited in Lorenz, 1994, p. 66).

Such events were not limited to Germany. In Rome, a "Higher Fascist School for Social Assistance in Industry" was established in 1928. In Spain, the Franco regime set up its own social work schools after closing down the existing school in Barcelona. Social welfare services were supported by the Fascists as part of their systems of social control.

Evidence suggests that some collusion was the result of active support for the policies, while others cooperated out of naïveté. There is evidence, too, of resistance from some social workers as they realized how their reports were being used. Involvement of the helping profession in such inhumane actions is difficult to comprehend and assimilate. Yet it is important to examine in order to prevent recurrence. Lorenz believes that the strong scientific emphasis in social work at the time and promotion of the belief in value-neutrality were at least partially to blame. The focus on technical methodologies for dealing with human problems and the absence of a human rights orientation allowed the methodologies of the profession to be used for evil purposes.

Elsewhere in the world, social work also coped with grave restrictions of human rights, such as in the internment of Japanese citizens and resident aliens alike in the United States. Articles in the *Social Service Review* give some indication of social work action—or inaction—over the internment:

> It is easy for us to forget about the Japanese—aliens and citizens—who were evacuated so many months ago. And the rejoicing over the Attorney General's announcement that Italian Americans who are still aliens would not be considered enemy aliens reminds us that the large numbers of Japanese-Americans, citizens and aliens alike, are still waiting for justice in our American republic. ("Child Welfare Problems and Japanese Evacuation," 1942, p. 673)

So complete was the suppression of Japanese rights in the West that even Japanese children were evacuated from orphanages and moved to the internment camps.

The Postwar Period

The postwar period brought several profound changes to social work around the world. First, Communist takeover of Eastern Europe led to the end of social work in several countries and the retarded development of social work throughout the Communist bloc. Second, devastation brought opportunities for social workers to become involved in the enormous relief and rehabilitation efforts in Europe and China. And third, nationalist and independence movements throughout the developing countries of Asia, Africa, and the Caribbean led to the birth of many new social work programs to accompany the birth of new nations.

Professional social work, as indicated by the presence of social work training institutions, had developed in Czechoslovakia, Hungary, Yugoslavia, China, and other countries later to fall under Communism. Soon after the Soviet takeover of Eastern Europe, social work was officially abolished as an unnecessary and bourgeois profession. The Chinese followed this pattern after the 1949 revolution. The Secretary's Report of the International Committee of Schools of Social Work in July 1950 reveals the beginning impact of the cold war on social work education while showing unrealistic optimism about the situation in China:

> From the Tsechoslovakian Schools, who were members before the last war, we hear no more. Of the East of Europe only the School of Mrs. Radlinska at Lodz in Poland has remained loyal to us. It may interest you to hear that Miss Schlat-

ter received a letter from Dr. Chen of Nanking, mentioning that his School did not in the least suffer from the new order. (Moltzer, 1950, p. 3)

Note that Miss Schlatter is Dr. Marguerite Schlatter of the School of Social Work in Zurich, Switzerland, and member of the International Committee of Schools of Social Work.

The secretary was correct about Poland. Although it did not flourish, social work continued in Poland throughout the era of Soviet domination. Yugoslavia also maintained social work education. In China, however, social work was soon abolished as an unnecessary and bourgeois profession. In still other cases, such as Armenia, Soviet domination isolated its republics and satellites from professional contact, thereby preventing the introduction of social work.

Devastation and Relief

The war brought devastation to the countries of Europe and to China and much of Southeast Asia. As Friedlander (1975) describes the situation in Poland:

> Poland was the most ravaged European country at the conclusion of the Second World War. Its railroads, power stations, highways and bridges had been destroyed, its ports made unusable, its factories stripped of machinery or burned, its livestock killed. Over six million Poles had died in the war and at least as many had been deported as slave laborers to Germany and to concentration camps. Almost the entire Jewish population had been murdered by the Nazis. (p. 14)

Social work, of course, did not escape, as the following plea for help for the Polish School of Social Work demonstrates:

> I appeal most warmly in the name of the Board, especially the French, English and German speaking countries to make their members send all they possibly can collect, books, papers reports, etc. regarding social work to Mrs. Helena Radlinska, one of the founders of our Committee, professor of the State University of Lodz (Poland). Mrs. Radlinska had the great misfortune to see destroyed besides her private house, the School of Social Work, founded by her at the University of Warsaw as well as the University itself, and to lose by death two-thirds of the teaching staff. In spite of this great misfortune starting anew at the age of 75 years Mrs. Radlinska does what she can to rebuild a School of Social Work at the University of Lodz. We cannot remain indifferent seeing this rare energy. (Moltzer, 1948, p. 2)

Devastation brought the need for relief and rebuilding. More interesting for social work history is that the need for extensive relief efforts were predicted and planned for long before hostilities ceased. Although it will be discussed more fully in the next chapter, social work involvement in the United Nations Relief and Rehabilitation Administration (UNRRA) programs in Europe was a high point of international social work activity. In November 1943, UNRRA was established by 44 nations, promising to organize relief and rehabilitation for the nations invaded by the Axis powers as soon as liberation occurred (Kollwitz, 1943). As soon as countries were liberated, relief efforts began. Efforts focused on the restoration of public services—water, sanitation, electricity, transportation—and reconstitution of health and social services. In many places, food relief was needed. It was an enormous undertaking. During its several years of operation, UNRRA was the largest exporter in the world and at its peak had a staff of 25,000 (Friedlander, 1975). The welfare division was set up in 1946. The emphasis was on aid to displaced persons, especially in Germany, Austria, Italy, Greece, North Africa, and, later, China. In Europe alone, 21 million persons had had to flee their countries or had been taken to Germany as prisoners or slave laborers. Special services were also developed to serve orphans and other needy children.

"For social work and social welfare, the restoration period following World War II can be described as a rich cornucopia filled with international programs, projects and opportunities" (Kendall, 1978, p. 178). A number of American social workers became involved in the relief and rehabilitation efforts of UNRRA in Europe and China. This was the first systematic program to send social welfare experts abroad to assist other countries in developing social legislation and social service programs. Training of indigenous social work personnel was a component of these efforts. The active consultation and training programs begun under UNRRA would continue for several decades under the auspices of the newly formed UN. Social workers also continued international work through the programs for children, refugees, and health care that were transferred to UN agencies such as the World Health Organization (WHO) and UNICEF.

Expanding Social Work in Developing Countries

Building on the UNRRA programs in social work education that sent educational consultants to devastated countries and provided funding for scholars to study in the United States and elsewhere, the UN soon became the largest contributor to the spread of professional social work throughout the world, taking responsibility for starting schools of social work in a number of developing countries (Younghusband, 1963). While the UN was only in its infancy, the then-temporary Social Commission of the Economic and Social Council (ECOSOC) encouraged attention to the training of social workers and to provision of technical assistance in social welfare. A series of studies and publications were initiated under the title "Technical Assistance for Social Progress" (vander Straeten, 1992). One of these, *Training for Social Work: An International Survey*, was issued in 1950, the first of five comprehensive studies in the field. Then, in 1959, the ECOSOC of the UN asked the secretary general to do "everything possible to obtain the participation of social workers in the preparation and application of programs for underdeveloped countries" (Garigue, 1961, p. 21).

The 1950s and 1960s were periods of independence movements through-out Africa, the Caribbean, and those parts of Asia still under colonial rule. Social welfare was identified as an important component of preparation for self-governance, as it was clear that populations held out hope for better standards of living under self-rule. In Jamaica, for example, Norman Man-ley, one of the "fathers of Jamaican independence," was responsible for the creation of Jamaica Welfare Limited in 1937, an organization devoted to community development. Through the political movement that grew out of the unrest of the 1930s, Manley secured an agreement for a tax on the export of bananas to fund community development programs (Maxwell, 1993). Community development was astutely selected for its contributions to community betterment while building an empowered populace crucial in moving independence forward. It became and remained a component of social work and social work education in Jamaica both at the University of the West Indies and at the Social Welfare Training Centre.

In her discussion of Africa, Asamoah (1995) observed:

> Perhaps the most significant event in the 1960s for both social work practice and social work education in Africa was the first International Conference of Ministers Responsible for Social Welfare, held in 1968. . . . The 1968 Conference of Ministers recommended that priority in developing countries be given to social welfare and that social welfare training prepare workers for carrying out developmental roles. (p. 225)

This conference, organized and held under the auspices of the UN, brought together top government officials in social welfare from 89 countries and observers from other nations and NGOs (United Nations, 1969). It is viewed as a landmark event in global social welfare.

Many countries in the developing world received consultative assistance for establishing social work training. Others secured fellowships to send faculty abroad for advanced training. In addition, grants through the UN and other sources directly assisted in establishing social welfare programs and social work training. Uganda, for example, established its social work program at Makerere University in Kampala with a UNICEF grant that financed the school through its first 4 years (Rao, 1984).

Era of Indigenization: The 1970s

The intense period of consultation, transplantation, and borrowing that occurred during the 1950s and 1960s was followed by a reaction characterized by rejection of Western models and a search for an indigenous form of social work. As proclaimed at the 1972 world meeting of social workers: "We have entered the era of 'indigenization'—of indigenous development based on the needs and resources and the cultural, political and economic landscape of each society—and the schools of social work are taking the lead, as they must, in carving out such new directions" (Stein, 1972, p. 161).

SYBIL FRANCIS: A MODERN PIONEER OF JAMAICA

Photo from personal collection of Sybil Francis

Sybil Francis is widely regarded as a central figure in the establishment of social work services and training in Jamaica and the Caribbean region. Born in 1914, her special talents were noticed early; she placed second in Jamaica in her High School Senior Cambridge examination. After several years of work experience in Jamaica, her talents were recognized and she was given a scholarship by the Colonial Development and Welfare Organization to study at the London School of Economics in 1943. Her schooling there actually took place in Cambridge, as the London school was evacuated to Cambridge due to the bombings during the war (Johansen, 1999). Francis began her work at the YWCA of Jamaica. Next, she worked as a secretary in the Land Department with a land settlement program for small farmers. When a social welfare section was formed, she was appointed to the position and began organizing women's groups, community organizations, and a settlers' association. All this was before Jamaican independence, but signs of change were apparent. She remembers sitting up in the mountains talking with farmers, speculating with them about what it would mean to live in an independent country. She also served as assistant secretary in the Social Welfare Ministry, working as liaison with the NGO sector and as administrator of the Child Care Division.

It is for her long career with the Social Welfare Training Centre at the University of the West Indies, which she headed from 1962 to 1989, that Sybil Francis is particularly well known. The core activity of the Training Centre was, and still is, to provide short-term training to social welfare personnel from the many countries in the Caribbean area. So thoroughly has the Centre done this that Francis once told a government minister that she could close down all the social services in the Caribbean by calling a strike of the graduates of her 4-month certificate course.

(continued)

A particularly remarkable feature of Francis's work at the Social Welfare Training Centre, however, is the number of other social service programs that were developed through her efforts and that continue today. These include the Child Development Centre, which grew out of UNICEF-sponsored efforts and now includes a day care center with research and education on the young child; WAND, the Women and Development program (now centered in Barbados), an organization doing research, publication, community development, and training on women and development; and a family planning project, initially taken on by Sybil under IASSW auspices and eventually transferred to Social and Preventive Medicine.

Now retired, Sybil Francis is tackling the topic of aging and is chair of the Jamaica National Council on Aging. She was a member of the Jamaican delegation to the World Assembly on Aging, representing her country on the main committee.

A side journey took her to the UN as part of newly independent Jamaica's delegation in 1963. Here, she became a member of the 3rd committee at the time work was being done on the Declaration on the Elimination of All Forms of Racial Discrimination. A particularly proud aspect of her service was that Jamaica proposed that 1968 be designated as International Human Rights Year.

She remains optimistic about social work and the potential for its contributions. Although dedicated to Jamaica and the Caribbean, she has also been a true internationalist. Francis served as vice president of the International Association of Schools of Social Work and was a member of the board of directors of the International Council on Social Welfare. A special feature of the 4-month training course at the Social Welfare Training Centre was the required cross-cultural field experience. A short-term project was completed in Jamaica by students from the other islands while Jamaican students were sent to Puerto Rico to do their projects. In this way, she shared her beliefs in international exchange with her students; she believes that each gained enormous insight about their own country through working in another.

(Based partly on personal communication with Sybil Francis, April 24, 1997)

Latin America began the indigenization trend. As described by an Argentine educator, the 1960s were perhaps the "most creative phase" as social work attempted to "grow from our own social reality" (R. Teubal, personal communication, March 13, 1997). According to Sela Sierra, "during the reconceptualization period, Latin America stopped searching for answers from Europe and the United States of America and engaged itself in the discovery of its own authentic potential to become a free continent" (cited in Queiro-Tajalli, 1995, p. 97). Strong anti-American feelings developed along with a rejection of the process of borrowing and using models from the industrialized countries. Social work became more political, more radical, and more focused on political consciousness. All social action was seen as having a political dimension. Whether the practitioner is conscious of it or not, the social worker is always siding with someone. The new message was that either you are on the side of the poor or you are not. Called the *reconceptualization movement,* it developed in two streams: the radical, which rejected capitalism, and the moderate, which moved away from the three accepted U.S. social work methods of casework, groupwork, and community organization toward a holistic perspective. In both streams, social work took on a more macro and more historical perspective (R. Teubal, personal communication, March 13, 1997). The ideas of Paulo Freire, a Brazilian educator exiled to Chile, helped Latin American social work develop a new emphasis on participation, organization, and consciousness-raising as methodologies (Jimenez & Aylwin, 1992). Liberation theology—the reinterpretation of Christianity through the eyes and experiences of the poor—as developed by Latin American Catholics, also influenced social work.

As social work developed, radicalization was often more a topic of discussion than an action agenda. It may have been the reestablishment of the dictatorship in Argentina or the coup in Chile—stifling all freedom of speech—that curtailed the move to active radicalism.

The Vietnam War intensified anti-Americanism around the world and brought new discussion of the dangers of imperialism. An intellectual campaign, waged in professional journals and at conference presentations, condemned the impact of the borrowing of American and British models of social work in Africa, Asia, and Latin America as irrelevant at best, damaging at worst. In some countries, the result was little more than protest, while in others, indigenization efforts yielded production of useful local case studies and teaching materials and the first development of culturally specific theories. In still other countries, there was more violent reaction against Western influences. As described in the brief biography of Sattareh Farman Farmaian, the Islamic Revolution in Iran resulted in the violent takeover of the school of social work. While attention to indigenization continues, it has been joined by more mutual efforts to cope with interdependence and by a new wave of borrowing set off by the dissolution of the Communist bloc.

The Fall of the Eastern Bloc and the End of the Cold War

The gradual thaw and then the dramatic end of Soviet domination in Eastern Europe set in motion an avalanche of new opportunities to establish social work services and educational programs in Eastern Europe and the former republics of the Soviet Union. As noted above, except in Poland and Yugoslavia, social work had officially been nonexistent in all countries of the Eastern bloc since World War II.

Social work in some form did exist in the USSR in the 1920s; indeed, representatives of the Soviet Union participated in the First International

SATTAREH FARMAN FARMAIAN:
FOUNDER OF SOCIAL WORK IN IRAN

Photo by L. Healy

When Sattareh Farman Farmaian returned to her native Iran to begin the first school of social work there, there wasn't even a word for social worker in the Persian language. Therefore, she invented one: *madadkar*, one who helps. She describes the tasks facing this new profession: "Social work in Iran would not be a desk job. It was going to be hard and dirty, practiced in discouraging circumstances amid conditions of the utmost wretchedness in a slum, a village or a public institution for the poor" (Farman Farmaian, 1993).

The personal story of this modern social work pioneer parallels the modern history of her country. She was born into the family of a prince of the Qajar family, the 15th of her father's 36 children. During her childhood, the family lived well in their compound in Tehran, but with uncertainty, as the new ruler, Reza Shah Pahlavi, was confiscating property of the Qajars and had briefly imprisoned Farman Farmaian's father after the fall of the Qajar dynasty. In her autobiography, she describes life in the harem and her close relationships with her mother, several of her father's other wives, and with many siblings and half-siblings (Farman Farmaian, 1992).

Her father, contrary to Muslim tradition, insisted that his daughters be educated as well as his sons. Sattareh was an enthusiastic student; during World War II, she left her sheltered home and traveled to the United States, where she became a student at the University of Southern California (USC) in 1944. She earned a BA and MSW from USC and began her career in social work.

For 4 years she worked with the UN in the Middle East, primarily as a social welfare consultant to the government of Iraq for the UN Educational, Scientific and Cultural Organization (UNESCO). She describes her experiences, first among the Bedouin and later in Iraq: "I had performed welfare work, training and research among the reed-hut slums of Baghdad, the mud dwellings of the Nile farmers, and in the dreadful Palestinian refugee camps in Lebanon" (Farman Farmaian, 1992, p. 206).

(*continued*)

Then, in 1958, she returned to Iran, determined to put her knowledge and experience to work for her own country. With the backing of the Shah's government, she opened a 2-year professional school of social work in Tehran and accepted her first class of 20 young Iranians for social work training later in 1958. The selection process was challenging. As she puts it, "a madadkar had to be a person whom I could teach to believe in something more than just himself and the future of his family and I could not afford to squander our meager resources on anyone uncommitted or opportunistic" (Farman Farmaian, 1993, p. 3). Her first task was to help the students—recruited from diverse social class, ethnic, and religious backgrounds, and sitting in a classroom with the opposite sex for the first time—accept each other.

The school became actively involved in social reform, tackling first the terrible conditions they discovered in an orphanage and a mental institution. Several years later, the School of Social Work established the Family Planning Association of Iran, introducing modern family planning into Iranian society. It took great skill in strategic accommodation and negotiation for this pioneer to further her agenda of family's and women's rights in a religious and very traditional society. The work, accomplished with help from an IASSW pilot project in family planning, was lauded in an IASSW report: "As a pioneer in the family planning movement in the country, it [the Tehran School of Social Work] has demonstrated to an unusual degree the effectiveness of social workers in promoting progressive policies, establishing effective programs, and providing needed service to a wide range of recipients" (Kendall, 1977, p. 20).

For 20 years, she devoted her efforts to furthering social work in Iran and to contributing to social work internationally. The Islamic Revolution in 1979 brought an end to her career in Iran and very nearly cost Farman Farmaian her life.

She arrived at work one morning to be told by one of the gardeners that students were waiting inside to kill her. Instead, they arrested her and delivered her to the headquarters of Ayatollah Khomeini. Among the charges leveled against her was that she had raised the living standard in Iran. By lifting many Iranians out of poverty, it was claimed that she had made them complacent and thereby delayed the overthrow of the Shah. Had the consequences not been so grave, it was a charge that would delight a social worker. After hours of waiting and of interrogation, she was released because another Ayatollah had interceded on her behalf. Warned to leave the country, she left Iran and went into exile in the United States.

Conference of Social Work in Paris in 1928 where they were outspoken against the individual charity approach and against religious influences on the profession (International Conference of Social Work, 1929). In the 1930s, however, social work was "condemned as a bourgeois artifact and eliminated" (Guzzetta, 1995, p. 197).

The end of the cold war brought a flood of consultants to Eastern Europe. As Guzzetta (1995) observed: "For vacationers and 'consultants' from the West, the Central and Eastern European countries were a dream come true. Prices were unbelievably low and outsiders were treated as honored guests, every utterance receiving attention and belief totally beyond the experience of academics in their home institutions. Once the borders were opened and the word was out, the stampede was on" (p. 200). While much of the consultation has been useful, other advice has been given uncritically and without understanding of the context. It is likely that another era of indigenization will emerge for the countries of the East.

A more gradual but still substantial opening up in China has led to about the same scenario. Following the Communist takeover in 1949, all social sciences were banned from Chinese universities by 1952, labeled bourgeois/capitalist subjects. For almost 30 years, there was no contact between China and world, relating to social work. Following the reestablishment of social sciences in Chinese universities in the early 1980s, explorations of social work began. By 1988, four universities had been given approval by the state to develop social work courses, and books and journals began using the term "social work" (Leung, 1995). The University of Hong Kong engaged in a 3-year cooperative project with Zhongshan University in China, involving teaching and fieldwork development. Chinese scholars were permitted to attend international social work meetings, and in 1988, China hosted the Conference on Social Work Education in the Asia and Pacific Region (Leung, 1995). Although the situation in China remains more controlled than in Eastern Europe, developments have been rapid since the mid-1980s.

The other major event of the 1990s was European unification. Its impact on social work has been considerable, especially on issues of personnel mobility and comparability of standards. As political and economic forces have brought about successively stronger agreements for a united Europe, a degree of professional integration is becoming necessary. Provisions now exist for the right to work in any member country, requiring mutual recognition of professional qualifications. "The European issue is now less the celebration of common values, knowledge and skills than how to best implement the right of social workers to practice in other member states" (Harris, 1997, p. 429). Numerous programs have offered grants to bring European social workers and social work educators together in joint programs. Interest in "European social work" has grown in the member states.

CONCLUSION

As social work enters its second century, challenges abound and new opportunities are evident. The promise of the end of the cold war has been diminished by worldwide fascination with the market economy and the resulting consequences of increased unemployment and greater personal insecurity for many. Cutbacks in welfare state commitments and lingering effects of financial crises in developing countries have led to continued scarcity of resources for meeting human needs and, therefore, to the widening gap between rich and poor. Yet during this period, social work has expanded to almost every nation and has increased its involvement in human rights and other significant international movements. Regional cooperation has increased, especially in Europe, creating new opportunities for cross-fertilization in the profession. Organized efforts at international action throughout the history of the profession will be discussed in more depth in the next chapter. Understanding both the global history of the development of the profession and of its international involvement will assist in charting the course of social work for the future.

REFERENCES

"Alice Salomon exiled," (1937), *Social Service Review, XI*(3), 510–511.

Asamoah, Y. (1995). Africa. In T.D. Watts, D. Elliott, & N.S. Mayadas, (Eds.), *International handbook on social work education* (pp. 223–239). Westport, CT: Greenwood Press.

Brown, G. (1991). The programme in the School of Continuing Studies. In J. Maxwell & E. Wint (eds.), *Contemporary social work education: A Caribbean orientation. Summary Proceedings of Social Work Symposium held May 27–29, 1991* (pp. 21–26). Mona, Jamaica: Department of Sociology & Social Work, University of the West Indies.

Child welfare problems and Japanese evacuation. (1942). *Social Service Review 16*(4), 673–676.

de Jongh, J.F. (1972). A retrospective view of social work education. In International Association of Schools of Social Work (IASSW), *New Themes in Social Work Education* [Proceedings] (pp. 22–36). XVIth International Congress of Schools of Social Work, The Hague, Netherlands, August 8–11, 1972. New York: IASSW.

Desai, A. (1987). Development of social work education. In *Encyclopedia of social work in India* (pp. 208–219). New Delhi: Government of India, Ministry of Welfare.

Farman Farmaian, S., & Munker, D. (1992). *Daughter of Persia: A woman's journey from her father's harem through the Islamic Revolution.* New York: Crown Publishers.

Farman Farmaian, S. (1993, February). *Social work in Iran.* Paper presented at the meeting of the Council on Social Work Education Annual Program, New York, NY.

Friedlander, W. (1975). *International social welfare.* Englewood Cliffs, NJ: Prentice-Hall.

Garigue, P. (1961). Challenge of cultural variations to social work. *Proceedings of the Ninth Annual Program Meeting* (pp. 9–22). Council on Social Work Education. New York: Council on Social Work Education.

Guzzetta, C. (1995). Central and Eastern Europe. In T.D. Watts, D. Elliott, & N.S. Mayadas (Eds.), *International handbook on social work education* (pp. 191–209). Westport, CT: Greenwood Press.

Harris, R. (1997). Internationalizing social work: Some themes and issues. In N.S. Mayadas, T.D. Watts, & D. Elliott (Eds.), *International handbook on social work theory and practice* (pp. 429–440). Westport, CT: Greenwood Press.

Jimenez, M., & Aylwin, H. (1992). Social work in Chile: Support for the struggle for justice in Latin America. In M.C. Hokenstad, S.K. Khinduka, & J. Midgley (Eds.), *Profiles in international social work* (pp. 29–41). Washington, DC: NASW Press.

Johansen, M. (1999, June 26). Sybil Francis reminisces on life and career. *The Daily Observer,* pp. 15, 17.

Kendall, K. (1977). *Final report: International development of qualified social work man-power for population and family planning activities.* New York: IASSW.

Kendall, K.A. (1978). The IASSW from 1928–1978: A journey of remembrance. In Kendall, K. (Ed.), *Reflections on social work education 1950–1978* (pp. 170–191). New York: IASSW.

Kendall, K. (1989). Women at the helm: Three extraordinary leaders. *Affilia, 4*(1), 23–32.

Kendall, K.A. (2000). *Social work education: Its origins in Europe.* Alexandria, VA: Council on Social Work Education.

Kollwitz, K. (1943). The United Nations relief and rehabilitation administration begins its work. *Social Service Review, 17*(4), 486–488.

Kudchodkar, L.S. (1963). Observations. *Indian Journal of Social Work, 24*(2), 96.

Leung, J. (1995). China. In T.D. Watts, D. Elliott, & N.S. Mayadas (Eds.), *International handbook on social work education* (pp. 403–419). Westport, CT: Greenwood Press.

Lorenz, W. (1994). *Social work in a changing Europe.* London: Routledge.

Manshardt, C. (1941). Education for social work. *Indian Journal of Social Work, II*(1), 12–22.

Manshardt, C. (1967). *Pioneering on social frontiers in India.* Bombay: Lalvani Publishing House for the Tata Institute of Social Sciences.

Maxwell, J.A. (1993, June). *Caribbean social work: Its historical development and current challenges.* Paper presented at the Caribbean Regional Social Work Conference, St. Michaels, Barbados.

Mazibuko, F., McKendrick, B., & Patel, L. (1992). Social work in South Africa: Coping with apartheid and change. In M.C. Hokenstad, S.K. Khinduka, & J. Midgley (Eds.), *Profiles in International Social Work.* Washington, DC: NASW Press.

Moltzer, M.J.A. (1948, March 12). Correspondence to members of the International Committee, Bloemendael, Holland. IASSW Archive, Social Welfare History Archives, University of Minnesota, Minneapolis, MN.

Moltzer, M.J.A. (1950, July). Secretary's report. International Committee of Schools of Social Work. IASSW Archive, Social Welfare History Archives, University of Minnesota, Minneapolis, MN.

Nitzsche, E. (1935). Letter to Alice Salomon. IASSW Archives, Social Welfare History Archives, University of Minnesota, Minneapolis, MN.

Ntusi, T. (1995). South Africa. In T.D. Watts, D. Elliott, & N.S. Mayadas (Eds.), *International handbook on social work education* (pp. 261–279). Westport, CT: Greenwood Press.

Popple, P.R. (1995). Social work profession: History. In R. Edwards (Ed.), *Encyclopedia of social work* (19th ed.) (pp. 2282–2292). Washington, DC: NASW Press.

Queiro-Tajalli, I. (1995). Argentina. In T.D. Watts, D. Elliott, & N.S. Mayadas (Eds.), *International handbook on social work education* (pp. 87–102). Westport, CT: Greenwood Press.

Radlinska, H.O. (1929). Training for Social Work in Poland. In *International Conference of Social Work* [Proceedings] (Vol. II, pp. 85–93). First Conference, Paris, July 8–13, 1928.

Ragab, I.A. (1995). Middle East and Egypt. In T.D. Watts, D. Elliott, & N.S. Mayadas (Eds.), *International handbook on social work education* (pp. 281–304). Westport, CT: Greenwood Press.

Rao, V. (comp.) (1984). *World guide to social work education* (2nd ed.) New York: Council on Social Work Education for the International Association of Schools of Social Work.

Richmond, M. (1917). *Social diagnosis*. New York: Russell Sage Foundation.

Salomon, A. (n.d.), *Character is Destiny*. Unpublished manuscript. (Available at the Leo Baeck-Institute, New York).

Stein, H.D. (1972). "Cross-national themes in social work education: A commentary on the sixteenth IASSW Congress. In IASSW, *New Themes in Social Work Education* (pp. 155–164). New York: IASSW.

United Nations. (1958). *Training for Social Work: Third International Survey*. New York: Author.

United Nations. (1969). *Proceedings of the International Conference of Ministers Responsible for Social Welfare*. New York: Author.

vander Straeten, S. (1992). *Oral history interview of Katherine Kendall*. Unpublished transcription of the interviews.

Van Wormer, K. (1997). *Social welfare: A world view*. Chicago: Nelson-Hall.

Walton, R.G. and El Nasr, M. (1988). The indigenization and authentization of social work in Egypt. *Community Development Journal, 23*(3), 148–155.

Wieler, J. (1988). Alice Salomon. *Journal of Teaching in Social Work, 2*(2), 165–171.

Wieler, J. (1989). The impact of Alice Salomon on social work education. In *60 Jahre IASSW* (pp. 15–26). Berlin: Fachhochschule fur Sozialarbeit und Sozialpadagogik.

Yelaja, S.A. (1969). Schools of social work in India: Historical development 1936–1966. *The Indian Journal of Social Work, 29*(4), 361–378.

Younghusband, E. (1963). Tasks and trends in education for social work: An international appraisal. *Social Work* (London), *20*(3), 4–11.

CHAPTER 3

INTERNATIONAL
PROFESSIONAL ACTION

A Selective History

In this chapter, the discussion of history continues with a focus on episodes of international professional action by social workers and with in-depth discussions of the brief notes that follow:

- more than 2,000 members of a new profession gather in Paris in 1928 to participate in the First International Conference of Social Work

- a social worker with the UNRRA meets with Mao Tse-tung and Chou En-lai to negotiate for delivery of postwar relief supplies in civil war–torn China in 1946

- the UN sponsors five major world surveys of social work education between 1950 and 1971

- a social worker advises the U.S. embassy in Brazil on important social conditions in 1963

- social work educators in Iran, Jamaica, the Philippines, and 17 other countries participate in an IASSW international project to develop curriculum on family planning in the 1970s

- in 1993, members of the International Council on Social Welfare (ICSW) Executive Committee approve an ambitious plan for involvement in the UN Summit for Social Development

- members of the International Federation of Social Workers meet in New York for an evening of letter-writing to Saddam Hussein, asking for the release of a Kuwaiti social worker

As the chapter title indicates, this will be a selective history, and one that will not follow a neat chronological order. The intent is to communicate some of the more interesting examples of social workers in action on the international scene and to discuss areas in which impact was considerable. After introductory remarks about social work involvement in social movements at the turn of the last century, the chapter begins with a discussion of the first effort to hold a worldwide social work conference, the 1928 First International Conference of Social Work. This meeting spawned the three major international social work organizations, now known as: the International Association of Schools of Social Work (IASSW), the International Federation of Social Workers (IFSW), and the International Council on Social Welfare (ICSW). Each organization will be discussed and a brief synopsis of their purposes and major activities will be given. One aspect of each organization's past or present work will be highlighted to illustrate how social work organizations have been differentially involved in international action, often having significant impact on social conditions. Selected for examination are: (a) the family-planning project conducted by IASSW in the 1970s, (b) the human rights work of the IFSW, and (c) ICSW's use of its consultative status with the UN to influence the Social Development Summit in the 1990s.

Three additional examples of particular importance to the history of international social work will also be presented. In UNRRA, social workers held a range of direct service, administrative, and planning positions in direct relief work in postwar Europe and China. The lessons of this experience suggest that social work skills can be successfully applied to relief and development work. In the early decades of the UN, social workers were involved as employees, trainers, consultants, and sponsored trainees in activities that spread social work education throughout much of the developing world. As "insiders," they had important opportunities to influence program directions at the UN. Finally, as an interesting example of policy influence, the experiences of the social welfare attachés in the U.S. State Department will be described. It demonstrates the potential value of social work in foreign policy.

Although the reader is reminded that this is far from a comprehensive history of social work's international involvement, the examples selected communicate a rich history of professional effort and impact. These will be further illustrated through several brief biographies of pioneers in international action.

ANTECEDENTS: ACTIVISM IN THE SOCIAL MOVEMENTS OF THE EARLY TWENTIETH CENTURY

The seeds of international professional action were sown by social work participation in the important international issues of the early 20th century. Women's issues, world peace, and labor conditions were dominant social concerns at the international level, and members of the new profession of social work were active in each of the related social movements. Through these movements, leaders in the social fields from different countries had opportunities to meet and exchange ideas while working for improved conditions for women and for workers. As noted in Chapter 2, among the social work pioneers who were also leaders in international women's organizations and international pacifism were Jane Addams and Alice Salomon. The two met at the 1909 International Congress of the International Council of Women in Canada (Lorenz, 1994) and were, with others, founders of the Women's International League for Peace and Freedom. Addams was

TIMELINE: HISTORY OF
INTERNATIONAL PROFESSIONAL ACTION

1919	Save the Children founded
1923	Jebb drafts Children's Charter
1924	Charter adopted by the League of Nations as Declaration on the Rights of the Child
1928	Social Welfare Fortnight held in Paris, including First International Conference of Social Work
1928–29	Founding of predecessors of ICSW, IASSW, IFSW
1932	Second International Conference of Social Work—Frankfurt
1936	Third International Conference of Social Work—London
1944–47	UNRRA conducts relief programs in Europe and China
1945	UN established
1946	Consultative status system for NGOs at UN established
1948	Fourth International Conference of Social Work—Atlantic City
1950	First UN survey of social work education
1955	Second UN survey of social work education
1958	Third UN survey of social work education
1963	Social welfare attachés appointed to U.S. embassies in Brazil and India
1965	Fourth UN survey of social work education
1971	IASSW family planning project begins
1971	Fifth UN survey of social work education
1976	IFSW Code of Ethics adopted
1970s	Inter-University Consortium for International Social Development (IUCISD) founded
1988	IFSW forms Human Rights Commission
1988	IFSW publishes policy papers
1994	IFSW/IASSW UN Manual on Human Rights published
1994	IFSW adopts *Revised Declaration of Ethical Principles*
1995	UN World Summit for Social Development held in Copenhagen

a leader of the Women's Peace Conference at The Hague in 1915 and continued her involvement in pacifism in spite of heavy criticism. Social workers were also concerned about conditions for children. Eglantyne Jebb led efforts for improving children's lives, through the Save the Children Fund, and initiated the first international policy on children's rights, a declaration adopted by the League of Nations in 1924.

It may have been from a natural outgrowth of these involvements that social work formed its own world organizations. There are indications that these social workers were in communication and visited with each other to examine developments in other countries. Seeking additional mechanisms for professional exchange and communication led to the call for a world conference and then for formal organizations. Within 30 years of the founding of professional social work, an international conference was held and the major international social work organizations were founded. Although earlier conferences provided opportunities for international exchange (e.g., the European International Conference on Charity and Welfare, founded in 1856, and the meeting on charities held in 1893 in conjunction with the Chicago World's Fair), the 1928 conference is seen as a watershed in the organization of international social work.

SOCIAL WORK TAKES THE WORLD STAGE: INTERNATIONAL ORGANIZATIONS

The idea for organizing an international conference of social work was suggested by European and Japanese social workers who were invited to attend the National Conference of Social Work held in the United States in 1919 and in 1923. An official proposal was made by Dr. René Sand of Belgium in a January 15, 1923, letter to Julia Lathrop; Dr. Sand was invited to attend the 1923 conference in Washington to explain his idea further. The conference approved the idea in principle and the endorsement by the American Association of Social Workers soon followed. Support was secured from the League of Red Cross Societies in 1925. In September 1926, an organizing committee met in Paris with representatives from 17 countries, from Europe, the Far East, and North America, and from the League of Nations, the International Labor Organization (ILO), the League of Red Cross Societies, the International Congress on Statutory and Voluntary Assistance, the International Migration Service, the Save the Children Fund International Union, and others. Funding was secured from various foundations, including Rockefeller and Russell Sage. Dr. Alice Masarykova of Prague led the conference and Dr. René Sand was secretary general.

Following several subsequent planning meetings in Paris and Prague, more and more social organizations asked to hold their conferences at the same time. Thus the planned event grew to become the International Social Welfare Fortnight and included not only the first international social work conference but also meetings of the International Child Welfare Congress, the International Congress on Voluntary and Statutory Assistance, and the

PIONEERS IN INTERNATIONAL ACTION: EGLANTYNE JEBB

Save the Children

Although she died at the relatively young age of 52, Eglantyne Jebb contributed extensively to international social action; she founded a major international NGO and drafted a document on children's rights that became the foundation for the 1989 Convention on the Rights of the Child. Jebb was born in 1876 in Shropshire, England, into a prosperous family. She was educated at Oxford and then took training as a teacher. However, she taught only briefly, soon becoming involved in social work with the Charity Organization Society (COS). In 1906, she conducted a study of poverty in Cambridge, "Cambridge: A Study in Social Questions," that is still recognized as sound and insightful research. Her career directions changed in 1913, when she went to Macedonia to do relief work after the Balkan Wars. It was during this visit that she found her life's work—emergency and development help to children in need—after seeing the appalling conditions of refugees displaced by the war.

Two accomplishments stand out among the many that can be attributed to Jebb. The first is the founding of the Save the Children Fund. News of the suffering caused by the Allied blockade in Europe at the end of World War I began to reach England. With her sister Dorothy, Eglantyne began to raise money to provide direct help to children in war-devastated Europe and called the effort the Save the Children Fund. Many thought it treasonous to assist enemy children. One of Jebb's supporters was well-known playwright George Bernard Shaw, who responded to criticism of his support of the enemy by saying "I have no enemies under seven." (Graham, 1978). Jebb was a masterful fund-raiser. One story tells of her arrest and conviction for publishing photographs of suffering children in Austria without proper permission from the censor still in place after the war. She was fined after vigorous prosecution but managed to talk the prosecutor into giving a donation to the Save the Children Fund (Gra-

(continued)

ham, 1978). She foresaw the phenomenon of "compassion fatigue" when she said "we have to devise means of making known the facts in such a way as to touch the imagination of the world. The world is not ungenerous, but unimaginative and very busy."

The Save the Children Fund became an international alliance that continues to this day. Jebb's ideas about aid, relief, and development were truly visionary; she advocated policies that are seen as the hallmarks of forward-looking development assistance for the 21st century. Two of the principles of the Fund was that aid should be based on need and that children should not suffer due to wars they had no part in. Jebb also believed that aid should be self-sustaining, be given in such a way as to stimulate self-help, and based on planning and research. She was concerned about mutuality, saying that: "The system of world organization . . . was not based on the principle of dividing up the countries into those which gave and those which received but on the policy of requiring the recognition of dual duty from all countries."

Jebb's other major accomplishment was the drafting of the "Declaration on the Rights of the Child" in 1923. It was adopted by the League of Nations and became the first in a series of global documents on children's rights, leading to the 1989 Convention on the Rights of the Child.

Jebb participated in international social work events and wrote about the nature of social work and globalism. The following quote exemplified her thinking: "Every social worker ought to be a scientist, and social workers all over the globe should feel that they are all members of one body engaged in laying the foundation of the civilisation of the future, working shoulder to shoulder and drawing upon a fund of common knowledge."

She suffered from chronic poor health and apparently from periodic depression. At times, her life seemed somewhat aimless, and she spent periods traveling with her mother. But during the last 9 years of her life, when her health was quite fragile, she pursued her mission to help children of the world vigorously. As noted above, it was during this 9-year period that she made her mark on social work, international development, and children's rights.

Her concerns for children were truly global. Prior to her death, she had intended to organize a conference on the needs of children in Africa and was studying Chinese to help with another project in the planning stages to develop alternatives to child labor in China. The conference she planned on Africa was held in 1931. Jebb intended to participate in the 1928 International Conference on Social Work in Paris but poor health prevented her from attending. However, the paper she prepared was read; in it she defined the essentials of international social work (Jebb, 1929). She died shortly after the conference in 1928.

In addition to the references noted, the biographical sketch of Jebb was prepared using documents from the archives of the International Save the Children Federation, including Save the Children, 1994, Information Sheet 15; Quotes from Eglantyne Jebb; 34 Facts About Eglantyne Jebb, and Save the Children Facts.

International Housing and Town Planning Congress. Funds for the Fortnight came from foundations in the United States, from the Czech and Japanese Red Cross Societies, and from national committees in Germany, Poland, and Spain.

The event itself was well attended. The International Conference of Social Work was held from July 8 to 13, 1928, in Paris, and drew 2,481 delegates from 42 countries, including 279 from the United States (Organization of the International Conference of Social Work, 1929, p. 14). One section of the conference was devoted to social work education.

It is interesting that these early conference organizers lauded the ease of modern transportation and communication that enabled them to meet. One speaker at the conference said:

> In the last hundred years, the technical application of human invention has wrought nothing short of a revolution in international relations. The high seas—obstacles for so long to the free interchange of goods and ideas—have become a great medium for the exchange of both. . . . Ships, railways, aeroplanes, telephones, wireless telegraphy, broadcasting—all these have made the world smaller, have brought us into close contact with one another for better or for worse. (Jebb, 1929, p. 637)

From the perspective of more than 70 years later, we marvel at the hardships endured to engage in professional exchange of ideas.

The 1928 Fortnight initiated what would become regular world meetings on social work and social welfare. The second conference was held in Frankfurt in 1932 in the midst of a worldwide depression. Discussions focused, not surprisingly, on the impact of unemployment on the family. The third conference in 1936 in London was also shaped by economic depression and unemployment, although the official theme was "Social Work and the Community" and featured discussion of the "new concept of community organization" (Katzki, 1988, p. 13). Ominous forewarnings were felt as representatives of the Nazi regime in Germany attended the conference and presented on the virtues of Nazi philosophy. Indeed, the war that followed interrupted all international activities and meetings until 1946, when remnants of social work and social welfare leadership came together to plan for the future. Conferences resumed in 1948, with the fourth conference in Atlantic City, New Jersey. The social work and social welfare professional organizations have held biennial conferences since 1948, continuing the important activities of knowledge sharing and professional networking across nations. In the two decades following the Atlantic City conference, milestones were the holding of world conferences in India (1952), Brazil (1962), and Kenya (1974); these events signified the expansion of social work organizations beyond Europe and North America to worldwide bodies.

The three major world social work organizations developed out of the 1928 conference and remain active today. Each will be discussed in the next section.

INTERNATIONAL SOCIAL WORK ORGANIZATIONS

International Association of Schools of Social Work

Acronym: IASSW

Founded in: 1928

Previous name: International Committee of Schools of Social Work

Members: Social work educational programs at the tertiary level throughout the world. Individual memberships also available

Purpose: To promote and develop quality education, training, and knowledge for social work practice worldwide and to promote social development

International Federation of Social Workers

Acronym: IFSW

Founded in: 1928 (predecessor organization); reassembled in 1956

Previous name: International Permanent Secretariat of Social Workers

Members: National professional associations make up the membership; individuals may join as Friends of IFSW

Purpose: To promote social work as a profession; to support national associations; to encourage and facilitate contacts between social workers of all countries; to represent the profession on the international level

International Council on Social Welfare

Acronym: ICSW

Founded in: 1928

Previous name: International Conference on Social Work

Members: National committees, other national associations, and specialized international organizations; individual memberships in national committees

Purpose: to promote social development and social welfare; to serve as a forum for exchange of knowledge in these areas; to maintain active liaison with the UN on social development matters

Inter-University Consortium for International Social Development

Acronym: IUCISD

Founded: In the late 1970s; inaugural symposium held in 1980

(continued)

Members: Institutional members (mostly educational institutions) and individual members

Purpose: An interdisciplinary organization founded by social work educators to promote social development, IUCISD brings scholars, practitioners, and students from the human services together to advance social development through teaching, practicing, researching, and networking

International Association of Schools of Social Work

Although Dr. René Sand was the prime mover behind the first conference, he asked Alice Salomon of Germany to lead a section on social work education. It was during this meeting that Dr. Moltzer of the Netherlands recommended that a committee be formed "to write to all the training schools of social work asking them whether they would be prepared to become members of an International Association of Schools," thus giving birth to the IASSW ("Fifth Question," 1929, pp. 233–234). Joining Salomon as founders of the International Committee of Schools of Social Work were Dr. M. J. A. Moltzer, the Netherlands; Mme Mulle, Belgium; and Mme Wagner-Beck and Mlle M. de Meyenburg, Switzerland. Miss Sophonisba Breckinridge and Mr. Porter Lee of the United States, Miss Elisabeth Macadam and Miss Elinor Black of England, Mme Edouard Fuster of France, and Professor Helena Radlinska of Poland were soon brought into the leadership group (Kendall, 1978). The letter of invitation to join a new organization of schools of social work that Dr. Salomon sent to the 111 identified schools of social work resulted in 46 founding member schools from 10 countries. By 1939, the number had grown to 75 member schools from 18 countries, including 29 schools from the American Association of Schools of Social Work (Kendall, 1978). By then, however, all German schools had dropped their membership in protest against the leadership of Dr. Salomon, a German of Jewish background.

The association (then named the International Committee of Schools of Social Work) immediately began to reach out to intergovernmental organizations. A working relationship was developed with the Commission on Social Questions of the League of Nations. The International Labour Office (Geneva) set up a Centre of Documentation for schools of social work to pull together statistics, research reports, and reports of seminars from schools of social work. Thus the setting up of working relationships with international intergovernmental bodies was identified very early as a strategy for international social work action.

Another early and continuing strategy for action, as noted above, is the holding of international conferences and seminars to facilitate interchange of information and ideas and the building of relationships across borders. This type of exchange is particularly important to an association of educators, which are seen as responsible for building knowledge and for research in the field. Exchange of information also contributes indirectly, if not directly, to the development of implicit general standards for social work education. In addition to the periodic world conferences, in the early years, international summer schools were held by the committee in Europe, focusing on various areas of social service (e.g., protection of minors, housing, and care and education of persons with disabilities) (Kendall, 1978).

World War II had a devastating, but temporary, impact on IASSW. Kendall (1987) notes that "the European network was shattered by World War II," (p. 992), leading to leadership changes in the organization. The founding president, Dr. Salomon, had been driven into exile and was not able to revive the board from her exile in the United States. She died in 1948, the year the IASSW met in Atlantic City in its first real postwar meeting. René Sand, still active after more than 30 years, became president until his death in 1953. The association began to mature into a world organization as it expanded its leadership group beyond Europe and added to the board members from Australia, Guatemala, Japan, and India in 1956. IASSW set up an independent secretariat in 1971, led by the first paid secretary general, Katherine Kendall.

The formation of a secretariat made it possible for the organization to take on expanded functions. A program initiative launched in the 1970s—a population and family planning curriculum project—demonstrates how social work education can contribute to international social change and development.

Family Planning in the IASSW: Program Development to Reshape Services. The IASSW population and family planning project provides an example of social work action through direct program development and implementation. Beginning in 1971, IASSW initiated a 5-year contract (extended to a 6th year) with the U.S. Agency for International Development (USAID) to develop qualified personnel for population and family planning work in developing countries. (The following section is summarized from the final project report, see Kendall, 1977.) The need for the program was defined at the International Conference on Social Work Education, Population and Family Planning held in 1970 and was twofold. First, population control and family planning were growing in importance as part of development programs; however, the approach of population experts was on meeting quantitative targets, with little attention to the human and cultural dimensions. Second, although social workers were strategically positioned to play important roles in family planning, there was little in social work education at the time to prepare them for these roles. The project goals were to define family planning in the context of social development and to prepare social workers for effective professional practice in family planning as part of their professional roles.

During the project, activities were carried out in 31 schools of social work in 13 developing countries, with less involvement in 7 other countries. In each of the project schools, population and family planning were formally added to the curriculum. Seminars and workshops (more than 100 over the life of the grant) were held to train faculty members to teach family planning, IASSW resource teams provided short-term consultation on curriculum development, and reference and teaching materials were provided to each school. The main activity was teaching social work students to use family planning information in their social work practice. Continuing education programs were developed for graduates and for related personnel. The project also resulted in interorganizational work both at the IASSW level and for the participating schools of social work, bringing social work into closer contact with governmental agencies and NGOs in population and development work. An important outcome was that social work defined its own approach to family planning: "Social workers hold the promotion of human welfare as a major goal of the profession; thus, they are concerned with family planning as a human right, as an essential element in family health and welfare, and as a significant aspect of social development. This means that the project has been just as much concerned with placing family planning into the full range of social welfare services as in placing social workers into family planning clinics" (Kendall, 1977, p. 3).

An impressive feature of the project was its geographic reach. Pilot schools were located in Turkey, Iran, Korea, the Philippines, Thailand, Indonesia, Jamaica, Sri Lanka, Bangladesh, Vietnam, Pakistan, Ecuador, Hong Kong, Sudan, Zambia, Ghana, Egypt, and Kenya. Project leadership was also diverse. Secretary General Kendall served as project director and was aided by a team that included Angelina Almanzor from the Philippines, E. Maxine Ankrah from Uganda, Barry Rigby, George Walmsley, Jacqueline Atkins, and Katherine Oettinger. The one area of disappointment was Latin America where the project failed to take hold. The one program established in the area was discontinued as performance was not satisfactory. In Asia, Africa, and the English-speaking Caribbean countries, considerable success was achieved. Asian schools reported that 7,000 students had been reached by the project. There were also increases in family planning-related field placements, in faculty community service activities, and in graduates securing related employment.

Another important outcome of the project was the strengthening of the national relevance of the social work curriculum as a whole. To prepare for integration of family planning content, many schools did a total curriculum review and used the challenge of integrating family planning and social development to link social work more closely with national social and economic development plans. Thus the family planning project strengthened the move toward indigenous curriculum, especially in the Asian schools. Regional differences in emphasis emerged; social development was accepted as the goal among Asian schools, whereas the African schools preferred an emphasis on family life education with a strong emphasis on community rather than the individual. The evaluators note that a later start limited African schools from realizing the full benefits of the project, although considerable progress was made.

The project generated a series of publications, some of which had lasting impact. An early publication was *Population and Family Planning: Analytical Abstracts for Social Work Educators and Related Disciplines* (1972, IASSW, New York). This volume brought acclaim from other professions and was deemed so useful that it was translated into Spanish by the Pan-American Health Organization. In 1973, a casebook was published of 22 Asian vignettes on social work in family planning: *Social Work in Action: An International Perspective on Population and Family Planning* (IASSW, New York). Proceedings of various international conferences and the regional seminars further enhanced the literature, especially the publication of volumes from regional perspectives in Asia and Africa. These include *A Developmental Outlook for Social Work Education* (1974) and *Asian Social Problems: New Strategies for Social Work Education* (1976) from the Asian region and *Education for Family Welfare: A Component of Development* (1977) and *Family Welfare in Africa: Educational Strategies* (1977) from seminars held in Africa (all published by IASSW, New York). Jamaica made a special contribution to the project in sharing its success with training paraprofessionals in social welfare and family planning. Through hosting an international workshop on paraprofessional training and publication of a manual on the subject, the work of the Social Welfare Training Centre at the University of the West Indies influenced similar developments in Asia.

The project was not without problems. Indeed, as mentioned earlier, efforts to establish pilot schools in Latin America failed; the project faced opposition to family planning from both the established church and from leftists who denounced family planning as an effort to limit populations of developing countries. Even in some of the schools with successful programs, small groups of students opposed family planning content on ideological grounds. Overall, however, the project provides an excellent example of international action to improve human well-being through the use of a curriculum and education project. The summary paragraph from the final report states:

> The project has laid the basic foundation for the development of qualified social work manpower for population and family planning responsibilities in Asia. An excellent beginning has been made in Africa. The IASSW view of family planning as positive family welfare and an integral aspect of social development has led to significant educational change in both regions. As a grassroots operation, the project has led to indigenous curriculum development related to national needs and priorities. This response to national development concerns through the new emphasis on family planning has broadened the purposes and scope of social work education to embrace a variety of community-based activities. (Kendall, 1977, p. 42)

Program efforts since 1977 have included further work on indigenous curriculum, assistance to the development and expansion of social work education in Eastern Europe and the former Soviet Union, attention to gender and women's issues in social work education, and an ambitious census project to catalog extensive information on social work education throughout the world. Co-sponsorship of the journal *International Social Work*, representation with the UN and UNICEF and regular biennial conferences continue. Additional activities are carried out by regional associations.

International Federation of Social Workers

The IFSW, an international organization of professional social workers, was founded in 1956. Its predecessor, the International Permanent Secretariat of Social Workers, was initiated in Paris in 1928 by social workers from England, France, Scandinavia, Switzerland, and Czechoslovakia; provisional statutes for the organization were approved at the Second International Social Work Conference in Frankfurt in 1932 by eight founding member countries (Belgium, Czechoslovakia, France, Germany, Great Britain, Sweden, Switzerland, and the United States) (Secretary General Tom Johannesen of the IFSW, personal communication, July 16, 1999). The Secretariat was active until the beginning of World War II; a conference planned for Prague in 1940 never took place. By 1950, plans began for a new organization, building on the legacy of the Secretariat—the International Federation of Social Workers.

The primary aim of the IFSW is to promote social work as a profession with professional standards and ethics. Thus, one of the major achievements of the organization has been development of ethical standards for the global profession. The International Code of Ethics was initially adopted in 1976 and represented the first code of ethics adopted to apply to social workers around the world. A number of national organizations have used the code as their own. In 1994, new ethical documents were adopted, the International Ethical Standards for Social Workers and the International Declaration of Ethical Principles of Social Work (IFSW, 1994; see Appendix A).

Another major goal of the IFSW is to "encourage contacts between social workers of all countries" and "to provide the means for discussion and exchange of ideas" (Johannesen, 1997, p. 154). Therefore, like the other professional organizations, the IFSW sponsors regular conferences at both the regional and international levels to promote communication and exchange among social workers.

An important part of IFSW's work has been to represent social work's views on major world issues through development of policy position papers and through its consultative status with the UN. As defined in its constitution, the IFSW aims to ensure social work involvement in international social policy, both by supporting national organizations in participating in social planning and policy formulation, both nationally and internationally, and by presenting the point of view of the profession on an international level through liaisons with various international organizations in the social welfare field (Johannesen, 1997). Through development and promulgation of policy positions on a number of significant global issues, IFSW has increased social work visibility on global policy. Among the problem areas addressed are: HIV/AIDS, migration, peace and disarmament, advancement of women, refugees, human rights, and indigenous people (IFSW, 1988).

Beginning in the late 1980s, IFSW adopted a strong program focus on human rights. Through case advocacy, policy advocacy, and member education, the Federation is making an impact in this important arena.

Human Rights: A Case of International Advocacy by the Profession. As explained by Secretary General Tom Johannesen (1997):

> Human rights are inseparable from social work theory, values, ethics, and practice. It is therefore difficult to perform social work in a society in which basic human rights are not met. The recognition of the interdependence between human rights and social work practice has led IFSW to focus its work in this area. (p. 155)

Although some activities began earlier, IFSW established its Human Rights Commission in 1988, with a human rights commissioner for each of the association's regions. The commission has an official liaison to Amnesty International. In 1996, the federation's policy statement on human rights was promulgated and publicized among members and related organizations (IFSW, 1996).

An important part of the IFSW's human rights program is direct advocacy on behalf of professional social workers and other social service workers who are victims of violations of human rights. An intensive campaign focused on Chile in the 1980s and South Africa in the latter part of that decade. More recent efforts have focused on social workers who are being held as political prisoners in Iraq, Myanmar, and other countries. One example is the case of Secretary General Feisal Al-Sane of the Kuwait Association of Social Workers, as documented in a 1999 issue of the *IFSW Newsletter* ("Saddam Hussein's Prisoner," 1999). He was apprehended by Iraqi troops during the invasion of Kuwait in 1990 after he had refused to join an opposition government under Iraqi protection. During the month following the initial invasion, Al-Sane took the lead in organizing men to plan for assistance to the people under the occupation. A spy infiltrated the meetings, leading to Al-Sane's arrest. He was taken to Iraq and has not been seen since 1990, although there was evidence reported by IFSW that he was still alive as of 1993. Using the methods popularized by Amnesty International, IFSW uses publicity and letter-writing to governments and other human rights bodies to call attention to the situation of those being illegitimately held for speaking out on injustices and other similar actions.

The IFSW, along with the IASSW, collaborated with the UN Centre for Human Rights on a curriculum project on human rights, resulting in the publication of a manual: *Human Rights and Social Work: A Manual for Schools of Social Work and the Social Work Profession* (United Nations, 1994). The manual was the first in a series planned to target human rights information to various professions and groups and served to expand the Centre's program of information and training beyond legal and criminal justice professionals. In the foreword to the manual, the assistant secretary general for human rights explains that it has been published "with the specific purpose of adding to the knowledge and understanding of this important professional group in respect of all aspects of human rights and the international mechanisms that have been developed to protect those rights" (p. iii).

The manual stresses the relevance of human rights to all levels of social work concern—the micro level of the individual, the meso level of community, and the macro or societal level. Social workers are encouraged to "examine the world and their role through a social justice lens" (p. 3). The recommended curriculum presents human rights as "inseparable from social work theory, values and ethics, and practice" (p. 5). Therefore, social workers are mandated to advocate for human rights even in authoritarian and oppressive contexts where it is dangerous to do so. The IFSW is developing a follow-up UN publication on the rights of the child.

In addition to the intrinsic importance of the work itself, IFSW's human rights efforts increase the visibility and credibility of social work in the community of international organizations.

International Council on Social Welfare

The third of the three organizations founded in 1928, the ICSW (first named the International Conference on Social Work) is now a "world organization for the promotion of social development" (Lally, 1987, p. 982). It does this by serving as a forum for exchange on knowledge on social welfare and social development; through liaison with relevant intergovernmental organizations, such as those of the UN, on social development matters; and by encouraging positive developments in social welfare around the world. Its mission statement defines its action strategies as follows:

> ICSW's main ways of pursuing its aims include gathering and disseminating information, undertaking research and analysis, convening seminars and conferences, drawing on grass-root experiences, strengthening non-governmental organizations, developing policy proposals, engaging in public advocacy and working with policy-makers and administrators in government and elsewhere. (ICSW, 1994)

Membership in the ICSW is through national committees. There are currently 51 national committees and 31 other national associations that belong to ICSW. International organizations can also belong to the Council and the 14 current NGO members include the International Federation of Red Cross and Red Crescent Societies, the International Federation on Aging, the International Planned Parenthood Federation, and the Salvation Army. ICSW reaches beyond any particular profession to involve practitioners from various disciplines and lay people interested in social welfare. This differentiates it from the work of its "sister" organizations, IFSW and IASSW. The three organizations often select the same location for their biennial conferences and co-sponsor a journal, *International Social Work*.

ICSW has held conferences regularly, except for the years during World War II. The organization has worked to ensure that work continues between

RENÉ SAND: ORGANIZATION FOUNDER

Social Welfare Archives, University of Minnesota

Dr. René Sand was a founder of the ICSW and the IASSW, an inspiration for the beginning of social work education in Chile, and a contributor to social work in his native Belgium; in addition, he made outstanding contributions in the field of social medicine. Truly a renaissance man, he was a leading figure in social work and social welfare for more than 3 decades and a leading figure in medicine for almost 5 decades.

Sand was born in Ixelles, Belgium, in 1877; he studied medicine at the University of Brussels and undertook postgraduate studies in hospitals in both Berlin and Vienna. One of his early posts was as a medical consultant to an insurance company dealing with accidents in the workplace. There he became aware of the everyday hazards in the life of ordinary workers, and his interest in social medicine was born. During World War I, he worked with the Red Cross of Belgium and aided refugees in London, deepening his social commitments. He was elected secretary general of the League of Red Cross Societies in 1921, an association he continued long into his career.

Sand made many trips abroad. He visited the United States twice in the years after World War I and was a presenter at the U.S. National Conference on Social Welfare. In 1924, he visited South America where he gave lectures in social medicine at the University of Santiago. As mentioned in Chapter 2, it was on his return to Europe that he met Dr. Alejandro del Rio and became involved in setting up the first school of social work in Chile. Working with the League of Red Cross Societies, he was involved in the creation of a number of international organizations, including the International Committee of Mental Health and the International Hospitals Association. In describing his special qualities as a leader, his obituary in *Lancet* read: "He had the knack of suppressing trouble-

(continued)

makers with a piece of well-timed and discriminating flattery; and he could shift readily from one language to another and produce a bon mot in each" ("Rene Sand," 1953, p. 576).

Social workers, however, remember Sand for applying these gifts to his founding activities in the field of social work. Sand was a prime mover in organizing the 1928 First International Conference of Social Work. In a paper he wrote proposing the conference, he expressed his belief in the importance of having those in the same field from different countries come together to share information about their daily practice and to meet each other. He worked with others for more than 4 years to make the conference a reality. Later, he said that the conference has "conferred on the social work profession a dignity and an authority that it had not enjoyed previously" (Anciaux, 1988, as translated from the French). He served as president of the ICSW from 1932 to 1948 and was president of the IASSW from 1946 until his death in 1953. He was credited with having been the "central source of power and inspiration behind the establishment" of both organizations (Kendall, 1978).

In 1937, Sand became secretary general of the Ministry of Public Health in Belgium. During World War II, he was taken prisoner by the Nazis in 1940 when they invaded Belgium and held in Tyrol, Austria, until May 1945 when he was liberated by the U.S. Seventh Army ("Obituary of Rene Sand," 1953). He returned to his activities in both social medicine and social work. He stepped down from the presidency of the ICSW in 1948, insisting that a younger member be named. But he continued on as honorary president and had, by then, been pressed into service as president of the IASSW to reorganize it after the war. Presiding at the 1952 Conference of Social Work in Madras, India, he oversaw the transformation of social work organizations into truly worldwide bodies.

Sand was also significantly involved in the founding of the World Health Organization (WHO). He presided over the committee of experts put together by the new UN to develop an international health organization; in 1950, he was appointed chair of the WHO expert committee for professional and technical education.

He died suddenly in 1953, and members of many organizations mourned his loss. In addition to his legacy of organizational leadership, he left extensive writings on the many topics of his expertise, including *The Advance to Social Medicine, La Medecine Sociale,* and *Health and Human Progress.* As noted in his obituary in the *British Medical Journal,* Sand "will be long remembered not only for his conceptions of the potentialities of international collaboration in medicine but also for his ideas of the part that medicine, as an art, should play in the social structure of every country" ("Obituary Rene Sand," 1953, p. 572). He believed that medicine would be fully developed only "if social and psychological aspects re-

(continued)

ceived a proper place in the training of medical students" ("Obituary René Sand," 1953, p. 572). His ideas on both international collaboration and on the importance of social factors in health are still current today. An award was established in his name by the ICSW and is awarded every other year to an individual or organization that has given outstanding service in social welfare.

Upon hearing of his death, Katherine Kendall, of the CSWE and later the secretary general of the IASSW, wrote:

> Dr. Sand was a hero to me and almost a myth long before I ever met him. From social work friends in Latin America, I had heard about him as the "father" of social work education there. They told me how he had traveled from one country to another awakening a deep and lasting interest in establishing schools for the preparation of social workers. When I did meet him at last, immediately after the war, the easily perceptible greatness of the man explained the myth and I knew why my South American friends had spoken of him with love and a respect amounting to reverence. ("In Memoriam," 1953)

conferences and has made efforts to increase the action components of its agenda (see box on René Sand). From 1964 to 1966, the organization considered ways to expand beyond a forum for biennial debate and exchange of ideas and to venture into action programs. In 1966, the name of the organization was officially changed to the International Council on Social Welfare to underscore that its scope is not limited to any one profession. The addition of a descriptive phrase to its name in 1982—International Council on Social Welfare: A World Organization Promoting Social Development—underscores the efforts of the organization to identify with the development movement and more closely identify with UN priorities (Katzki, 1988).

ICSW has always maintained relationships with major world organizations. It has successfully used its consultative status with the UN to increase the voice of social welfare in important recent deliberations, as will be explained next.

United Nations Consultative Status: Action to Influence Global Policy. ICSW maintains consultative status in Category I (explained below) with the UN, allowing the organization to participate with UN bodies in New York, Geneva, and Vienna. Indeed, ICSW was one of the first NGOs to receive consultative status with the UN shortly after its founding. The system for NGOs to interact with the UN was established in 1946 and remains largely unchanged today. Organizations are permitted to apply for consultative status with the ECOSOC if they meet several conditions: They must focus on issues related to ECOSOC, have aims consistent with the UN Charter, and broadly represent those in their field (with a preference for worldwide organizations rather than national bodies). NGOs can be accepted into one of three classifications, with varying privileges. ICSW is a Category I organization, designated as an organization "with a basic interest in most of the activities of the Council" (Willetts, 1996, p. 32). Category II organizations are those with competence in selected areas of ECOSOC's scope and are granted fewer privileges of interaction. Still other organizations are placed on the roster, a list of specialization organizations that ECOSOC may consult on an ad hoc basis.

Over the years, efforts have been made to limit the number of NGOs with consultative status and to put some restrictions on their activities. In the specialized work of the UN, however, the importance of NGO contributions and expertise is recognized. As a Category I organization, ICSW can attend ECOSOC meetings, circulate written statements to members, and address a council committee and, if recommended, the full council. In addition, Category I organizations can submit agenda items for ECOSOC consideration. Access to information is an important benefit of consultative status; NGOs have access to UN documents and have passes to enter UN facilities, although recent concerns with security may limit the number of persons with access.

Social Development Summit (1995): Effective Use of Consultative Status. The specialized conferences held by the UN have created additional opportunities for NGO participation. One of these was the World Summit on Social Development, held in Copenhagen in 1995. Falling squarely within the expertise of ICSW, the organization mobilized and implemented a series of special efforts to make an impact on world deliberations and, beginning in 1993, made the summit its major priority. Since the summit, the ICSW program has emphasized follow-up efforts to implement its plan of action.

Activities began several years prior to the actual summit, as the optimal time to influence UN deliberations is during the preparatory work that precedes major world meetings. Working with other key NGOs, ICSW developed plans at its February 1993 executive committee meeting to organize an NGO consultation meeting during the first UN Summit Preparatory Committee meeting and to organize a global NGO preparatory meeting to coincide with the 1994 International Conference on Social Welfare in Finland (ICSW, 1993). A special summit newsletter was initiated; over the next several years, six issues were produced and thousands distributed to members, NGOs, governments, and intergovernmental agencies. The NGO preparatory meeting drew over 60 NGO leaders for a 3-day meeting in Helsinki in July 1994. Later that summer, ICSW participated in the second preparatory committee meeting for the official UN Summit. At the meeting, it organized an NGO issues forum and disseminated several thousand copies of ICSW speeches and policy papers related to poverty and other Summit topics (ICSW, 1995). Through this lengthy process of monitoring official deliberations, disseminating speeches and policy suggestions, and organizing NGOs for participation, ICSW was able to influence the official plan of action of the UN meeting. According to Julian Disney, chair of the ICSW Summit Working Group, "ICSW widely circulated about a dozen policy papers and proposals for inclusion in the Summit agreements and we are pleased that many of our recommendations are reflected in the final documents" (ICSW, 1996).

Activities continued after the summit, focusing on implementation of the summit recommendations and plan of action. ICSW initiated the *Social Development Review*, a quarterly publication dedicated to summit follow-up and other social development issues. Following the summit, ICSW developed a policy paper on social development to guide its actions in the field (ICSW, 1998). Another important activity was the organization of regional follow-up meetings for NGOs to work on implementation issues and seminars on summit implementation for each ICSW regional meeting.

In 1997, a "Memorandum of Understanding Between the U.N. Development Programme and the International Council on Social Welfare" was adopted to realize greater collaboration between the UN body and the Council. As stated in the document: "The principal areas for collaboration and interaction will concern reduction and eradication of poverty throughout the world, with special emphasis on pursuing and monitoring implementation of the relevant agreements made at the World Summit for Social Development and other global conferences" (ICSW, 1997, p. 1). The memorandum commits the two organizations to work together to implement the summit recommendations on the eradication of poverty by promoting the use and discussion of UNDP's annual Human Development Report and ICSW's *Social Development Review*, producing and distributing expert papers on strategies for poverty reduction, increasing NGO involvement in intergovernmental meetings relating to poverty eradication, and preparing for the year 2000 UN General Assembly review of progress on the implementation of the Summit plan (ICSW, 1997).

Thus, through this work, ICSW has successfully launched and maintained an action agenda focused on influencing global policy and mobilizing other NGOs to do likewise. The ICSW experience is a useful example of effective use of UN consultative status, which is discussed again in Chapter 10.

DIRECT WORK IN INTERNATIONAL ORGANIZATIONS: THREE EXAMPLES

UNRRA: A Case Example of Direct Social Work in Relief and Development

Social workers continue to make an international contribution through direct work in relief and development, and the UNRRA (discussed briefly in Chapter 2) was a particularly important international direct service experience for the profession. It was not the first such experience however; social workers had been active in voluntary organizations such as the Red Cross and the international YWCA for decades prior to World War II. Social workers also participated in the founding of the Save the Children Fund in 1919, and in 1924, founded the International Migration Services, later renamed International Social Service, to aid those displaced by World War I and the Great Depression that followed. The work of this organization demonstrated the value of social casework techniques in addressing problems of migration and family separation.

UNRRA, however, was active during a unique period in the history of international social work. Social workers joined in the postwar relief efforts, especially under UNRRA, giving many professionals their first experience in international social work.

> UNRRA organized the first systematic program to delegate experts in social welfare on the request of governments of liberated nations where UNRRA missions started the training of key workers, in order to enable them to organize their own welfare and health services. (Friedlander, 1949, p. 207)

Although much of the work of the UNRRA was to manage large-scale import of relief supplies and to rehabilitate public utilities and the infrastructure for transport, the necessity for relief services was also recognized. Most UNRRA social workers were involved in work in relief services, defined in the council resolution as:

> health and welfare; assistance in caring for, and maintaining records of, persons found in any areas under control of any of the United Nations who by reason of war have been displaced from their homes and, in agreement with the appropriate governments, military authorities or other agencies, in securing their repatriation or return; and such technical services as may be necessary for these purposes. (Howard, 1944, p. 5)

The need for qualified personnel was recognized: "First consideration must be given to technical competence. Whether the task is to care for orphaned or other disadvantaged children; to provide for aged or disabled persons; to feed masses of men, women, and children; or to render any of the wide variety of services likely to be needed, the primary requisite should be knowledge of the work to be done and skill in its performance" (cited in Howard, 1944, p. 6). The requisites for international social work are further identified and remain true today:

> Second in importance only to technical competence is a sympathetic understanding of the economic and social situation of the people among whom welfare work is to be done . . . and a knowledge and an appreciation of the normal customs and ways of life of the people among whom they work. . . . Furthermore, since UNRRA is a truly international organization, its welfare staff should be comprised only of persons possessing an international viewpoint and willing to dissociate themselves from any national interests or objectives which might conflict with their responsibility to the family of nations by which they are employed. (cited in Howard, 1944, p. 7)

Voluntary social service agencies joined the international relief efforts. At least 40 private agencies formed the American Council of Voluntary Agencies for Foreign Service to coordinate planning for relief among themselves

DONALD HOWARD: SOCIAL WORKER IN UNRRA

Social Welfare Archives, University of Minnesota

Many social workers left their regular posts to join the UNRRA in the years between 1944 and 1946. One of them was Donald Howard, who took a leave from the Charity Organization Department of the Russell Sage Foundation to join UNRRA in 1944. Over the next 2 years, he made significant contributions to postwar relief efforts.

Howard helped to draft materials for the UNRRA council that defined the relief and welfare functions of the organization. His first official UNRRA assignment was in the Washington office, where he headed up research and planning for the Welfare Division. Next, he was deployed to London and Paris. There he helped to develop the postwar welfare programs for Eastern Europe. The Welfare Division focused on assisting displaced persons and addressing the breakdown of social services infrastructure in countries that had been occupied. However, sound planning for resettlement and for infrastructure development were often overshadowed by pressing needs for relief supplies. Arranging for delivery and distributions of food and medicines occupied much of UNRRA staff's attention.

After 6 months in England and France, Donald Howard was transferred to China as the chief welfare officer for the China office. Soon, he was named deputy director of the UNRRA China Mission in charge of health, welfare, and displaced persons services.

His UNRRA assignments led to some unusual social work experiences. In Europe, Howard worked with SHAEF—the Supreme Headquarters, Allied Expeditionary Forces. All planning for welfare services to displaced persons in Germany had to be done in coordination with the U.S. Army (Howard, 1946b). Logistical problems increased with the increasing East/West divide in Europe; political problems also intensified as citizens in the West grew less supportive of sending supplies to Soviet-controlled areas. Work in China was greatly complicated by the ongoing civil war between the Nationalist forces and the Communists. UNRRA's

(continued)

mission was to distribute aid equitably, without regard to political allegiances. In his 1946 article about relief work in China, Howard discusses an important meeting he held with Mao Tse-tung, Chou En-lai, and Nationalist representatives to arrange for relief to be allowed into Communist-held territory (Howard, 1946a). Through his writings on UNRRA for social work journals, Howard conveyed the difficulties of the work. A worldwide food shortage and tremendous need for relief resulted in famine conditions in China. Relief workers were called on to decide who could be saved by a ration of scarce food: "The decision to abandon the principle of aiding those persons who are in greatest need is perhaps the most difficult choice a relief worker can ever be called upon to make. And, once he has determined that these shall be saved but that those shall be allowed to die, a worker feels a sickening sensation, as if something vital inside him had given way, as if something sacred had been debased." (Howard, 1946a, p. 308)

After the UNRRA mission, Howard returned to the Russell Sage Foundation as director of the Department of Social Work Administration, overseeing studies in domestic, international, and foreign social welfare. He was elected president of the AASW in 1947. During his presidency, he remained extensively involved in international affairs. Under his leadership, the AASW developed policy statements on major international issues of the day. His correspondence files include drafts for AASW policy statements on foreign relief and on long-term aid to displaced persons. To these he applied the principles learned through the UNRRA experience, advocating aid without regard to politics and the importance of addressing human needs. He highlighted the similarities between administration of foreign aid and sound social work principles that had evolved from the depression-era programs.

Howard helped to draft the postwar constitution for the International Conference of Social Work and was a leader in efforts to organize and implement the long-delayed Fourth International Conference of Social Work. Originally planned for Brussels in 1940, the conference was cancelled due to the war. It was finally held in Atlantic City, New Jersey, in 1948. The Social Welfare Archives house an extensive file of letters written by Howard to solicit speakers for the conference. Those about the emergence of the rift with the Eastern Bloc and the deteriorating situation in China are particularly illuminating.

Howard's international interest may have derived from his parents. He was born in Tokyo, Japan, in 1902, where his parents were serving as missionaries. He returned to the United States at the age of 10 and was educated in Ohio. Howard received degrees from Otterbein College in Ohio and the University of Denver; and a Ph.D. in 1941 from the University of Chicago School of Social Service Administration. Prior to be-

(continued)

ginning at Russell Sage Foundation in 1936, he worked at community organizing in Colorado and worked as director of adult activities at a settlement house in Chicago. In the mid-1930s, Howard worked for the Emergency Relief Administration in Colorado. Howard left the Russell Sage Foundation in 1948 to become the founding director of the University of California at Los Angeles (UCLA) Department of Social Welfare (UCLA, 1948); within a year, the program became the School of Social Welfare, and Howard's title changed to dean (UCLA, 1988).

and with government agencies. By mid-1944, the council had recruited 67 experienced social workers from the staffs of member agencies to work in the UNRRA, with their salaries continuing to be paid by their employing voluntary agencies. (Larned, 1945). The council formed working committees on geographic areas, on displaced persons, and on material aid. An important aspect of its work was to set personnel standards and, in liaison with UNRRA, to encourage careful selection of welfare workers.

Social workers participated in UNRRA work throughout Europe and held some leadership roles; Irving Fasteau, an American social worker, directed the UNRRA program in Finland (Friedlander, 1978).

UNRRA was also active in China. According to Howard (1946a, p. 310), there were probably 100 "highly competent American social workers" involved in relief efforts in postwar China. These included general relief workers plus specialists in such areas as child welfare, work with the aged, work relief projects, and work with refugees.

> These ambassadors of American social work are achieving signal success, not only in helping to work out technical methods of meeting China's staggering needs, but also in providing the spark and impetus so essential to get relief work under way in areas where wide-scale and fast-moving operations are a novelty. To see these workers in action gives one a new appreciation of the validity of American social work principles, of the soundness of our technical skills. (Howard, 1946a, p. 310)

In the article, Howard also discusses the difficulties of ensuring distribution of relief in China due to the ongoing conflict between the Communists and Nationalists for control of territory. He describes his own involvement in negotiations with the Communists:

> The most heartening experiences which the writer enjoyed in China included visits with Mao Tze-tung and Chou En-lai to discuss possibilities of getting relief to Communist areas; more detailed discussion with lesser Communist officers; and finally, conferences between local Communist representatives and Nationalist army officers to plan means of getting relief supplies into a specific Communist area. (Howard, 1946a, p. 300)

As noted by Wickwar (1947), the achievements of the UNRRA Welfare Division "are highly instructive to all who have at heart the further development of international welfare action" (p. 363). It is also clear from the accounts of participants that the UNRRA experience launched many social workers into international careers; others continued a part-time interest in internationalism through teaching, consultation, and research. Social workers who began their careers in the 1940s cite UNRRA as the most significant force in expanding internationalism within social work. Some of the work, especially consultations and aid to social work education, were continued under the UN and its constituent agencies.

Inside Influence at the United Nations

Precedent for liaison with the UN was established under the League of Nations. Social workers from various countries participated in discussions of international social questions with the League. Within the various sections and committees of the League, social workers were "frequently invited to sit with government officials as observers or to participate as experts, thus affording opportunity for fusion of official and voluntary agency points of view" (Larned, 1945, p. 194). Involvement of the international professional organizations in the UN through consultative status has already been described, but in the early years, social workers were directly involved in the work of the UN as employees and consultants. Kendall talks of her work at the temporary headquarters of the new body at Lake Success, New York:

> It was a fabulous experience working at the U.N. in those early days of 1947 as all the programs were shining new and idealistic. We were located at Lake Success in a barn of a building that had produced material for the war effort and now it was a peace factory. In that period, people there were so imbued with the promise of the U.N. that there they had no question that the world would eventually, if not soon, be safe from the scourges of war and other evils." (Billups, 1997, p. 68)

In another speech, she added: "We were there as international civil servants and we were international. If we did not think and act as internationalists we could not have survived in the heady international atmosphere of those first years. It was really quite wonderful" (Kendall, 1994, p. 7). For at least 2 decades following the Second World War, the UN "was unquestionably the most significant of the internationalizing influences on the social work profession, not only in this country [U.S.] but throughout the world" (Kendall, 1994, p. 6). At its first meeting in 1947, the Social Commission of ECOSOC followed up on the work of UNRRA by encouraging development of social work and social services.

In 1950, the UN Social Commission adopted an important resolution on the necessity of training for social work. The resolution read:

> that social work should in principle be a professional function performed by men and women who have received professional training by taking a formal course of social work theory and practice in an appropriate educational institution . . . and that these courses, whether provided in universities or special

schools, should be of the highest possible quality and should be sufficiently comprehensive to do justice to both the variety and the unity of social work. (cited
in Billups, forthcoming)

The resolution was sent to ECOSOC and to the General Assembly; it was
adopted in 1950. This put the UN on record as recognizing social work as
a profession requiring specialized training—an important development
(Billups, 2000).

In 1959, the ECOSOC expanded its interest in social work and asked the
UN secretary general to do "everything possible to obtain the participation
of social workers in the preparation and application of programs for underdeveloped countries" (Garigue, 1961, p. 21). These strong statements
demonstrate that in the early days of the UN, social workers had important
roles inside the organization as employees and consultants working on expansion of social work education and development of social programs.
Eileen Younghusband (1963), too, acclaimed the UN's role as the biggest contributor to the spread of social work education around the world and, therefore, because of the close link between training and profession, to the spread
of the social work profession. Major world surveys of social work training
were conducted and published by the UN in 1950, 1955, 1958, 1965, and 1971;
training seminars were held on social work; and social welfare officials from
developing countries were given UN support to study social work in the
United States and Great Britain. The UN lent support to several conferences
exploring aspects of international social work education, sending representatives to the 1964 Conference on International Social Welfare Manpower
(Washington, DC) and to the 1970 Conference on Social Work Education,
Population and Family Planning (Hawaii).

Social work involvement in the early UN inspired the careers of some
important actors in international social work, as the following quote indicates. A social worker from Egypt, who became chief of social welfare at the
U.N. and then chief of UNICEF for Europe, explained her introduction to
international work in this way:

> My interest was stimulated when I was a student at Bryn Mawr from 1946–50.
> The U.N. was developing during this time period and this was a frequent topic
> of discussion at the School of Social Work. Some of the social work pioneers at
> the U.N. came to speak to us; others had developed materials for teaching from
> their U.N. experiences. Professors were involved in training relief workers for
> the Quakers to work in war torn areas and this affected their teaching of us.
> There were quite a few foreign students enrolled in the social work program.
> We both caught the excitement of these international developments and then
> contributed to it through sharing our ideas. (A. Gindy, personal communication,
> September 22, 1982)

Decline of Inside Influence. Positions as staff and consultants enabled social
workers to have a direct impact on design and implementation of UN programs. More recently, social work influence and activity inside the UN has

PIONEERS IN INTERNATIONAL ACTION:
DAME EILEEN YOUNGHUSBAND

Katherine Kendall, personal collection

Dame Eileen Younghusband of Great Britain "changed the character of social work education in her own country and, as a consultant and author of the third U.N. international survey of social work education she contributed enormously to the development of schools of social work around the world" (Kendall, 1989, p. 24). Born in 1902 in London, her father was a mountaineer and explorer. Younghusband studied sociology and social studies at the London School of Economics and joined the faculty there (Quam, 1995).

Younghusband's international contributions were many. Her primary arenas for international action were the UN and the IASSW. She also had a significant but controversial career in Britain, where she played a major role in establishing the social work course at the London School of Economics. The conclusions she drew in her major survey of social work in Britain (sponsored by the Carnegie U.K. Trust) were that training was deficient in lack of emphasis on fieldwork and practical aspects of the profession, that there was a serious lack of literature and research, and most significantly, that social work was splintered into many separate specializations and lacked a core identity. She advocated a general approach rather than specialization, saying: "It would be dangerous to overstress divisions within the course; it may be that they are a concession to our ignorance rather than to our knowledge" (Jones, 1984, p. 54). The recommendations were unpopular, especially with psychiatric social workers and almoners who had considerable clout within social work. Thus at the time, much of Eileen's leadership was rejected by her colleagues in Britain, and she was chided by the psychiatric social workers in particular for her lack of a social work credential. As her biographer noted, "To say, as the professional social workers did, that she 'wasn't qualified' was rather like complaining that Florence Nightingale was not a State Registered nurse. She was creating the profession they belonged to" (Jones, 1984, p. 60).

(continued)

On the international scene, she was almost venerated as a leader and friend to social work educators. Soon after World War II, Younghusband began to get involved in international social work activities. She worked with the UNRRA and attended the first postwar International Conference on Social Work in the Netherlands in 1947. She spent part of 1948 in Geneva as a consultant to the Social Welfare Fellowship program of the UN Bureau of Social Affairs. During this year, she also traveled to UN headquarters, which was then at Lake Success, New York. There she met Katherine Kendall, another pioneer in international action, and the two began a long friendship and productive professional association. It particularly flourished through their involvement in the IASSW. Younghusband participated in the 1950 congress in Paris and was soon identified as a leader in the IASSW; she served as vice president from 1954 to 1961, as president from 1961 to 1968, and then as Honorary President until her death (Quam, 1995).

From 1956 to 1959, the UN engaged Younghusband to conduct and write the "Third International Survey on Training for Social Work," produced in 1959. The report remains "one of the most thoughtful, exhaustive and thorough attempts to analyzse the nature of social work education, the teaching methods, the content and the objectives" (Jones, 1984, p. 96). As Kendall explained, "As the author of a landmark U.N. study that dealt in depth with the organization and content of social work education, she helped to give the social work curriculum a distinguishing identity, thus making it possible for social work to claim legitimacy as an international discipline" (Kendall, 1989, p. 30).

It is not surprising that Younghusband was sought after as an international consultant on social work. She assisted many countries—including Hong Kong, Jamaica, and Greece—in their efforts to improve the profession and professional education. As she reflected: "It was a time for world experts. Colonialism was being phased out and the newly independent nations still looked to the West for help and support" (as quoted in Jones, 1984, p. 92).

In her work both in Britain and throughout the world, she viewed social work as a "Gestalt" in which knowledge from many fields was brought together and the result was a synthesis that was more than its individual parts: "This knowledge may be comparatively elementary in any one of the social or behavioral sciences, but the total synthesis results in an understanding of man and his social functioning, refined by constant practice, which is certainly not elementary" (as quoted in Jones, 1984, p. 97).

Younghusband died in a traffic accident in 1981 at the age of 79 while on a visit with friends in the United States. She left a wealth of important publications on British and international social work. At her memorial service held in the beautiful church of St. Martin-in-the-Fields in London,

(continued)

hundreds of colleagues and friends from the United Kingdom and other countries paid tribute to her unique place in the history of social work in Britain and in the world (Kendall, 1982). Tributes to her outstanding contributions to international action continue, especially through the biennial Eileen Younghusband memorial lecture at the world congresses of the IASSW.

declined greatly. Several reasons can be advanced. One is that the UN shifted its emphasis away from human resources to economic development, a field to which social work has less to offer. Even as the focus moved toward social development, social work was slow to adapt to the development movement and was unable to compete in the interdisciplinary environment. As one expert expressed it: "We spent too much time promoting social work instead of promoting strategies to meet human need" (S. Pettis, personal communication, November 11, 1982). Was this due to lack of experience with the mass poverty characteristic of developing nations? To the individual focus of American social work? To overconcern with protecting social work's sphere of influence? Whatever the mix of reasons, the profession was not successful in specifying how it could contribute to the goal of development and therefore was left behind in the mainstream movement toward development programs within the UN. The failure to define social work responsibility in the international arena, beyond spreading social work education around the world, was a shortcoming that ultimately brought a decline in influence. As another expert sadly noted, "The fading influence of U.N. activities in the field of social welfare is an example of what can happen when the vision is gone and only the bureaucracy remains" (Kendall, 1978, p. 191).

The Social Welfare Attaché Program

An even more short-lived but interesting opportunity for work and influence was realized in the social welfare attaché program in the United States. Although the impact of the attaché program was limited due to the brevity of the experiment, the lessons of the relevance of social work expertise to foreign policy are important. Embassy positions, called attachés, exist for experts in fields such as labor and military affairs to advise the embassy staff on key matters. In the 1960s, the U.S. State Department experimented with a program that placed social welfare attachés in two U.S. embassies. There was an earlier version of this program just after World War II when there were welfare attaché positions in France and India. Mary Catherine Jennings was appointed attaché to the Brazilian embassy in 1963; shortly thereafter, Ruby Pernell was appointed to be social welfare attache to the embassy in India under Ambassador Chester Bowles. Bowles was ambassador to India after World War II when that embassy had a social welfare attaché. He valued the contribution so highly that he specifically requested reinstitution of this position when he accepted a return assignment in India in the 1960s

(Bowles, 1965). The profession was enthusiastic about the appointments. An article in the *NASW News* reporting the appointment of Jennings indicates that the professional association had lobbied for this: "This appointment is the first tangible result of the years of work done by NASW in co-operation with the U.S. Department of Health, Education and Welfare (DHEW) since the two positions for social welfare attachés established in 1947 were discontinued" ("Mary Catherine Jennings," 1963, p. 1).

The overall function of the attaché was to provide the ambassador and other staff members with reports based on observation and evaluation of social conditions and social services. The attachés were to maintain contacts with local social agencies, interpret and represent U.S. social welfare policies and services, provide consultation to the embassy on intercountry services, increase U.S. participation in international social welfare activities, and promote exchanges in the field of social welfare. The job description also indicates that they may be called on to provide consultation to the U.S. Agency for International Development to evaluate requests for social development aid and to provide consultation to the staff of the embassy on intercountry social service issues, such as repatriation of stranded Americans, intercountry adoptions, or arranging for social services for separated families. This last task was limited; the attachés had to be on guard not to become social workers to the embassy staff (Mary Catherine Jennings Holden, personal communication, March 4, 1997).

One benefit of the program to the U.S. government was that social welfare attachés were in contact with groups that did not normally interact with the embassy. In Brazil, for example, Jennings was an important link to movements for social progress and to the Catholic Church. This, she believed, helped to balance public perception that U.S. interests in Brazil were about militarism and materialism. One of the key functions of the attaché was to observe and report what was going on in social development. The topic was of interest to the State Department and other government agencies at the time, as President Kennedy's Alliance for Progress initiatives had a social development component. Therefore, a study of social work education in Brazil that illuminated attitudes toward social development was shared with the Department of Health, Education and Welfare (DHEW) as well as the State Department.

The posts were evaluated very positively by the ambassadors. Recommendations were made to add social welfare attachés at other key embassies in the developing world, including the Philippines and Indonesia. Instead, by the late 1960s, the program fell to budget-cutting pressures. Jennings left her post in Brazil in 1968 to become chief of the International Training Section at DHEW; she was not replaced. The position in India ended at about the same time. Quite possibly these budgetary pressures were complicated by the political environment of the times, with substantial unrest at home and both domestic and worldwide antiwar agitation over the Vietnam War, then at its height. These events diminished support for international interventions.

The social welfare attaché program is an important model for international action. In an evaluation of the importance of the post, the ambassador in India noted that the social welfare attaché broadened the embassy's contacts with government and the wider society, building relationships that no other unit in the embassy had. Perhaps surprisingly, the attaché was seen as important in building a positive image of the United States. "Due to the earlier work of the first Social Welfare Attaché, a tremendous amount of goodwill towards the United States had been created which, without a social welfare specialist, we were unable to continue to cultivate" (Bowles, 1965). Social work brought expertise to a wide range of important issues, including status of women, children, and youth; poverty; and social planning. The example and lessons of the social welfare attaché program should not be forgotten, whether or not they can ever be revived in the same format. The value of provision of social welfare expertise to governmental bodies in international relations and the centrality of issues of social development to social, economic, and political relations should be promoted in all nations.

CONCLUSION

The profession of social work has had a long history of international action, beginning almost at the inception of the profession. There have been impressive accomplishments, both by organizations and by individuals. If there is a negative side, it is that it is a history of ups and downs, not a seamless story of progress. The diminution of inside involvement in the UN represents a loss of professional influence and a reduction in the centrality of social welfare in UN work. Presently, social work influence in the UN is primarily external, through the consultative status of the professional organizations. The UN has relatively few social work employees and no special social work programs.

Responsibility for this reduction rests both within the UN and within the profession. When the UN turned away from the promotion of social work education and social welfare programs toward development and then toward an emphasis on special populations through its special years and conferences (see Chapter 6), social work lost its arena of uncontested leadership. The profession was not successful in defining a new role in development or in taking the lead in its areas of expertise on women, children, and poverty.

Initially, social workers made their international impact in broad global social movements, such as the peace and women's movements at the beginning of the 20th century. It appears that social work leadership in major global movements has lessened, although it may be too soon to fully evaluate this. And there are examples of significant individual involvement, such as the work of social workers from Africa and the United States in world AIDS work, and organizational involvement, such as the work of ICSW on social development described above.

On the positive side, the international social work organizations have shown remarkable resiliency, and certainly their survival and continued work are important. They have been particularly successful in actions to en-

sure exchange of professional knowledge by regularly holding world conferences and by sustaining publication of *International Social Work* for more
than 40 years. Recently, the organizations have shown renewed initiative by
using their consultative status with the UN and by joining with other NGOs
in preparatory work and NGO forums at some of the special UN world conferences.

Continued development of vehicles for professional action is another
positive action. A fourth vibrant international social work organization was
founded less than 30 years ago, the Inter-University Consortium for International Social Development (IUCISD). It was originated by a group of U.S.
social work educators in response to what they saw as neglect of the critical issues of social development by the established social work organizations. It has grown into an international, interdisciplinary organization with
a focus on development theory, research, teaching, and practice. The addition of IUCISD to the list of human service organizations has created additional opportunities for international involvement and may well have
spurred increased attention to development by the mainstream social work
organizations.

Important successes of the past may inform action for the future. The
IASSW family-planning project demonstrated how a concerted response to
a social need through the seemingly modest strategy of curriculum development can make an impact on the shape of social and health services. If
significant funding had been available more recently, could similar levels of
success have been achieved in other areas, such as HIV/AIDS?

The positive evaluation of the brief social welfare attaché program points
to the value of advisory roles for social workers in international relations.
While it may never be revived in the exact form of the attaché experiment,
the profession and individual professionals may use lessons learned to identify new advisory roles through which contributions can be made.

As international organizational action for the future is considered, the
policy role may well grow in importance. Policy advocacy in human rights
and other areas should continue. Social work professional organizations also
need to develop national action agendas on their own nations' foreign policy. In 1947, in discussing postwar relief proposals for aid to Europe and
China before Congress, Howard (1947) told the social work profession in the
United States:

> Because of deep interest in and special knowledge of social welfare needs and
> services, social workers must take a leading part in helping the American peo-
> ple fully to understand the issues at stake and to do all in their power to see
> that the course taken by our government is the best that can be pursued under
> prevailing circumstances. (p. 7)

His message led to a resolution of support for foreign assistance by the
AASW. Today, it can be applied to the social work profession in all countries where governments take action that has international impact.

REFERENCES

Anciaux, A. (1988). Rene Sand—Fondateur de L'ICSW. In ICSW *1928–1988: ICSW, Celebration of the 60th anniversary* pp. 25–28. Vienna: International Council on Social Welfare.

Billups, J. (1997). Reflections on a professional's life as an internationalist: An interview with Katherine A. Kendall. *Reflections, 3*(2) 65–85.

Billups, J. (forthcoming). *Faithful angels: International social work notables of the late 20th century.* Washington, DC: NASW Press.

Bowles, C. (1965, Sept. 15) correspondence to D. Wilken, Director, Inter-departmental Relations Staff and GAO Liaison, Department of State.

Fifth Question: Co-education or separate schools for men and women. The plan for an International School of Social Work. (1929). In *International Conference of Social Work* [Proceedings] (Vol. II, pp. 223–238). First Conference, Paris, July 8–13, 1928.

Friedlander, W.A. (1949). Some international aspects of social work education. *Social Service Review, XXIII*(2), 204–210.

Friedlander, W.A. (1978). *International social welfare.* Englewood Cliffs, NJ: Prentice-Hall.

Garigue, P. (1961). Challenge of cultural variations to social work. In *Education for Social Work* [Proceedings] Council on Social Work Education (Ninth Annual Program Meeting). 9–22.

Graham, J. (1978, December). Saviour to the world's children. *Readers Digest,* 121–128.

Howard, D.S. (1944). U.N.R.R.A.: A new venture in international relief and welfare services, *Social Service Review, XVIII*(1), 1–11.

Howard, D.S. (1946a). Emergency relief needs and measures in China. *Social Service Review, XX,* 300–311.

Howard, D. (1946b, June). Personal vitae. Social Welfare Archives, NCSW Collection, Box 7-folder 5.

Howard, D.S. (1947, May). "Urgent international welfare measures—Our responsibility. *The Compass,* reprinted in "From the archives" (1998). *Journal of Progressive Human Services 9*(1), 65–72.

In memoriam: Dr. Rene Sand, 1877–1953. (1953). *Social Service Review, 27*(4), 427–428.

ICSW (1993). Executive Committee Meeting, Draft Minutes. Vienna, February 10–14, 1993. (Available from ICSW, 5 Tavistock Place, London, UK.)

ICSW (1994). ICSW Mission Statement. ⟨www.icsw.org/mission.htm⟩ (accessed 7/31/98).

ICSW (1995). Report of the Activities of the General Secretariat, January 1994–March, 1995. Prepared for the Executive Committee Meeting, Copenhagen, March 13–15, 1995. (Available from ICSW, 5 Tavistock Place, London, UK.)

ICSW (1996). Biennial report, 1994–1996. Montreal: Author.

ICSW (1997). Memorandum of understanding between the United Nations Development Programme and the International Council on Social Welfare (www.icsw.org/policy_memorandum.htm) 7/31/98.

ICSW (1998). Policy paper on social development. ⟨www.icsw.org/policies_social.htm⟩ (accessed 7/31/98).

International Federation of Social Workers (1988). *International policy papers.* Geneva: Author.

International Federation of Social Workers. (1994). *The Ethics of Social Work.* Oslo: Author. (Full text available www.ifsw.org.)

International Federation of Social Workers (1996). *International statement on human rights.* ⟨www.ifsw.org/4.5.6.pub.html⟩ (Accessed 11/8/98).

Jebb, E. (1929). International social service. In *First International Conference of Social Work* [Proceedings] (Vol. I, pp. 637–655). First Conference, Paris, July 8–13, 1928.

Johannesen, T. (1997). Social work as an international profession: Opportunities and challenges. In M.C. Hokenstad & J. Midgley, (Eds.), *Issues in International Social Work* (pp. 146–158). Washington, DC: NASW Press.

Jones, K. (1984). *Eileen Younghusband: A biography.* Occasional Papers on Social Administration Number 76, London: Bedford Square Press. (Note: Jones quotes Younghusband throughout the biography but does not identify the works from which the quotes are taken.)

Katzki, K. (1988). 60 Years of ICSW. In ICSW, *1928–1988: Celebration of the 60th Anniversary* (pp. 11–20). Papers from the conference, Frankfurt and Berlin, July 29–August 2, 1988. Vienna, ICSW.

Kendall, K. (Guest Editor). (1982). *International Social Work, XXV*(1).

Kendall, K. (1977). *Final report: International development of qualified social work manpower for population and family planning activities.* New York: IASSW.

Kendall, K. (1978). The IASSW 1928–1978: A journey of remembrance. In K. Kendall, *Reflections on Social Work Education* pp. 170–191. New York: IASSW.

Kendall, K.A. (1987). International social work education. In A. Minahan (Ed.), *Encyclopedia of Social Work* (18th ed., pp. 987–996). Silver Spring, MD: NASW Press.

Kendall, K. (1989). Women at the helm: Three extraordinary leaders. *Affilia, 4*(1), 23.32.

Kendall, K.A. (1994). The challenges of internationalism in social work: Past, present, and future. In L. Healy (Ed.), *The global-local link: International challenges to social work practice.* West Hartford, CT: Center for International Social Work Studies, University of Connecticut School of Social Work.

Lally, D. (1987). International social welfare organizations and services. In A. Minahan (Ed.), *Encyclopedia of Social Work* (18th ed., pp. 969–986). Silver Spring, MD: NASW Press.

Lorenz, W. (1994). *Social work in a changing Europe.* London: Routledge.

Larned, R. (1945). International social work. In *Social Work Yearbook 1945* (pp. 188–194). New York: Russell Sage Foundation.

Mary Catherine Jennings is appointed new social welfare attaché in Brazil. (1963). *NASW News, 8*(3), 1.

Obituary of René Sand. (1953). *Journal of the American Medical Association, 153,* 1028, 1111.

Obituary René Sand, M.D. LL.D. (1953). *British Medical Journal, 4835,* 571–572.

Organization of the International Conference of Social Work. (1929). In *International Conference of Social Work* [Proceedings] (Vol. I, pp. 5–17). First Conference, Paris, July 8–13, 1928.

Quam, J.K. (1995). Younghusband, Dame Eileen (1902–1981). In R. Edwards (Ed.), *Encyclopedia of social work (19th ed.,* p. 2619). Washington, DC: NASW Press.

René Sand. (1953). *Lancet* (London) *265,* 576.

Saddam Hussein's prisoner for over 8 years: The case of Feisal Al-Sane. (1999, January). *IFSW Newsletter, 7.*

United Nations (1994). *Human rights and social work: A manual for schools of social work and the social work profession.* [Professional training series No. 1] Geneva: UN Centre for Human Rights.

University of California, Office of Public Information, Biography—Donald Howard, 9/1/48. Social Welfare Archives, AASW Collection, Box 21.

UCLA (1988). Issue on the 40th Anniversary of the UCLA School of Social Welfare [Special issue]. *UCLA Social Welfare, 3*(1).

Wickwar, W.H. (1947). Relief supplies and welfare distribution: UNRRA in retrospect. *Social Service Review, XXI*(3), 363–374.

Willetts, P. (Ed.) (1996). *The conscience of the world: The influence of non-governmental organisations in the U.N. system.* Washington, DC: Brookings Institution.

Younghusband, E. (1963). Tasks and trends in education for social work: An international appraisal. *Social Work* (London) *20*(3), 4–11.

CHAPTER 4

SOCIAL WORK AROUND
THE WORLD TODAY

The term social work includes every effort to relieve distress due to poverty, to restore individuals and families to normal conditions of living, to prevent social scourges and to improve the social and living conditions of the community, through social case work, through group activities, through community action in legislation and administration, and through social research.

[DEFINITION OF SOCIAL WORK AGREED UPON FOR USE AT THE
FIRST INTERNATIONAL CONFERENCE OF SOCIAL WORK, 1928.]
"ORGANIZATION OF THE SOCIAL WORK," 1929, P. 5.

In examining social work in various countries around the world, one is struck by both similarities and differences. While indigenization has increased local variations in method and increased attention to local problems, globalization has heightened professionals' awareness of common issues and increased opportunities for communication and exchange.

There are no international standards that regulate the profession of social work or accredit its educational programs across nations. There are, however, a number of commonalities in social work throughout the world. Although relative emphasis varies, social work everywhere recognizes a dual emphasis of responsibility to individuals in need and responsibility for social reform or social change. Values play an important part in defining social work, with human dignity as a core value. And social work practice in all countries is strongly influenced by the social environment and the larger political/economic context.

This last commonality, the strong social environmental, or contextual, component of social work, leads to unique local patterns. Thus, one of social work's most important and distinguishing features—that it is *the* profession that recognizes the interaction of individuals with their environments—leads to differences in social work practice among countries and regions. In addition, resource availability is a facilitating or constraining factor that varies greatly by country.

In this chapter, examples of current social work practice and issues will be discussed, drawing on countries facing many different social problems with varying levels of financial and professional resources. These range from

Denmark, a high-income country where social work is practiced in the context of a universalist welfare state, to Jamaica, a relatively resource-poor country that has achieved respectable standards of health and education, yet where social workers now struggle with the impact of structural adjustment. In Armenia, the profession of social work has emerged since 1990 and has had to cope with war, extreme political change, and resource shortages. Mauritius can best be described as a society in transition, creating new challenges for a 30-year old profession. Social workers in Argentina work, along with the rest of civil society, to overcome the effects of their long period of military oppression while facing new challenges of privatization. And in Japan, social workers address the problems of a postindustrial, consumer-oriented society that has undergone a demographic transition. Through these examples, similarities and differences in social work will be illustrated. A brief analysis will conclude the chapter.

CURRENT SOCIAL WORK IN SELECTED COUNTRIES

Denmark

Social workers in Denmark practice within the context of a comprehensive, universalist welfare state. The proportion of the population living in poverty is small, estimated at 4% to 8%. Families are protected by a set of social insurances that provide for health care, education, and protection from poverty due to unemployment or old age. In addition, the social welfare system takes a preventive approach to problems that arise from normal living, for example, providing a system of health visitors to provide support and advise on child-rearing and child health matters to new parents.

The majority of social workers are employed by local social service agencies run by municipalities or by counties. Health services, both general and psychiatric hospitals, employ social workers, as do the prisons. Social work with the elderly is relatively new but is growing with the aging of the Danish population. School social work is just beginning and where it exists is under local authority. Smaller numbers of social workers are employed by private organizations, such as battered women's crisis centers and settlement houses. In Denmark, however, a relatively small number of agencies are private and even those get some public funds.

Although it is important to underscore that most social work services are delivered by public agencies, policy changes are under way. Corporations are now being encouraged by the Ministry of Social Affairs to take social responsibility for their employees, and as a result, some are employing social workers to assist with this function. Private organizations are also becoming more important in social work as Denmark looks for ways to address the growing costs of the welfare state and problems of unemployment and social exclusion that have not been effectively handled by traditional services. Revisions to the Social Services Act adopted in 1997 included provision for active cooperation of the public sector with various private organizations in the municipalities. There are many unresolved problems in efforts to establish a mixed public and private sector welfare system. These include the division of labor between the sectors and "myths and prejudices within these two sectors" (Halskov & Egelund, 1998, p. 19).

The major functions of social workers are social counseling and case management, especially those employed by municipal social services. Referral is another important social work function, that is, assisting the client to access the available benefits and services. Referrals are made to services offered by the public sector as well as by private organizations. Therapy is not considered part of the social work task and function. Perhaps 10% to 15% of social workers do become therapists, but only after receiving advanced training; they then typically find work in hospitals, crisis centers for women or men, and other treatment institutions. In such settings, part of being a social worker is being able to offer professional therapy (I. Hjerrild, personal communication, April 17, 1997).

In Denmark, only trained persons with diplomas in social work can call themselves social workers or be hired to do social work. Social pedagogy here is a more narrow field, emphasizing training to care for children in day care and other institutions.

Social Work Education. Social workers are educated at four National Danish Schools of Social Work at Esbjerg, Odense, Aarhus, and Copenhagen and in a program at Aalborg University. The programs at the National Danish Schools accept students with at least 9 months' work experience for a 3-year, postsecondary course, leading to a diploma of "Social-rådgiver." Education combines academic courses in social work methods and theories, social welfare legislation, psychology and sociology, economics, and law with a 5-month field placement and two small-group projects. Typical field placements are in the social welfare and health services of local and county authorities, including social and health service departments, hospitals, correctional services, trade unions, housing associations, and residential institutions. The goal is to prepare students for employment in both public and private organizations; the majority of graduates are employed by local and county social welfare departments.

Several recent changes to social work education have been adopted. A course of advanced studies in social work began in 1998, offering a 10-month course in advanced social work methods; supervision, consultation and teaching; research; and administration and management. The initiation of this program signals recognition of the need to prepare social workers for leadership positions in the field. In 1992, a master's program was piloted as a cooperative program between the school at Copenhagen and Aalborg University. In 1996, a new government act introduced modifications in the academic program and governance structure of social work education. The change was to be fully operational by July 1999 ("Social Work Education in Denmark," 1998). A stronger emphasis on interdisciplinary education is now required. Teams of faculty from various disciplines will develop curriculum in each of the four main areas of social work: counseling theory and practice; human development; law; and political science, economics, labor, and other supporting social sciences. The law also demands higher-order integration of theory and practice and requires evaluation of students' practice and personal competencies as well as their academic progress. Schools of social work will be governed by local boards, made up of local political representatives as well as social service agency representatives, faculty, and a student (Inger Hjerrild, personal communication, April 17, 1997).

In spite of the official recognition, social workers have relatively low pay; the Danish Association of Social Workers, with approximately 10,000 members (95% of all professional social workers), negotiates with the government at local and national levels on pay and working conditions (Information sheet on Danish Association of Social Workers, 2000). In addition, the Association runs conferences and becomes involved in legislative issues affecting social work.

Future Issues. In the future, social workers in Denmark will continue to work on identity issues and intend to work to strengthen research. Changes in Danish society are posing new professional challenges, especially a new conservatism in the political-economic culture and an increase in the number of the unemployed and of minorities in society. Unemployment has grown in Denmark and is particularly severe among the young and among immigrants. A survey showed that 75% of all youth received some form of cash assistance before the age of 26; unemployment among young immigrants is 25%, and many of these youth have poor prospects for future employment due to low levels of education (Halskov & Egelund, 1998). New strategies aimed at "activating" the unemployed and other marginalized populations are being developed, along with a strong emphasis on employment. Local authorities have recently restructured to separate services for the unemployed from service for general problems. The general caseload tends to include more low-income clients. Will this signal a turn away from the universalism that has brought social harmony to Denmark? (I. Hjerrild, personal communications, April 17, 1997, June 1998). A concern about the emphasis on employment is that it "ignores the need for broader and more personally-targeted initiatives in relation to more vulnerable young people— for instance young, single mothers" (Halskov & Egelund, 1998, p. 15). The current content of social work education may not prepare professionals for work in employment-focused programs.

Jamaica

In Jamaica, the majority of professionally trained social workers are employed in government programs, including youth and community programs of the Government Social Development Commission, probation and correctional services, and children's services. Relatively few opportunities exist in hospitals, in contrast to the Caribbean island of Trinidad where medical social work is the predominant field. Until recently, some social work graduates went to work in schools as guidance counselors, but teachers' colleges are now beginning to train their own counselors and school social work does not exist as such. A few pilot employee assistance programs have begun in selected industries; at least one bauxite company and the national telephone company each employ a professionally trained social worker as a "welfare officer." Approximately three quarters of trained social workers are in the public sector, primarily with the services named above, with slightly less than 25% in NGOs often as managers, consultants, and researchers. Only about 2% work in the profit-making commercial/industrial sector, usually in human resource development.

While many of the problems social workers deal with are common to any society, others reflect the particular circumstances of Jamaica. Migration to the United States and Canada is a common phenomenon and often separates families, sometimes for years. Social workers encounter children whose parents are overseas or who are preparing to migrate themselves. Children are an important focus for social work and Jamaica's NGO community has mobilized to implement the Convention on the Rights of the Children (CRC) since its adoption by the UN in 1989. Interest in parenting education and public attention to child protection have increased in recent years.

Identity and Contributions. Social work leaders in Jamaica see many universals in social work practice. However, they also note that social workers in Jamaica, especially those who are untrained, tend to be more directive and prescriptive than social workers in the United States. This is partly explained by the pressures of large caseloads but is also due to cultural expectations on the part of clients who expect the expert to have knowledge and to solve

CAREER PATH: A SOCIAL WORKER IN JAMAICA

One experienced social worker described her career as follows. For years she was employed by an NGO named VOUCH—Voluntary Organization for the Upliftment of Children. She worked with families experiencing problems with child-rearing. The clients were inner-city families living in poverty; often, they were long-term clients of the agency. She did casework, assisting parents (usually mothers) in working out solutions to their children's distresses, and made referrals for other services. At that time, the agency temporarily assigned its social workers to work 2 days a week in the maternity hospital and the children's hospital. As a result, these hospitals have since added social work services. Now employed by the United Way, she sees her function as educating corporate people and United Way volunteers about the social problems of Jamaica and consulting with private voluntary agencies to help them to improve their programs.

(Sheila Nicholson, personal communication, April 22, 1997)

their problems. In addition, the ability to truly use a democratic empowerment approach is societally determined. The ideal is present in Jamaica, but its practice may be hampered by traditions of social stratification and traditional authority patterns (John Maxwell, personal interview, April 25, 1997). Others believe that social work principles, though generally applicable across nations, have been interpreted through the "filters of the culture and with a particular Jamaican scene" (Sybil Francis, personal communication, April 24, 1997).

Another important area of contribution has been through involvement in community development. Beginning in the years of unrest and political awakening in the 1930s, community development has been important in involving social workers in attacking severe rural poverty and later, urban problems. As noted, an early organization was Jamaica Welfare, founded in 1937 by Norman Manley with funds negotiated from the Banana Producers' Association. The organization established that the funds were "not for charitable purposes . . . but for real help in the development of the island and its peasants" (Girvan, 1993, p. 7). As early as 1940, Jessie Irwin, "an outstanding social worker," advocated for the focus to be on community organizing at the village level to strengthen local capacity, rather than on the building of community centers (Girvan, 1993, p. 10). This was accomplished through many organizations—farmers' organizations, women's groups, cooperatives, study clubs, and youth groups. Community development continues to be a social work function today in a number of small NGOs throughout the island. In the late 1980s, the Association of Development Agencies in Jamaica utilized a community development approach to rebuilding after Hurricane Gilbert, mobilizing residents to engage in self-help reconstruction and institution building, rather than passive relief work. Case 4.1 illustrates the development approach.

In a more recent community development effort, social workers affiliated with the University of the West Indies have worked in a squatter community on leadership development and community capacity building to enable the community to plan for its relocation. In Jamaica, perhaps as many as 20% of the population are living on land that they do not own or formally rent; these settlements are commonly referred to as squatter communities.

Current leaders in the profession assess the contributions of social work to national development as positive. One commented that through social work NGOs "we have jolly well kept the lid on the kettle" in many instances, by tackling issues the government won't or can't deal with. If these efforts had not been made, catastrophic problems could have resulted (S. Nickolson, personal communication, April 22, 1997). Another stated that social work has made a particularly important contribution to Jamaica's development by making people more aware that things can be done to improve conditions. Social work's stance is that people can change, that they can be helped, and that they can learn to help themselves; through this message, social work has done a lot for Jamaica and is recognized even by government (Elsye Sayles, personal communication, April 24, 1997).

CASE 4.1: COMMUNITY DEVELOPMENT AFTER A DISASTER

A social worker heading the Association of Development Agencies (ADA) in Jamaica was faced with a practice dilemma in the wake of Hurricane Gilbert in 1988. Gilbert was a devastating hurricane, causing the worst destruction in Jamaica in 30 years. Needs for assistance were enormous. Yet ADA was a development agency, committed to enhancing community capacity for self-help. Its challenge after Gilbert was to sustain this focus in the face of such great need and donor pressure to engage in relief—the distribution of commodities.

Devastation was particularly bad in poverty areas, where poorly constructed dwellings were no match for high winds. ADA therefore decided to organize a series of shelter clinics to teach local agencies and residents how to build or rehabilitate homes to make them less prone to hurricane damage. A team was put together, including architects and a builder from the Women's Construction Collective—selected purposefully to increase female participation. Funding was quickly secured from several external and regional sources.

The clinics included preparatory meetings in the community to define roles and responsibilities; a community-wide workshop to mobilize participation; workdays to construct a building; and an evaluative workshop that included evaluation of both the extent of learning about disaster preparedness and about community building. Community participants learned by doing—by constructing a simple structure with a hurricane resistant roof to be given to a particularly needy individual or used as community space. Before construction could begin, the community had to decide the disposition of the finished product. During the project, ADA held 13 clinics in "rural to deep rural" locations, with an average of more than 50 participants in each. Outcomes included more than 600 residents having learned safe building skills, increased personal efficacy, and the development of new and/or strengthened community organizations in most locations.

Social work roles for the director and her associates were many. The most important may have been to guide the agency to stay true to mission in difficult times and to find a way to use crisis to strengthen, rather than divert, the agency. Social work beliefs in resiliency and empowerment were definitely put into practice. Much time was spent in coalition building and in guiding and facilitating local involvement, being vigilant not to take control of community decisions. Finally, the project was designed and implemented to pay attention to the needs of those often left out—women, rural residents, and the disabled. The model's success led to a request to take it to Montserrat the next year after Hurricane Hugo hit the eastern Caribbean.

(Case adapted from Baker, 1998)

Social Work Education. Social work education was initiated at the University of the West Indies in 1961 at the Mona campus as a 2-year certificate course. The university serves 14 English-speaking Caribbean countries from three campuses in Jamaica (Mona), Barbados, and Trinidad. Social work was initiated at the Mona campus, but programs have developed in Trinidad and Barbados more recently. A baccalaureate degree has been offered since 1969/70 (or 1973/74 in current form) and a master's degree program, the only one in the English-speaking Caribbean, was begun in 1993. The master's program is small and draws students from throughout the English-speaking Caribbean. Two concentrations are offered—direct practice and management—in alternating years.

The majority of trained social workers receive their education through the baccalaureate program in the Department of Sociology and Social Work. Approximately 80 are enrolled at any one time, and by 1991, it was estimated that about 600 social workers had been educated by the department. Content includes core courses in sociology and other social sciences, psychology of the individual and society, and social work methods and practice, taught both in academic classes and in field practica. Caribbean realities are addressed in sociology courses and in the courses on social policy. However, indigenous social work literature is less available. As Maxwell (1991) indicates, "there remains, still largely unanswered, a challenge to develop local theoretical formulations as a basis for advancing the understanding of . . . the Caribbean personality, individual and interpersonal behavior patterns, the effectiveness of techniques directed at assisting individuals, groups and community to improve social functioning or to effect changes on oppressive environmental forces" (p. 20).

Short-term, more paraprofessional, training has been available in social services through the Social Welfare Training Centre, established in the Department of Extra Mural Studies at the University of the West Indies in Mona in 1962. This "Four-month Course in the Principles and Practice of Social Work" was first offered in 1963 to 12 students from five Caribbean countries (Brown, 1991). The Training Centre continues to offer the 4-month course and other short-term practical training to persons working in social services throughout the English-speaking Caribbean.

Mauritius

Mauritius, an island nation in the Indian Ocean, has undergone tremendous change over recent decades. After years of colonization by France and Britain, independence was achieved in 1968. More recently, the biggest change has been a shift from a predominantly agricultural economy overwhelmingly dependent on a single crop (sugar) to an economy with a sizable manufacturing sector and considerable tourism. The growth of manufacturing, initially textiles, brought job opportunities for women, ushering in changes in gender and family roles. Mauritius is therefore described as a society in transition—from an agricultural to manufacturing economy, from an unskilled to skilled labor force, from extended families to nuclear families, and toward status as a newly industrialized country (NIC) (Republic of Mauritius & UNICEF, 1994). It is not surprising that the president of the Mauritian Association of Social Work said that "at the threshold of the third millennium, the social work profession in Mauritius is preparing to face the challenges of change affecting every sphere of life of the Mauritian citizen" (Ramgoolam, 1996, p. 1).

UNICEF describes Mauritius as in transition from a society concerned with child survival to a society concerned with child development and protection (Republic of Mauritius & UNICEF, 1994, p. 2). This description is useful in examining changes in social work functions and priorities, both in Mauritius and in other countries at similar levels of development. Originally focused on community development and then on probation services, social work is increasingly concerned with behavioral and emotional aspects of individual and family well-being. Mental health counseling, work with families experiencing domestic violence, child protection, suicide prevention— these are services now beginning to attract social work attention. This transition can be observed not only in Mauritius but in many developing countries as they successfully reduce infant mortality, improve literacy and sanitation, and wipe out widespread malnutrition. Once the survival issues are satisfactorily addressed, quality of family life and developmental issues can be tackled.

Social work is a relatively recent profession in Mauritius, but social welfare entitlements and social services have a long history. An old "Poor Law" provided indoor and outdoor relief as early as 1830, and the modern Mauritian welfare system was influenced by British Fabian socialism. Several decades before independence, Labour Party leader and future Prime Minister Seewoosagur Ramgoolam began to advocate for food subsidies, health insurance, publicly financed education, and old age pensions (University of Mauritius, 1986). Labour Party support was bolstered by the two influential social welfare studies conducted in Mauritius around 1960. The first, conducted by J. E. Meade, examined the economic and social structure of Mauritius; the second, by Richard Titmuss and Brian Abel-Smith, focused on social and demographic issues (Meade, 1961; Titmuss and Abel-Smith, 1961). The reports led to development of strong programs in family planning and related social services and to social welfare legislation. Although constrained by the IMF's structural adjustment requirements in the 1980s, the commitment to social welfare remains strong. Examination of the welfare indicators for Mauritius (see Table 1.1, Chapter 1) shows the island's success in child survival, with an infant mortality rate of 19, and life expectancy of 71. As noted above, current "typical social work cases" show increased concern with child development, family life, and mental health.

Most social workers in Mauritius are civil servants, and the largest numbers are employed in social security and the probation service. A network of social welfare centers and community centers throughout the country employ social workers who engage in a variety of roles to encourage community action to solve problems. There are a few medical social workers in the major hospitals and a small number at the mental hospital. A smaller number of social workers are employed by the larger nongovernment agencies, including the Mauritius Family Planning Association and the Mauritius Alliance of Women.

Certainly no single case is typical of social work in a country. Case 4.2 is included because it illustrates Mauritian social work in transition, recognizing child development needs yet hampered by incomplete service development and lack of resources.

A case such as Jean's could occur in many societies. It illustrates the functions of the social worker in investigation, efforts at family intervention,

CASE 4.2: A CASE OF CHILD NEGLECT IN A FAMILY IN POVERTY IN MAURITIUS

Jean is a 4-year-old boy who lives with his father, 7-year-old sister, and grandmother in a three-room corrugated iron house. The parents are separated and his mother lives elsewhere. The case was reported to the Child Development Unit of the Ministry of Women, Family Welfare and Child Development by a medical worker in the hospital. A caseworker visited and found that Jean, mentally retarded, was being "grossly neglected." The house was filthy; according to the grandmother, the father is an alcoholic. She said she is too old to care for such a child who needs constant care. The caseworker discovered that Jean could not speak. He made noises and followed the caseworker everywhere, touching him frequently. To the worker, the child seemed to be deprived of affection. Making a second visit, the caseworker interviewed the father. The father said he had no objection to the child being placed in a home. The mother was summoned to the office, but she refused to take Jean.

The caseworker tried to admit Jean to an institution but could not find a vacancy in a place equipped to care for handicapped children.

Soon thereafter, Jean was left tied to a bed, unfed and unattended. He became ill and was admitted to a hospital. During his 2-month stay, no relative visited him. Discharge planning was challenging, because no placement could be found. The caseworker attempted to admit Jean to the Shelter for Women and Children in Distress, a temporary shelter, but the agency refused him admission. The agency claimed it was not equipped to cope with Jean's multiple needs. The caseworker took the case to the Ministry's Permanent Secretary and to the Magistrate to get an order to admit Jean to the shelter. He is now waiting for SOS Children's Village, a residential facility operated by an NGO, to determine whether it will admit him for longer-term care.

(Boodajee, 1997)

referral, and finally, case advocacy to secure needed services for the client. It points out the need for further advocacy for service development to ensure that the needs of children with disabilities can be addressed. The case also illustrates the transition being experienced in Mauritian social work. Rather than focusing on child survival, the caseworker is focusing on child protection. As more appropriate services can be developed, child development will increase in importance.

Unlike in most other countries, social work in Mauritius has been a male-dominated profession. Within the last few years, however, the number of women has increased significantly, and female social work students now outnumber their male counterparts in the classroom. The most likely factor influencing this change is the changing role of women in society.

The Mauritius Association of Professional Social Workers was formed in 1984 and is affiliated with the IFSW. Its structure calls for an executive committee of representatives from the six major areas of social work: social security, probation, youth, medical social work, municipality welfare, and social welfare. Given the expansion of new settings for social work discussed above, some modifications may be expected in the future.

Social Work Education. Social work education is offered at the University of Mauritius. Until 1995, the highest credential offered was a Diploma in Social Work Studies, earned through a 2-year course of academic classes and field placement. In the diploma program, only students with at least 2 years of social work experience were admitted, and slots were allocated to various ministries and agencies, including the Ministry of Social Security, the Ministry of Reform Institutions, the Ministry for Women's Rights and Family Affairs, Mauritius Family Planning Association, the Sugar Industry Labour Welfare Fund, and the Mauritius Council on Social Service. The professional association and personnel from social agencies lobbied for several years for upgrade to a degree program, citing the need for upgrading of skills and improved status and "the need in our society for intervention by professional social workers in various problems thrown up by the complexity of life in present day Mauritius" (Manrakhan, 1990). In 1995, the university responded and began a degree program. The first students graduated in 1998 with a bachelor of science degree in social work.

Argentina

Although social work at schools does not exist in Jamaica or Mauritius, it is a common first job for a social worker in Argentina. While providing the new graduates with excellent opportunities to use their knowledge and initiative in serving both children and parents, it is a difficult job. School social workers are paid very little, and the children they work with in the public school system are very poor. In addition, a worker may be assigned to serve several schools. The best-paid social work jobs are in the judicial system, working with juveniles or working in jails and the courts. Other employment opportunities are in general and mental hospitals and in centers for the aged. Argentina had an important system for pensioners, called barrio centers. Here, social workers worked with old age pensioners providing social, cultural, recreational, and food distribution programs. With funding cutbacks, poverty among the aged is a growing problem. Argentine social workers have practiced within a welfare state; 95% were employed by the government. Now, however, the country is following the world trend toward privatization. Little clinical work has been done by social workers in Argentina, where the profession is not therapy oriented. Some private practice is beginning now that social workers have lost jobs through the government cutbacks resulting from privatization and are seeking new roles.

The roots of social work in Argentina are in the early work of charity groups, religious organizations, and mutual aid societies. Formal education for social work, as mentioned in Chapter 2, was adapted from European models and emphasizes the role of social worker as assistant to other professions, especially medicine. Religious traditions remain influential, as does a focus on the family. The theme of freedom from oppression is also significant—initially freedom from repressive governments, more recently from the oppression of international debt (Queiro-Tajalli, 1995).

Social workers are about 90% female, although about 40% of social work professors are male. Identification as a women's profession has kept salaries low. In addition, "the profession's roots in charity work, its primary mission of helping the poor and the oppressed, and its dependence on other disciplines do not help to improve the public image of social work" (Queiro-Tajalli, 1995, p. 93). Legislation adopted in 1989 does recognize social work's broad functions, including supervision, research, planning, and programming as well as direct services; both agency- and nonagency-based practice are recognized (Queiro-Tajalli, 1995).

An Association of Social Workers exists, and it recently developed a code of ethics for social workers in Argentina. The profession is described by one professor as "politically minded but not politically active" (R. Teubal, personal communication, March 13, 1997). There is a strong philosophical belief that social workers in practice are either on the side of the poor or they are on the side of the rich. This is reflected in the definition of social work advanced by Sela Sierra, an Argentine educator: "Social work is a change process seeking the humanization of social conditions and a progressive social liberation" (as quoted in Queiro-Tajalli, 1995, p. 97). Thus, a macro vision exists, yet there is little overt social reform or social action probably because of the high percentage of professionals who are government employees, fear of losing jobs in this era of cutbacks, and the residue from the oppression of the 1970s. Under the military dictatorship, no freedom of speech existed and Argentina entered a "long, horrifying journey of terrorism, counter-terrorism, riots, abductions and tortures" (Queiro-Tajalli, 1995, p. 98). Liberal and radical ideas, such as those of Paulo Freire that had changed social work in Latin America, were banned. Social workers tell of burning their books to avoid suspicion, spies in the classroom, and colleagues who "disappeared." Social work educators and practitioners were among those who were fired, jailed, killed, or exiled. Not only was advocacy suppressed, but even the teaching of group work was dangerous. Social work educators had to be sure not to promote radical action by students, which could result in the students' deaths. Thus, for survival reasons, social work would "think radically but act conservatively" (R. Teubal, personal communication, March 13, 1997).

Social Work Education. From its beginnings in 1930, social work education has expanded considerably and is now offered at 68 schools of social work (Queiro-Tajalli, 1997). These include schools at two levels: university degree programs and programs offered by religious and governmental organizations. As noted above and in Chapter 2, the content of social work education has been influenced by both philosophical and political developments within the country. Recent emphasis has been on "integrating theory and practice, the need to work at the micro and macro levels, and the necessity of interventions that respond to the socioeconomic and political realities of those being served" (Queiro-Tajalli, 1995, p. 101). Students in university programs receive education in the social sciences, including sociology, psychology, and scientific thought, and content on Argentine social problems, research, social work practice, and field practica. Placements are in clinics, community centers, and schools. The University of Buenos Aires has its students begin with macro practice and move to more micro practice settings, first with a placement in community work, then in groupwork, and finally work with individuals and families (R. Teubal, personal communication, March 13, 1997). Now that the controls of the military government are gone, students are allowed to participate in university governance. A renewed focus on relevance and indigenous concerns can therefore be expected, tempered, however, by economic realities of reduced educational funding and scarcity of professional jobs.

Armenia

On September 21, 1991, Armenia ended 70 years of Soviet rule and voted to declare itself a sovereign state. Reforms and changes that had begun earlier intensified, particularly the move from a centrally controlled economy to free enterprise. While transition has been difficult in many of the former Soviet republics, Armenia has faced particularly enormous challenges. Conflict with neighboring Azerbaijan led to an influx of refugees and to a blockade of Armenia by Turkey as well as Azerbaijan, causing shortages of fuel and raw materials, which further devastated the economy. In addition, Armenia was still reeling from the effects of a 1988 earthquake that killed 25,000, left a half-million homeless, and destroyed most of the country's second largest industrial city (Manjikian, 1996). Ironically, the earthquake planted some of the seeds for the development of social work, as will be explained.

As part of the Soviet system, the state controlled social welfare and provided a set of subsidies and cash payments to protect against social and medical crises. Other than one's family, the government was the only source of solutions to problems. No private charitable organizations existed or were permitted; indeed, even the Armenian church did not have a well-developed tradition of charitable works. Armenia, therefore, like the other former Soviet republics, suffered from significant gaps in human service infrastructure to support the introduction of social work.

The crisis created by the 1988 earthquake shocked Armenians into realizing how unprepared they were to deal with needs for social services. This great tragedy has also been described as an opportunity. "It might sound callous to characterize such a tragedy as an opportunity, it was in the sense that it shook and collapsed social and political structures as effectively as it did material structures" (Moushigian, 1991, p. 1). Although Armenia was still under Soviet control, international aid organizations moved in to help, as "the disaster crumbled the barriers of this garrison state" (Moushigian, 1991, p. 2). Among these were the International Committee of the Red Cross, UNICEF, UN High Commissioner for Refugees (UNHCR), Oxfam, the Peace Corps, and aid agencies of the European Union (EU). The external assistance—with modern medical technologies and mental health and trauma counseling—revealed just how unprepared and ill-equipped the Soviet system was to cope with the emergency. Thus, in Armenia, the earthquake opened the way to outside influences, including the introduction of mental health and social services, before the dissolution of the Soviet Union.

Rapid change has shaped the context for the introduction of social work to Armenia. In the larger economic and political arenas, Armenia has moved rapidly toward a market economy and democracy. The first few years of independence brought the birth of a dozen political parties; initiation of a free press; privatization of farms, housing, and small business; introduction of a national currency; opening of a stock exchange; and development of a new tax system (Manjikian, 1996). The rapidity of change, coupled with the blockade and the earthquake, resulted in a 55% decline in national income from 1988 to 1992. Just as expectations were rising, the living standards of most Armenians fell.

With no prior history of social work nor even a religious charitable tradition, the majority of the Armenian population had no understanding of what social work was or how this newly introduced profession could contribute to the society. Yet, in just a few years from 1991 to 1998, a profession has been established. Social work education has not only begun but has graduated several classes of entry-level paraprofessionals and has moved into full university status.

Social Work Education. Efforts to establish the profession began in 1990 when Dr. Ludmila Haroutunian, Head of the Department of Applied Sociology at Yerevan State University and active in women's affairs in the USSR, began to organize training for social workers. She sent each of her faculty members to the London School of Economics to study social work for 6 to 12 months and to gain practical experience in social welfare settings. Contacts were also initiated with the University of Connecticut, which led to design and implementation of 6-month training courses for employees of the Ministry of Labor and Social Welfare. With the graduation of the first 15 trainees in June 1994, Armenia had its first group of trained social workers. An undergraduate social work major has now been introduced at Yerevan State University, and the first group of professional social workers graduated in spring 2000.

As in other Eastern European countries and former Soviet republics, establishing field placements has been a challenge. Yet, in the spring of 1998, there were 41 students in field placements. Settings included children's residential programs, an old age home, children's hospitals, a juvenile detention facility, the civil and criminal courts, the Ministry of Social Welfare, a mental health facility, and a community-based agency serving battered women. This last agency was founded by a faculty member and is staffed by social work graduates and current field students. Two new sites for field placements are being developed: a gynecological clinic serving adolescent girls and a prison/probation program (Nancy Humphreys, personal communication, February 11, 1999). With the help of the University of Connecticut and an Armenian-American social worker, staff at Yerevan State University have written a fieldwork manual and provided training and orientation to the new field instructors. Most of the field instructors are psychologists; orientation and training provided have emphasized the differences and similarities between their profession and the "new" profession of social work (Nancy Humphreys, personal communication, February 11, 1999).

An Armenian Model? Significant challenges remain. One observer defined Armenia as a "case example of a country subscribing to a world culture" (Manjikian, 1996, p. 42), as she saw "no characteristics within the curriculum particular to its own political, economic and social life" (p. 44). The world culture argument sees the establishment of social work as part of the effort of Armenia "to establish itself in the world community by modeling other programs which are regarded as successful" (Manjikian, 1996, p. 42). An alternative explanation is the functional argument that views the initiation of social work as a response to the enormous social and economic dislocation brought about by the dissolution of communism. New problems arose, or were being documented for the first time, and established programs and patterns of help were disrupted by change. Social work, with its theories of helping and practical skills, was brought in to fulfill the helping function. This explanation has parallels to the explanation of the evolution of social work as a force to replace changing family and neighborhood helping patterns and the disruptions caused by industrialization in earlier times in Europe and North America.

Whichever theoretical explanation is correct, and probably elements of both apply, Armenian social work has work to do to define its own niche within its society and to further refine the type of practice approaches and theoretical perspectives that fit its own context. The recognition of social work as an occupation in the new Armenian constitution should assist future efforts.

Japan

Social work in Japan is caught between tradition and demographic change, and both are influencing the roles and functions of professionals. Social welfare services have been established and organized through a set of major national laws, and most social work is practiced in agencies established by these laws. Three of the laws were passed in the immediate post–World War II period: Child Welfare Law (1948), Law for the Welfare of Physically Handicapped Persons (1949), and Daily Life Security Law (1950). During the 1960s, three more were added: Law for the Welfare of Mentally Retarded Persons, Law for the Welfare of the Aged, and Law for Maternal and Child Welfare (Okamoto & Kuroki, 1997). Although Japan does not have a comprehensive welfare state, Article 25 of the constitution guarantees the right to an acceptable standard of living: "the state has the responsibility to ensure that the people maintain a minimum standard of wholesome and cultural living" (Maeda, 1995, p. 395). Trained social workers, chiefly graduates of baccalaureate programs, work mainly in child welfare, services for the disabled and the elderly, and government services; other settings include hospitals and health centers, youth organizations, and community agencies (Maeda, 1995).

The major social work functions are social casework and case management; community work exists but plays a secondary role (Matsubara, 1992). Social casework is the common method in welfare offices, hospitals and health care centers, and child guidance centers. The approach to public assistance combines financial assistance with counseling of clients. Case management is growing in importance, especially in the field of welfare of the elderly. The increased popularity of case management is attributed to lack of coordination and cooperation among social welfare institutions; inefficient services; lack of knowledge of services among the populace; and the cultural rejection of counseling as negative and stigmatizing (Matsubara, 1992). Thus, referral, service advocacy, coordination, and reassurance are more common and acceptable social work roles than in-depth counseling to individuals.

As noted above, community work is less common. However, there are important roles for community work within the profession: to identify needs for social services, to promote the establishment of more private agencies to provide needed services, because development of the nonprofit sector has been slow; and to expand "mutual support and assistance" in local communities (Matsubara, 1992, p. 90).

Social workers generally receive low wages, although the profession is organized and recognized by laws. The Japan Association of Social Workers was formed in 1960 and adopted a code of ethics in 1986 (Maeda, 1995). In 1987, the government passed the Certified Social Worker Law and the Certified Care Worker Law and established state exams for each. Confidentiality is protected by the first law and has increased the recognition of social workers as qualified professionals.

Social Work Education. Education for social work is provided in 104 undergraduate schools, 24 junior college programs, and 19 technical schools, for a total of 147 programs (Kasumi Hirayama, personal communication, July 30, 2000). The Japan Association of Schools of Social Work (JASSW) was founded in 1955 to upgrade educational standards and to join the IASSW. The association focuses on the areas of (1) promotion of professionalization of social work and related occupations; (2) curriculum development for social work; and (3) international activities (Hirata, 1986). JASSW curriculum standards require education in four areas: foundation (including principles and concepts of social work, social welfare policies and services, history of social welfare); methods and techniques (direct service, community organization, planning, administration, and social survey); fields of practice (family, child welfare, aged, handicapped, medical, etc.); and fieldwork.

Postgraduate education has been slow to develop, but there are now 23 doctoral programs and 40 master's programs. Enrollments remain small, although they have grown beyond Maeda's (1995) estimates of only about 150 students enrolled in graduate education. Thus, few social workers are trained for leadership roles. Other educational dilemmas are that colleges are not permitted to grant a bachelor of social work; therefore, students receive a bachelor of art or a bachelor of sociology degree. Also, some students select social work just to get a place in a university, with no intention of practicing. A 1983 study showed that more than a quarter of social work students did not intend to work in the field (Maeda, 1995).

Issues and Challenges. Challenges for Japanese social work grow out of demographic change, the conflicts between tradition and change, and the relatively low status of the profession.

Traditional Japanese culture is family oriented and group oriented. Values that are stressed in the family and in the workplace are loyalty, conformity, and unity (Okamoto & Kuroki, 1997). Yet Japanese society has been undergoing major changes. Modernization has led to new family patterns; more young Japanese live in nuclear families rather than remaining with parents. In the mid1960s, 80% of elderly parents lived with their children; by 1996, this had fallen to 57% (Bass, 1996). "The breakup and perhaps passing of the traditional family in Japan—in other words, the movement in recent decades toward the nuclear family as society's paradigm—is related to Japan's economic success, as more families become transient in the pursuit of employment" (Matsubara, 1997, p. 87). At the same time, the number and proportion of aged people in the population has increased dramatically. In 1940, only 4.7% of the population was over 65; by 1990, this figure had increased to 12%. Predictions are that the percentage will increase until 2021 when almost a quarter (23.6%) of the population will be over 65 (Matsubara, 1992). The need for services for the elderly has increased and will continue to expand; Matsubara (1992) predicted that 200,000 additional social workers will be needed by early in the 21st century just to serve this population. As the dependency ratio (the number of working age adults available to support children and elderly) increases, concern over paying for services will intensify and may result in reductions in social welfare benefits. Yet the government is pursuing policies to ensure opportunities for productive and meaningful aging. According to Bass (1996), the Japanese gerontologic emphasis on "expanding opportunities for enhanced meaning and purpose in life is a far more complex and challenging goal, and one which has received scant attention in Western societies" (p. 11).

It is also possible that demographic realities will cause modifications in traditional attitudes about the roles of families, government, and other service providers as the burden of family care grows more onerous. At the same time, "the system of mutual aid, which has traditionally existed in historically stable communities, is a potential casualty of Japan's new economic prosperity" (Matsubara, 1992, p. 87). Even more than other Japanese, the elderly see using social services as an embarrassment, not a right. Social workers will need to find ways to reach the reluctant elderly and help them to use the services they need. This is an important professional challenge for the present and near future.

Underutilization of social work training is another problem area. Many social work graduates work in residential institutions where they are assigned direct care work. In these roles, there is little or no professional autonomy and professionals are asked to perform hands-on care rather than counseling or case management. Although there are benefits to the clients in that abuse and neglect are rare, "this relative upgrading of the quality of care is achieved at the expense of social workers who are trained to do more" (Matsubara, 1992, p. 91). Lack of job mobility compounds this inefficient use of skilled social workers.

Social work services are not provided in schools, and there is little contact between the educational and social service sectors. Yet social work is needed to address growing problems among children caused by intense academic competitiveness.

Finally, social work in Japan continues to struggle to adapt imported social work theories. The reliance on foreign, mostly U.S., theories has impeded the development of a responsive profession. As a result:

> There is a considerable gap between the theory and the practice of social work. The shared responsibility for this lack of fit lies with the incongruous match between American theories and the Japanese sociocultural environment and culture-bound practice situations. This makes it hard to accommodate theories from cultures foreign to Japanese values in Japanese social work practice. (Okamoto and Kuroki, 1997, p. 279)

Matsubara predicts that because traditional ideologies are deeply rooted, it will take perhaps several decades for true change to occur, in spite of the fact that economic and social changes make traditional values somewhat dysfunctional. He concludes that in order to enhance the impact of the profession, "social work in Japan must acknowledge and accommodate the elements of Japan's culture" and give increased attention to theory development (Matsubara, 1992, p. 95).

SIMILARITIES AND DIFFERENCES
IN THE WORLD OF SOCIAL WORK

Now that social work has been briefly explored in six very different countries, we can turn to an analysis of the difficult questions raised by comparative efforts. What are the similarities and differences in social work as it is conceptualized, organized, and practiced in our six example countries and beyond? Can social work legitimately be called a worldwide profession? And can a globally applicable definition of social work be developed? As the president of the IFSW remarked: "After 100 years or more of professional social work we still have to ask the question: What is social work?" (Envall, 1998, p. 2).

It may be argued that the similarities in social work worldwide are superficial and exist only at highly abstract levels. It is equally legitimate to argue that it is the differences that are superficial. Social work continues to endure and to expand into a growing number of countries. Identification with a worldwide profession through organized associations has intensified, and many national associations have collaborated through the IFSW to develop a revised code of ethics and statement of ethical principles, a manual on human rights, and position statements on social issues. The difficult work on a new worldwide definition of social work began in 1996. It should be noted that efforts at defining social work within nations have also been challenging. The fact that no worldwide definition existed for many years is not, in itself, an indicator that the profession has only superficial commonalities.

Commonalities and Differences Among the Example Countries

A number of specific commonalities and differences in the profession can be identified. To some degree, social work in all six countries examined had external roots. The founder of social work in Denmark sought inspiration and knowledge from the United States and Germany, but social work in Denmark developed along a particularly Danish path. In Argentina, a sustained and vigorous rejection of foreign theory has led to considerable independent development of professional ideology. Mauritius, Jamaica, and Japan are still heavily influenced by foreign literature and imported models of social services. The Japan case suggests that early introduction of the profession does not automatically lead to its taking root firmly in the culture. The situation in Armenia is emerging; as Manjikian (1996) noted, a truly "Armenian" strain is not yet detectable. The dearth of indigenous literature remains a problem in much of Africa and Asia. In countries such as the United States, Britain, France, and Germany, locally produced research and literature have played significant roles in shaping the profession.

Hokenstad, Khinduka, and Midgley (1992) identified four sets of commonalities from their analysis of social work in 10 countries:

1. Social work takes on a broad range of roles and responsibilities in each country where it is present.
2. In all countries examined, social work defines itself as an agent of social change and reform.
3. Work with the poor is a part of social work in almost all countries. (The authors do not identify any countries where this is not true.)
4. There are shared values of "promoting human dignity and social justice, empowering poor and vulnerable peoples, and encouraging intergroup harmony and goodwill" (p. 182).

The authors concluded that in spite of many differences among nations, social workers face similar issues in most if not all countries. On the other hand, they also claimed that "the universality of social work does not mean that the pattern of social work's organization, roles and fields of service, modes of educational preparation, or degree of social recognition are uniform throughout the world" (Hokenstad, Khinduka, & Midgley, 1992, p. 181). Next, the areas of commonality and difference will be examined in greater detail.

Breadth and Variety of Roles and Settings for Practice. Context—including the role of government in social welfare, the pattern of development of complementary professions, and the structure of societal institutions—influences the specific fields of practice and roles of social work. As described above, school social work is prevalent in Argentina but unknown in Mauritius or Japan. In Jamaica, some social workers formerly worked in schools, but these functions are now being taken over by counselors trained at teachers' colleges. These differences probably have little to do with social work competence in the various countries, but are shaped by societal definitions of the nature of problems of children and structural decisions about where psychosocial problems should be addressed. The involvement of social workers in direct care work in institutions in Japan is a similar type of difference in professional role. In the United States, direct care work is considered nonprofessional or paraprofessional work; in Denmark, it is the work of a separate profession of social pedagogy. Social work roles are therefore influenced by professional status and by the development of other professions in the social welfare arena.

In all countries, social work is broad and has shown flexibility in expanding into new roles and new fields of service. This has been another enduring characteristic of the profession. The definition developed in 1928, quoted at the beginning of this chapter, speaks to social work's wide range of roles in treatment, prevention, and improvement of social conditions. The full range of social work methods—casework, groupwork, community action, legislative work, administration, and research—are included in this definition written more than 70 years ago. Harris views flexibility as a key to social work's success. He also notes that it is related, perhaps unavoidably, to definitional difficulties: "A precondition for its [social work's] flexibility and utility is a certain lack of precision and an embarrassing degree of definitional elusiveness" (1997, p. 437). Flexibility and growth are amply demonstrated in the case studies cited here, such as the recent expansion into counseling and mental health work in Mauritius and social work leadership on issues of child welfare and children's rights in Jamaica.

Social Change. The belief in positive change and in people's capacities to change are important hallmarks of social work. As expressed by one of the social work leaders from Jamaica, social work's stance that people can change, that they can be helped, and that they can learn to help themselves is a valuable contribution to individual, community, and national development (Elsye Sayles, personal communication, April 24, 1997). In the face of daunting and overwhelming social problems everywhere, social work's optimism and emphasis on possibilities are important commonalities. Empowerment may not yet be a commonality in the way social work is practiced, but the ideology of empowerment is one of the shared values of the profession.

A related dimension is the social work profession's commitment to social change and social reform, mandated in the international code as well as most national codes of ethics. The action agendas to bring about change differ according to national context. Lobbying and legislative action predominate in the United States where social reform is seen as part of the profession's dual commitment to client service and societal improvement within a democratic system of government. In Argentina, social workers have a more radical ideology, but a cautious approach to change actions shaped by many years of repressive government. Social workers under apartheid South Africa and military governments elsewhere have struggled to find ways to bring about change when peaceful protest and even words, including speeches, letters, articles, and class discussions, could result in arrest and imprisonment. Thus social change ideology is universal; social change strategies and the level of the profession's involvement in change efforts are determined by the local context.

Social Problems and Interventions. Social workers are coping with similar social problems in many if not most countries. "The extraordinary similarity of issues that social workers face all over the world is probably the most salient conclusion one can draw from a review of social work in different countries" (Hokenstad, Khinduka, & Midgley, 1992, p. 191). Poverty and its related difficulties are important concerns for social workers everywhere. Other common challenges include child and family problems, cultural diversity and conflict, and social exclusion.

Yet, differences in scope and severity of these problems cannot be overlooked. Poverty affects only about 4% of Danish citizens, but it is a mass

SOCIAL EXCLUSION

Social exclusion is a term used to describe social and economic marginality. Those who are socially excluded are usually unemployed and often live in poverty; in addition, their exclusion extends to social and civic participation. Social exclusion means that segments of the population no longer participate in opportunities available in society (Gore, 1995).

phenomenon in India, sub-Saharan Africa, and in many countries of the former Soviet Union. Many of the clients of social work services in Jamaica and Argentina are desperately poor. Difference in the scope of poverty or other problems, in resources available, and in social welfare structures differentially shape the social work response. Mass poverty requires a social or community development approach; individual poverty in a welfare state can be addressed through referrals for entitlements. Thus, common problems provide a global agenda for social work, but interventions continue to be locally determined.

Payne argues that social work exists and gains societal acceptance because it "allows society to deal successfully with social issues which have been identified and which cannot otherwise be resolved" (1998, p. 447). Globally, social work is therefore a profession that responds to identified social issues, which most scholars believe are becoming more commonly experienced around the world. The specific forms that social work takes in any country, however, are shaped by that society's views of the social issue and by the possibilities for intervention, including resources, institutional support, and societal approval. "Societies construct the kind of social work that responds to their views of social issues and the way it would be possible to deal with them" (Payne, 1998, p. 447). (For further discussion of global social problems, see Chapter 5.)

Shared Values. Value commitments and ethical principles are at the core of social work as a profession. At least in general principles, there is a global commonality of values. Social work in every country stands for respect for the worth and dignity of all people. Social work also shares a concern for vulnerable groups, with particular attention to the poor, and identifies efforts to end discrimination and move toward equal treatment for all as professional goals. As discussed above, a commitment to social reform and change is a universal value of the profession, at least at an abstract level. Participation and self-determination of those being helped are widely accepted principles, although they may be put into practice with different levels of tolerance for paternalism. Values differences are most likely found between communally oriented societies and the individualistic-oriented Western societies. The similarities and differences in values will be discussed in depth in Chapter 7.

Theoretical Underpinnings. Determining the common or different theoretical underpinnings of social work is more complex. Social work everywhere draws upon a range of social and behavioral sciences to inform its practice. Curricula in social work educational programs across the six countries examined for this text included human behavior and the social environment; social service policies and programs, and social research methods. The specific theories emphasized differed.

Lorenz (1994) identifies four philosophic traditions as the key forces that shaped social work in Europe: Christianity, philanthropy, feminism, and socialism. Clearly, as a group, these cannot be claimed as globally relevant or dominant theories. The lack of fit is obvious, for example, in Mauritius with its Hindu majority, in Armenia, which lacks a philanthropic tradition, or in Japan where feminism has been a late and relatively weak development and where Christianity is embraced by only a minority of the population.

In Latin America, social work has incorporated elements of liberation theology and the conscientization ideas of Paulo Freire. This has given Latin American social work a locally relevant identity that supplements the elements it shares with social work elsewhere. African social workers and social work educators have made efforts to identify social work as social development. This has clarified the importance of linking professional goals with development goals; however, the theory base of social development is vague and draws from many disciplines. Social development requires an emphasis on community and national problems rather than on individuals and a shift from welfare of specific disadvantaged groups to broader community welfare. Competence in social development requires a theoretical background from many disciplines with "specific attention to theories of adult education and literacy, social change, social structure, social order, social development and modernization, attitude development and change, motivation, and family systems and kinship networks" (Asamoah, 1997, pp. 310–311). The knowledge areas on Asamoah's list could be relevant to social work anywhere; what is distinctive is the emphasis on social systems and macro theories rather than on theories of individual behavior.

There is clearly no single theoretical base for social work as a global profession. Yet many theories used have broad relevance. Continued efforts at practice theory development in Africa, Asia, Latin America, and the countries of the former Soviet Union are needed and will contribute to the evolution of a constellation of applicable theories.

At the IFSW General Meeting in July 2000, a new international definition of social work was adopted. Adoption followed 4 years of work by a task force to develop a definition that would be brief, yet universally applicable. The definition follows:

> The social work profession promotes social change, problem solving in human relationships and the empowerment and liberation of people to enhance well-being. Utilising theories of human behaviour and social systems, social work intervenes at the points where people interact with their environments. Principles of human rights and social justice are fundamental to social work. (IFSW, 2000)

The 1928 definition cited at the beginning of this chapter remains a fairly accurate description of the profession, although it contains some outdated language. As the 2000 definition is circulated and used, it will be interesting to see if it has as much staying power. Although the definition communicates the aims of social work, it does not convey what social workers do; it may therefore be of limited use in introducing the profession to global policy makers and professionals in other disciplines.

REFERENCES

Asamoah, Y. (1997). Africa. In N.S. Mayadas, T.D. Watts, & D. Elliott (Eds.), *International handbook on social work theory and practice* (pp. 303–319). Westport, CT: Greenwood Press.

Baker, P. (1998). Staying focussed on development. In Wint, E. & Healy, L. *Social work reality.* (pp. 46–57). Kingston, Jamaica: Canoe Press.

Bass, S.A. (1996). Introduction: Japan's aging society. *Journal of Aging and Social Policy, 8*(2/3), 1–12.

Boodajee, K.Y. (1997). A critical appraisal of the functioning of the Child Development Unit of the Ministry of Women, Family Welfare and Child Development with reference to case studies showing strengths and weaknesses of the unit. Unpublished paper, University of Mauritius, Social Work Diploma course.

Brown, G. (1991). The programme in the School of Continuing Studies, In J. Maxwell & E. Wint, Eds. *Contemporary social work education: A Caribbean orientation* (pp. 21–26). Mona, Jamaica: Department of Sociology and Social Work, University of the West Indies.

Envall, E. (1998). President's message. *IFSW Newsletter,* issue 2, p. 2.

Girvan, N. (Ed.) (1993). *Working together for development: D.T.M. Girvan on cooperatives and community development 1939–1968*. Kingston, Jamaica: Institute of Jamaica Publications.

Gore, C. (1995). Introduction: Markets, citizenship and social exclusion. In G. Rodgers, C. Gore, & J. B. Figueiredo, *Social exclusion: Rhetoric, reality, responses* (pp. 1–40). Geneva: International Labour Organization/International Institute for Labour Studies.

Halskov, T., & Egelund, T. (1998). Social work in Denmark. In S. Shardlow & M. Payne (Eds.). *Contemporary issues in social work: Western Europe* (pp. 11–24). Hants, England: Arena Ashgate Publishing.

Harris, R. (1997). Internationalizing social work: Some themes and issues. In N.S. Mayadas, T.D. Watts, & D. Elliott (Eds.), *International handbook on social work theory and practice* (pp. 429–440). Westport, CT: Greenwood Press.

Hirata, T. (Ed.) (1986). *Guide to Japanese social work education.* [Prepared by the Japanese Association of Schools of Social Work] Tokyo: National Council of Social Welfare.

Hokenstad, M. C., Khinduka, S., & Midgley, J. (Eds.) (1992). *Profiles in international social work.* Washington, DC: NASW Press.

Information sheet on Danish Association of Social Workers. (2000). http://socialrdg.dk/Startside/engelsk.htm. [accessed 2/17/00].

Lorenz, W. (1994). *Social work in a changing Europe.* London: Routledge.

Maeda, K.K. (1995). Japan. In T.D. Watts, D. Elliott, & N.S. Mayadas (Eds.), *International handbook on social work education* (pp. 389–402). Westport, CT: Greenwood Press.

Manjikian, G. (1996). *The spread of social work education: Case study of Armenia.* (Monograph). Stanford, CA: International Educational Administration and Policy Analysis, School of Education, Stanford University.

Manrakhan, V. (1990, September). Letter to the University of Mauritius Regarding the Degree Course in Social Work. The Mauritius Association of Professional Social Workers, September, 1990.

Matsubara, Y. (1992). Social work in Japan: Responding to demographic dilemmas. In M.C. Hokenstad, S.K. Khinduka, & J. Midgley (Eds.), *Profiles in international social work* (pp. 85–97). Washington, DC: NASW Press.

Maxwell, J.A. (1991). The Professional Programme in the Department of Sociology and Social Work. In J. Maxwell & E. Wint (Eds.), *Contemporary social work education: A Caribbean orientation* (pp. 11–21). Mona, Jamaica: Department of Sociology and Social Work, University of the West Indies.

Meade, J.E., Foggon, G., Houghton, H., Lees, N., Marshall, R.S., Roddan, G.M., & Selwyn, P. (1961). *The economic and social structure of Mauritius.* London: Methuen & Co.

Moushigian, G. (1991). *Armenia, the earthquake of December, 1988, and the role of American social work.* Unpublished paper.

Okamoto, T. and Kuroki, Y. (1997). Japan. In N.S. Mayadas, T.D. Watts, & D. Elliott (Eds.), *International handbook on social work theory and practice* (pp. 263–281). Westport, CT: Greenwood Press.

The organization of the First International Conference of Social Work and of the First International Social Welfare Fortnight. (1929). In International Conference of Social Work [Proceedings] (Vol. I, pp. 5–7). First Conference, Paris, July 8–13, 1928.

Payne, M. (1998). Why social work? Comparative perspectives on social issue and response formation. *International Social Work, 41*(4), 443–453.

Queiro-Tajalli, I. (1995). Argentina. In T.D. Watts, D. Elliott, & N.S. Mayadas (Eds.), *International handbook on social work education* (pp. 87–102). Westport, CT: Greenwood Press.

Queiro-Tajalli, I. (1997). Argentina. In N.S. Mayadas, T.D. Watts, D. Elliott (Eds.), *International handbook on social work theory and practice* (pp. 76–92). Westport, CT: Greenwood Press.

Ramgoolam, K.C. (1996, July). *Social work profession meeting the challenges of change in Mauritius—Community workers in action.* Paper presented at the Joint World Congress of IFSW and IASSW, Hong Kong.

Republic of Mauritius and UNICEF. (1994). *Situation analysis of women and children in Mauritius.* Mauritius: Henry Printers Ltd.

Social work education in Denmark. (1998). Available at http://www.dsh-aa.dk/edueng1.htm. Accessed December 10, 1998.

Titmuss, R.M., & Abel-Smith, B. (1961). *Social policies and population growth in Mauritius.* London: Methuen & Co.

University of Mauritius, School of Administration. (1986, October). Mauritius: The Welfare System Environment. Internal document, October, 1986.

CHAPTER 5

GLOBAL INTERDEPENDENCE
AND SOCIAL WORK

Global interdependence needs to be recognized as "an irrefutable fact of life on which action must be based" (Joint Working Group on Development Education, 1984). The impact of global interdependence has been widely recognized in economic and environmental matters. It has been less well understood as a force affecting social work practice and professional action. This gap in comprehension is particularly acute in Western nations. Social workers in less economically powerful nations and former colonies have lived with the impact of global interdependence for many years. Borrowing of social work curriculum from the industrialized nations, presence of foreign experts in social and educational programs, and involvement with the social services initiatives of UNICEF, World Health Organization (WHO), United Nations Development Program (UNDP), and other organizations have all contributed to a more global perspective for social work in the developing world. In the 1980s and 1990s, the impact of global economic interdependence has been great as social workers in Africa and the Caribbean have coped with structural adjustment, bringing them into personal and professional contact with International Monetary Fund (IMF) policies.

Only more recently has global interdependence been recognized as a force affecting social work in the industrialized countries of Europe, North America, and Japan. Yet, does global interdependence truly matter to the individual social worker in North America? In this chapter, several theses are put forth and elaborated: (1) as a citizen and as a social worker, your health security, and well-being and that of your clients are directly affected by interdependence; (2) the forces of globalization have led to increased similarities in the social problems experienced in the countries of the world, creating a large shared agenda for knowledge and action; and (3) countries can no longer "solve" their social problems (or protect their environments or economies) in isolation but must take other nations into account. Social workers, too, must be cognizant of global matters in order to understand the problems they face in working with clients and communities and in contributing to problem resolutions. Finally, it is argued that these three points are true in most if not all countries.

The dimensions of interdependence and their indicators will be discussed first. Then, two issues—migration and AIDS—will be discussed as manifestations of global interdependence in the social welfare sphere. This will be followed by a brief discussion of poverty, women's issues, and street children as examples of the growing shared agenda in social welfare. The impact of national policies on other nations, an important but less recognized dimension of interdependence, will be illustrated through a discussion of ways in which nations model social welfare policies after those adopted elsewhere.

WHAT IS INTERDEPENDENCE AND WHAT FORMS DOES IT TAKE?

John Maxwell Hamilton (1990), author of *Entangling Alliances* and *Main Street America and the Third World*, defines interdependence simply as "a nation's increased sensitivity to external forces" (p. 21). Midgley (1997) says that globalization is "a process of global integration in which diverse peoples, economies, cultures and political processes are increasingly subjected to international influences . . ." (p. xi). It also includes "the emergence of an inclusive worldwide culture, a global economy, and above all, a shared awareness of the world as a single place" (p. 21). As suggested in the definitions, there are many aspects of interdependence; these include human migration; trade; international investments and banking; the range and reach of military weapons; use of foreign labor; dependence on resources from other countries; and a broad range of environmental concerns, including biodiversity, pollution, and natural resources. Interdependence is aided by fast, cheap means of travel, by networks of telephone and computer communications, and by viewing of television programs which reach far beyond the originating nation (Hamilton, 1990).

As discussed by Hamilton and others, there are several main arenas of interdependence: environmental, cultural, and economic. Surprisingly, Hamilton leaves out security interdependence—the threat of nuclear war, terrorism, and other assaults on physical security—which is included here. In this chapter, social welfare interdependence is also added to the list of dimensions to be explored and is given special emphasis.

Environmental Interdependence

Environmental problems in one country are truly the problems of neighboring countries and, quite possibly, of all of us. There are two main environmental problems: pollution and resource depletion. Air pollution and ocean pollution do not respect national boundaries. Pollution of the ocean in any part of the world can wash onto the shores of other nations or taint fish eaten throughout the world. Pollution from industrialized cities in the northern United States affect air quality in Canada, and towns on the southern U.S. border are increasingly worried about the environmental hazards of industrial development in northern Mexico. Possibly no event catalyzed world realization that environmental damage crosses borders as much as the nuclear accident at the power plant in Chernobyl in the Ukraine. Dangerously high radiation levels were detected in Finland, Poland, Sweden, and many other nations, shocking policy makers into the realization that whatever environmental safeguards may be adopted at home are not sufficient to protect their populations.

Air pollution is linked to increases in lung cancer, asthma, bronchitis, and pneumonia. These ailments are particularly serious in crowded cities and in areas of rapid and relatively unregulated industrial development such as China. Pollution also contributes to global warming, causing predictions of significant climate change and a rise in sea level. All nations need to be concerned about these predictions; some are more immediately imperiled. The tiny Republic of Maldives, a nation of islands in the Indian Ocean, would lose 80% of its land if sea level rises 1 meter ("Maldives on the Beach," 1999). Maldives cannot address this problem alone or even make a significant contribution to its resolution; instead, it must depend on policies and actions of the rest of the nations of the world to prevent the sea from swallowing it up.

Pesticides provide another example. Pesticides banned for use in the United States are still being exported to countries with fewer regulations. These pesticides then re-enter the U.S. food supply on imported fruits and vegetables. Still others, such as DDT, travel by rain and wind to affect areas where their use has been banned (Hamilton, 1986).

According to the UN, over 1 billion people lack access to clean water and almost 2 billion lack essential sanitation (Hoff, 1997). Through globalization, unsanitary conditions in one part of the world can affect food imported by another or can lead to infections' being passed through international travel and migration. Tuberculosis is prevalent in crowded and unsanitary conditions; it then fans out to other places with the migrants from the slums. "Tuberculosis travels across the border between El Paso, Texas, and Ciudad Juárez, Mexico, as does malaria, cysticerosis, typhoid, leprosy, schistosomiasis, viral hepatitis, and Chagas' disease" (Keigher & Lowery, 1998, p. 155). Once again, the conditions of sanitation and pollution become everyone's concern. Thus a suburban businessman may be sitting next to an undocumented immigrant with drug-resistant tuberculosis on the New York subway. The conditions in the immigrant's homeland and the U.S. policy of denying health care to undocumented immigrants may cost the businessman his health or even his life. The personal impact of environmental interdependence can be devastating.

Depletion is the second dimension in environmental degradation. Depletion of the world's resources through overuse and carelessness includes mineral resources, forests, water, and soil. There are now 26 countries classified as water-scarce (Hoff, 1997). Soil loss and desertification (the loss of agricultural land to encroaching desert) contribute to food shortages and push rural people into already crowded cities. Deforestation contributes to increased erosion, pollution, and global warming and to the extinction of species. It is estimated that deforestation in the tropics may cost the world 15% to 20% of its species by 2000 (Hoff, 1997). Conservation efforts or lack thereof in other countries affect all of our futures. Quoting a small farmer in

Costa Rica, "I know I can destroy the future of the forest and the people, but I have to eat today" (Hamilton, 1990, p. 91). In 1950, 75% of Costa Rica was natural forest; by 1977, this had been reduced to 33%. At the current rate of deforestation, it is predicted that by the middle of the 2000–2010 decade, the only forest in Costa Rica will be in the national parks and the country will be forced to import timber (Hamilton, 1990).

Environmental interdependence affects all peoples of the world and is a major challenge to world policy processes and goals. The loss of biodiversity and the increase in deforestation and desertification are causing immediate severe hardships for people in the affected areas. Famine and regular food shortages, displacement of communities, and increasingly harsh daily routines of water and fuel gathering for women and children are among the effects. Environmental challenges complicate development efforts and have led to demands for development models that emphasize sustainability—the preservation of the future capacity for development.

Cultural Interdependence

Advancements in communications technologies, inexpensive world travel, and international movements of populations have brought cultures into frequent contact with each other. Speaking of the Caribbean region, Robotham (1996) says that transnational culture has invaded even the masses: "Able to access relatively cheap travel, to exploit the wide extension of modern digital international telephone linkages in the region, and to receive substantial remittances from relatives in North America and Britain, a whole informal transnational culture has been generated among this group" (pp. 23–24). Exchange of cultural influences and consumer goods is spread by legions of women in the Caribbean who travel throughout the region to the Cayman Islands, Martinique, Panama, and even New York and Miami, buying and selling produce, crafts, and other consumer goods; their activities are so extensive that they have earned the title of informal commercial importers (ICIs).

The influence of these cross-cultural exchanges is seen in changes in food, entertainment, and lifestyles. The impact of these changes can be viewed as enriching, homogenizing, or evil. Hokenstad and Midgley (1997) discuss the importance of "international roots" of culture in countries that are increasingly diverse. Celebrating diversity is the theme that expresses the enrichment view of cross-cultural influence.

Cross-cultural influence can, however, have a homogenizing effect on mass culture. Rock, rap, and reggae music can be heard in Boston, Bucharest, Bujumbura, and Bogotá. Teens wear jeans and U.S. sports team T-shirts from Uruguay to Uganda. The spread of franchised fast-food chains means one can eat the same food in most countries of the world. Cross-cultural influence is both welcomed and rejected. In Kenya, the popularity of Western rock music led television critic Amboka Andere to comment: "Kenyan culture suffers as the nation is bombarded by foreign styles of music and dance—as though Kenyans are incapable of making their own" (Hamilton, 1990, p. 128). Although much of this cultural impact is superficial, it causes concern that deeper cultural traditions and values may be lost if the homogenizing influence of mass culture expands.

Globalization as an evil influence is expressed in the book *Social Strains of Globalization in India* (Taber & Batra, 1995): "Globalization is first of all, a threat to accustomed ways of living and solving problems. . . . While globalization means more consumer goods and better incomes for many, it also means, for example, increased materialism with higher dowry demands and more degradation for female infants" (p. 24). Thus global influences are seen as attacks on positive aspects of traditional cultures, resulting either in loss of tradition or in strange mutations, for example, dowry demands for television sets, VCRs, and cars.

The UNDP concurs that consumption is having negative effects on culture as well as on health and the environment (UNDP, 1998). Particularly noted are "the pressure of competitive spending and rising social standards of consumption, with worrying trends showing the consumption of 'luxuries' rising faster than the consumption of 'necessities' " (p. 65). These developments mean that consumption becomes a force for social exclusion rather than inclusion.

Tourism—the quintessential transnational industry—brings other forms of cultural influence. Robotham (1996) asserts that tourism is so important to the Jamaican economy that the nation "re-oriented" itself from British culture to American culture to attract nearby travelers. The elites involved in the tourist industry "changed the way (they) sought to present Jamaica, Barbados and the whole region to the outside world. It has had a dramatic effect on how the rest of the world perceives the region" (Robotham, 1996, p. 21).

There are real and potential benefits to tourism. Promotion of tourism provides a means for countries without an industrial base to use its natural assets, such as beaches, forests, and animal and bird life, to generate jobs and earn income. In a number of countries, tourism is a leading source of foreign exchange. Tourism potentially provides opportunities for cultural enrichment and intercultural exchange. Visitors may learn about new places, explore historical sites and museums, experience different natural environments, and learn about cultures, including meeting people from cultures very different from their own. These experiences can affect tourists' attitudes and build global-mindedness. Still other tourist locations, such as Disney theme parks, New York, and Paris, are potential meeting places for visitors from many parts of the world.

But there is a darker side to this "quintessential transnational industry." Sex tourism is perhaps the darkest. In Thailand, for example, rural poverty and unemployment drive women into cities to seek work, where "sex tourism has created a great demand for women in the 'service sector' " (Mensendiek, 1997, p. 173). Traditional family and religious ideologies are upset as poor women become prostitutes to support their families. Whereas the cost to society is high, the cost to the women themselves is higher because AIDS and other sexually transmitted diseases are rampant. And "for those who profit from the sex industry, women are commodities easily replaced if they become ill or die" (Mensendiek, 1997, p. 173). In other parts of the world, young boys are also lured into prostitution as part of the sex tourist industry and face early death from AIDS, ostracism from societies hostile to homosexual activity, and the typical risks to prostitutes of exploitation and physical abuse.

When tourism is not respectful of local peoples and traditions, the potentials for positive cross-cultural contact are violated. Tourists may stay in opulent fortresses while local residents are banned from entering the premises and using their own beaches. Or tourists may snap pictures of residents as if they were oddities or mere parts of the scenery. Environmental damage also results from tourism, for example, from the chemicals used on newly constructed golf courses and from the careless destruction of coral reefs.

Economic Interdependence

The most recognized dimension of interdependence is the global economy. Because the impacts are of particular importance to social workers and their clients, extra attention will be given to economics here. Currently, the flaws of the global economy—long-term unemployment, labor insecurity, debt, and low incomes—are having a negative impact on human welfare around the world. In countries where the impact is serious, social cohesion is being affected (Wagner, 1997). Economic interdependence is demonstrated through world trade, investments, currency regulations, aid, and lending. Multinational corporations produce products through complex arrangements in many countries, blurring the concept of domestic and foreign production. Indeed, half of the world's largest economic units are not nations but multinational corporations (Day, 1989).

Countries have long recognized their dependence on other nations for access to raw materials that could not be produced domestically and to markets for selling products produced in abundance. Countries that have few mineral resources, limited land for agricultural production, or short growing seasons are highly dependent on trade with other nations to obtain goods for survival. Some countries grow or produce only one or two major commodities for trade, leaving them highly vulnerable to market forces determining the price for their products and for importation of other goods. In 1968, for example, newly independent Mauritius received nearly all of its foreign exchange earnings from sugar, which constituted 93% of annual exports (Bowman, 1991). In a table labeled "Desperate Dependence," UN Conference on Trade and Development (UNCTAD) statistics showed that Burundi earned 84% of foreign exchange from coffee; Zambia, 88% from copper; Ghana, 66% from cocoa, and Netherlands Antilles, 92% from oil products (United Nations, 1990). As prices fall, these countries experience a major drop in income and therefore well-being for the population.

The growth of multinational companies and the internationalization of the economy mean that jobs can be moved from country to country in search of lower costs and higher profits. Industrialized countries and some of the more successful newly industrializing countries have seen plant closings and loss of jobs to other countries, resulting in high unemployment and severe dislocation for workers in effected industries. These trends affect many, prompting Day (1989) to write that social workers need to understand that "even in the most individual casework efforts, the international economy has an effect" (p. 232).

Oil and Debt: Economic Interdependence at the Crisis Level. Two world crises during the last 30 years of the 20th century underscore the impact of global economic interdependence and the interaction between global economic forces and social welfare. These are the "oil crisis" of the early 1970s and the debt crisis, which began shortly thereafter and still continues. According to Isbister (1998), the oil crisis and the debt crisis demonstrate the extent to which economies of poor countries are "enmeshed in an increasingly globalized economy" (p. 184).

Oil is recognized as one of the world's most crucial and essentially nonrenewable resources. Although oil reserves are concentrated in the Middle East, multinational oil companies controlled production and pricing until the early 1970s, with oil prices fixed at about US$3 per barrel. In 1973, Saudi Arabia and its allies, angered by U.S. support of Israel, realized that oil was a potent political weapon. They joined together in the Organization of Petroleum Exporting Countries (OPEC) and first instituted a boycott of sales to the United States and then a large oil price increase to US$13 a barrel. These actions touched off shortages known in the United States as the oil crisis (Isbister, 1998). By 1979, the price had risen to US$30 per barrel, a 10-fold increase in just 6 years. According to Isbister (1998), "the price increase was easily the biggest shock the international economy had sustained since the Second World War" (p. 179). In the industrialized countries, recession, inflation, and a scramble for conservation resulted. There were human casualties as well. Sharp increases in utility costs for home heating, cooking, and lighting produced a new class of homeless people—those forced out of their homes by astronomical utility bills, which caused them not to be able to pay rents or mortgages. Still others lived in apartments or homes without heat or lights after utilities were turned off for nonpayment. A demand for new social services resulted, spurring development of fuel banks and utility assistance programs across the United States.

In poorer countries, the impact was much greater. Non-OPEC countries began to borrow money to pay for the greatly increased costs of imported oil. Their options were limited, as most oil in developing countries was used for industry not personal home or transportation consumption. Thus consumption could not be curtailed without harming productivity. Indeed, "the origin of the third world debt crisis was the OPEC price increases of the 1970s . . . price increases which produced a tidal wave of change in international monetary relations" (Isbister, 1998, p. 181).

The urgent need for money to buy oil in poorer countries coincided with the availability of money for loans because OPEC countries were investing the huge sums of cash they had earned from oil sales into Western banks. Soon, a new crisis, the international debt crisis, eclipsed the oil crisis. National governments took on big loans, and these debts were increased by rising interest rates; falling commodity prices impaired ability to repay. Many countries in Latin America and Africa were soon faced with debt repayments that were so large they were impossible to pay. This, in turn, was a threat to banks in industrialized countries and, potentially, to the world banking system because the loans were so large that for a time they exceeded the net worth of the banks. Interdependence was painfully obvious to officials in borrowing and lending countries alike, and it was making an impact on ordinary people through appeals for bank bailouts, cuts in production in the industrialized countries, and rapidly falling standards of living in developing countries. The heaviest burden fell on the poorer countries: "For the developed countries, the debt crisis was only a potential danger [of bank collapse], but for the third world it was a monumental present disaster" (Isbister, 1998, p. 183).

As the amount of principal and interest that a country was expected to pay back each year reached or even exceeded half the total value of their exports in any one year, it was clear that these countries were in deep trouble. Imports had to be cut, government spending for services was reduced, and as a result, standards of living fell—often dramatically. In Mexico, for example, real wages fell by 40% from 1982 to 1988. More shocking is the decrease in per capita annual income in Nigeria, an oil-exporting country that borrowed to expand development projects and was devastated by falling oil prices and poor management of funds, which fell from US$800 to US$380 in the 2-year period from 1985 to 1987. The numbers are shocking, but they do not begin to express the human misery that resulted.

The remedy for the debt crisis was structural adjustment, a set of reform policies designed by international financial institutions and imposed on indebted countries as a condition of eligibility for future loans and refinancing of existing debt to permit lower payments. As defined by Hoy (1998), structural adjustment is a cluster of policies that "demand that governments spend within their means, keep exchange rates competitive, let markets determine prices, withdraw from regulation and subsidy, and privatize industries that had previously been nationalized" (p. 163). Therefore, governments have been required to spend less on health and education, to remove subsidies on food and transportation, and to devalue their currencies—a move that results in drastic declines in purchasing power for wage earners. The structural adjustment cure has been as painful as the disease of debt for the people in many countries.

In Jamaica between 1977/78 and 1988/89, the percentage of public expenditures on debt payments rose from 17.7% to almost 40% while the percent spent on education dropped from 16% to 12% (Anderson & Witter, 1994, p. 20). In discussing the impact of structural adjustment in Jamaica:

The losers were clear. They were seen in the increased numbers of homeless and mentally ill searching routinely through garbage containers, they were absorbed among the numbers of youth recruited into criminal posses, they were included among the fixed income pensioners whose private poverty could not be relieved by food stamps, they were numbered among those who stood grimly in visa lines, and they were to be found among those whose incomes were increasingly inadequate for the purchase of basic food requirements. (Anderson & Witter, 1994, p. 52)

The impact of cutbacks in education included increased teacher to pupil ratios, lower attendance, declines in performance on standardized tests, and crumbling facilities. Although major health indicators do not always reveal short-term changes, statistics showed an increase of certain infectious diseases and the children's hospital reported that the rate of admissions of children for malnutrition changed from 3.5 per 1,000 admissions in 1975 to 8.3 in 1985 (Anderson & Witter, 1994, p. 49).

These results were not confined to Jamaica. Indeed, throughout the "structurally adjusted world," researchers and field staff from UNICEF and NGOs found increased poverty; rising rates of infant mortality in countries such as Ghana and Brazil; reappearances of diseases thought to be eliminated, including yellow fever in Ghana and malaria in Peru; and falling school enrollments (Hoy, 1998, p. 54). The economic policies imposed on poorer countries by the international financial institutions were having and continue to have a demonstrable effect on the social well-being of people and the social welfare services of the affected countries. Increased poverty along with decreased access to health care and education caused rises in infant mortality, infectious disease, and illiteracy. Additional social problems arise as secondary results, including increased homelessness, street children, child labor, youth unemployment, and youth violence.

Structural adjustment has had an impact beyond the economic ones and has created what Anderson and Witter (1994) call a new and dangerous belief system:

Structural adjustment was viewed as a set of externally-imposed measures designed to swing the balance further in favour of the propertied classes, and to extract resources from the country through increasing foreign penetration and international indebtedness. The prevailing ethos at all levels of society was consequently one of negativism and futility. What needs to be explored is the extent to which this ethos becomes entrenched and unsurmountable. (Anderson & Witter, 1994, p. 54)

Why did countries agree to adjust their economies in such damaging ways? Most likely they had no choice if they were to remain within the international economic system at all. "As first Mexico and then Venezuela discovered and now South Africa is discovering, within the space of a day, a state whose finances loses the confidence of transnational finance capital faces the immediate collapse of its currency. It has little choice but to adopt the fiscal austerity measures demanded by the global market or to face financial ruin and the collapse of its ability to rule" (Robotham, 1996, p. 15)

While the crisis has eased somewhat—especially from the perspective of Northern financial institutions which no longer face collapse due to debt—many countries remain heavily indebted, and debt continues to weigh down prospects for development. As reported in the 1998 UNDP *Human Development Report*, Jamaica has an external debt of US$4.3 billion, which is 135% of its gross national product (GNP), earning it the distinction of being a severely indebted low-income country (SILIC). Mauritius owes US$1.8 billion, and Argentina owes a staggering US$89.8 billion, 46% and 33% of the countries' GNP, respectively. (For an in-depth discussion of global economic issues, readers are referred to Prigoff, 2000.)

Security Interdependence

During the many years of the cold war, people in the United States and the Soviet Union knew that their security depended on a standoff and restraint between the two nuclear superpowers. The euphoria that greeted the breakup of the Soviet Union and the turn of the newly independent parts of that nation toward democracy was short-lived. What replaced the standoff of superpowers was the potential decentralization of conflict and lessened control in ensuring nuclear restraint. With nuclear weapons held in various parts of the former Sovient Union—new and relatively politically unstable countries—and in Pakistan and India, neighboring countries with a history of hostility toward each other, nuclear insecurity has increased. Global interdependence is obvious in the face of the nuclear threat, both in terms of the inability to contain the effects of a nuclear explosion and the likely spread of regional conflicts into wider attacks.

International terrorism is a newer threat to security. A tool often used by groups who are oppressed and feel powerless in the larger world system, terrorist attacks have been carried out against military bases, commercial airliners, a cruise ship, department stores, embassies, and crowded market areas of city streets. International cooperation is needed not only to improve security and detection but also to work on resolutions for persistent situations of deprivation and conflict, such as those in Palestine and in Northern Ireland.

Social Welfare Interdependence: Selected Examples

The dimensions of global interdependence discussed above—environmental, cultural, economic, and security, have significant implications for social work. But interdependence is also evident in the social welfare issues that are the focus of social work professional responsibility. Migration and the AIDS crisis will be discussed as two examples of interdependence in social welfare issues. The interplay of dimensions of interdependence should be obvious in examining one of the most significant social manifestations of interdependence, migration.

Migration. The international movement of peoples is undoubtedly the most dramatic social indicator of global interdependence, especially to the people-focused profession of social work. Among these international populations are refugees forced from their countries by war or by various forms of political and religious oppression. Others flee famine, internal strife, and severe economic deprivation, including that caused by structural adjustment. Still others migrate, temporarily or permanently, to seek better opportunities in education or employment. According to Estes (1997), 100 million people are currently involuntarily living outside their country of origin. Of these, only 13,236,500 were classified as refugees by the UN in 1996, with another 13 million listed as being "of concern" to the UNHCR (UN High Commission on Refugees, 1996).

Figures for recent years show that the United States admitted 54,707 refugees in 1998 (down from 112,000 in 1997), and Canada admitted 24,214 in 1997 (U.S. Department of Justice, 1999; Citizenship and Immigration Canada, 1999). It is important to understand, however, that "the large majority of refugees from the developing nations have fled to other developing countries" (Mupedziswa, 1997, p. 112). The impact of refugee influx on the world's poorest countries is significant. Although the international community provides assistance, the burden on the countries hosting the refugees is often hard to manage. Mupedziswa cites the case of the Mozambican refugees who fled into Malawi at such a rate that at one point there was one Mozambican refugee to every nine Malawians—both countries are among the world's poorest. Pakistan, rated 138th on the Human Development Index (HDI) rankings and therefore struggling to meet its own development needs, has had to cope with Afghan refugees for many years. As of 1998, Pakistan was providing asylum to 1,202,700 refugees (UNDP, 1998). The influx of Rwandan refugees into the Democratic Republic of the Congo (formerly Zaire) was a destabilizing force, contributing to that country's 1997 coup. In 1996, 1,700,000 refugees from tiny Rwanda were in neighboring Burundi, Tanzania, Uganda, and Zaire (UNDP, 1996).

Even in wealthy countries, providing refugee asylum or resettlement is difficult and costly. The practice implications of resettlement will be discussed further in Chapter 9.

A far larger number of international migrants are legal and illegal immigrants. While they migrate voluntarily, many do so only because opportunities are severely limited in their own countries or because they are enduring oppression and persecution not officially recognized by the UN or the receiving countries. For example, the number of legal "conventional" immigrants admitted into the United States in 1993 was 725,721. Over 500,000 of these came under family reunification and preferences categories, with another 147,000 admitted as employment preferences (Isbister, 1996). Temporary migrants—guest workers—are prevalent in Europe and the Middle East. In times of labor shortage in northern Europe, laborers from Greece, Turkey, and other countries are recruited to work in Germany, Sweden, and elsewhere. While some guest workers return to their home countries, others stay on, becoming targets of resentment and discrimination as economic conditions worsen in the host countries. Workers from developing countries, including Mauritius and the Philippines, were recruited to work in the Gulf States when work opportunities there expanded rapidly due to oil prosperity.

In addition to legal immigrants, there are a large number of illegal immigrants in many countries. For example, although numbers cannot be accurately determined, the number of undocumented immigrants in the United States was estimated at 3.4 million in 1992 and was said to be growing by about 300,000 per year according to an INS study (Isbister, 1996). A more recent estimate from the U.S. Immigration and Naturalization Service was 5 million people living in the United States illegally and 275,000 more entering each year (U.S. Department of Justice, 2000). Although most (54% of the total) come from Mexico, there are also significant numbers who enter from Europe and Asia and overstay tourist visas. A final group making up "international populations" are visitors and students, diplomats, and employees of foreign companies and their families residing temporarily in another country.

These various groups are the willing and unwilling ambassadors of global interdependence. Their presence demonstrates that political and economic conditions in one country affect the population makeup of other countries. Increases in international population movements in the 1980s and 1990s have turned formerly homogeneous countries, such as Denmark, into multicultural ones and have further diversified already diverse populations, such as those in Canada and the United States. In 1997, 9.7% of the population of the United States was foreign-born. This is an increase from 7.9% just 7 years earlier and from a low of 4.8% in 1970 (World Almanac, 1999). The contribution to diversity can be seen in the list of the top 10 countries of origin of the foreign-born in the United States: Mexico, the Philippines, China, Cuba, Vietnam, India, Dominican Republic, El Salvador, Great Britain, and Korea (World Almanac, 1999).

Often, only part of a family migrates, creating multinational families. The interactions of these families create new sets of interdependencies at both micro and macro levels. Within the family, phone calls and visits are made, plans may be made for other family members to migrate, and money and gifts are sent home. Cumulatively, these activities have an impact at the macro level. Remittances—payments sent to family members in other countries from their kin and friends residing in the United States—totaled $12,230,000,000 in 1995 (UNDP, 1998). Remittances make up the second largest source of foreign exchange for Jamaica. Modifications in immigration policy in the United States, Canada, or Great Britain will thus have a direct impact on Jamaica's balance of payments.

Some migrants return to their countries of origin, especially for their retirement years. Many of them experience another period of resettlement and readjustment. Others return involuntarily through deportation. This, too, can have impact at the macro level. Officials in Jamaica believe that the stricter provisions adopted in 1996 for deportation of immigrants who commit criminal offenses in the United States have led to a measurable increase in violent crime in Jamaica—crime committed by "drug-dealing 'posse' members deported home to Jamaica from the United States" (Maxwell, 1990, p. 24).

AIDS. The rapid spread of HIV/AIDS to every country in the world has been another stunning health and social indicator demonstrating that no country is a fortress. Throughout the early and mid-1980s, a number of countries denied that they had AIDS cases. Today, HIV infection has been acknowledged around the world, and AIDS is recognized as a major global problem with health, economic, and social dimensions. AIDS has crossed borders with ease, moving along routes of international transport and travel. Describing its spread across Africa, a writer for the *Economist* said: "It marched with rebel armies through the continent's numerous war zones, rode with truckers from one rest-stop brothel to the next, and eventually flew, perhaps with an air steward, to America" ("AIDS in the Third World," 1999, p. 42). Thus global interdependence—in transport of goods, the impact of armed conflict, and air travel—was and is a force in the spread of AIDS.

While universally present, AIDS, like poverty, is differentially affecting the countries of the world. Since HIV was identified in the 1970s, more than 47 million people have been infected and approximately 14 million have died. AIDS is now the world's fourth leading killer disease ("AIDS in the Third World," 1999). Daily 16,000 new infections occur, and 90% of them occur in developing countries (UNDP, 1998). Although India has the largest number of people living with HIV (estimated at 3 to 5 million), the countries of southern and eastern Africa have the highest proportion of infection; in Botswana, for example, 25% to 30% of the population between the ages of 15 and 49 are HIV-positive (UNDP, 1998). Rates this high means that life expectancies have been dramatically lowered for Botswana, Zambia, Kenya, Zimbabwe, Guyana, Honduras, and other countries. Life expectancy in Guyana is projected to fall from 60 years in 1998 to 50 years in 2010; without AIDS, the projected life span would be 68. The statistics for Botswana are even worse. Infants in 1998 could only expect to live 40 years; without AIDS, the life expectancy would have been 62. By 2010, an infant born in Botswana will face a life span of 30 to 40 years (UNDP, 1998).

Social workers are particularly concerned about the number of children orphaned by the AIDS-related deaths of their parents. Counted at 8.2 million in 1997, the projection for 2000 is 16 million orphans under age 15 due to AIDS. In Africa, "households headed by children have begun to appear" (UNDP, 1998, p. 34). Child mortality has also increased. Children die both directly from AIDS and indirectly from the effects of the disease—malnutrition and lack of care either because of the death of parents or because of impoverishment of families and communities when breadwinners die.

The economic impact of AIDS affects families, businesses, and even national economies. The death of large numbers of workers in their prime productive years means shortages of skilled labor, wasted investments in train-ing, and the expense of hiring and training new laborers. Absenteeism for illness and funeral attendance impairs productivity; in Zambia, one cement plant experienced a 15-fold increase in absenteeism caused by funeral at-tendance between 1992 and 1995 (McNeil, 1998). AIDS-related health care costs strain national budgets, even though in poor countries most people have no access to life-prolonging drugs. The World Bank estimates that the cost of the AIDS drug "cocktail" for just one patient would provide school-ing for 400 children for one year in Africa. Health care systems thus have to make harsh choices, which usually means that those infected will die sooner than they would if they lived in richer countries. Burial expenses are also a burden, both for families and for those employers who pay for them as em-ployee benefits. Due to all these factors, the gross domestic product (GDP) of Kenya will be 14.5% smaller in 2005 than it would have been without AIDS, and the country's per capita income will be 10% less ("AIDS in the Third World," 1999). It is obvious, then, that HIV/AIDS is a global problem of such magnitude that it is reversing the development progress in some countries and impeding it in many others.

There are some success stories with HIV education and prevention, sug-gesting ways for social work to contribute. Many of the factors fueling the rapid spread of AIDS exist in all countries, rich and poor alike: taboos on talking about sex, myths and misinformation about the disease and how it is spread, stigma associated with HIV infection, and sexism that forces women to submit to men's sexual demands. While researchers look for a cure or vaccine, education and prevention remain the key strategies for fight-ing AIDS.

The Joint UN Program of HIV/AIDS—UNAIDS—documented the suc-cess of education in Uganda, a poor country with low levels of literacy. One of the first African countries to admit to the threat posed by AIDS, the gov-ernment commissioned low-cost but useful surveys of sexual behavior and mounted an AIDS public information campaign. A key ingredient was to give "free rein to scores of non-governmental organizations, usually foreign-financed, to do whatever it took to educate people about risky sex" ("AIDS in the Third World," 1999, p. 44). As a result, the "potholed streets of Kam-pala are lined with signs promoting fidelity and condoms," frank informa-tion is widely distributed, and schools use role-playing to teach adolescents how to deal with risky situations ("AIDS in the Third World," 1999, p. 44). Surveys show that Ugandans are delaying sexual activity, using condoms more frequently, and having fewer sexual partners. The result were impres-sive; HIV rates among women tested at prenatal clinics fell from about 30% to 15% in just 5 years ("AIDS in the Third World," 1999).

Social workers have been among the active professionals in the Ugan-dan struggle against AIDS; indeed, no human service profession in Uganda has been able to ignore AIDS (Ankrah, 1992). Social workers have taken on a variety of roles, including provision of supportive counseling to AIDS suf-ferers and their families, development of community support networks to assist those with AIDS, health education, and research (Ankrah, 1992). Health education activities have been extensive. Social workers have worked through the Red Cross, through churches, and with a local AIDS information center to prepare educational materials, conduct supportive studies, and train key people on AIDS prevention, including local leaders, religious leaders, teachers, police, women's groups, and agricultural extension staff. Training of trainers (TOT) is another social work role. The Department of Social Work and Social Administration at Makerere University has conducted research into "social, cultural and behavioral aspects of AIDS" (Ankrah, p. 58). Students have been involved in this field research, resulting in a number being employed full-time as AIDS researchers after graduation. The department's work was recognized; the government granted the department a seat on the National Committee for the Prevention of AIDS (Ankrah, 1992).

Although international migration and AIDS have been highlighted, there are other examples of global interdependence in the social arena, for example drug trafficking. The desperate situation of farmers in Bolivia and the addictions of city dwellers throughout the world are linked through a profitable and often violent international trade in drugs.

In addition to the problems whose very nature and substance are shaped by interdependence, there are many problems that can be classified as global in nature in that they are shared by many or all nations and require multinational action. One of the most pervasive is poverty. The problems of women and children are also often at the center of social work worldwide.

A SHARED AGENDA OF GLOBAL SOCIAL PROBLEMS

Poverty

Widespread poverty is now a global phenomenon and certainly one of the greatest challenges to international social work. Of all the global problems, poverty is the most pervasive and intractable. It is the root of many if not most other social problems: Poverty plays a strong role in migration; it is a growing factor in the spread of AIDS; it is linked to drug production and use; and it is the direct cause of street children, homelessness, child labor, and malnutrition. According to the UNDP (1996), "poverty is no longer contained within national boundaries. It has become globalized. It travels across borders, without a passport, in the form of drugs, diseases, pollution, migration, terrorism and political instability" (p. 2). In 1990, the World Bank estimated that the number of people living in poverty was 1.2 billion people; half of these were estimated to be living in absolute poverty, defined as having insufficient resources to obtain basic daily requirements of water, food, fuel, and shelter (Estes, 1997).

The gap between rich and poor has been growing. The share of the world's income controlled by the richest fifth of the world's population increased in 1991 to 85%, from 70% in 1960. At the same time, the income share for the poorest fifth decreased from 2.3% to a meager 1.4% (Crosby & Van Soest, 1997, citing UNDP figures from 1994). The gap between rich and poor within nations as well as the gap between rich nations and poor nations contribute to these statistics.

If there is any good news about poverty, it is that it is possible for very poor countries to avoid famine and to achieve acceptable levels of human well-being (Sen, 1993). Conversely, achieving higher national income is not sufficient to guarantee improvements in life expectancy, infant mortality rates, or education and nutritional statuses. UNDP differentiates income poverty from human poverty, a broader measure of well-being. Concurring with Sen, the UNDP states that human poverty can be addressed even in countries with very low incomes. Sen cites the example of Kerala State in India, with a population of 29 million. Life expectancy is more than 70 years (compared to that for all of India of 61.6), literacy rates are high, and women have comparable life chances to men's—unlike the rest of India. These achievements have come about through state-level policies of expanded public education, an emphasis on universally provided basic health services, and subsidized nutrition, even though the GNP per capita is lower in Kerala than the average for India (Sen, 1993). Similar policies and results have been achieved in Sri Lanka, Costa Rica, Jamaica, and China.

The UNDP Human Poverty Index for industrialized countries (HPI-2) is comprised of four statistics: the percentage of people not expected to survive to age 60; the percentage of people 16 to 65 who are functionally illiterate; the percentage below 50% of the median personal income; and social exclusion, as measured by the number of long-term unemployed as a percent of the total labor force. Using this measure, the United States has the greatest incidence of human poverty among the 17 industrial countries—16.5%—followed by Ireland (15.2%) and the U.K. (15%). Sweden has the lowest at 6.8% (UNDP, 1998).

Poverty does not respect equal opportunity. The poorest of the poor are mostly women and their children, especially those living in rural areas of developing countries. Poverty is both a cause and result of the disadvantaged position of women around the world.

The Status of Women

Throughout the world, the status of women is another issue of common concern to social work. Although some have observed that for women there may not be any truly developed countries, women fare much worse in some countries than in others. Maternal mortality—deaths due to complications of pregnancy and childbirth—claims more than one half of a million lives a year; almost all of the deaths are in developing countries. In sub-Saharan Africa, 1 in every 13 women dies from pregnancy/childbirth-related causes, while the rate in Canada is only 1 in 7,700. Illegal abortion contributes to women's death toll too. In a recent year, 1.6 million legal abortions were performed in the United States, resulting in 6 deaths. In Mexico, where abortions are illegal, 1.5 million were performed anyway, causing 140,000 deaths (Ginsberg, 1990). Two-thirds of the world's illiterates are female; the male-female literacy gap is largest in South Asia, sub-Saharan Africa, and the Middle East. In South Asia, for example, only 36% of women are literate compared to 63% of men (UNICEF, 1998). An even lower percentage of girls has access to secondary or higher education.

The lower "value" accorded to girls is reflected in their poorer nutritional status. In families in some parts of the world, girls eat last. A study in the Punjab region of India showed that 20% of girls were malnourished as compared to only 0.1% of boys (MacCormack, 1988). Poor nutrition and less access to health care result in higher death rates for female children than for their brothers; the World Bank says that every sixth infant death in India is due to gender discrimination.

Amartya Sen (1993) shocked the world when he announced that 100 million women were missing from global population figures—the victims of overt and violent discrimination against female children through sex-selection abortion and infanticide combined with the "staunch anti-female bias in health care and nutrition" (p. 46). Girls who survive early childhood may be subjected to other forms of gender violence. Two million girls a year suffer female genital mutilation (FGM), labeled by UNICEF (1996) as "one of the worst violations of the Convention on the Rights of the Child" (p. 7). While 75% of cases of FGM are in only 6 countries (Egypt, Ethiopia, Kenya, Nigeria, Somalia, and Sudan), the practice has migrated with its practitioners, prompting laws against FGM in Australia, Norway, Sweden, and the United Kingdom (UNICEF, 1996). In all countries of the world, domestic violence and rape continue to be major threats to women's health, security, and survival. Poverty among women is another universal problem. Women-headed households are poorer in all countries; women's poverty affects the lives of their children and becomes a major contributor to special problems of disadvantaged children.

Street Children

Globally, poverty and worsening economic conditions have caused an increase in the number of street children. Some of these children are members of homeless families; others may live only part of the time on the streets, working to add marginal amounts to a family's subsistence income. The most disadvantaged, however, have no home other than the streets and little or no contact with their families. They may be the boys who sleep on the streets of Columbia, stealing or carrying out small jobs for money and sniffing glue to dull the pain of their existence; they may be the street children of Brazil, facing extreme oppression and, for a time, even death at the hands of police bent on ridding the streets of these small nuisances; they may be the barrel children of Jamaica, left by mothers who emigrated and who support themselves by selling the barrels of goods their mothers send to them; or they may be adolescent runaways in the cities of America, living in shelters or turning to prostitution to survive. Whereas the young children who live permanently on the street represent extreme cases of poverty and abandonment by families and societies, the problems of many street children differ only by degree from the problems of much larger numbers of undereducated, unemployed youth. Youth unemployment and social exclusion are growing problems from Europe to the Caribbean islands. Hopelessness—youth without a vision of a future—leads to drug use and violence in many cases. There is a pressing need for social work attention to homeless, futureless children around the world.

Social Policy Emulation

The final aspect of global social welfare interdependence to be considered here is the phenomenon of social policy emulation. Interdependence can also be seen in the extent to which policies adopted in one country affect other countries. In some cases, the effect is due to the conditions caused by provisions of a policy; in other cases, the effect is felt when one nation models its social welfare policies on those of another nation.

Nations around the world shape and reshape their own social policies to fit with trends elsewhere. In some places, this homogenization has been encouraged or even pressured by regional economic groups (such as the European Union) or required by the IMF, as described earlier in this chapter. Other instances of emulation have been voluntary, as countries look to others as models. Until the early 1980s, the modern welfare state was regarded as the model toward which developing countries aspired; the Scandinavian and northern European welfare state provisions were seen as standards of excellence in social welfare against which other systems could be measured. In the 1980s, privatization and austerity grew in popularity. Initiated in the United Kingdom under Margaret Thatcher's administration and in the United States under President Ronald Reagan, privatization and reductions in entitlements and subsidies for the poor increasingly became the policies emulated by other nations and institutionalized as part of the IMF's structural adjustment plan. More recently, policies of managed care in the health sector are being exported.

Social policy homogenization has been a concern among social welfare experts throughout the development and strengthening of the European Union (EU). As mobility between states has become less regulated, there are strong forces encouraging adoption of social policy modifications. Although these modifications would likely improve provisions in the countries with the least developed social welfare, states with generous and comprehensive benefits would be pressured to reduce them. It is increasingly likely, therefore, that innovations, advances, or retrenchments in social welfare in one nation will reverberate through this process of policy emulation to create like changes in other nations' policies. The process itself is neutral; however, global economic competition tends to support conservative trends toward less welfare. As suggested in Chapter 1, the policies of one nation increasingly affect the well-being of people in other nations. This occurs not only from direct impact but from the influence of the policies as models for other countries' policies.

PROSPECTS FOR ACTION: OPPORTUNITIES IN INTERDEPENDENCE

Global interdependence also offers positive opportunities for exchange and mutual problem solving. Advances in technology have eased international communications through telephones, computer links, and videoconferences. It is now easier than ever before to exchange information and ideas and to work with colleagues around the world—without leaving one's office. The challenge is to seize these opportunities by accepting interdependence as an irrefutable fact and to overcome tendencies toward isolationism that prevent this recognition. In later chapters, strategies for professional action for mutual problem solving will be discussed in more depth.

REFERENCES

AIDS in the Third World: A global disaster. (1999, January 2). *Economist*, 43–44.

Anderson, P., & Witter, M. (1994). Crisis, adjustment and social change: A case study of Jamaica. In E. LeFranc (Ed.), *Consequences of structural adjustment: A review of the Jamaican experience* (pp. 1–55). Kingston, Jamaica: Canoe Press.

Ankrah, E.M. (1992). AIDS in Uganda: Initial social work responses. *Journal of Social Development in Africa, 7*(2), 53–61.

Bowman, L.W. (1991). *Mauritius: Democracy and development in the Indian Ocean*. Boulder, CO: Westview Press.

Citizenship and Immigration Canada (1999). Canada—A welcoming land. 1999 Annual Immigration Plan. ⟨http://cicnet.ci.gc.ca/english/pub/anrep99c.html⟩ (accessed 10/7/99).

Crosby, J., & Van Soest, D. (1997). *Challenges of violence worldwide: An educational resource*. Washington, DC: NASW Press.

Day, P.J. (1989). The new poor in America: Isolationism in an international political economy. *Social Work, 34*(3), 227–233.

Estes, R. (1997). World social situation. In R.L. Edwards (Ed.), *Encyclopedia of social work* (19th ed., 1997 suppl., pp. 343–359). Washington, DC: NASW Press.

Ginsberg, L. (1990). Selected statistical review. In *Encyclopedia of social work* (18th ed., 1990 Suppl., pp. 256–288). Silver Spring, MD: NASW Press.

Hamilton, J.M. (1986). *Main street America and the third world*. Cabin John, MD: Seven Locks Press.

Hamilton, J.M. (1990). *Entangling alliances: How the third world shapes our lives.* Cabin John, MD: Seven Locks Press.

Hoff, M.D. (1997). Social work, the environment, and sustainable growth. In Hokenstad, M.C., & Midgley, J. (Eds.), *Issues in international social work* (pp. 27–44). Washington, DC: NASW Press.

Hokenstad, M.C. and Midgley, J. (Eds). (1997). *Issues in international social work.* Washington, DC: NASW Press.

Hoy, P. (1998). *Players and issues in international aid.* West Hartford, CT: Kumarian Press.

Isbister, J. (1998). *Promises not kept: The betrayal of social change in the third world* (4th ed.). West Hartford, CT: Kumarian Press.

Isbister, J. (1996). *The immigration debate* West Hartford, CT: Kumarian Press.

Joint Working Group on Development Education (1984). *A framework for development education in the United States.* Westport, CT: Save the Children [for InterAction].

Keigher, S.M., & Lowery, C.T. (1998). "The sickening implications of globalization. *Health and Social Work, 23*(2), 153–158.

MacCormack, C.P. (1988). Health and social power of women. *Social Science and Medicine, 26*(7), 677–683.

Maldives: On the beach. (1999, January 9). *Economist,* p. 39.

Maxwell, J.A. (1990, September). *Development of social welfare services and the field of social work in Jamaica.* Paper presented at the Caribbean Conference for Social Workers, Paramaribo, Surinam.

McNeil, D.G., Jr. (1998, November 15). AIDS stalking Africa's struggling economies. *The New York Times,* pp. 1, 20.

Mensendiek, M. (1997). Women, migration and prostitution in Thailand. *International Social Work, 40,* 163–176.

Midgley, J. (1997). *Social welfare in global context.* Thousand Oaks, CA: Sage.

Mupedziswa, R. (1997). Social work with refugees: The growing international crisis. In M.C. Hokenstad & J. Midgley (Eds.), *Issues in international social work* (pp. 110–124). Washington, DC: NASW Press.

Prigoff, A. (2000). *Economics for social workers: Social outcomes of economic globalization with strategies for community action.* Belmont, CA: Brooks-Cole.

Robotham, D. (1996, April 20). Transnationalism in the Caribbean: Formal and informal. AES Distinguished Lecture, Spring Meeting, San Juan, Puerto Rico.

Sen, A. (1993, May). The economics of life and death. *Scientific American,* 40–47.

Taber, M.A., & Batra, S. (1995). *Social strains of globalization in India.* New Delhi: New Concepts International Publishers.

UNICEF (1996). *The progress of nations 1996* Wallingford, Oxon, UK: P&LA.

UNICEF (1998). *The state of the world's children* 1998. New York: Oxford University Press.

United Nations (1990). *The world economy: A global challenge.* New York: U.N. Department of Public Information.

United Nations Development Program (1996). *Human development report 1996.* New York: Oxford University Press.

United Nations Development Program (1998). *Human development report 1998.* New York: Oxford University Press.

United Nations High Commission for Refugees (1996). *UNHCR by the numbers.*

United States Department of Justice (1999). *Legal immigration, fiscal year 1998* (I.N.S. Annual Report No. 2), Washington, DC: Office of Policy and Planning.

United States Department of Justice. (2000). Illegal alien resident population. Immigration and Naturalization Service. Available at www.ins.usdoj.gov/graphics/aboutins/statistics/illegal alien/index.htm. Accessed August 25, 2000.

Wagner, A. (1997). Social work and the global economy. In Hokenstad, M. C., & Midgley, J. *Issues in international social work* (pp. 45–56). Washington, DC: NASW Press.

World almanac and book of facts. (1999). Mahweh, NJ: World Almanac Books, Primedia Reference Inc.

CHAPTER 6

INTERNATIONAL SOCIAL WELFARE ORGANIZATIONS AND THEIR FUNCTIONS

The challenges of global interdependence outlined in Chapter 5 are addressed by a wide range of international organizations that work in the social welfare field. These organizations are at work on projects such as planning and implementing income-generation projects to address poverty; providing emergency food, clothing, and medical care in crisis situations; conducting education and prevention campaigns to slow the spread of HIV; promoting low-cost primary education models; developing standards to encourage equal rights for women; and tackling child labor through standards setting and negotiation. Although comprehensive descriptions are not feasible here, this chapter provides an overview of a selected number of international organizations in order to increase understanding of the context of international social work. Selection is challenging because international social welfare activities are conducted by myriad organizations. Some specialized organizations deal only with international issues related to social welfare. Other international social welfare activities are carried out by domestic organizations with international linkages and by international organizations in other fields of specialty, such as economics, health, or agriculture. Three major groups of organizations are the intergovernmental agencies of the United Nations (UN) system, governmental agencies of individual countries, and private or nongovernmental organizations (NGOs).

Most international agencies do not have a specific set of roles or functions labeled "social work." However, they are engaged in development or social development work, the enhancement of social welfare, the promotion of standards for social and economic well-being throughout the world, and the sponsorship of professional exchanges. Thus their work fits within the definition of international social work used in this book, and understanding the functions of these organizations is essential for professional action in an interdependent world.

INTRODUCTION TO DEVELOPMENT AND DEVELOPMENT ASSISTANCE

Most international social welfare organizations are involved in development and/or promotion of human rights. These two movements have been pri-

126

orities in post–World War II international relations. The emergence of numerous newly independent countries in the 1960s—countries that had poorly developed economies, mass poverty, and little physical or institutional infrastructure—led to identification of development as a priority. Initially, development was understood to mean economic growth. The belief, based on a theory by Walt Rostow and others, was that all problems of poverty and underdevelopment would be solved as a country's GNP grew; that is, the benefits of economic growth would "trickle down" to the whole population (McGowan, 1987; Rostow, 1960). By the end of the 1960s—the UN's 1st Development Decade—it was becoming obvious that economic growth was difficult to achieve and that, where achieved, benefits often did not trickle down to the poor. Development has therefore matured over the following decades into a complex concept intertwining social, economic, and environmental factors. Progress has been uneven and major challenges remain.

The provision of development assistance has spawned a large network of international organizations. Development assistance can be provided through bilateral agreements—the provision of aid or technical assistance by one country to another—or through multilateral efforts. Although bilateral aid can address humanitarian objectives and is based partly on notions of obligation of the rich nations to assist the poor, the foreign policy goals of the donor country are often intertwined with the more explicit program goals. At least partly for this reason, recipient countries often prefer multilateral aid—assistance provided through intergovernmental organizations with varied members, often including the recipient country. Although they exist, there are fewer foreign policy "strings" and obligations attached to multilateral aid, and at the broadest level, the concept of global cooperation is present. Both bilateral and multilateral governmental organizations also channel development assistance through NGOs similar to the way national and state government agencies deliver programs domestically through private agencies by means of grants and contracts.

Individual descriptions will be provided for key intergovernmental agencies and selected governmental agencies. Because of the large number of NGOs, relatively few examples can be included; the section on NGOs will be organized to describe the major functions carried out by such bodies: relief and development, advocacy, development education, exchange, and cross-national- and international-related casework.

UNITED NATIONS AGENCIES AND ACTIVITIES

The UN and its agencies are major players in international social welfare and the provision of multilateral assistance. Indeed, some scholars identify accomplishments in the social field as the major successes of the UN, rather than its intended major goals of peace-keeping and conflict resolution. As noted by Altschiller (1993), "the founders of the United Nations gave it . . . a wide mandate in economic and social affairs" (p. 196).

Activities within the social mission were among the first UN activities. Prior to the official establishment of the UN, a number of countries worked through the UN Relief and Rehabilitation Administration (UNRRA) to provide relief and reconstruction in war-torn Europe and Asia. These efforts were described in Chapters 2 and 3. As noted, social work experts were substantially involved in the UNRRA programs and leadership, and for many social workers, experience gained through UNRRA launched their careers in international social welfare. The activities and success of UNRRA provided an important backdrop for the evolution of the social development mission of the UN.

Current UN Structures and Agencies

The UN was created with the signing of the charter on June 26, 1945 (effective October 24, 1945). The charter defines the following as the purposes of the UN:

> 1) to maintain international peace and security; 2) to develop friendly relations among nations; 3) to achieve international cooperation in solving international problems of an economic, social, cultural, or humanitarian character and in promoting respect for human rights; and 4) to be a center for harmonizing the actions of nations in the attainment of these common ends. (U.S. Government Manual, 1998, p. 754)

The third purpose—wide in scope—legitimizes the many social welfare/social development efforts of the UN.

There are presently 185 member nations, up dramatically from the 51 founding members. The work of the UN is done thorough the General Assembly, comprised of all member states; the Security Council, whose 15 members are charged with the responsibility of maintaining international peace and security; and the Economic and Social Council (ECOSOC), which is described below. A substantial amount of the UN development effort is carried out by the specialized agencies and special bodies of the UN, including UNICEF, the World Health Organization (WHO), and the UN Development Program (UNDP). After the description of the ECOSOC, the major UN agencies related to social welfare are described, followed by a discussion of how the UN uses special events and commemorations to extend its impact on the problems of special groups, such as women, children, and families.

The Economic and Social Council. ECOSOC reports to the General Assembly and has been given coordinating functions over a range of economic and social matters (Altschiller, 1993). According to its charter, its purposes are to promote higher standards of living, full employment and conditions of economic and social progress and development; solutions to international economic, social, health, and related problems and international cultural and educational cooperation; universal respect for and observance of, human rights and fundamental freedoms for all without distinction as to race, sex, language, or religion (United Nations, 1945). ECOSOC has representatives from 54 member states and operates through four standing committees: Program and Coordination, Human Settlements, Non-Governmental Organizations, and Negotiation with Intergovernmental Agencies (United Nations, 1998). It also utilizes Regional Commissions, Functional Commissions, and additional expert bodies. Among the nine Functional Commissions are the Commission for Social Development, the Commission on Human Rights, the Commission on the Status of Women, the Population Commission, and the Commission on Narcotic Drugs (UN, 1998). ECOSOC's functions include coordination of the activities of the specialized UN agencies in the social field.

A major social welfare report, *The Report on the World's Social Situation,* is issued every 4 years by the Department of Economic and Social Development of the UN, and endorsed by ECOSOC. The 1997 report, the 14th in the series that began in 1952, focuses on the major themes of the 1995 World Summit for Social Development—poverty, unemployment, and discrimination (United Nations, 1997a). In calling for strategies to eradicate poverty, the report documents that one fourth of the world's population currently lives in severe poverty. In many nations, unemployment has soared since the previous report. More optimistically, the report describes the world labor force as being better educated, more skilled, and more mobile than at any previous time (United Nations, 1997a). The concluding chapter of the report addresses discrimination and other forms of social exclusion and their relationship to poverty and unemployment. It calls for policies and strategies to increase social integration.

The Centre for Social Development and Humanitarian Affairs, previously located in Vienna, had been a focal point of social welfare activity in the UN, serving, among other capacities, as the organizing force behind the 1987 Interregional Consultation (described later in this chapter). In 1991, ECOSOC adopted a resolution calling for strengthening and restructuring the Centre for Social Development, noting the growth in interest and activities in the social development arena. The Centre has now been reorganized, with most of its functions incorporated into the new Department of Policy Coordination and Sustainable Development, located in New York.

The UN Children's Fund (UNICEF). UNICEF is an important agency of the UN Founded in 1946 for post-war relief in Europe and China, it became a permanent agency with a focus on development. UNICEF operates programs in most of the world's countries, 161 in 1995, with program expenditures in 1995 of $804 million (United Nations, 1997b). The agency's goal is "to improve the lives of children and youth in the developing world by providing community-based services in primary health care, social services, water supply, formal and nonformal education, nutrition and emergency operations" (Hoy, 1998, p. 88). Since the passage of the Convention on the Rights of the Child by the General Assembly and its subsequent ratification by almost all nations of the world, UNICEF's major emphasis has been "to ensure the survival, protection and development of children within the framework of the Convention" (United Nations, 1997b, p. 1034).

UNICEF's efforts in the area of child protection are of particular interest to social work. The agency has addressed issues of abuse and exploitation through its initiative on "Children in Especially Difficult Circumstances"; it is now working to integrate these efforts "into mainstream programs, leading to a holistic response" (United Nations, 1997b, p. 1203). UNICEF assists children affected by armed conflict, hazardous or exploitative child labor, sexual exploitation, childhood disability, and those children and families affected by HIV/AIDS. UNICEF has supported NGO programs on prevention, protection, and rehabilitation regarding sexual exploitation of children in Brazil, Costa Rica, and Thailand; a national trauma recovery program for war-affected children in Rwanda; and a coordinated project providing alternative care, education, and life skills training for AIDS orphans in Uganda.

A major compiler of statistics on the status of children, UNICEF publishes useful data for comparative research and planning in its annual report, *State of the World's Children.*

UNICEF has achieved some notable successes. In 1991, UNICEF and the World Health Organization (WHO) announced that they had surpassed their goal of immunizing 80% of the world's children against six major killer diseases (United Nations, 1992). The campaign for simple interventions in cases of diarrheal disease—oral rehydration therapy (ORT)—has gained ground in many countries. UNICEF's success in drawing attention to children's issues was underscored by the UN's adoption of the Convention on the Rights of the Child in 1989 and by the World Summit for Children, held in 1990. Both have been major tools for advocating for children and will be briefly discussed below. Successful advocacy by UNICEF through its campaign for "Adjustment with a Human Face" forced lending institutions and governments to recognize the human and social costs of structural adjustment (Cornia, Jolly, & Stewart, 1987).

Unfortunately, UNICEF has had to devote a large share of its funds and efforts to emergency relief. In 1995, UNICEF spent 25% of its budget in 21 armed conflict situations and during 10 natural disasters. This is up from only 8% in 1990 (United Nations, 1997b).

United Nations Development Program. UNDP was created in 1965 and since then has grown into the largest source of multilateral grant assistance, "providing a greater variety of services to more people in more countries than any other development institution" (Hoy, 1998, p. 84). UNDP is also the largest source of technical assistance grants for developing countries (Altschiller, 1993). Almost half of the agency's program expenditures are used to provide technical expertise to projects in developing countries, especially for feasibility studies, to strengthen local institutions, and to upgrade planning capabilities (Morrison & Purcell, 1988). The world's poorest nations are the major recipients; 87% of UNDP grants go to the poorest countries (Hoy, 1998). The largest sector aided by UNDP is agriculture, followed by industrial development, transportation and communications, and natural resources, leaving about 25% of the projects in areas such as education, population, health, employment, and other human development areas (Morrison & Purcell, 1988).

In 1986, UNDP set up the Division for Women in Development, responding to criticisms that development programs not only overlooked the role of women but sometimes worsened their condition. It administers the UN Development Fund for Women (UNIFEM), a special fund to support projects for low-income women in poor countries. As part of a reorganization in 1996, the agency identified six priorities for its work: "poverty elimination and grassroots participation; environmental and natural resource management; management for development; women in development; technology transfer and adaptation; and technical cooperation among developing countries" (Hoy, 1998, p. 84).

The annual UNDP publication, *Human Development Report,* a volume referenced liberally in this book, provides useful information for international social work. A feature of the reports is a rating of countries' progress on the Human Development Index (HDI), a rating that combines life expectancy, adult literacy, mean years of schooling of the population, and gross domestic product (GDP) per capita. Development of this index has been significant in increasing the recognition that development must include social and human resource elements, not just economics.

World Health Organization. WHO is another specialized agency of the UN. The goal of WHO is to encourage the greatest possible level of health for all. As such, this agency monitors international health issues, works to control communicable diseases, sets international health standards in such areas as drugs and vaccines, conducts research, and engages in more direct efforts to solve health problems and strengthen national health systems (Morrison & Purcell, 1988). A special focus is primary health care, a campaign launched in recognition of the fact that the most gains in overall health status come from simple interventions in sanitation, water, immunization, and maternal-child health.

WHO has now been called on to lead in the campaign to control the spread of HIV. With the estimated number of persons infected by HIV in 1998 at 33 million, including almost 6 million new cases in that year, AIDS education, prevention, and research have become major WHO priorities ("The Worldwide AIDS Toll," 1998). Africa, with almost 50% of the total world cases of HIV infection and grossly inadequate health resources, is a special target. Increasing attention is also being paid to the enormous social welfare impact of AIDS, especially the growing population of orphaned children and other disruptions in normal family roles and responsibilities.

WHO is credited with a major role in the successful eradication of smallpox. It has been working to eradicate polio, as part of the long-term "Health for All by the Year 2000" campaign—a campaign to provide basic health services to all people in the world and to make progress on eradicating major preventable diseases.

United Nations Fund for Population Activities. UNFPA is the largest source of funds for family-planning-related programs in developing countries (Hoy, 1998). Over half of program funds go into family planning services. Education accounts for about 15% of funds spent, and a little less than 10% is spent on collection of population data, with emphasis on developing countries (Morrison & Purcell, 1988). Recently, the agency has emphasized the importance of linking family planning and reproductive health with development goals, following the recommendations from the 1994 UN International Conference on Population and Development. The concept of demographic targets has been deemphasized in favor of meeting the family planning needs of individuals (Hoy, 1998). Another accomplishment has been to provide family planning and reproductive health services in refugee crisis situations.

Funding support from the United States was greatly curtailed beginning in 1984 when the United States refused to contribute to organizations that supported or permitted abortion services. This ban was reversed in 1993.

The United Nations High Commission for Refugees. UNHCR celebrated its 40th anniversary in 1991. Originally created as a temporary agency, the UNHCR shows no sign of completing its tasks of protection and service to refugees. In 1995, for example, the agency had responsibility for the fate of about 24 million people, 14 million of them refugees; other populations under UNHCR programs are the internally displaced (3.2 million), returnees following disasters or conflict (2.8 million), and others with special humanitarian needs (3.5 million). (United Nations, 1997b). The functions of the UNHCR include refugee protection, assistance and aid to refugees in transit, voluntary repatriation where possible, resettlement, and integration into countries of first asylum. In 1995, the agency assisted about 800,000 people to repatriate, primarily to Afghanistan, Rwanda, and Myanmar. UNHCR works on standards regarding the treatment of refugees worldwide in addition to its direct work to solve specific refugee problems of relief and settlement. In fact, for the first few decades of its existence, the agency emphasis was on setting standards for the identification and treatment of refugees, rather than provision of assistance. UNHCR became more involved in direct work during the 1975 crisis when Cambodian refugees flooded into Thailand.

The budget of UNHCR was 1.17 billion in 1995 (United Nations, 1997b).

Food and Agriculture Organization (FAO) and World Food Program. The first of the UN specialized agencies created, the FAO's goal is to work toward global food security. The organization provides technical assistance and advice on agricultural planning, production and food distribution, and, through a Global Information and Early Warning System, it identifies areas at risk of food shortage. With the UN, the FAO sponsors the World Food Program, which supplies 25% of the world's food aid. The goal of the program is to provide food not only for crisis situations but also to support development. In the mid-1980s, about two thirds of the food aid was used to support development. By 1994, 70% was being used for emergency situations. The primary role of the agency now is "the coordination of large scale relief operations" (Hoy, 1998, p. 90).

There are other UN organizations that conduct activities related to social welfare. However, a complete and comprehensive description of these is beyond the scope of the present volume. Through the *Yearbook of the United Nations*, other UN publications, and the many websites maintained by the organization, readers can expand their knowledge about UN agencies and activities.

Special Years, Conferences, Declarations, and Conventions

The UN utilizes designations of special years and decades and global conferences both to draw attention to important issues and to bring world leaders together to work on acceptable strategies and commitments (see e.g., Bennett, 1988; Taylor & Groom, 1989). Many of these have emphasized social welfare. Some have resulted in significant forward-looking plans of action. Historically, two special meetings stand out in their importance to international social work: the UN Conference of Ministers Responsible for Social Welfare, held in 1968, and the Interregional Consultation on Developmental Social Welfare Policies and Programmes, held in 1987.

The UN International Conference of Ministers Responsible for Social Welfare, held at the UN headquarters in New York in 1968 is viewed as a watershed event. The conference brought together 89 high-level national delegations, including many government ministers. Additional representatives attended as observers from 8 other nations, from UN agencies, and from other international bodies and NGOs in consultative status with ECOSOC (United Nations, 1969). The conference focused global attention, at the very highest levels of government, on social welfare needs and strategies. In addition to specific recommendations, the conference unanimously adopted a resolution underscoring that "effective social welfare policy and programmes have a vital role to play in national development" and that "social progress, higher levels of living and social justice are the ultimate aims of development" (United Nations, 1969, p. 23).

The next global intergovernmental meeting on social welfare took place nearly two decades later in Vienna in 1987—the Interregional Consultation on Developmental Social Welfare Policies and Programmes. Official representatives from 91 countries, including 30 government ministers, participated along with representatives of UN organizations and of more than 50 NGOs (United Nations, 1987). The meeting resulted in adoption of "Guiding Principles for Developmental Social Welfare Policies and Programmes in the Near Future" (United Nations, 1987). As described by the director general of the UN Vienna office, the adoption and subsequent endorsement by the General Assembly of the "Guiding Principles" "denotes growing international consensus on the vital importance of social issues in any genuine and sustainable development process" (United Nations, 1987, preface). It also clearly identified social development as the thrust of the UN in the area of social welfare, a focus that continues to the present.

Recent Special Years and Conferences of Significance. In 1995, two major social welfare events occurred, the World Summit on Social Development (Copenhagen) and the Fourth World Conference on Women (Beijing). The Social Development summit, a landmark event in the future of social development and social welfare, convened heads of state to develop means to put the needs of people, especially the poor, at the center of development efforts. According to Kofi Annan, secretary general of the UN, this Summit "represented a turning point in our collective consciousness regarding social issues" (United Nations, 1997a, p. v.). Issues addressed included achieving sustainable development with social justice, enhancing social integration, reducing poverty, and expanding opportunities for productive employment (United Nations, 1993b). NGOs participated actively in preparations for the summit (the ICSW's involvement was discussed in Chapter 3) and in the NGO Forum held in conjunction with the actual meeting. An important outcome of the summit was agreement on "Ten Commitments" by the participating governments, including commitments to work for eradication of poverty, full employment, promotion of social integration, respect for human dignity and achievement of equality and equity for women, and universal access to education and primary health care (United Nations, 1995a).

The other 1995 meeting was the Fourth World Conference on Women, held in Beijing, China, in September. The focus of this meeting, with a theme of "Action for Equality, Development and Peace," was a second 5-year review of the plan adopted in Nairobi at the World Conference to Review and Appraise the Achievements of the UN Decade for Women in 1985, the "Nairobi Forward-Looking Strategies for the Advancement of Women to the Year 2000" (United Nations, 1991). The conference called for universal ratification of the Convention on the Elimination of All Forms of Discrimination Against Women (CEDAW), by 2000 (United Nations, 1995b).

Among other major conferences that have recently focused the world's attention on issues important to social welfare were the World Summit for Children, which in 1990 was the first world gathering of heads of state to focus on children and adopted goals to improve the lives of children including reduction of child deaths, improved nutrition, basic education for all children, reductions in adult illiteracy, and extension of family planning services; the 1992 UN Conference on Environment and Development, held in Rio de Janeiro, which explored the interrelationships between environmental preservation and sustainable development; the 1993 World Conference on Human Rights; and the 1994 Conference on Population and Development, which, as noted earlier, linked family planning with development.

The UN also designates international years and international decades to call attention to issues and to mobilize planning and action. The goals of the

International Year of the Family in 1994, for example, were to increase awareness of family issues and "to improve the institutional capability of nations
to tackle serious family-related problems with comprehensive policies"
(United Nations, 1993a, p. 18). The recommendation for the year was developed at the 1987 Interregional Consultation on Developmental Social Welfare Policies and Programmes, described above. International Year of Older
Persons, 1999, was designated to "recognize humanity's demographic coming of age and the promise it holds" (United Nations, 1993a, p. 17).

Declarations and Conventions as International Social Policy

Policy documents issued by the special meetings, developed in preparatory
work, and those developed at the UN take a variety of forms. The most significant are the conventions, which are statements of international law ratified by member nations. In 1989, the UN adopted the Convention on the
Rights of the Child, a major piece of international "legislation" in the area
of child welfare that identifies standards for survival, protection, and development of children. As of 1999, all but two countries (Somalia and the
United States) have ratified the convention, making it the most widely ratified piece of international law. This follows other significant conventions
on human rights, including the CEDAW (1979) and the Convention on the
Elimination of All Forms of Racial Discrimination (1969). Declarations, such
as the Copenhagen Declaration of the World Summit on Social Development,
state the goals to which country leaders commit themselves. In the Copenhagen Declaration, leaders committed their countries to work to eradicate
absolute poverty and to work toward full employment. Details are spelled
out in the Programme of Action emanating from the conference (United Nations, 1995a). Declarations do not include the monitoring and enforcement
provisions of conventions, but they state goals and principles.

World Bank and International Monetary Fund

The World Bank and IMF are not social welfare organizations. Because of
the significance of their loans and policies, however, they deserve brief mention here. In 1944, representatives from the United States and Europe met in
Bretton Woods, New Hampshire, to establish new economic policies to address the needs of the post–World War II world. The World Bank, IMF, and
a series of trade agreements resulted from these meetings; the financial institutions are sometimes called the Bretton Woods organizations, in reference to the historic meetings.

The IMF and World Bank have similar philosophies, members, and activities. Their major goals differ however. The IMF provides technical assistance to countries on banking, balance of payments, taxation, and related
matters. The major goal of the World Bank is "to provide loans to encourage economic development, whereas the IMF oversees monetary and exchange rate policies" (Hoy, 1998, p. 77). Therefore, the World Bank can be
viewed as a development organization, whereas the IMF aims to ensure an

orderly world economic system. Both organizations make loans, but there are differences in their loan policies. Any member country can borrow from the IMF—usually to address balance-of-payments problems—but only developing countries can borrow from the World Bank.

Several organizations comprise the World Bank group, including the International Bank for Reconstruction and Development (IBRD), and the International Development Association (IDA). The IBRD loans money for economic development. The terms of these loans are only "slightly better than average market rates and only slightly concessional; thus, they are not considered official development assistance" (Hoy, 1998, p. 46). Because of this, the poorest nations can seldom afford IBRD loans. They borrow instead from the IDA, often interest-free and with lenient terms. These loans are considered to be development assistance and go to countries that cannot borrow elsewhere; funds for the loans come from donor nations (Hoy, 1998).

The majority of loans have been devoted to infrastructure projects, but the World Bank also funds projects in rural and urban development, housing, education, health and nutrition, and population planning. UN member countries are members of the World Bank, but the United States, Japan, and the EU control 55% of the votes. World Bank influence was substantial in the 1970s and is still considerable in some countries. Overall, its influence has lessened due to the strong role of private capital. In 1995, for example, the World Bank lent $21 billion to developing countries, whereas $170 billion was invested in these countries by private companies (Hoy, 1998). Private investment seldom flows to countries considered poor risk; in these countries, the World Bank remains the primary source of credit.

The loan policies of the World Bank group and the IMF greatly affect the development prospects of poor nations and the climate within which international social welfare efforts are made. As explained in Chapter 5, since the 1980s, the IMF has insisted that nations with poor balances of payments and large debt adopt programs of "structural adjustment" in order to qualify for additional credit. Requiring broad-scale changes in economic structure, structural adjustment often leads to cutbacks in publicly supported, universal services, such as health and education, and worsens the plight of the poor within the poorest countries. As such, monetary policies have negatively affected social welfare conditions in much of Africa and Latin America, as least in the short run (Cornia et al., 1987; Jacobson, 1989). The impact of the IMF's policies falls largely on poor countries. As summarized by Hoy (1998): "Its power over developing countries is immense, but it has little more than the power of advice over the economies of industrialized nations" (p. 69).

GOVERNMENTAL AGENCIES

Governments, including the U.S. government, carry out international programs through their national agencies and through participation in multilateral organizations, including those just described. International social welfare functions of governments include foreign assistance, professional and educational exchange in social welfare, research on comparative social welfare, direct services to international populations, such as refugee assistance, and participation in various international programs and conferences.

In the United States, social welfare was included in the government's very first technical assistance program. Established by the Technical Assistance for Foreign Countries Act passed by Congress in 1939, the Department of State, the Children's Bureau, and the American Association of Schools of Social Work collaborated in a program that brought 15 directors of Latin American schools of social work to the United States for training (Hilliard, 1965). Thus at the very earliest stages of giving aid, the importance of social work was recognized.

Key U.S. government agencies in international aspects of social welfare today are the International Development Cooperation Agency and the Department of Health and Human Services (DHHS). They, as well as agencies from other countries, will be explained briefly below.

Governmental Bilateral Aid Programs and Agencies

The Nature of Bilateral Foreign Assistance. Foreign aid, or international development assistance, in part fulfills a social welfare function. Aid is viewed as one mechanism, along with investment and favorable trade prospects, that can assist poor countries in their development efforts. In 1968, the Pearson Commission, an international panel appointed by the president of the World Bank to recommend improved policies for international development, set a target for the level of aid effort for industrialized nations of 0.7% of each nation's GNP—a figure adopted by the UN as part of its strategy for the Second Development Decade (Isbister, 1998). Aid effort is the amount of aid given as a proportion of the donor country's GNP. Few nations, however, have ever contributed at the recommended level—to date only Denmark, the Netherlands, Norway, and Sweden have met this goal.

It is important for social workers to understand that international assistance serves many purposes for the donor nations and that humanitarianism is often not the major consideration. Bilateral aid in particular is an instrument of foreign policy, used to gain allies and shape policy decisions in other countries. During the cold war era, aid was used by Western countries to build allies against communism and by the Soviet Union and China as a tool to secure allies for the Communist bloc. Aid also may be used to open up new markets for donor country products. Hoy (1998) charges that in the United States, "replacing the cold war rationale for aid as a means to contain communism is today's rallying call for international aid to help the United States compete successfully in the global marketplace" (p. 40). In justifying giving aid to an increasingly skeptical Congress and public, the U.S. Agency for International Development (described below) boasted that 70% of bilateral aid money is spent in the United States and fully half of the money the United States allocates for multilateral aid is spent on U.S. goods (Hoy, 1998). Historically, U.S. generosity in distributing surplus food has been important to maintenance of farm prices at home. Thus aid is used partly to benefit the domestic economy; these considerations may lessen the effectiveness of the international mission of assistance by increasing the cost of commodities and services donated, adding excessive regulations about utilization of U.S. carriers and businesses, and by depriving countries in the recipient country's region of much-needed business. In addition, the end of the cold war did not end the use of assistance for security and military reasons. Recipients are often selected for strategic reasons rather than on a basis of need for help. For many years, therefore, Israel and Egypt have topped the list of recipients of U.S. aid dollars, receiving almost half of the aid budget while the world's poorest countries receive only about a quarter (Isbister, 1998).

Bilateral Aid Agencies: The U.S. Agency for International Development (USAID). In the United States, the foreign aid program is administered by the USAID, which is part of the International Development Cooperation Agency. The Overseas Private Investment Corporation is a separate part of the umbrella agency; it facilitates U.S. private investment to promote economic development in 140 countries. USAID currently administers economic and humanitarian aid programs in developing countries, Eastern Europe, and in the newly independent states of the former Soviet Union. Although an emphasis on strengthening private sector development shifted USAID away from traditional social welfare projects during the 1980s, the agency remains involved in many social initiatives.

In a reorganization of USAID in the early 1990s, five goals for the agency were defined: (1) Provision of humanitarian relief; (2) stabilization of population growth; (3) promotion of democracy; (4) environmental protection; and (5) broad-based economic growth (Hoy, 1998). Fitting with the goals, programs are organized into five development areas: Population and Health, Economic Growth, Environment, Democracy, and Humanitarian and Crisis Assistance. USAID also encourages "building indigenous capacity, enhancing participation and encouraging accountability, transparency, decentralization, and the empowerment of communities and individuals" (cited in Hoy, 1998, p. 35). Clearly, these are very compatible with social work methods and purposes.

When President Clinton took office in 1992, he expressed a commitment to restoring U.S. leadership in aid for true development. This promise has not been realized. Instead, the aid budget has been repeatedly cut, and the poorest countries are receiving an even smaller share. The USAID focus in the mid to late 1990s has been on strengthening democracy and capitalism, especially in the countries of the former Soviet bloc. In 1996, the former Soviet republics received 17% of the U.S. bilateral aid budget, while all of Africa, undeniably the area where need is greatest, received less than 12% (Hoy, 1998). Funds for overall humanitarian and development aid have been reduced, with the greatest reductions in aid for Africa. Since 1995, the U.S. has ranked last among the industrialized nations in aid effort, giving only 0.1% of its GNP.

USAID carries out some of its international relief and development work by providing funding to NGOs. Recognizing the need to build a constituency of support for aid, development education has also been part of the agency's agenda.

Peace Corps. The U.S. Peace Corps is an unusual program that fits both in the category of development assistance and in the category of exchange. Established to involve Americans directly in providing assistance in poor nations, many have asserted that the Corps is really an international cultural exchange effort, with benefits largely flowing to the volunteers themselves in terms of cultural enrichment and career preparation.

When the Peace Corps was founded in 1961, social work organizations attempted to play a major formative role and to convince Peace Corps founders that the building of social services in developing countries should be a major component of Peace Corps services. Their efforts were largely unsuccessful (Katz, 1962). Nonetheless, through the Peace Corps, the United States conducts volunteer projects, some of which are related to social welfare, such as primary health care promotion, urban development, and community development. The Peace Corps was made an independent agency by the International Security and Development Cooperation Act of 1981.

Bilateral Aid in Japan, Nordic Countries, and Canada

Bilateral aid is provided by many nations, including all of the industrialized countries. There are some differences in approach in various nations. In 1989, Japan became the largest donor of bilateral aid in terms of absolute funds. In 1995, for example, Japan spent $15.5 billion on development aid compared to U.S. expenditure of $7.3 billion. Japanese aid tends to emphasize large infrastructure projects, unlike the capacity-building projects favored by the United States and European countries. As is true for U.S. aid, Japanese aid is often tied to the purchase of Japanese goods.

"Sweden, Finland, Norway, and Denmark are commonly perceived as having the most pro-development, altruistic and progressive aid programs" (Hoy, 1998, p. 32). Sweden, Norway, and Denmark are leaders in level of effort, consistently surpassing the target of 0.7% of GNP. In addition, their aid agencies have focused on development goals and have conceptualized recipient countries as partners. They also strongly support multilateral agencies such as UNICEF.

The Canadian International Development Agency (CIDA) was established in 1968. The agency's ideals stress cooperation with recipient countries in order to contribute to economic growth and improve social systems. Following an important review of Canadian foreign assistance efforts in 1987, the resulting Charter on Overseas Development Assistance defined four key principles: (a) putting poverty first—helping the poorest; (b) helping people to help themselves; (c) priority for development goals in setting aid objectives rather than other foreign policy considerations; and (d) partnership between Canada and people and institutions in the Third World (Gilcrest & Splane, 1995). Furthermore, this document defined poverty as "a lack of choice," a "lack of access," and "inequity in opportunity in the distribution of the benefits of growth and in social justice" and "underdevelopment of human potential" (as cited in Gilcrest & Splane, 1995, p. 583). Social workers in Canada hailed this progressive definition of poverty as well as the CIDA emphasis on putting poverty first.

At the same time, Canada reaffirmed its earlier commitment to meet the 0.7% target for assistance. However, that figure has not been achieved to date; instead, Canada, like other countries, has reduced its level of spending in the face of economic difficulties at home. In an assessment of the current aid program, social work authors Gilcrest and Splane (1995) say that the important goals expressed in the 1987 charter are not likely to be reached "in this century" (p. 584). Rather, Canada's program has the characteristics criticized in a UNDP report, *The Reality of Aid:* a decline in aid budgets, of "increased diversion of aid from long-term development projects to short-term emergency relief; diversion of aid from Africa to eastern and central Europe; and the continuing use of aid to promote domestic imports from industrialized countries" (as cited in Gilcrest & Splane, 1995, p. 583).

A unique feature of governmental aid in Canada is that provincial governments also give aid. The national government permits provinces to sponsor aid projects as long as they are consistent with overall Canadian social and foreign policies. Thus the government of Alberta, for example, spent about $2 million on projects in 56 countries in 1992/93 (Gilcrest & Splane, 1995).

Government Agency Exchange Efforts

Although aid is a particularly significant welfare-oriented function of governments, national agencies are extensively involved in international exchange efforts under a variety of auspices. Exchange is an important international social work function. Therefore, some of the activities of the U.S. government that relate to social work are very briefly summarized below.

Department of Health and Human Services. Within DHHS, the international affairs staff in the Office of Public Affairs of the Administration for Children and Families (ACF), previously organized as part of the Office of Human Development, is the contact point for the international activities of the U.S. government most closely related to social work. The office organizes U.S. participation in intergovernmental international meetings and organizations, administers several bilateral programs in social welfare, is involved in comparative research, and arranges the programs of international visitors in social welfare. Under the Coordinated Discretionary Funds Program, the ACF has periodically made grants to support the transfer of international innovations in social services to the United States.

The ACF has participated with social welfare ministries in several countries in cooperative social welfare projects. In the 1990s, several special initiatives focused on Eastern Europe and the countries of the former Soviet Union. ACF regularly participates in meetings of international organizations, such as UNICEF, ECOSOC, and the European Centre for Social Welfare Policy and Research. Additionally, ACF provides experts for special UN efforts; one example is the provision of support and expertise to the UN group that developed the Declaration on Social and Legal Principles Relating to Adoption and Foster Placement of Children Nationally and Internationally (U.S. DHHS, 1993).

The Social Security Administration, also part of DHHS, conducts research on social security programs worldwide. The research is published in a biennial volume, *Social Security Programs Throughout the World*. The agency also serves as the U.S. link to the International Social Security Association.

The United States Information Agency. The United States Information Agency (U.S.I.A.), under its Bureau of Educational and Cultural Affairs, had been responsible for administering educational and cultural international exchanges. Through the USIA, many social welfare leaders came to the U.S. for professional visits and meetings with counterparts. The agency also sponsored academic linkage and exchange projects in many fields, including social welfare, sending U.S. scholars to study or teach abroad and sponsoring international scholars in the U.S. The agency was abolished and its functions transferred to the U.S. Department of State as of October, 1999.

Agencies Dealing With Migration and Refugees

The Office of Refugee Resettlement (ORR) is part of the ACF, within DHHS, and has responsibility for planning and directing the implementation of national programs to resettle refugees in all the states and advising the secretary of DHHS on resettlement policies (*United States Government Manual*, 1998). Among the programs for which ORR is responsible are: Refugee and Entrant Resettlement, State Impact Assistance Grants, and the U.S. Repatriate Program. Within the State Department, the Bureau of Population, Refugees and Migration is charged with developing policies on refugees and migration and for overseeing programs for refugee admissions. In addition, this bureau administers U.S. contributions to agencies that serve refugees around the world, including UN organizations and NGOs. Further, the bureau "coordinates U.S. international migration policy within the U.S. government and through bilateral and multilateral diplomacy" (*U.S. Government Manual*, 1998, p. 397). Resettlement will be discussed in more depth in Chapter 8.

Other agencies are less involved in international social welfare but still carry out related functions. These include the Department of Labor, the lead agency on International Labor Organization (ILO) matters, and extensive programs in international health administered by the National Institutes for Health, Fogarty International Center, and the Office of International Health at the Public Health Service. The Department of Agriculture shares responsibility for international food assistance efforts with USAID. Key programs in agriculture include the Food for Peace Program, established in 1966, and the more recently founded Food for Progress Program to provide food to developing democracies.

NONGOVERNMENTAL ORGANIZATIONS

NGOs play a significant role in international social welfare. Also called *Private Voluntary Organizations* (PVOs), they are organized to serve a range of functions, including:

- relief and development
- advocacy for causes such as human rights and peace
- development education
- exchange
- international networks of social and youth agencies
- the cross-national work of domestic agencies targeted at international problems such as adoption, child custody, and refugee resettlement
- professional associations (as described in Chapter 3)

In addition to their major functions, many of these NGOs have consultative status in the UN (defined in Chapter 3) and its specialized bodies and may collaborate with and receive funds from intergovernmental and national government agencies to conduct their work. Too numerous to describe all, this section will give examples of NGOs that fulfill the functions just identified. (The international professional organizations were described in Chapter 3 and will not be covered here.)

Relief and Development

NGOs plan and implement relief and development work in developing countries, and, increasingly, in poverty-stricken areas of industrialized nations. One of the earliest private relief organizations was the International Committee of the Red Cross, which was founded in 1863 to provide relief services and ensure humane wartime treatment of prisoners and civilians.

The Red Cross has been joined by numerous international private organizations emphasizing relief to refugees, famine victims, and victims of war and natural disasters. Usually provided under emergency conditions, relief involves provision of basic necessities of food, water, shelter, clothing, and medical care to sustain life. Increasingly, the large-scale relief organizations have worked to refocus their efforts toward development—the initiation of self-sustaining efforts that will contribute on a long-term basis to improvements in quality of life. Some examples of development activities are forming local cooperatives and introducing improved farming techniques, preventive health care projects, and local sanitation improvements, such as digging wells and building latrines. Some NGOs are moving further into what has been called *sustainable systems development* (Morrison & Purcell, 1988). In this approach, more interventions target policy and institutional changes at the regional or national level to create an environment in which sustainable people-centered development is feasible. The line between relief and development is seldom absolute. Most development NGOs still engage in some relief work, especially in times of crisis. This stems from the recognition that development is impossible without the guarantee of human survival. As expressed by Mabub ul Haq (1982), former head of UNDP, if an individual dies from hunger, there is no chance that he can be developed.

Among the larger U.S.-based NGOs in development work are CARE (the Cooperative for American Relief Everywhere, now known by its acronym), Catholic Relief Services, PLAN (formerly Foster Parents Plan International), and the Christian Children's Fund. All have annual budgets of over $100 million. Most receive considerable amounts of government funding to carry out relief and development work on-site in developing countries. In fact, 29% of U.S. government aid is channeled through NGOs and the same is true in other Organization of Economic Cooperation and Development (OECD) countries (Hoy, 1998). Innovative work, often in politically difficult climates, is also done by smaller NGOS, such as the American Friends Service Committee (AFSC), Oxfam, and the Unitarian Universalist Service Committee. Many of these agencies do not accept government money in order to remain free to advocate for policy changes and to assist in areas not approved by government agencies. The AFSC, for example, began projects in Cambodia shortly after the fall of the Khmer Rouge, during a time when the U.S. government prohibited official aid to Cambodia.

There is increasing realization that development efforts must be self-sustaining in order to have impact. This favors participatory, community-level efforts that are "bottom-up"—strategies planned and implemented with and by people experiencing the problems being addressed. There is a perception that NGOs are more innovative, flexible, and cost-effective and that they are better able to reach the poor through grassroots work than is true for governmental or intergovernmental organizations. In general, NGOs are less bureaucratic and are less tied to the changing priorities of legislatures than the bilateral agencies. For those with significant dependence on government funding, these advantages are partially erased; these NGOs also become limited by the priorities and "strings" of government regulations.

The work of international NGOs is complemented by Southern NGOs—those based in developing countries. Some Southern NGOs are very small, village-based organizations, whereas others are national cooperatives, environmental groups, or women's organizations. Among the more well-known

NGOs are the Grameen Bank of Bangladesh, an organization that has spurred micro-enterprise development, especially for women, and the Green Belt Movement in Kenya, a women's environmental movement in which over 50,000 women have participated in planting more than 10 million trees to stem soil erosion (Hoy, 1998). There are also some international organizations based in the South. Development Alternatives With Women for a New Era (DAWN), based at the University of the West Indies in Barbados, is a network of Third World women activists. These developing country NGOs are important players in development successes and their activities—both independent projects and partnerships with Northern NGOs—need to be encouraged.

To further their goals, Northern NGOs have formed several coordinating bodies. InterAction is a coalition of more than 150 U.S. NGOs that have joined together to coordinate their work in disaster situations, to work toward improved U.S. development assistance and general development policy, and to collaborate in development education efforts (InterAction, 1997). InterAction has developed and published PVO standards covering governance, finance, and management practices (InterAction, 1993). The International Council of Voluntary Agencies (ICVA), is an international membership organization for national and international PVOs engaged in development work. The organization provides information exchange and management assistance, as well as serving as a liaison to UN bodies.

These coordinating bodies have been particularly active in assisting NGOs to carry out their supplementary purposes of policy advocacy and development education, which are presented in the following sections.

Advocacy

Most NGOs include advocacy as one of their functions. Increasingly, U.S.-based NGOs have identified the need to serve as voices for more effective international assistance programs and for responsible international policies in general. A recent initiative is the InterAction campaign to encourage U.S. ratification of the UN Convention on the Rights of the Child. NGOs led a successful campaign against the sale of baby formula in developing countries in the 1980s through massive public education on the value of breast feeding and the dangers of using baby formula in areas with poor sanitation. The campaign included pressure on multinational corporations involved in the manufacture and promotion of baby formula. A more recent campaign was initiated by Oxfam UK to press for debt relief for poor countries. More typical of the NGO lobbying agenda is advocacy for development priorities and adequate funding for foreign assistance.

Another form of advocacy is carried out at the intergovernmental level through consultative status with the UN. More than 2,300 NGOs were accredited by the UN for participation in the Copenhagen World Summit for Social Development, and the Beijing Conference on Women included participation of more than 4,000 NGOs.

Some NGOs are devoted primarily to advocacy, especially in human rights. An example is Amnesty International, an organization that documents abuses of human rights and sponsors campaigns to improve human rights treatment and obtain prisoner release. Another human rights NGO, Defense for Children International, was active in the 1980s and early 1990s in over 60 countries to monitor and advocate for children's rights. The organization was a major actor in the campaign to draft and adopt the UN Convention on the Rights of the Child.

Development Education

Many NGOs conduct development education programs—efforts to educate the public on conditions in the developing world and to motivate action on behalf of the needs of the world's poor. Partly motivated by the need to appeal to donors and the realization that there is large-scale public ignorance of development realities, agencies also recognize the contribution they can make in sharing their knowledge and experience in development with the general public. Between 1982 and 1993, the Biden-Pell Amendment to U.S. foreign aid legislation provided special grants for development education. The YWCA and NASW were among the organizations that received these grants from USAID, funds were used for materials and educational campaigns on global issues aimed at their memberships. Development agencies were also involved. Save the Children (SC), for example, produced educational materials to sensitize children to the needs of other children around the world and implemented action projects in schools. Bread for the World is an organization dedicated solely to development education and advocacy, with a focus on world hunger. This Christian-based citizens' group produces action alerts, background papers on hunger issues, and videos for education; it also lobbies the government on domestic and world hunger policies.

The American Forum is an NGO that sponsors and promotes development education. It sponsors an annual forum on development education and publishes books, manuals, teaching aids, and a newsletter to assist educational efforts.

Exchange Programs

Exchange is used in social welfare, as in other fields, as a mechanism for transfer of knowledge and service models as well as a means of bridging cultural barriers and increasing understanding. The Council of International Programs (CIP) is one example of an exchange organization. Founded in 1956, CIP sponsors educational exchanges for human service professionals and youth leaders. Participants are engaged in both educational seminars and fieldwork in social agencies and youth programs. The placements and seminars are operated by local affiliates that are linked to universities. Professionals from more than 100 countries have participated in CIP exchanges (Alliance for International Educational and Cultural Exchange, 1998).

Agencies such as World Learning, founded in 1932 as Experiment in International Living, have sponsored youth exchanges to enhance cross-cultural understanding. Academic exchanges, some in the social welfare field, are supported under the Fulbright Scholar program, and formerly by the U.S. Information Agency—its exchange functions have been assumed by the State Department. The Fulbright program has been one of the major sources of support for U.S. scholars to teach, consult, and do research in other countries. In addition, many exchanges have developed between universities or from personal contacts between professionals.

Social and Youth Agencies With International Counterparts

Although they will not be discussed in depth here, there are a number of social and youth development agencies that have branches in many nations. These include the Boy Scouts, the Girl Scouts, the YMCA, the YWCA, the Salvation Army, the Red Cross, and others. Each has functions that relate to status as an international organization. The U.S. YWCA, for example, maintains World Mutual Service committees in many of its branches and has a headquarter's division to address collaborative efforts with the World YWCA. Red Cross branches in many nations send volunteers to assist in disasters in other parts of the world.

Agencies Engaged in Cross-National Social Work

A growing number of private social welfare agencies are engaged in cross-national social work, including international adoption, child custody problems, divorce and other family problems involving citizens and laws of more than one country, and sponsorship and resettlement of refugees. Although some agencies specialize in such work, others are introduced to international dimensions of social welfare through their involvement with individual cases.

International Social Service (ISS), located in Geneva with branches in 16 countries, specializes in cross-national casework. With an emphasis on migration, the agency intervenes in individual and family problems that can be solved only through coordinated efforts in several countries. The agency maintains a documentation center on migration, refugees, family law, and children's rights (Encyclopedia of Associations, 1999).

Many international adoptions are arranged through social agencies and all such adoptions in the United States involve a home study, as required by the Immigration and Naturalization Service. Agencies such as Holt International Children's Services, founded in 1956, specialize in international adoption. Such services, however, are also available from many general adoption agencies. The adoption of children from other countries is also common in Europe. Wherever it occurs, the practice of international adoption involves agencies in cross-national work.

Refugee resettlement programs have also engaged many private social agencies in international work. Although not always conceptualized as international social work, competent refugee work is impossible without knowledge of the refugee's culture of origin, international transit experiences, and the receiving country's policy regarding refugees, including reunification and family sponsorship issues. Among the agencies significantly involved in refugee resettlement in the United States are Migration and Refugee Services of the U.S. Catholic Conference, Lutheran Immigration and Refugee Service, and many specialized agencies serving particular national, religious, or ethnic groups. Practice issues concerning refugee resettlement, immigration, international adoption, and intercountry casework will be discussed in Chapter 9.

CONCLUSION: MOVING FORWARD

The social work–related functions of international organizations cover an enormous scope, and there are many such organizations. Assessments of need and the growing importance of social factors in development suggest that the level of activity is likely to increase significantly in the future.

All recent surveys of current social welfare needs in the international context indicate that a full agenda remains, and grows. Basic-needs issues persist: Food, shelter, primary health care, and primary education are still inadequately provided in much of the developing world. Ensuring respect for the rights of children, women, persons with disabilities, and minority ethnic and racial groups remains a challenge. At the same time, demographic changes and modernization influences are causing new concerns with issues of aging, mental health, and substance abuse. There is a growing recognition that the social dimensions of development decisions and policies are key to meeting the ultimate objectives of development strategies—improved living standards for all. Thus social welfare and social development should grow in importance.

If there is a counterindication, it is that trends in reducing domestic social safety nets and curtailing the Western welfare state are having and will have an impact on development assistance. As explained by Roger Riddell (1996) in a study of the role of aid:

> [A] factor adversely influencing aid lies in the ripple effects of changing perceptions within donor countries about the nature of the state, the welfare state, and society; the nature of responsibility for assisting those which do not have the means to help themselves; and how best to prioritize the use of state funds. . . . As state aid, including hand-outs, are viewed less and less sympathetically as solutions to domestic problems, it is asked why these solutions should continue to be used to help solve development problems of poorer countries. (p. 2)

These "ripple effects" are further evidence of the social policy emulation discussed in Chapter 5. Clearly, emphases on privatization, increased role of the market, and reduced social welfare roles for governments are already having an impact on attitudes and practices in international development.

In order to move forward, the organizations involved in international social development and social work must appropriately assess accomplishments and failures. The problems facing the field of international social welfare appear overwhelming—seemingly intractable poverty, especially in Africa; the devastation of AIDS in suffering, costs, and family disruptions; ethnic conflicts; and a continuing flow of refugees. However, there have been major successes, such as lengthening the life span, eliminating diseases such as smallpox, reducing hunger in Asia, increasing the number of literate adults, recognizing standards for human rights, and introducing new strategies to improve child survival. The social mission of the UN has been one of its major successes. Governments have demonstrated a willingness to come together and work on strategies for human betterment, even if with imperfect results. International agreements have been reached on the broad outlines of human rights policy covering women, children, and racial and ethnic minorities. While implementation lags, it is no small achievement to have secured wide international agreement on principles of human rights and human development. There have also been millions of small social development successes in terms of individual lives saved, refugees resettled, villages mobilized to help themselves, artisans helped to start small businesses, and persons educated about HIV risks.

Thus in considering the future of international social welfare efforts, it is important that both the successes and the failures, the challenges and the victories, be reported and analyzed.

Chapter 8 will look more specifically at practice in international social development and implications for social work. Although there are many challenges ahead for international social welfare, one that may shape social work participation in international work is success in reducing the dichotomy between international and domestic social welfare issues. There are currently two separate fields with different personnel, terminology, and policy concerns. Particularly in the United States, social work, the dominant profession in domestic social welfare, has remained mostly uninvolved in international social development agencies, mostly untouched by the development education movement, and mostly uninterested in social welfare policy with international implications. Chapter 8 will detail the roles and functions involved in development work that are relevant for social work. It will also identify the lessons learned from international development that can be applied to social work wherever it is practiced.

REFERENCES

Alliance for International Educational and Cultural Exchange (1998). *International exchange locator: a resource directory for educational and cultural change.* Washington, DC: Author.

Altschiller, D. (1993). *The United Nations' role in world affairs.* The Reference Shelf (Vol. 65, No. 2). New York: H.W. Wilson Company.

Bennett, A.L. (1988). *International organizations: Principles and issues* (4th ed.). Englewood Cliffs, NJ: Prentice Hall.

Cornia, G., Jolly, R., & Stewart, F. (Eds.). (1987). *Adjustment with a human face.* New York: UNICEF.

Encyclopedia of associations: International organizations. (1999). Detroit, MI: Gale Research.

Gilcrest, G., & Splane, R. (1995). Canada's role in international social welfare. In J. Turner & F. Turner (Eds.). *Canadian Social Welfare* (3rd ed., pp. 574–596). Scarborough, Canada: Allyn and Bacon.

Hilliard, J.F. (1965). AID and international social welfare manpower. In *Proceedings of the Conference on International Social Welfare Manpower, 1964.* Washington, DC: U.S. Government Printing Office.

Hoy, P. (1998). *Players and issues in international aid.* West Hartford, CT: Kumarian Press.

InterAction (1993). *InterAction PVO standards.* Washington, DC: Author.

InterAction (1997). *InterAction member profiles 1997–1998.* Washington, DC: Author.

Isbister, J. (1998). *Promises not kept: the betrayal of social change in the third world.* West Hartford, CT: Kumarian Press.

Jacobson, J. (1989, July–August). Paying interest in human life. *WorldWatch*, pp. 6–8.

Katz, A. (1962). Social work's contribution to the Peace Corps. In *Proceedings of the 1962 Annual Program Meeting CSWE* (pp. 75–85). New York: Council on Social Work Education.

McGowan, P. (1987). Key concepts for development studies. In C. Joy & W. Kniep (Eds.), *The international development crisis and American education.* New York: Global Perspectives in Education.

Morrison, E., & Purcell, R.B. (Eds.) (1988). *Players and issues in U.S. foreign aid.* West Hartford, CT: Kumarian Press.

Riddell, R. (1996). *Aid in the 21st century.* (Discussion Paper Series No. 6). New York: UNDP.

Rostow, Walt W. (1960). *The Stages of Economic Growth: A Non-Communist Manifesto.* New York: Cambridge University Press.

Taylor, Paul and Groom, A.J.R. (Eds.) (1989). *Global Issues in the United Nations' Framework.* New York: St. Martins Press.

The worldwide AIDS toll. (1998) *The Hartford Courant* November 25, 1998, p. A 17.

ul Haq, Mahbub (1982, July). "Beyond the Cancun Summit" Unpublished presentation at the Society for International Development Conference, Baltimore, Maryland.

United Nations (1945). United Nations Charter. Available at http://www.un.org

United Nations (1969). *Proceedings of the International Conference of Ministers Responsible for Social Welfare,* September 3–12, 1968. New York: Author.

United Nations (1987). *Interregional Consultation on Developmental Social Welfare Policies and Programmes.* [Special Issue of the *Social Development Newsletter*, vol. 1987-1-25.] Vienna: Centre for Social Development and Humanitarian Affairs.

United Nations (1991). *Women: Challenges to the Year 2000.* New York: Author.

United Nations (1992). *Yearbook of the United Nations, 1991* (Vol. 45). Dordrecht, Netherlands: Martinus Nijhoff Publishers.

United Nations (1993a). *United Nations Conferences and Observances.* (Reference Paper No. 32, Communications and Project Management Division and Meetings Coverage Section). New York: Author.

United Nations (1993b). World Summit for social development to be held in Denmark in 1995. *UN Chronicle, XXX*(1), 82–85.

United Nations (1995a). *Copenhagen Declaration and Programme of Action. World Summit for Social Development*. New York: Author.

United Nations (1995b). *Platform for Action and the Beijing Declaration: Fourth World Conference on Women*. New York: UN Department of Public Information.

United Nations (1997b). *Yearbook of the United Nations 1995*. Vol. 49. New York: Author.

United Nations (1997a). *Report on the world social situation 1997*. New York: Author.

United Nations (1998). *Basic facts about the United Nations*. New York: Author.

U.S. Department of Health and Human Services, Administration for Children and Families (1993, March 30). Staff memo.

United States Government Manual 1998 (1998). Washington, DC: Office of the Federal Register, National Archives and Records Service, General Services Administration.

CHAPTER 7

VALUES AND ETHICS
FOR INTERNATIONAL
PROFESSIONAL ACTION

It is never the people who complain of human rights as a Western
or Northern imposition. It is too often their leaders who do so.

KOFI ANNAN, 1997, UN SECRETARY GENERAL

Values are potentially both unifying and divisive factors in international social work. In the search for commonalities in social work around the world,
the strong value base of the profession is always cited as one of the key aspects of its universal identity. Social workers in all countries espouse commitment to professional values, and social work professional associations in
many countries have adopted or are currently working on codes of ethics.
The profession has come together through its international organization, The
International Federation of Social Workers (IFSW), to develop and adopt an
international code of ethics, comprised of an International Declaration of
Ethical Principles of Social Work and International Ethical Standards for Social Workers (IFSW, 1994) (Appendix A). Yet the commonality of values and
ethics may be superficial. There is a strong current of criticism that social
work values and ethical codes are too grounded in Western-oriented individualistic values to the exclusion of other perspectives. It is undeniable that
issues of values and ethics become complex and controversial as one moves
among various social and cultural contexts.

In this chapter, values and ethics that relate to the full range of international professional actions—cross-cultural practice, practice in the global
arena, professional exchange, and international policy advocacy—are discussed. Questions to be addressed include:

1. To what extent are social work values universally applicable? What are
   the areas of agreement and the areas of tension and conflict in attempting to define universal social work values?
2. How do these issues within social work relate to the broader philosophical arguments for universalism and the polar position of cultural relativism in the study of values and ethics?

3. If values are not universal, are there alternative values that would inform social work in contexts that differ along the key dimension of emphasis on individuals as contrasted to emphasis on the collectivity?

4. What social work values are needed to support and guide international professional action as defined in this book? To what extent are current national and international codes adequate, and what revisions would be helpful in furthering a global profession?

UNIVERSALISM VERSUS CULTURAL RELATIVISM

An understanding of universalist and cultural relativist perspectives on ethics is a prerequisite to advancing discussion of ethics for the global profession. Can a universal set of social work values be defined that applies to professional work in any country? This question raises philosophical issues with very practical consequences for social workers in practice in multicultural as well as international environments.

Two competing schools of thought within ethics are the deontologist school that "stresses the overriding importance of fixed moral rules," arguing that "an action is inherently right or wrong" and therefore that ethical principles apply to all situations, and the teleologist view that ethical decisions should be made "on the basis of the context in which they are made or on the basis of the consequences which they create" (Loewenberg, Dolgoff, & Harrington, 2000, p. 46). In the language of international human rights, these viewpoints are called the universalist and the cultural relativist, respectively. In the universalist view, "all members of the human family share the same inalienable rights" (Mayer, 1995, p. 176) and "culture is irrelevant to the validity of moral rights and rules" (Donnelly, 1984, p. 400). Cultural relativists, on the other hand, argue that "culture is the sole source of the validity of a moral right or rule" (Donnelly, 1984, p. 400) and that "members of one society may not legitimately condemn the practices of societies with different traditions," especially practices considered culturally based (Mayer, 1995, p. 176). At the extremes, each position is rigid.

Universalism and relativism can more usefully be seen as a continuum. Mixed positions occupy the center of the continuum, combining the notion of a set of universal rights with consideration for the maintenance of cultural traditions. The IFSW code of ethics identifies with this middle ground. In the statement of the purposes of the International Declaration of Ethical Principles, the first is "to formulate a set of basic principles for social work, which can be adapted to cultural and social settings" (ISFW, 1994, Section 2.1).

Adapting principles, however, is not easy. Practitioners in the field often encounter situations that cause moral discomfort and raise ethical dilemmas as they interact with different cultures. They struggle at the practical level with the universalism-relativism debate, asking themselves, "When is different just different and when is different wrong?" (Donaldson, 1996, p.

48). This question suggests a mixed approach, and indeed, Donaldson argues that it is wrong to fully adopt either a universalist or relativist approach.

The universalism-relativism debate is highly relevant to social work values and ethics. Much of this value systems debate has taken place over human rights, concerning issues central to social work interest and practice. These include the rights of children, the disabled, gays and lesbians, ethnic minority groups in many host countries, and, perhaps particularly, the rights of women. The role and status of women and children within the family and within their economies and societies are often at the heart of social work value clashes over the principle of self-determination and the social work commitment to equity. For example:

- A female Cambodian refugee living in a U.S. city asks for help at a shelter for battered women. The local Cambodian Mutual Assistance Association criticizes the shelter, charging that its focus on counseling the woman on her rights and on preparations for independence are destroying the fabric of Cambodian family and social life.

- Iranian social work educators were instrumental in bringing family-planning services to Iran in the 1970s. Were the mullahs right that this represented a fundamental threat to the Islamic way of life, or was it essential practice to meet the needs of women and their families?

- West Indian politicians in a U.S. city speak out against the child protection agency's investigations of child abuse in families using corporal punishment, asserting that West Indians don't want their children to grow up undisciplined.

- Local community development workers in Bangladesh encounter a group of enraged local leaders, charging that their micro-enterprise and literacy programs for women are destroying family roles and violating the Koran.

- Efforts to ensure nondiscriminatory treatment for gays and lesbians encounter hostility in Jamaica, Zimbabwe, the United States, and elsewhere.

These brief examples show that the social work values that drive practice interventions are enmeshed in the dilemmas of universalism versus cultural relativism.

Equality and Culture: Can They Be Reconciled?

As noted above, issues concerning the role and status of women have often been at the heart of the values debate. Social work codes of ethics, including the IFSW's, express a commitment to equality and specifically mention gender equality. Feminist human rights scholars warn of the dangers of cultural relativism. Ketayun Gould (1989), a social worker, sees the problem as "advocacy of a 'cultural' viewpoint that assumes a defensive posture by not only tolerating the oppression of women in one's own and other societies, but coming repeatedly to the defense of this oppression in the name of eth-

nic solidarity" (p. 12). In 1979, the UN adopted the Convention on the Elimination of All Forms of Discrimination Against Women (CEDAW). As of the
1999 report from the UN Centre for Human Rights, 163 countries had ratified CEDAW and an additional 3 had signed it (United Nations Development Program [UNDP], 1999). But CEDAW has had more reservations
entered by countries ratifying than any other human rights treaty, indicating "widespread and deep-rooted resistance to the concept of full equality
for women" (UNICEF, 1997). Furthermore, some of these reservations, such
as those entered by Bangladesh, Egypt, Libya, and Tunisia contradict the
purposes and essential protections of the treaty. Twenty-four nations filed
reservations against Article 16, the guarantee of equality between women
and men in marriage and family life. "Such reservations strike at the heart
of CEDAW. They reject the extension of human rights protection into the
private domain and entrench the inferior role of women" (UNICEF, 1997,
p. 49). Thus "the UN tolerated a situation where some Middle Eastern countries would be treated as parties to a convention whose substantive provisions they had professed their unwillingness to abide by" (Mayer, 1995,
p. 179).

An interesting aspect of CEDAW is that it specifically calls for cultural
change. Article 5 states that ratifying countries should take measures to
"modify the social and cultural patterns of conduct of men and women with
a view to achieving the elimination of prejudices and customary and all other
practices which are based on the idea of the inferiority or the superiority of
either of the sexes or on stereotyped roles for men and women" (United Nations, 1979, Article 5). Principle 2.2.7 of the IFSW International Declaration
of Ethical Principles of Social Work states that, "Social workers respect the
basic human rights of individuals and groups as expressed in the United
Nations Universal Declaration of Human Rights and other international conventions derived from that Declaration" (IFSW, 1994), which includes
CEDAW. It can be argued, therefore, that the social work ethical code puts
social workers on the side of advocating for changes in cultural practices
when those practices are discriminatory or are based on stereotypical ideas
of gender roles.

An alternative argument is provided by the Afrocentric scholar Josiah
Cobbah. The Universal Declaration of Human Rights, he charges, is "a product of Western liberal ideology," adopted during a time when "most of the
population of Africa south of the Sahara was still under colonial domination" (Cobbah, 1987, p. 316). Thus, the declaration is grounded in individualism and its values are a poor fit in the communalist societies of Africa.
Cobbah is concerned that human rights may be a "Trojan horse" sent in to
change African civilizations. "Africans emphasize groupness, sameness and
commonality" rather than individual freedom (Cobbah, 1987, p. 320). The
prosperity of the community is more important than the prosperity of the
individual. The values that emanate from communalism are hierarchy, respect, restraint, responsibility, and reciprocity. Some elements in the mix are
easily embraced by social work, such as generosity and cooperation in daily
life. Others are more problematic, especially the notion of a hierarchical vil-

lage and family organization in which social roles are rigidly assigned, almost invariably assigning women to roles of lesser economic and social influence. Aspects of the concept of restraint may also be problematic; restraint means that "a person does not have complete freedom. Individual rights must always be balanced against the requirements of the group" (Cobbah, 1987, p. 321). Would a social worker therefore encourage a client to show restraint in seeking to resolve a problem, suggesting that the client's individual need should recede in the interests of group cohesion?

What Is Culture?

One difficulty in assessing the validity of claims for cultural relativism are the vexing questions of what represents culture and who are the legitimate interpreters of a culture. In the following box, Arati Rao suggests considering questions about the nature of culture and participation when faced with a claim for cultural relativism in human rights.

Rao's questions ask practitioners to evaluate the extent to which cultural practices are shaped through participation of all sectors of a population and to examine who benefits from the defense of a particular cultural practice. For example, were women and young girls involved in the definition of female sexuality that gave rise to genital mutilation/female circumcision in East Africa? Although it is true that many women are involved in the continuation of the practice, this does not prove that the practice grew out of female views of sexuality or that women had or have power to shape tribal practices. Women's role in continuation of the practice today may well be more indicative of extreme dependence on male approval and marriage customs for survival than on intrinsic support for the practice. Another aspect of the analysis is to determine whether women benefit from this ritual circumcision. Clearly, many women suffer severe health problems, even death, and others endure lifelong pain and discomfort. The "benefit" to women is continued acceptance into traditional marriage patterns. True beneficiaries of the practice are male society members who continue to control the sexuality of females through circumcision.

The question—"What is culture?"—can also assist in assessing whether practices should be challenged or defended. The social worker can look, with the clients, at the extent to which the practice in question is core or central

EVALUATING CULTURAL CLAIMS

1. What is the status of the speaker?
2. In whose name is the argument from culture advanced?
3. What is the degree of participation in culture formation of the social groups primarily affected by the cultural practices in question?
4. What is culture, anyway? (Rao, 1995, p. 168)

to the maintenance of culture. For example, when a West Indian parent says that child beating is important to maintaining the culture, the social worker can encourage exploration of whether it is corporal punishment that is the cultural value or well-disciplined children. Reframed in this way, mutual problem solving may be enhanced and may permit movement beyond culture clash.

Cultural relativists tend to present culture as static. In reality, cultures are dynamic: "Culture is a series of constantly contested and negotiated social practices whose meanings are influenced by the power and status of their interpreters and participants" (Rao, 1995, p. 173). Mayer (1995) responds to the charge that feminist views are compatible with Western ideology but alien to Eastern and Middle Eastern cultures by arguing that feminism was also "alien" to Western countries and required long periods of struggle and cultural change in order to gain acceptance. Thus, cultures evolve and receive new ideas—a process that can have both positive and negative consequences.

The Concept of Harm and Cultural Relativism

Donaldson (1996), speaking from an international business perspective, warns that one cannot act from a "when in Rome" position without the danger of committing serious violations of fundamental values. He implies that the question of doing harm should be used as a criterion to evaluate whether practices encountered when crossing cultural boundaries can be accepted. Although his advice is targeted at those with multinational business ventures, it is applicable to social work.

Those who live and work abroad will need to "grapple with moral ambiguity" because practice considered ethical in one country or cultural setting may be unethical in others (Donaldson, 1996, p. 56). According to Donaldson, the important question for social workers is to "learn to distinguish a value in tension with their own from one that is intolerable" (p. 58). In international work, social workers will encounter some value differences that can be accommodated but others that must be rejected because they stray too far from respect for human dignity, and they do harm. Donaldson cites the example of nepotism in corporations in India and gift-giving in Japan as examples of the first, and forced labor, physical abuse of employees, and toxic waste dumping as examples of practices that stray too far from essential values and cannot be condoned. The first instances are practices that would be unacceptable in U.S. business and would cause discomfort when encountered; however, nepotism and gift-giving probably do not violate core human values. Again, respect for cultural differences is encouraged *unless* the practice causes significant harm. Thus opposition to female circumcision may be more easily justified by the practice's record of causing serious physical harm to many who undergo it rather than attacking the practice's roots in denial of female sexual pleasure. Using the material above, judgments would also be influenced by the fact that the victims of female circumcision are children, who are unable to participate in the dialogue about cultural formation and preservation.

Core Social Work Values and Universalism/Relativism

In reviewing the International Code of Ethics and the codes of ethics from social work groups from various countries, common or nearly common elements are evident. These include statements of commitment to the inherent worth and dignity of people, commitment to equality and nondiscrimination, the concepts of multiple responsibilities of the professional (to self, profession, clients, society at large, co-workers and employers), self-determination, and confidentiality. Self-determination, confidentiality, and equality and nondiscrimination will be examined next in more depth in order to consider how cultural context influences the operationalization of the value in question.

Self-Determination. Self-determination—fostering the ability of the client to make his or her own life choices and decisions—is an important principle in Western social work. The capacity to make one's own decisions is viewed as central to full adult functioning in an individualistic society. Thus social work practice is often oriented toward assisting individuals, groups, and communities to become more self-directed. This applies whether working with a battered woman to help her realize that she has choices and a right to make them or working with a poor community to help it mobilize and set its own priorities. The principle of self-determination is also intended to prevent the social worker from making decisions and choices for the client. The most revered forms of professional intervention facilitate the client's journey to discovery of his or her or their own options and choices with only gentle guidance and support from the social worker.

Yet, even in Western countries, the emphasis on self-determination varies. Denmark is characterized by a strong tradition of communitarianism, "which stresses responsibility of the society for the welfare of all" (Lane, 1998, p. 7). Fitting into the group is more important than standing out as an individual. According to Lane (1998) the value of self-determination is present in Danish social work, however, it is not emphasized: "Deference to decisions by experts, such as medical personnel and social workers, is more acceptable to both Danish citizens and to Danish professionals. The ideal of the individual's rights to self determination, self empowerment and self actualization are not as strong" (p. 10). Protective payments—direct payment of a client's bills by welfare authorities to prevent money mismanagement— are commonly used by welfare offices, a practice rejected in the United States as a violation of client rights to self-determination.

Social workers in Asia and Africa view self-determination as a particularly problematic ethical principle, advocating actions ranging from discarding it as irrelevant in a communalist society to modifying it to permit more worker-directed interventions in highly role-stratified cultures.

In her study of casework in India, Ejaz (1989) found that caseworkers tended to be directive and to give advice and suggestions to their clients. Almost all workers thought that their clients expected the social worker to make decisions for them (Ejaz, 1991). As one student expressed it: "There is a tendency in me to guide too much. If I don't give suggestions or show ways out, they [clients] gape at me. They tend to lean on us and the easy way out is to provide solutions" (Ejaz, 1991, p. 134). In so doing, however, the social workers reported feeling conflicted about their practice because they saw their approach as violating the concept of self-determination. The Declaration of Ethics for Professional Social Workers, developed by the Tata Institute Social Work Educators' Forum in Bombay, includes self-determination: "I shall respect people's right for self-determination, and shall ensure that they themselves play an active role in relation to the course of action to be taken about their life situation" ("Declaration of Ethics," 1997, p. 339). Ejaz (1991), however, believes that the more directive approach is consistent with sociocultural and religious traditions. She discusses the *guru-chela* relationship, which is similar to a priest-disciple or teacher-student relationship, as a model for social work. It is customary for Indians to look up to elders and to seek and accept advice from those who are more experienced or schooled. Social workers, on the basis of their education and professional expertise, are in the position of elders (regardless of age) and are seen as givers of advice and guidance. In other societies, for example, Jamaica (as mentioned in Chapter 4), social workers also tend to be more directive and prescriptive in response to cultural expectations that experts are there to solve problems. Thus the limits of self-determination are stretched, but not abandoned, in response to client expectations.

The widespread belief in fate in Hindu societies also affects self-determination. In Hindu philosophy, fate, or karma, explains that a person's status and misfortunes are ways through which they atone for misdeeds committed in a prior life (Ejaz, 1991). Clients may therefore accept their problems with resignation and apathy and be resistant to taking charge of their own futures, that is, being self-determining. Some Indian social workers report using fate as a positive force in encouraging clients to take action, however:

> Yes, karma can be used as a double-edged weapon. Either you fight it or succumb to it. I would empathize [with the client] and say—maybe—I'm here to help you and that's part of fate. Maybe you are suffering now but it's fated you are going to get cured. . . . Your good karma can save you. (quoted in Ejaz, 1991, p. 137)

Thus, again, the social worker is able to adapt the concept of self-determination in culturally acceptable ways.

Silavwe (1995) takes a stronger position, stating that the concept of self-determination is inappropriate in solving personal problems in Africa "because it assumes concepts of individuality which are not applicable in an

African culture or society" (p. 71). He explains African communalism as follows:

> African society is characterized by the prevalence of the idea of communalism or community. The individual recedes before the group. The whole of existence from birth to death is organically embodied in a series of associations, and life appears to have its full value only in these close ties. Individual initiative is discouraged. . . . Self-initiative or self-determination in resolving personal problems is collectively sanctioned by the community. (pp. 72–73)

Africans' emphasis on "groupness, sameness, and commonality" leads to values of "cooperation, interdependence and collective responsibility" (Cobbah, 1987, p. 320) rather than individual initiative and self-determination. Silavwe recommends that group determination replace self-determination as the dominant value in African social work.

Group determination is embodied in the principles of community development. The values of participation, local leadership, democratic decision making, and self-guidance are evident in the following definition:

> Community development . . . aims to educate and motivate people for self-help; to develop responsible local leadership; to inculcate among the members of rural communities a sense of citizenship and among the residents of urban areas a spirit of civic consciousness; to introduce and strengthen democracy at the grass-roots level through the creation and/or revitalization of institutions designed to serve as instruments of local participation; to initiate a self-generative, self-sustaining, and enduring process of growth; to enable people to establish and maintain cooperative and harmonious relationships; and to bring about gradual and self-chosen changes in the community's life with a minimum of stress and disruption. (Khinduka, 1975, p. 175)

In addition to participation in decision making, the community members themselves accomplish the selected projects through their own actions. The role of the social worker in community development is to assist, facilitate the "self-choosing" of goals, promote indigenous leadership, and work with the community to prevent leadership from being authoritarian. Therefore, this is group determination for addressing community problems and aspirations. Its applicability to the problems of individuals remains more unsettled.

The International Code of Ethics takes a moderate relativist stance on self-determination. The term is not used in the document. Two elements of the standards relative to clients, however, apply. One says: "Within the scope of the agency and the client's social milieu, the professional service shall assist clients to take responsibility for personal actions" (IFSW, 1994, Section 3.3.3). The next standard reads: "Help the client—individual, group, community or society—to achieve self-fulfillment and maximum potential within the limits of the respective rights of others" (IFSW, 1994, Section 3.3.4), a modest attempt to blend individual rights with communalist ideas. These

CASE 7.1: VALUES AND CULTURE CONFLICT— A CASE OF MISPLACED CONFIDENTIALITY

A young social worker returned to Zambia after completing his MSW in the United States and was assigned by his agency to take an adolescent boy back to his home village. The boy, a runaway, had committed several minor thefts and had been arrested by the police in Lusaka. As the social worker and the boy neared the end of the 10-hour drive into the rural area, they approached the village. The official car was spotted pulling into the village, and the village headman and several other elders came rushing toward the car. As the social worker slowed to a stop the headman cried out: "How's our boy? What has happened to our boy?"

The social worker answered quickly: "I cannot tell you. It's confidential. I must see his parents and discuss it with them." Looking up, he saw a look on the older man's face that was at once both stunned and bemused. The young social worker was suddenly overcome with a feeling of estrangement. How removed he felt from his culture; his remarks suddenly seemed foolish in the face of the older man's obvious concern. As the social worker relayed the story, that moment in the rural village marked the beginning of his journey to indigenize his practice and to adapt his recently gained professional knowledge and to search for ways to blend the principles of social work with the strengths of Zambian society.

(Personal story told to author, August 27, 1982, anonymous)

flow from the Statement of Principles that says, "Each individual has the right to self-fulfillment to the extent that it does not encroach upon the same right of others, and has an obligation to contribute to the well-being of society" (IFSW, 1994, Section 2.2.2). In putting the concept of the right to self-fulfillment within the context of the rights of others and well-being of society, the IFSW appears to give only moderate endorsement to self-determination, showing sensitivity to countries where others and society are emphasized.

Confidentiality. Silavwe also challenges the relevance of confidentiality. In traditional Africa, problems are resolved through open discussion, with involvement of extended families and village or tribal elders. The Western notion of confidentiality—that problems of individuals are secret and private matters to be protected, even from the circle of caring others—is harmful in this context. A social worker from Zambia related Case 7.1, an experience with confidentiality upon returning from his studies in the United States.

Case 7.1 does not indicate that confidentiality is a meaningless concept. Silavwe believes that clients must be protected from careless and ill-meaning use of their personal information. In different cultural contexts, however, confidentiality may have different limits. The rules of confidentiality are not meant to cut the client off from support and assistance. The headman's question—"How's our boy?"—signaled his right to information as part of the boy's circle of caring others, indeed, in Africa, as part of his "extended" family.

To learn from this example, U.S. child welfare social workers might want to think about ways to avoid the situations in which confidentiality sometimes "protects" a child's information to the detriment of the child. Potential care-giving relatives have sometimes been kept unaware of family crises and unnecessary foster placements have resulted. The cases in which this occurred are examples of values interpretation at the far end of the individualistically oriented continuum.

Some African social workers discuss traditional networks and methods of problem solving that require modification of confidentiality. Marriage problems, for example, may be discussed by the elders of the village in an open forum; Silavwe recommends that social workers endorse and utilize these methods, giving the example of a "social casework and remedial services committee" in Zambia in which personal cases are brought to a group where they are discussed by community members including elders, clergy, doctors, and social workers. Even research interviews may need to be conducted in the open, with village members watching, rather than in confidential settings (Silavwe, 1995). Not all agree. Jacques (1997) argues that some clients may not wish to have their problems resolved or even discussed by the village elders, who may be particularly ill-equipped to cope with the issues that bring people into counseling. Individuals struggling with modern issues in Africa, especially conflicts arising between changing roles of women and traditional expectations, such as cases of spouse abuse, and problems related to AIDS, may not find the advice of village elders adequate. Thus even within the same cultural context, different cases may require differential use of both confidentiality and self-determination principles.

The IFSW Code of Ethics is more directive about confidentiality, specifying that the social worker must "maintain the client's right to a relationship of trust, to privacy and confidentiality and to responsible use of information. . . . No information is released without the prior knowledge and informed consent of the client, except where the client cannot be responsible or others may be seriously jeopardized" (IFSW, 1994, Section 3.3.2).

Equality and Nondiscrimination. Social work codes of ethics contain strong statements of equality and nondiscrimination. The International Code and a number of national codes commit social workers to support equality and oppose discrimination on a variety of grounds, including gender, age, disability, color, social class, race, religion, language, political beliefs, or sexual orientation (IFSW, 1994, Section 2.2.6). The Indian Social Workers' Declaration of Ethics emphasizes the special responsibility of the profession to serve and advocate for oppressed classes, specifying that the profession is "committed to solidarity with the marginalised peoples" ("Declaration of Ethics," 1997, p. 336). It is clear from codes of ethics that social workers must practice equality of treatment and nondiscrimination in their work. In addition, a number of national codes require social workers to take steps to oppose discrimination and promote social justice and equity in the broader society.

These commitments bring the profession into conflict with operative values in many societies. Social workers in the European Union (EU) recognize the trends toward social exclusion, increasingly turning the EU into a fortress denying access to immigrants and socially and economically isolating the minority populations already within their borders. Still other policies may deny rights to cultural integrity. In Denmark, for example, policies aimed at promoting integration of refugees and immigrants into Danish society require dispersed settlement, "without regard to personal preferences about where to live" on the part of the immigrants themselves (Lane, 1998, p. 12). Lane found a surprising absence of concern with community participation, empowerment of immigrant groups, or of their self-determination in debates about work with immigrants. Multiculturalism and respect for diversity were relegated to secondary concerns, with the emphasis on helping people from other countries to become Danish (Lane, 1998). Issues of discrimination were often overlooked and had not been a focus of social work discussions.

Extending equality on the basis of sexual orientation puts social work at odds with their societies in a number of countries and has led to some divisions within the profession along religious lines. Reflecting majority views in many Caribbean nations, the director of the Caribbean Council for Europe blasted pressure on Caribbean countries to liberalize their laws on homosexuality as a form of human rights imperialism (Jessop, 1998). Religiously affiliated colleges in the United States pressured the Council on Social Work Education (CSWE) to modify the accreditation requirements of nondiscrimination against lesbians and gays. Yet the obligation of the individual social worker to practice nondiscrimination is clear. The Canadian Association of Social Workers' Code of Ethics specifically states that its requirements exceed those in legislation; thus social workers' professional responsibility for nondiscrimination on sexual orientation is greater than their legal responsibility. (Canadian Association of Social Workers, 1994).

Distributive Justice

Social work's role in distribution of scarce resources is related to the equity value commitment. All social workers are involved in distributive justice as they make decisions about who is to receive what services, material aid, or even professional time. For social service planners and administrators, distributive justice considerations are frequently at the heart of practice actions. Pursuing one program often means not pursuing others; allocating funds or staff resources in one area will mean that other options go underfunded or unstaffed; providing one client or one group of clients with more resources means fewer resources available for other claimants. Whether guided by con-

CASE 7.2: DISTRIBUTIVE JUSTICE—AIDS AWARENESS

An international development agency has funding available for an AIDS program in the target country. The possibilities are:

1. a media campaign to make high-school age youth aware of the dangers of AIDS and modes of transmission
2. an outreach education and intervention program for prostitutes and long-distance truck drivers who frequent prostitutes, the groups with the country's highest incidence of AIDS and HIV infection
3. a community residential program for persons suffering from AIDS, who are typically shunned by family and society and die homeless

scious or unconscious principles, social workers are involved with distributive justice as they make these decisions. There are a variety of approaches to distributive justice, that is, principles by which scare resources can be allocated: merit, productivity, equal distribution to all, utilitarian (benefitting the largest number), need, and Rawlsian principles, which allow inequality in distribution if the most disadvantaged people benefit (Congress, 1996). Imagine the set of program choices outlined in Case 7.2.

In making this decision, principles of distributive justice and equity will be considered. How will one choose between prevention and palliative care for those who are suffering acutely? Between reaching large numbers of youth, or reaching the groups at highest present risk? Between serving the "innocent" or groups such as prostitutes who are stigmatized by society? Considerations of merit, productivity, justice, benefit to the largest number, or benefit to the most disadvantaged will need to be weighed.

Practice decisions will be shaped by differing cultural views on acceptable principles of distribution. Whereas equal access is an accepted (although not always practiced) value in the United States, in India, taking care of one's own family is the first responsibility; therefore, assisting one's brother-in-law in getting a job is quite acceptable. Status considerations may also enter the equation. Deference to an applicant's high status may lead a social worker to give him or her a position at the top of the waiting list. Whatever the cultural context, awareness of the principles underlying distributive justice is important for social workers, especially those in administrative, policy, and planning roles.

VALUES AND ETHICS FOR INTERNATIONAL PROFESSIONAL ACTION

One dimension of preparing for practice in today's interdependent world is clearly that social workers need to address and wrestle with the universalism-cultural relativism issue. However, this alone is only a piece of international social work values. The various codes of ethics for social workers need improvement in order to serve as effective guides for international professional action.

As mentioned earlier in this text, the Joint Working Group on Development Education (1984) called for acceptance of global interdependence "as an irrefutable fact of life on which action must be based" (pp. 3–4). Accomplishing this requires a major shift in attitudes and values. This working group from InterAction, comprised of development professionals, identified the following as relevant values: concern for global justice and equity; respect for differing cultures, traditions, beliefs and expressed needs; sense of personal responsibility for promoting development; clarification of personal values related to world hunger and poverty; and acceptance of sharing and cooperation as the means to improved global security. These could readily be adopted as values for international social work.

A recent *Human Development Report* (UNDP, 1994) proposes another ethical principle relevant to social work: the universalism of life claims. This principle is defined as the belief that no child "should be doomed to a short life or a miserable one merely because that child happens to be born in the 'wrong class' or in the 'wrong country' or to be of the 'wrong sex'" (p. 13). Universalism of life claims globalizes the value of equity and nondiscrimination and could serve as a starting point for redefining social work values for international professional action. Most social work codes of ethics include principles of equity. The International Code of ethics, however, contains no mention of country of origin in its nondiscrimination principle that does include gender and social class, along with other characteristics. In the United States, the NASW (1996) Code of Ethics specifies that social workers should not practice or condone discrimination and, in addition, that they should "act to prevent and eliminate domination of, exploitation of, and discrimination against any person, group or class on the basis of race, ethnicity, *national origin*, color, sex, sexual orientation, age, marital status, political belief, religion, or mental or physical disability" (p. 27). Application of this clause, however, has been interpreted to mean that social workers should prevent discrimination against those persons already in the United States regardless of their national origin. The implications for social work practice and advocacy of an ethical obligation to eliminate discrimination on a global scale have not been explored, yet would be far-reaching. Adopting universalism of life claims as a social work value would require the profession to commit to improving the lives of children living in misery anywhere in the world and to consider the global implications of equity for its practice, knowledge development, and, especially, policy development and advocacy efforts. It is also clear that although adding such a statement to the International Code of Ethics would be a fairly easy task, the challenge would be to make it operational and define the policy, practice, and advocacy responsibilities for social workers in all countries that could emerge from this value commitment. Implications for distribution of resources, immigration and refugee policies, giving aid, trade, and more would be far-reaching.

The International, Canadian and U.S. codes do reflect a level of increased global awareness in their most recent editions. Under the section on responsibilities to the broader society, the U.S. code now says social workers "should promote the general welfare of society from local to global levels, and the development of people, their communities, and their environment" (NASW, 1996, p. 26). The Canadian code says "a social worker shall advocate change for the overall benefit of society, the environment and the global community" (CASW, 1994, p. 9). The International code contains two references to international responsibilities. The preamble contains a list of goals that social workers are dedicated to, including "development of resources to meet individual, group, national and international needs and aspirations" (IFSW, 1994, Section 3.1). And one of the general standards of ethical conduct is to "identify and interpret the basis and nature of individual, group, community, national and international social problems" (IFSW, 1994, 3.2.8). What is missing from all of these codes is interpretation of the implications of these rather ambiguous statements. However, they do provide a starting point by identifying world-mindedness as a social work value.

International value commitments also carry with them ethical obligations to be knowledgeable and skillful. In a paper on world hunger, Haru (1984) calls for adding the concept of effectiveness to practitioners' ethical obligations. Morally justified ineffective action on serious global problems, such as hunger, is not truly moral, she argues. This is reflected in the social work codes of ethics as the principle of professional competence. Adding universalism of life claims to social work ethics would require considerable work on new knowledge and skills for social workers around the world in order to ensure effectiveness.

CONCLUSION AND RECOMMENDATIONS

In concluding this discussion of values for international social work, we must return to the question of whether there are universal social work values. There is considerable agreement that some level of universality exists. Indeed, without fundamental value agreements, it is questionable whether international social work is a viable concept. Among the brave authors writing on the topic of universal social work values, Gray (1995) identifies the profession's altruistic mission of helping others and responding to human needs and the pursuit of social justice as universals. Taylor-Larsen (1996) agrees and adds "social work's radical respect for the clients themselves as being experts on their own life situations" (p. 2), although this moves into more controversial territory.

Moving away from the polar positions on the universalism-cultural relativism continuum, social workers can find comfort either in Donaldson's

(1996) moderately relativist position or Donnelly's (1984) moderately universalist one. According to the former, there are a set of core human values that must be respected "as an absolute moral threshold"; these should be mixed with "respect for local traditions and a belief that context matters when deciding what is right and what is wrong" (Donaldson, 1996, p. 52). Donnelly recommends a framework within which there would be a form of "weak relativism" that "would recognize a comprehensive set of prima facie universal human rights and allow only relatively rare and strictly limited local variations and exceptions" (Donnelly 1984, p. 401).

It does seem evident that social work must reject a purely relativist stance. Human right abuses cannot be condoned, and cultural change may be called for in some situations. The questions raised by Rao (1995) on participation and representation in cultural formation are important considerations for social workers in their assessment of culture-specific values. Answering these questions, however, is very difficult for a "cultural outsider."

Also clear is that the profession must move beyond ethical principles bound up in individualistic values. The cult of individualism, especially in its "rugged" and competitive forms, negates reciprocity, generosity in social relations, cooperation, and other-directedness as values. Needed are ethical codes that not only encourage cooperation and generosity but also respect fundamental and equitable human rights. To date, development of codes of ethics based on communalist values has lagged. The following statement from the CASW code is a beginning: "The social worker will consider the client as an individual, a member of a family unit, a member of a community, a person with a distinct ancestry or culture and will consider those factors in any decision affecting the client" (CASW, 1994, p. 4). Earlier in this chapter, statements from the IFSW code that suggest communalism were discussed. These need to be specified in more detail in order to offer alternatives that could be used to guide ethical decisions.

Identifying practice principles is somewhat easier. Silavwe's (1995) description of African communalism contains important implicit practice principles: "The whole of existence from birth to death is organically embodied in a series of associations, and life appears to have its full value only in these close ties" (pp. 72–73). This statement is instructive for practice in many cross-cultural cases. In work with a refugee woman from Cambodia or from Ethiopia at a battered women's program, the social worker should make a special effort to understand the woman's ties to her family, extended family, and community. Counseling, while still respecting her dignity and right not to be abused, should also involve the client in a search for ways to maintain her connectedness. Otherwise, the outcome of intervention may be to protect her from abuse but also to diminish the value of life itself through severing of crucial close ties.

Link (1999) identified four common principles that she believes apply to social work throughout the world: (1) Be responsible in professional actions; (2) act in a way that enhances peoples' lives [note here that 'enhance' will be differentially defined]; (3) focus on the process as well as the task; and (4) act with cultural understanding. Her more detailed set of universal ethical principles instruct the practitioner to focus on self-awareness of cultural bias and "geocentrism." Dialogue is crucial to ethical cross-cultural practice throughout the intervention and in evaluating both the process and outcome of the professional action (see Figure 7.1).

Finally, new values of world-mindedness and global social work competence must evolve to position the profession for assuming its responsibilities in the global era. In knowledge development, practice, and policy advocacy, nationalistic limits on value commitments must be removed. Concern for equity must extend beyond national boundaries, and this concern should be reflected in the ethical obligations of social workers wherever they practice.

Widest perspective for assessment

- Before acting, review personal value, history, and cultural bias; ask the question, "How am I influenced personally and professionally by this question or problem?"
- Review the value base, history, and culture of the other(s) concerned with the ethical question.
- Question geocentrism and the impact of the location of people involved; what would be different if this dialogue were happening elsewhere in the world and why?

Inclusion of the service user in dialogue and decisions

- Discuss the "right to reality" of the service user and their family or community; spend time defining this reality.
- Acknowledge the "power" of the professional.
- Attend to the use of clear language.
- Consider the question of "conscientization": To what extent is the immediate ethical tension reflective and part of wider societal and global issues?

Joint evaluation

- Was the outcome lasting in its resolution of the ethical questions in the workers', service users', and community view?
- Which actions by the workers worked best?
- Which actions by the service user(s) worked best?
- Did all members feel included and respected?
- What would be different in a future instance of this ethical decision?

Link, 1999, p. 90

Figure 7.1 Principles: Global Ethics

REFERENCES

Annan, K. (1997, October 20). Speech delivered to the Communications Conference, Aspen Institute, Aspen, Colorado. Available at www.unhchr.ch. Accessed November 11, 1998.

Canadian Association of Social Workers (CASW) (1994). *Social Work Code of Ethics*. Ottawa, Ontario: Author.

Cobbah, J.A.M. (1987). African values and the human rights debate: An African perspective, *Human Rights Quarterly, 9,* 309–331.

Congress, E.P. (1996). *Social work values and ethics: Identifying and resolving professional dilemmas*. Chicago: Nelson-Hall.

Declaration of ethics for professional social work. (1997). *The Indian Journal of Social Work, 58*(2), 335–341.

Donaldson, T. (1996). Values in tension: Ethics away from home, *Harvard Business Review, 74*(5), 48–62.

Donnelly, J. (1984). Cultural relativism and universal human rights. *Human Rights Quarterly, 6,* 400–419.

Ejaz, F.K. (1989). The nature of casework practice in India: A study of social workers' perceptions in Bombay. *International Social Work, 33,* 25–38.

Ejaz, F.K. (1991). Self-determination: Lessons to be learned from social work practice in India. *British Journal of Social Work, 21,* 127–142.

Gould, K.H. (1989). International perspective on women, development and peace. *Swords and Ploughshares* [Bulletin of the program in Arms Control, Disarmament and International Security], *III* (4) 11–13. Available from the University of Illinois at Urbana-Champaign.

Gray, M. (1995). The ethical implications of current theoretical developments in social work. *British Journal of Social Work, 25,* 55–70.

Haru, T. (1984). Moral obligation and the conceptions of world hunger: On the need to justify correct action. *Journal of Applied Behavioral Science, 20*(4), 363–382.

International Federation of Social Workers (1994). *International Code of Ethics for the Professional Social Worker*. Oslo, Norway: Author.

Jacques, G. (1997, July). *The baby and the bathwater: The dilemma of modern social work in Africa*. Paper presented at the Third Conference of Caribbean and International Social Work Educators, Port of Spain, Trinidad.

Jessop, D. (1998, February 1). Caribbean norms vs. European ethics. *The Sunday Observer* [Jamaica], p. 13.

Joint Working Group on Development Education (1984). *A framework for development education in the United States*. Westport, CT: Save the Children [for InterAction].

Khinduka, S. (1975). Community development: Potentials and limitations. In R.M. Kramer & H. Specht (Eds.), *Readings in community organization practice* (2nd ed., pp. 175–183). Englewood Cliffs, NJ: Prentice-Hall.

Lane, T.S. (1998, March). *Social work values and ethics from an international perspective*. Paper presented at the Annual Program Meeting, Council on Social Work Education, Orlando, Florida.

Link, R. (1999). Infusing global perspectives into social work values and ethics. In C.S. Ramanathan & R.J. Link (Eds.), *All our futures: Principles and resources for social work practice in a global era* (pp. 69–93). Belmont, CA: Brooks Cole/Wadsworth.

Loewenberg, F.M., Dolgoff, R., & Harrington, D. (2000). *Ethical decisions for social work practice*. Sixth Edition, Itasca, IL: Peacock.

Mayer, A.E. (1995). Cultural particularism as a bar to women's rights: Reflections on the Middle Eastern experience. In J. Peters & A. Wolper (Eds.), *Women's rights, human rights: International feminist perspectives* (pp. 176–188). New York: Routledge.

National Association of Social Workers, (1996) *Code of ethics.* Washington, DC: Author.

Rao, A. (1995). The politics of gender and culture in international human rights discourse. In J. Peters and A. Wolper (Eds.), *Women's rights, human rights: International feminist perspectives* (p. 167–175). New York: Routledge.

Silavwe, G.W. (1995). The need for a new social work perspective in an African setting: The case of social casework in Zambia. *British Journal of Social Work, 25,* 71–84.

Taylor-Larsen, Z. (1996, July). *International social work: Is there a body of values, theories and methods in social work education which is culturally transferable?* Paper presented at the Congress of the International Association of Schools of Social Work, Hong Kong.

UNICEF (1997). *The progress of nations 1997* New York: Author.

United Nations (1979). *Convention on the elimination of all forms of discrimination against women.* Full text available at www.unhchr.ch.

United Nations Development Program. (1999). *Human development report 1999* New York: Oxford University Press.

United Nations Development Program. (1994). *Human development report, 1994.* New York: Oxford University Press.

CHAPTER 8

INTERNATIONAL RELIEF AND DEVELOPMENT PRACTICE

Lara Herscovitch, MSW

Director of Programs, Greater Bridgeport Area Foundation;
Education Specialist, Save the Children/USA

In the world of international relief and development, NGOs apply skills and knowledge that are partly drawn from, and are relevant to, the field of social work, yet these organizations do not necessarily consider themselves social work or social welfare institutions. Similarly, as discussed earlier in this book, the social work field in industrialized countries has not traditionally targeted the international domain as central to its mission. However, there is significant crossover between the two, in terms of both principles and implementation methodologies. The goal of this chapter is to help readers bridge that gap between international and traditional domestic social work practice. The following topics will be addressed:

- the specific context and content of international relief and development work

- role that social workers play in international relief and development practice

- key lessons learned from international relief and development practice and the ways these lessons can be applied to social work practice in industrialized countries

THE CONTEXT AND CONTENT OF INTERNATIONAL RELIEF AND DEVELOPMENT PRACTICE

Traditionally, international NGOs focused on either relief or development. Historically, the relief domain is social assistance work that is conducted under emergency circumstances—in a war environment or in response to a natural disaster, such as famine, an epidemic, or an earthquake. Generally, relief work involves a rapid response to basic human needs: shelter, food, water, safety, and family reunification. Relief interventions emphasize immediate responses to immediate needs, and practitioners struggle with the questions about how to serve populations in emergencies without creating a "hand-out," or dependency, dynamic. This is particularly the case in long-term refugee camp situations in which need for relief is protracted.

Development work, on the other hand, has traditionally been looked at as that which is carried out under normal (i.e., nonemergency) circumstances. Applications of development work include such areas as:

- the environment: wildlife, ecology, agriculture, pollution/industrialization, desertification
- human development: education and early childhood development, health, population
- economic development: agriculture, microbusiness development, group loan programs
- democracy building: citizenship, local governance/decentralization
- infrastructure: water systems, wastewater disposal, irrigation systems.

It is important to note that although a program can focus on a single theme, most focus on more than one in order to respond to real-life situations in communities in which needs are multiple and linked. Furthermore, many development approaches in the past successfully targeted medical interventions and are moving beyond the minimal goals of the Health for All campaign, which aimed at basic health services and communicable disease control. As stated by Ennew and Milne (1990) "If the future is to be viable, today's adults must meet the challenge not only of ensuring their [children's] physical survival but also of preventing that survival being a mockery of human dignity because of exploitation, poverty and violence" (p. 8).

The modern "relief vs. development" landscape has changed. Much of the dialogue among international practitioners is now around the "relief to development *continuum*." There is an increasing understanding of the issues that connect relief and development work and how one can pave the way to the other. For example, poorly planned agricultural practices—typical development work—can cause soil erosion or deforestation, which can cause severe landslides during a heavy rainy season or hurricane thus leading to the need for relief work. Similarly, well-executed relief work, conducted through and in full cooperation with community groups, rather than simply handing out goods, can pave the way to solid development work during nonemergency times by building local capacity to identify and create solutions for local problems. The example of relief after Hurricane Gilbert in Chapter 4 demonstrated this principle. Other areas of clear overlap include land mine education and removal of land mines, activities that can be conducted in times of political peace but clearly are connected to war situations—traditionally considered to be the clear territory of relief workers.

International relief and development practice aims to facilitate change on a number of levels—behavioral, cultural, institutional, or political. To achieve these goals, development practitioners employ a range of strategies.

Practitioners work at different times with individuals, communities, institutions/organizations, and policy makers in order to leverage change (Midgley, 1995). While some organizations focus more on direct community-based work and others more on policy-level work, most work on a number of different levels simultaneously, and expatriate social workers are expected to

IS INTERNATIONAL RELIEF/DEVELOPMENT SOCIAL WORK?

Yes

The process of international development was originally conceived of as largely economic and physical and emphasized large-scale infrastructure projects. Since the 1960s, there has been increasing emphasis on the need to build human capacity as a proactive strategy in facilitating large-scale change (Levinger, 1996). The "social" or human dimension of development has links to social work, which has from its founding emphasized the centrality of positive change on individual and family levels and the importance of holistic approaches. An example of this is the move in development away from a narrow health focus in child survival programming to holistic early childhood development programs that benefit the 12 out of 13 children who do survive (Myers, 1992).

A survey of development agencies found a high degree of fit between social work qualifications and the skills and knowledge sought by the agencies (Healy, 1987). The planning, management, training, and community organization skills often taught in macropractice curricula are highly valued in development work along with interpersonal competence and cultural sensitivity. The success of earlier social workers, from Eglantyne Jebb to the workers in UNRRA, suggest that relief and development work are social work.

No

Social work is a "caring" profession that is responsive to human suffering but in a reactive and palliative manner not consistent with the aims of development. The development community perceives social work as preoccupied with individual treatment and ill-prepared or disinterested in addressing problems of mass poverty. The profession usually focuses its attention on those who are the most marginalized—addicts, the mentally ill, offenders, teen mothers—much like Mother Theresa's work in India; although the intentions of social work are good, they have little impact on mainstream social development. Thus a survey of development agencies conducted in 1981 found that "none of the agencies . . . felt they had any particular need for social workers" (National Association of Social Workers, 1981). Although the respondents may have based their opinions on misconceptions, social work has a lot of work to do before it can define its work as international development.

be able to interact on most levels. The major strategies for international development are:

- *Direct implementation*, also known as a bottom-up or grassroots approach, involves designing and directly delivering community-based programs and services.
- *Community mobilization* stimulates communities to organize, plan, carry out, evaluate, and sustain actions to address the problems that they identify.
- *Partnering and institutional development* are becoming more common in international work (see "Social Work Roles in International Relief and Development" for further details) and involve collaborating with other organizations in pursuit of common goals as well as assisting other organizations in the development of skills that will enable them to better plan, carry out, and sustain their programs.
- *Policy and advocacy* focus on working with governments and donors in order to influence policies and practices to impact more positively on the client(s).

SOCIAL WORK ROLES IN INTERNATIONAL RELIEF AND DEVELOPMENT

Although some may still debate the relevance of the profession in international work, in fact social workers hold many and diverse roles within international NGOs. These include program implementation, casework, program development/technical specialist, program management, program monitoring and evaluation and research, training/training of trainers , organizational development/network building, and advocacy/policy making. Central to each role is the focus on building the capacity of the client—whether an individual, family, community, government, organization, or network. In addition, although many of these roles are distinctive, in many cases there is functional overlap. This is particularly true in the advocacy arena; all social workers serve as advocates on many levels—with families, local leaders, community groups, NGOs, and government officials at local, regional, and/or national levels. There are similarly overlapping responsibilities in the other areas. For example, in many cases a fieldworker will be responsible for collecting data to be used for monitoring and evaluation (M&E) purposes, a program manager may implement or facilitate a field training event, and a technical advisor or specialist may help manage a field program. Because social work is rooted in the *holistic,* or *ecological model,* of human development (Germain & Gitterman, 1996), practice seeks to influence decision making and practice in many arenas. Each particular role is described below.

Program Implementation: Community-Level Work

Staff members who are responsible for program implementation on the community level are based *in the field* (i.e., overseas) and work directly with program participants. They may work on a number of levels, depending on the objectives of the program. Typical tasks of a program implementer are organizing after-school activities, teaching literacy classes, building the capacity of a women's microbusiness group, organizing communities around women's rights, forming school management committees, educating youth about reproductive health and HIV/AIDS, or building potable water systems. Usually these positions are held by individuals who are nationals of the country in which the program is located, because they are the ones who understand local culture, language, values, and so on. Sometimes a successful implementer can be an expatriate as well, as in the case of the U.S. Peace Corps' animators, or community organizers.

Educational training of implementers may focus on a number of different areas but normally includes learning about social services or one particular social sector or technical area. It is important to note that educational opportunities can be limited for nationals, either for access or economic reasons, and thus experiential learning is often a meaningful substitute or complement. The role of the community implementer can overlap with that of *institutional development*, in which the focus is on building the capacity of local or national organizations to do their work more effectively. Organizational development is described below.

Casework

The casework function is a subset of the community-level program implementation role, and associated tasks can be viewed on a continuum. Caseworkers respond, as appropriate, to clients' needs for short-term psychological "first aid," long-term therapy or rehabilitation, or psychiatric interventions for individuals suffering from clinically diagnosed post-traumatic stress disorder (Garbarino, Kostelny, & Dubrow, 1991). The role of the caseworker tends to be more prevalent in relief work or in urban programs, for example, dealing with street children. This role is only carried out effectively by those caseworkers or clinicians who have a deep understanding of local and cultural issues—and thus can empathize with needs vis-à-vis the unique ways in which a given population normally copes and "heals." Expatriate clinicians, therefore, need to be fully bilingual and bicultural. In some cases, instead of providing direct service, it is more appropriate for an expatriate caseworker to support national staff in their own delivery of casework/therapy. It is important to note that, especially in emergency and war situations, program *staff* also need psychological support to effectively cope with their roles as helping agents. Educational training for a caseworker often includes groupwork as well as individual casework and may include an area of specialization that targets a particular population. Case 8.1 describes a casework project.

Success of the project was aided by a number of factors, including the social worker's language competence, her openness to receiving new information and redefining the scope of the project, and her embrace of mutuality in the training process. Thus mental health services to Cambodian refugees were improved in both the Thailand camp and a social service agency in Connecticut where the social worker was employed.

CASE 8.1: IMPROVING CASEWORK
THROUGH NATURAL HELPERS IN A REFUGEE CAMP
Vichhyka Ngy, MSW, Director, Asian Family Services

A social worker, herself a Cambodian refugee, received a small grant to improve mental health service in Site II, a large refugee camp in Thailand. The social worker did not intend to do counseling herself, as seeking counseling for personal problems from a professional is unknown and culturally inappropriate to most Cambodians. Therefore, the initial goal of the project was to improve casework services by training Buddhist monks on mental health assessment and referral, assuming that they were a main source of help to camp residents. During the study phase of the project, the social worker discovered in her interviews of Buddhist monks that women in the camps were more likely to go to Buddhist nuns for help with personal and relationship crises and that the nuns had longer relationships with people in need. Cultural taboos prevented the refugees, especially women, from discussing sexuality or relationship problems with the monks. The monks' role was primarily to perform rituals to deal with the spirits causing the illness or depression. Support and "counseling" were done by the nuns.

The second phase of the project, the training of natural helpers, therefore shifted to a different target group—the Buddhist nuns. The social worker reported that the training was actually mutual training. She provided the nuns with knowledge on the causes and symptoms of depression, on mind/body links, on assessment techniques, and on when and how to refer (after discovering that there were few links between the temples and the formal mental health service in the camp). The nuns taught her meditation techniques and their role in alleviating stress and Buddhist concepts of health and illness. She was able to apply these in her work in the United States with Cambodian refugees, especially older and more traditionally religious refugees.

Program Development/Technical Specialist

The role of program development or technical specialist is focused on the programmatic *content* of projects as contrasted with administration or management, to be discussed next. It can be based in the field where actual program implementation is taking place or in a headquarters office. Program development focuses on strategizing and designing program approaches either in a single sector, such as education or health, or in multiple sectors that are integrated in their implementation, such as in a project for life skills development for youth. Specific tasks associated with program development include conducting needs assessments and designing projects, developing and writing program or project proposals, representing the program in technical fora and with donors, providing technical assistance and guidance, documenting program progress, and designing and writing technical publications. The educational training for a technical specialist normally includes an advanced degree in a particular program area, complemented by in-depth experience implementing or managing programs in the same sector. Case 8.2, while lengthy, illustrates both the tasks of a program developer and the content of the work.

Program Management

The role of the program manager is more administrative in function than that of program development/technical specialist. This role can also be field-based or headquarters-based, but tends to be field-based in order to effectively oversee day-to-day operations. Specific tasks associated with program management include representation of the program with partner agencies and donors; oversight of program budget and personnel; oversight of implementation, including monitoring and evaluation, as well as oversight of technical assistance provided to the program; and assistance with fund-raising, including large-scale proposal development. One challenge for program managers is how to balance decentralized, participatory decision making and management with the need for quick decision making and efficiency (Latting & Gummer, 1994). Educational training of program managers often concentrates on general macro functions such as administration, financial management, program planning and monitoring, and staff supervision.

The social worker who is employed overseas as a program manager will have a broad range of responsibilities and the opportunity to exercise a variety of skills encompassing administrative, program, and community functions. The next case, 8.3, was written by a social worker deployed as a program manager in the Sudan, implementing food security programs for war- and drought-affected people; he had overall responsibility for all aspects of program support. He describes his role and experiences in a typical day.

As the case demonstrates, the role of program manager requires multiple skills in planning, negotiation, and fiscal and personnel management; the setting in isolated rural Sudan required additional adaptation and cross-cultural learning.

Program Monitoring and Evaluation (M&E) and Research

The program evaluator may be employed by the agency for which the evaluation is being conducted or may work for a research-focused organization that is contracted externally to conduct the work. Program evaluations are often conducted by outside/external evaluators because those individuals do not have a stake in whether the evaluation results are positive or negative and thus are viewed to be more objective; therefore, the evaluation is viewed to be more credible. Normally, staff working on direct implementation of programs collect data on a day-to-day basis, with guidance from an evaluator or technical specialist. The M&E data may be fed into an impact

CASE 8.2: DEVELOPING A PROGRAM
FOR REGIONAL APPLICATION IN AFRICA
(Case contributed by Amilia Russo de Sa,
Communication Officer, UNICEF/Mozambique)

The Sara Communication Initiative (SCI) is being developed by UNICEF for application in 15 countries located in the eastern and southern regions of Africa. Ms. Russo de Sa, communication officer for UNICEF/Mozambique, is the point person for developing the Sara program. SCI is being developed in response to assessments of the situations of female children in several countries of the region, which indicated common problems of sexual harassment and abuse as well as inequity in access to education. SCI is a multimedia project with animated film as its core. Complementing the program's animated videos, each episode has one accompanying comic book and a poster to reinforce the positive messages for children and their families. Animation was chosen as a medium because it can illustrate difficult issues in a less threatening way than real-life film.

Sara, the heroine of all the stories, is a 14-year-old schoolgirl living in a peri-urban environment. Her skills include communication, negotiation, critical thinking, and decision making, but she expresses a wide range of human emotions and is resilient in the face of challenge. Sara's stories provoke debate among peers and parents, teachers, and community leaders about the status and rights of adolescent girls in modern African society. Employing the 90% entertainment 10% education formula, SCI promotes the protection, status, and self-esteem of girls in the countries of the eastern and southern regions of Africa. To date the following four episodes have been produced:

- Episode 1: "The Special Gift"—on importance of girls' education

- Episode 2: "Sara Saves Her Friend"—on sexual harassment

- Episode 3: "The Daughter of a Lioness"—female genital mutilation

- Episode 4: "The Trap"—on "sugar daddies"

Additional episodes, focused on child labor and HIV/AIDS orphans will be produced. *A Manual for Life Skills Education*, using Sara characters, was produced and tested. It is a resource book designed to be used independently of the comic books but serves an important function in elaborating on the themes and issues raised in core episodes.

As the point person for the development of the Sara project, de Sa is coordinating implementation, including:

- advocating for and promoting the initiative with donors within UNICEF and with partner agencies, including potential implementing agencies *(continued)*

- providing technical and financial support to partners (mainly NGOs and schools), including conducting or coordinating research around adolescence and associated problem areas on which to base new local stories

- providing comprehensive training to partners on the use of the program materials and to writers for the production of local Sara stories

- ensuring the production of the core materials in Portuguese (they were also produced in French, English, and Swahili), and ensuring the local production and dissemination of the 13-part radio series, with the support of BBC and Radio Mozambique (the radio series was produced in Portuguese as well as three other local languages by local radio stations with UNICEF support)

A key challenge in developing this kind of regional project is that the core materials cannot address all the critical issues for girls in every country. At the regional level compromises need to be made in order to produce stories that have the same level of interest and acceptance in each individual country. In order to address this challenge, locally produced materials are developed, focusing mostly on issues of adolescent sexuality. In addition, research is conducted to determine which issues are most appropriate and of most interest and concern for country-specific (and in some cases locality-specific) young audiences. After the themes have been identified, UNICEF works with writers and illustrators for the production of appropriate materials.

The overall goals of the Sara initiative are first to provoke discussions about challenging issues relating to girls and second to spark changes in behavior around those issues. In an isolated district within Zambezia Province (the highly populated center of Mozambique, with approximately 4 million people), UNICEF staff attended a meeting with members of Community-Schools Linkages Committees, National and Provincial Ministry of Education staff, community mobilizers from the National Institute of Social Communication, and numerous community members. Over the course of two nights, UNICEF projected the Sara video on a large screen for the audience, which numbered in the hundreds. This showing represented the first time in 10 years that many audience members had seen a film, and for most it was the first time they had ever seen an animated film. During the fourth showing, one teacher began interacting with other audience members and through questions and answers made the story clear to the other viewers. After the viewing, UNICEF staff noted that male community members were openly discussing their opinions and regrets about why their girls did not attend school (many were blaming themselves). Current statistics show that the level of girls' schooling in this district has increased. Although evaluations cannot prove whether this change is due solely to the Sara project, most involved believe it played a stimulating role.

CASE 8.3: A DAY IN THE LIFE OF A PROGRAM MANAGER
David Bourns, MSW, Save the Children

The Sudan has been torn by civil war for several decades, with the current phase beginning in the mid-1980s. Many people who rely on traditional subsistence farming and herding for their livelihood have been displaced or have been subject to frequent attacks by roving military squads. Food stocks and essential household items have been stolen and destroyed, and traditional planting areas have become inaccessible due to insecurity. Working in this environment requires not only sound program design but also detailed attention to a reliable program support infrastructure, including human, mechanical, and administrative, and to security precautions for staff working in the field. Save the Children sponsored a food program, comprised of seed distribution, tools, relief food, and food for work. I was hired to provide overseas on-site management of the project.

A typical day might be as follows: I awaken around dawn to join program staff in visiting several target communities within a few hours drive of the office (over rough or nonexistent roads). The visits will entail observing project implementation and meeting community members to discuss their thoughts and concerns. Such dialogue might take place only with community leaders or might involve a larger group discussion with many residents. Site visits also provide the opportunity to meet with staff members who are based in the field to discuss pending issues related to implementation. In this predominantly Muslim area, the visits are scheduled so as not to conflict with the regular prayers that take place five times a day. Occasionally we may be invited to a breakfast, traditionally at 10:00 AM, that may include roasted camel meat or boiled camel liver.

On return to the office, a meeting is held with available program staff to discuss the morning's observations and plan follow-up, and to review the status of monitoring and evaluation activities. New program opportunities will also be identified and tasks assigned for data collection and proposal development. It will eventually fall on the program manager to refine and finalize the new proposal, based on discussions with beneficiaries, government counterparts, and staff, for submission to donors. The program manager will participate in meetings with existing and potential donors throughout the year in order to report on existing projects, to strengthen the case for additional funding, and to pave the way for new proposals.

Once the program meeting has ended, it is time to review and approve administrative documents related to such things as supplies procurement, vehicle repair and maintenance, personnel issues such as evaluation and recruitment, and local legal issues. Some matters will require further discussion with the administrative staff, the review of in-

(*continued*)

ternal procedures and guidelines, and occasionally the physical monitoring of routine procedures. Vehicles, which take a hard beating in an environment of poor roads and ever-present sand, require particular and constant attention to ensure that they are properly maintained, that parts are procured efficiently, and repairs completed at the lowest possible cost. Time is then required to complete additional paperwork such as the editing of regular project reports written by field staff for donors, the preparation of internal reports to be submitted to the field office director and other senior staff, and correspondence to/from partners and counterparts.

Next, I have scheduled an afternoon meeting with the manager of a program suboffice who is visiting for several days. This manager runs a program office located in a particularly insecure and politically sensitive area, and there are always a number of important issues to review. In this case I am especially concerned with reports that staff from this office are ignoring security guidelines and beginning the day-long drive to this office too late in the day and traveling through insecure areas after dark. For emphasis, I remind him of the two staff from this office that were killed in an ambush 2 years previously and of the vehicle we now have parked in the compound that is full of bullet holes from an attack a number of months ago. In the latter instance, amazingly, no one was injured. The office manager is a dedicated and hardworking staff person whose enthusiasm is the cause of this problem. Although all staff are strongly committed to our mission, we have no wish to compromise their safety while implementing programs. We take this opportunity to review with the senior administrative officer all security guidelines and make sure that preparations for an upcoming visit of USAID personnel, including a visit to a suboffice, are on schedule.

Near the end of the day a meeting is held with the staff finance officer to review monthly budget reports, which must be submitted to headquarters, and to monitor project spending against grant line items. Because there are several grants and other funding sources that make up the entire office budget, monitoring is essential to ensure that costs are being allocated properly and that project spending requirements are being met. Findings from the recent internal audit of the field office conducted by headquarters have just been received and also require written responses. Funding is very difficult to find in northern Sudan, and it is especially important to maintain meticulous financial records and monitor funds closely.

As the office closes for the day, the administrative officer reminds me that government visitors are expected that evening in time for dinner and will be spending the evening in the agency's guest house. (I try to ignore the chicken clucking in the compound that I know will be the evening's meal.) Over dinner I respond to their questions and comments about pro-

(continued)

grams and government regulations, and we plan a joint site visit for the following week. They invite me, and other senior staff, to attend a local football match the following week as their guests (only after we arrived, following a long drive, did they add that they would like us to participate in half-time activities, which revealed to the entire town my complete lack of athletic prowess).

evaluation, but normally individuals assessing program impact will collect data independently as well. Specific tasks can include setting up baseline surveys and training field staff in data collection; analyzing data collected; holding focus groups with program participants and/or program staff; writing evaluation reports for NGOs, governments, or donors. Program evaluation and research have gained much attention in recent years because implementing organizations have realized that while they *want* to focus on "program learning," often there are insufficient resources to support it. As a result, individuals conducting program research are supported, in many cases, by specific grants that are associated with a university. These research studies may use a number of different methods and may occur over different lengths of time; they may include cross-sectional or longitudinal studies, quantitative or qualitative studies, and various methods including sampling, experimental or single-subject designs, or surveys, among others (Rossi & Freeman, 1993; Rubin & Babbie, 1993). The following case tells of an "in-house" effort and the difficulties of obtaining an objective evaluation.

One way to reduce this kind of disruption to a program is to plan a visit on a day when group activities are already taking place. For example, the same social worker mentioned in Case 8.4 visited a Mozambican land mine

CASE 8.4: EVALUATING CHALLENGE— "A TYPICAL PROGRAM DAY?"

Getting a true sense of the quality of a program can be challenging for a technical specialist who is based in a headquarters office. One such social worker/technical specialist in education was visiting a number of El Salvador schools with colleagues in order to monitor the implementation of a new primary education program. Generally, these visits unfold as follows: (a) before a guest's arrival at a program site, she or he is perceived as important and in a position of authority, with some control over the fate of the program, especially its funding; (b) the visit is announced in advance and is planned in detail, including songs, gifts, food, and a formal presentation; (c) the program participants (in this case, school administrators, students, teachers, and parents) stop the implementation of the program to tend to (b); and (d) the visitors are supposed to evaluate how the program looks on a "typical day."

awareness program on a day when a community theater event was also taking place. The skit performed was intended to raise awareness of community members about the dangers of land mines, as well as educate them
about how to spot a land mine and what action steps can be taken after one
is spotted. The visitors, in this case, were audience members along with community members; program implementation was not compromised due to
the external visit. Another suggestion is for visitors to encourage program
activities to continue, to show interest in "regular," day-to-day activities,
and, of course, to view them as unobtrusively as possible.

Training/Training of Trainers (TOT)

The trainer's role involves building the capacity of other individuals in order that they conduct their work more effectively. The trainer sometimes targets those individuals who are providing direct service, other times those
who are managing or developing programs, and in some cases those who
are responsible for training activities. This latter category is called training
of trainers (TOT). The trainer is responsible for facilitating active learning as
well as modeling effective training techniques. For example, during a training for youth workers around reproductive health activities, the trainer not
only is teaching the content about reproductive health practice but also is
modeling the training techniques that she or he hopes the youth will learn
as a result of participating. Some of this training content includes designing
and planning training that responds to the needs of multiple stakeholders;
group dynamics and learning; stimulating discussion; team building; use of
role-playing and small groups; feedback and evaluation, including self-as-
sessment; awareness of adult nonformal education theory and techniques to
support it (e.g., traditional banking-style education—where learners are seen
as passive and empty of knowledge and teachers are seen as the holders of
all relevant information who thus "deposit" the knowledge into learners—
versus more progressive problem-posing education—where learning takes
place as a result of active participation and dialogue by teachers and learners alike). TOT workshops focus on teaching individuals training techniques
that can in turn be applied to any sector area (Silberman & Lawson, 1995;
Vella, 1989).

Organizational Development/Network Building

The role of organizational development/network building is becoming more
common although it often is linked to other social worker roles, particularly
training. The role of an individual working in organizational development
usually focuses on two levels. The first level is working to build the capacity of one client organization: organizing, building, and supporting the development of organizational vision and developing positive organizational
values and culture, work processes, and organizational learning. The second
level is to build the capacity of local organizations to allow them to more ef-

fectively conduct their direct implementation. Most organizations working internationally are moving toward institutional/organizational development in order to increase the scale of their work, as will be discussed later in the chapter.

When focusing on network building, an individual seeks to link, connect, and facilitate interorganizational collaboration. Network building is becoming a more popular organizational practice due to an increased recognition that organizations can complement each other's work as well as increased pressure from donor agencies to work cooperatively. There remains considerable tension around collaboration though, because funding environments are very competitive and organizations struggle with whether to invest limited resources in developing coalitions or to focus on their own organization solely (Rosenthal, Mizrahi, & Sampson, 1994). For this reason, networks are a popular trend. As part of a network, organizations can jointly plan and advocate, but they do not have to outwardly compete for limited resources. In addition, networks help build the understanding and trust that is helpful for further joint work. The education of those working on organizational development/network building usually focuses on macropractice, including administration, management, policy/planning, or specifically, in organizational development.

Advocacy/Policy Making

The advocacy/policy-making role seeks to leverage change on a macro level and can be viewed as three somewhat different subroles. The *lobbyist* works to influence congressional actions and/or voting behavior of legislators. More often social workers play the role of the *advocate*, working for an organization that seeks to leverage its field practice into larger scale change by demonstrating to other organizations, donors, and governments which types of approaches are most effective and thereby influencing them on what types of activities they should fund or otherwise support. The third role, the *policy maker*, can be broadly defined. Policy makers may lead NGOs but more often hold roles within globally influential institutions, such as the World Bank, a UN agency, or a bilateral donor organization.

Cross-Cutting Practice Skills

In any social work position—in any country—there are skills that are central to the successful execution of the above-described roles. Social workers will be engaged in a number of different tasks with clients—whether individuals, organizations, communities, or nations. These tasks typically include engagement; assessment(s); selection/design of intervention(s), including the formulation of goals and objectives; implementation; M&E; and termination and follow-up. There may be some instances in which one task is completed before the next; however, often the process is not linear. Thus social workers engaged in relief or development work may be focusing on

BOX 8.5: POLICY AND ADVOCACY
FOR REFUGEES AND CRISIS SITUATIONS
Dr. Neil Boothby, Senior Coordinator for Refugee Children,
UN High Commission for Refugees

As UNHCR's senior coordinator for refugee children, I am responsible for developing policy, program priorities, and strategic initiatives for refugees worldwide. In this context, I work closely with governments, NGOs, and other UN agencies to ensure the rights and needs of refugee children and adolescents are prioritized in all phases of UNHCR's operations. Central to successfully reaching the organization's goals are analytical, interpersonal, and negotiation skills. A policy maker needs to be able to understand complex situations quickly and make decisions about what strategies will be most effective, based on lessons learned from past interventions. I was actively involved in developing UNHCR policy on how to effectively intervene and to coordinate NGO activities in response to the Kosovo refugee crisis.

In my work on the Kosovo situation, I was able to draw on my past policy experience with numerous UNHCR initiatives. These include (a) the establishment of rights-based, child-adolescent-specific performance objectives for emergency, postemergency, and reintegration phases of emergencies; (b) the Liberian Children's Initiative, which placed a major emphasis on reintegration education and access to health services for all returnee children; (c) the ARC—Action for the Rights of the Child—training and capacity building initiative, undertaken in partnership with the International Save the Children Alliance; and (d) the establishment of a $US5 million trust fund to strategically reorient UNHCR programming and protection activities to better address at-risk refugee children. Each of the initiatives required a systematic involvement of stakeholders from UNHCR and beyond, requiring the need to strike the difficult balance between participatory planning and quick decision making in order to move large-scale projects forward. As a specialist in crisis, the policy work has taken me to many places where children have been affected by armed conflict, including Mozambique, Sierra Leone, and Liberia to address the problem of child soldiers and to Bosnia, Uganda, and Rwanda to develop programs for children who were separated from their families as a result of ethnic violence.

one or more of these practices at any given point. As an illustration of the cycle, a social worker may:

- engage a certain population (e.g., impoverished families living in rural West Africa)
- assess what "problem(s)" to target (e.g., girls do not attend or drop out of primary school)

- select and/or design the intervention to be applied, including the formulation of goals and objectives, in relation to local conditions, constraints, and resources (e.g., in partnership with local community members, the creation and sustaining of safe, relevant, high-quality primary schooling opportunities for girls)
- implement the intervention
- monitor and evaluate the effectiveness and quality of the school(s) (e.g., collect data on a day-to-day basis and periodically evaluate program quality)
- terminate the intervention and provide follow-up support as needed (e.g., phase out external support to the schools and support local school management committees to take on more intensive roles; set up systems within the Ministry of Education to continue to support teacher training and local community management) (adapted from Kettner, Moroney, & Martin, 1990; Meyer & Mattaini, 1995; University of Connecticut School of Social Work, 1998)

The skills needed to successfully build the capacity of a client, whether that client is an individual, a community, or an organization, include strong interpersonal and communication skills (including language capability where applicable) and critical thinking and analysis, presentation, organizational, writing, decision making, and collaboration/teamwork skills; knowledge of human behavior and cross-cultural knowledge that allows the worker to adapt their general principles of human behavior to local culture(s) are also necessary. Social work training provides a solid foundation in human be-

CASE 8.6: MEETING THE COMMUNITY

Social workers who are not from the communities where they are working need to be aware of how they may be perceived. One social worker, engaged with a rural Haitian community, was staying in an NGO guest house. During her free time, she left the grounds (which were completely surrounded by a tall fence and gated door) to sit and read in a gazebo-type structure in the community's central area. Although she was eager to interact with community members, she was approached very cautiously at first, usually by children. Over time, she built relationships with parents and children alike. She discovered that most expatriates never left the guest house grounds except to go to work—usually in an expensive four-wheel-drive vehicle. Thus the community members had not experienced an expatriate who spent time sitting and getting to know them on their terms. Although cautious, the community members were happily surprised when the social worker made attempts to interact with them. The informal conversations turned into a giving and receiving of informal Kreyol/English language lessons, and lasting friendships were built.

havior and interactions, but it is important to recognize that workers need to bring humility and openness to all interactions, particularly with individuals from different cultures, as Case 8.6 illustrates.

This is just one result of social work training that instructs on how to learn to communicate in cross-cultural situations, how to be patient with others and self, and how to adapt knowledge and experience to fit new situations.

LESSONS LEARNED FROM INTERNATIONAL RELIEF AND DEVELOPMENT: PROGRAM PRINCIPLES

All effective international work, whether relief or development, seeks to create sustainable solutions. To do this, certain principles may be applied that are based on key lessons that have been learned by both domains.

Whereas many organizations working in international relief and development share program principles and strategies, each has its own particular goals and objectives and, thus, strategies to accomplish its mission. Similarly, different international organizations target their interventions on different levels and with different emphases—whether with policy-making institutions, national governments, local or national NGOs, directly with communities, or others (as discussed above). Although institutional practices are becoming more similar as organizations learn what is effective, there remain some significant differences between organizations. To illustrate, an international NGO, Save the Children/USA, is described in Case 8.7.

While program principles and strategies are distinct among international NGOs, there are some similarities. Following is a description of broad principles and strategies that are employed by international NGOs, based on significant lessons that have been learned over decades of international relief and development work. The principles have considerable applicability to social work in both developing and industrialized countries.

Focus on a Disadvantaged Population Within a Holistic, Multisector Approach

Most NGOs have a primary area of activity such as the environment/ natural resources, education, health, or economic development. Because real-life issues are connected, most NGOs working through direct service strategies ultimately focus on numerous cross-cutting issues. A multi-sector approach is increasingly required. One illustration of this dynamic is in the area of basic education. Many children do not attend school because their families need their labor in order to earn income. Even though their long-term earning potential would be higher if they attended and stayed in school, many families cannot afford to do without children's short-term assistance in harvesting crops or performing other work tasks. Other families have enough resources to send only one child to school (because of costs associated with school uniforms, basic supplies, etc.), and parents choose to send

CASE 8.7: SAVE THE CHILDREN/USA

The Save the Children/USA (SC/USA) mission is *to create lasting, positive change in the lives of disadvantaged children.* The nonprofit, nonsectarian organization is actively working in 40 countries, including the United States. The international work of SC is conducted in Africa, Asia, Eastern Europe, Latin America, the Middle East, and Russia and the newly independent states. Guiding the international programs are two goals:

1. to secure the well-being of the world's poorest children by strengthening the capacity of children, caring adults, communities, and partner organizations to improve education, health, and economic opportunities for children and families
2. to meet the basic needs of children in war and crisis by improving the well-being of children in life-threatening situations

In SC/USA's development practice, the empowerment of marginalized women, families, and communities, is addressed in the work of three key sectors: (a) Strong Beginnings education program, which focuses on access to and success in basic education (early childhood development, primary education, youth development, and adult literacy); (b) Economic Opportunities program, which targets microenterprise development through Group Guaranteed Lending and Savings (GGLS), allowing women to manage group-based credit and increase their control over local economic resources; and (c) Health, Population and Nutrition program, which has demonstrated low-cost, community-based ways to improve reproductive health and reduce maternal and infant mortality. These initiatives are integrated into SC's core strategy, Woman/Child Impact (WCI). WCI promotes the needs and rights of women and children through changing policies, building institutional capacity in gender relations analysis, and developing tools for impact measurement.

In SC/USA's relief practice, the Division for Humanitarian Response (DHR) exists to secure the needs and to protect the rights of children in crisis. To achieve this goal, DHR focuses its efforts on three strategy objectives: (a) effectively integrating food security objectives in emergency relief, transition, and development programs in regions and sectors; (b) strengthening the capacity of communities and local groups to deliver emergency, rehabilitation, and reconstruction services to children and women; and (c) minimizing the adverse effects of disasters or transitional situations on the lives of children and women. During disasters, DHR places special emphasis on meeting the needs of children because they are at greatest risk. During an emergency, food and water are often the critical elements that are needed. DHR, however, works to address a

(continued)

broader range of issues, particularly in times of war. Under its Children and War initiative, DHR addresses such issues as providing psychosocial assistance for child soldiers, helping to reunite unaccompanied children with their families, and training children to avoid land mines and other dangers.

Save the Children Annual Report, 1998

sons instead of daughters because sons stay with the immediate family while daughters are "married off" to other families. In addition, research has proven that healthy children in school learn more than sick or hungry children. Thus education programs focus not only on quality issues within a school, such as curriculum development and teacher training, but also on health, gender, and economic issues. Indeed, one can argue that on a national or international level, "sustainable development requires economic growth" and all development issues are linked (Stoesz, Guzzetta, & Lusk, 1999, p. 157). Families therefore have more children to work in fields, but the increase in workers further degrades the soil, which requires more workers to reap the same yields, and so on. Applying the lessons from development, social work can learn to simultaneously focus on oppressed or marginalized populations while looking holistically at needs and problems.

Capacity Building and Empowerment

Capacity building as a social work task, built on the core principles of enabling and facilitating self-help, can take many forms at different levels in varying international relief or development situations. Building the capacity of the client is central to creating approaches that will last over time. What this means in practice is that all work done *for* a client, should be done *in collaboration with* the client. In many situations it is easier to focus on capacity building in a development setting in which the luxury of time and peace allows for participatory planning. In some emergency circumstances, especially when health needs are at stake or clients are traumatized, it is much more difficult to engage clients substantively in planning and implementation. To the extent possible, however, it is critical that all interventions be planned, implemented, and evaluated in partnership with the client, whether an individual, family, community, or organization. This ensures program relevance as well as program sustainability.

Impact, Sustainability, Cultural Relevance, and Scale

Programs are designed to achieve maximum positive impact on the group or issue of concern. Because all social programs are difficult to implement successfully due to the large number of factors that are outside the control of the program, many programs adopt Freire's concept of praxis, that is, implementing, reflecting, and adapting the program (or activity) based on lessons learned regarding what went well and what did not (Freire, 1992). One challenge with using this approach is that most major fund providers, particularly bilateral donor agencies, require a project to predetermine program outcomes. There is greater flexibility today in *how* to reach the outcomes, however, which allows a project to adapt its implementation to meet any unforeseen circumstances. Nevertheless, "NGOs who wish to remain effective and accountable . . . should diversify their funding sources and pursue strategies to raise funds locally—the only way to promote sustainability (and associated legitimacy) in the long term" (Edwards & Hulme, 1996).

Organizations working in development and relief have learned that in order for programs to be successful, they must first create positive change, and then positive change must continue to be made in the absence of the external support. For this reason, achieving large scale is widely perceived as central to having a maximum impact. That is, programs seek to reach the maximum number of beneficiaries, or clients, with vital benefits while also retaining the highest quality. A major challenge facing relief and development work is that of maintaining high quality as a program becomes larger (Herscovitch, 1997).

In addition, programs need to be culturally relevant if they are to succeed and continue. As discussed above, if programs are designed and implemented in partnership with the client(s) (including men and women, youth, teachers, community leaders, and so on), they will be culturally relevant. Partnerships with communities provide insight into relevant local needs—ensuring program relevance and cultural sensitivity. UNICEF's 1989 State of the World's Children report summarizes the issue as follows: "One of development's 'Seven Sins' is Development without participation: Sustained development ultimately depends on enhancing people's own capacities to improve their own lives and to take more control over their own destinies" (in Myers, 1992, p. 309). Although it is difficult to plan relief activities to be sustainable (i.e., the hope is that refugees living in camp situations will eventually return home), this goal is furthered when activities in emergency circumstances are planned and implemented in partnership with the affected population(s).

Gender Equity

Most programs that are focused on human development seek to promote increased equality, opportunity, and leadership of women and men to ensure maximum benefits for all. As discussed above, programs that seek empowerment and sustainability work to increase the capacity of disadvantaged individuals and groups to make choices and take actions *on their own behalf* from a position of strength. This can be particularly challenging in cultures where men and women are not seen as equals. For example, in Afghanistan under the Taliban, women were ordered to leave their jobs and return to their homes. NGOs working during this situation were forced to choose whether to continue to help the disadvantaged in, arguably, greater need, or whether to evacuate their staff in the hopes of putting more macro political pressure on leaders who are viewed as oppressing the population. As discussed in Chapter 7, tensions between gender equity and culture raise numerous ethical dilemmas.

Costs

One issue central to the sustainability of programs is that they be low cost. If local communities and national/local governments are to sustain program activities, these activities need to be affordable. One way of achieving this is to draw on locally available materials and resources. For example, in building schools, local materials such as wood, straw, bamboo, tin, and so on may be used rather than importing foreign materials. Where a community has no hard resources to contribute, in-kind contributions such as labor can be an effective substitute. Thus in some cases, external materials may be given as part of a larger cost-sharing strategy. For example, one national NGO, in its reconstruction efforts after Hurricane Mitch devastated parts of Central America, provided the raw materials needed to rebuild housing, schools, water systems, and other structures. The communities receiving the goods took the lead in planning and implementing all rebuilding efforts, with technical support provided (as needed) by NGO staff.

CONCLUSION: WHAT INTERNATIONAL PRACTICE MEANS FOR SOCIAL WORK DOMESTICALLY

There is some difficulty in transferring particular program models between social work in industrialized and developing nations because the specific contexts—needs and resources—between the two can be radically different. However, many, if not all, of the principles and strategies are effectively used across and between borders. The lessons learned in relief and development are equally applied to Western social work settings: focus on a disadvantaged population or issue of concern; a holistic approach to capacity building, empowerment, and gender equity; achievement of impact and sustainability; and keeping costs as low as possible.

The roles that social workers play in international relief and development work are the same ones they play in industrialized countries. These include casework, program implementation, program development/technical specialist, management, monitoring and evaluation/research, training, organizational development/network building, and advocacy/policy making. Just as in nonindustrialized countries, the central focus of fulfilling any role successfully is focusing on the self-help philosophy of capacity building so that clients are able to create positive change(s) on their own behalf. Within the roles played by social workers internationally, the same tasks are undertaken: engagement, assessment, selection and design of an intervention, implementation, M&E, and termination and follow-up. While the content or focus of the tasks will differ from country to country and community to community, the skills required to successfully complete them are the same.

Thus the work that social workers are conducting internationally, whether in relief or development settings, is applicable to the work that social workers are conducting in industrialized country settings. This trend is increasing in this age of rapid globalization and industrialization, with populations more mobile than ever before (Valle, 1994). Children growing up in urban environments in developing countries are facing the same challenges as children in more industrialized settings. As more children are left on their own because both parents have to work, they become more susceptible to violence and other negative influences, or what has been called a "socially toxic environment" (Garbarino, 1995, p. 115; Kotlowitz, 1991). Social workers in all settings, working within the ecological framework of human development, have the opportunity to counteract some of these trends through the positive and sustainable approaches learned through relief and development practice. And social workers who devote their careers to international work will find ample relevance from their professional training. Thus it may be appropriate to state that international relief and development work is social work.

REFERENCES

Edwards, M., & Hulme, D. (1996). Too close for comfort? The impact of official aid on nongovernmental organizations. *World Development, 24*(6), 961–973.

Ennew, J. & Milne, B. (1990). *The next generation: Lives of third world children.* Philadelphia, PA: New Society.

Freire, P. (1992). *Pedagogy of hope: Reliving pedagogy of the oppressed.* New York: Continuum.

Garbarino, J., Kostelny, K., & Dubrow, N. (1991). *No place to be a child: Growing up in a war zone.* Lexington, MA: Lexington Books.

Garbarino, J. (1995). *Raising children in a socially toxic environment.* San Francisco: Jossey-Bass.

Germain, C.B., & Gitterman, A. (1996). *The life model of social work practice* (2nd ed.). New York: Columbia University Press.

Healy, L.M. (1987). International agencies as social work settings: Opportunity, capability, and commitment." *Social Work, 32*(5), 405–409.

Herscovitch, L. (1997, April). *Moving child and family programs to scale in Thailand: Integrated program for child and family development* [Program Review]. Bangkok: UNICEF.

Kettner, P.M., Moroney, R.M., & Martin, L.L. (1990). *Designing and Managing programs: An effectiveness-based approach.* Newbury Park, CA: Sage.

Kotlowitz, A. (1991). *There are no children here.* New York: Doubleday.

Latting, J.K., & Gummer, B. (1994). Can administrative controls and pressure for efficiency and effectiveness be balanced with the staff's demand for decentralization and participation? In M. J. Austin & J. I. Lowe (Eds.), *Controversial issues in communities and organizations* (pp. 251–266). Needham Heights, MA: Allyn and Bacon.

Levinger, B. (1996). *Critical transitions: Human capacity development across the lifespan.* Newton MA: Education Development Center.

Meyer, C.H., & Mattaini, M.A. (Eds.). (1995). *The foundations of social work practice: A graduate text.* Washington, DC: NASW Press.

Midgley, J. (1995). *Social development: The developmental perspective in social welfare.* London: Sage.

Myers, R. (1992). *The twelve who survive: Strengthening programmes of early childhood development in the third world* (rev. ed.). Ypsilanti, MI: High/Scope Press.

National Association of Social Workers (1981). *International social work program plan.* Washington, DC: Author.

Rosenthal, B., Mizrahi, T., & Sampson T. (1994). Should community-based organizations give priority to building coalitions rather than building their own membership? In M.J. Austin & J.I. Lowe (Eds.), *Controversial issues in communities and organizations* 9–22. Needham Heights, MA: Allyn and Bacon.

Rossi, P.H., & Freeman, H.E. (1993). *Evaluation: A systematic approach* (5th ed.). Newbury Park, CA: Sage.

Rubin, A. & Babbie, E. (1993). *Research methods for social work* (2nd ed.). Pacific Grove, CA: Brooks/Cole.

Save the Children (1998). *Annual report.* Westport, CT: Author.

Silberman, M., & Lawson, K. (1995). *101 ways to make training active.* San Francisco: Pfeiffer.

Stoesz, D., Guzzetta, C., & Lusk, M. (1999). *International development.* Needham Heights, MA: Allyn and Bacon.

University of Connecticut School of Social Work (1998), Foundations of Social Work Practice. Unpublished Course Outline. West Hartford, CT.

Valle, I. (1994). *Fields of toil: A migrant family's journey.* Pullman, WA: Washington State University Press.

Vella, J. (1989). *Learning to teach: Training of trainers for community and institutional development.* Westport, CT: Save the Children.

CHAPTER 9

INTERNATIONAL/DOMESTIC PRACTICE INTERFACE

Global interdependence has increased the number and variety of internationally related aspects of domestic social work practice in most countries. Although relatively few social workers will have the opportunity to engage in the full-time development practice discussed in Chapter 8, all are likely to engage in internationally related social work within their usual jobs. For some this will occur frequently, while for others it will involve only an occasional case or administrative challenge. This chapter will discuss social work practice with refugees, immigrants, and other international populations; international adoption; social work in border areas; intercountry casework; and administrative and community organizing issues. Practice principles will be emphasized and illustrative cases used.

SOCIAL WORK WITH INTERNATIONAL POPULATIONS

The Migration Process and Its Impact

As migration continues to bring large numbers of refugees and immigrants to new countries, social workers encounter them in schools, hospitals, child welfare agencies, and community organizations. Many professionals are unprepared to provide informed and skilled assistance to individuals and families from other countries and cultures. Faced with cultural and language gulfs between them and their prospective clients, workers may retreat in fear and avoid providing needed services or may deliver inappropriate services. At the time, the amount of knowledge required for cross-cultural competence may seem overwhelming.

It is well accepted that social workers should have knowledge about the cultures of those they serve, but gaining and utilizing such knowledge about multiple cultures is a large task. Matthews (1994) found that even social workers who have specialized knowledge about an immigrant population may not always apply this knowledge in practice. Drachman (1992) suggests using a stages-of-migration framework to aid in assessment and intervention planning with immigrant populations. The framework specifies that the knowledge and information needed to effectively assist a foreign-born individual or family must address the three stages of their journey—

TABLE 9.1 Stage of Migration Framework

Stage of Migration	Critical Variables
Premigration and departure	Social, political, and economic factors
	Separation from family and friends
	Decisions regarding who leaves and who is left behind
	Act of leaving a familiar environment
	Life-threatening circumstances
	Experiences of violence
	Loss of significant others
Transit	Perilous or safe journey of short or long duration
	Refugee camp or detention center stay of short or long duration
	Act of awaiting a foreign country's decision regarding final relocation
	Immediate and final relocation or long wait before final relocation
	Loss of significant others
Resettlement	Cultural issues
	Reception from host country
	Opportunity structure of host country
	Discrepancy between expectations and reality
	Degree of cumulative stress throughout migration process

Drachman, 1992, p. 69.

premigration and departure; transit; and resettlement—and may include many dimensions, as outlined in Table 9.1 (Drachman, 1992, p. 69).

In applying the framework to an individual case, the worker seeks information about critical history that has shaped the individual's current reality, cultural influences, and particularly traumatic events that may have occurred. Experiences in each of the stages will vary considerably between groups and individuals. A Cambodian refugee may have endured a dangerous trek to the Thailand border during which one or more children may have perished, and the transit phase may have included several years of deprivation in a refugee camp. For a Jamaican immigrant, the transit phase may have been a 4-hour flight from Kingston to New York. But the Jamaican is likely to endure a lengthy period of family separation during resettlement because children are often left behind until the parent(s) is economically established and can secure visas for his or her children. A social worker who attempts to treat either client for depression without understanding his or her experiences in premigration, transit, and resettlement is unlikely to provide effective intervention.

Social workers need to gain knowledge of immigration statuses and rules, appropriate cultural knowledge, and skill in working through interpreters. Each area will be discussed below.

Immigration Statuses

The immigration status of foreign-born individuals affects their rights and access to social and health services and may restrict other rights, such as the right to travel out of the country of current residence. Professionals who interact with international populations need information about the various immigration statuses that apply and the rights and duties associated with each. To advise without proper information could jeopardize a family's status and even lead to deportation. Immigration restrictions may restrict optimal social work practice, preventing or delaying family reunification, for example. In Case 9.1, an undocumented client's fear of deportation was misinterpreted as child neglect and resistance to help.

Work with the undocumented must be done carefully to balance social work ethical obligations for safeguarding self-determination and confidentiality, legal and agency obligations, and client safety and well-being. In the United States, all government-supported services except public education

---

CASE 9.1: IMMIGRATION STATUS MISUNDERSTOOD
Ada Sanchez, Department of Child & Family Services

A child welfare supervisor, herself an immigrant from Peru, relates this case. A 6-year-old Hispanic girl was referred by her school to our child protection agency as at risk of medical neglect. The child had a rash; although the mother had been advised by the school nurse to take the child to a doctor, she had not. The social worker tried to interview the child, but the child seemed afraid and would not answer questions. The social worker then visited the mother with an interpreter and provided a list of doctors. The mother promised to take the child the next day; however, when the social worker visited the mother a week later, she had not followed through. The social worker told me that she was planning to recommend a protective services follow-up for medical and emotional neglect. During her visits, she had become concerned that the mother was always sleeping, could never find her medical or Social Security cards, and provided very little information. In addition, the worker suspected that the child could be developmentally delayed because she would not engage with the worker. I decided to accompany the social worker on a home visit. As soon as the mother opened the door, and her mouth, I realized she was from South America. Everything suddenly made sense to me. The mother and father were illegal residents. Mother worked third shift so that she could be home with her child and the father could work during the day. They had no insurance and no money to pay for medical care. The mother was putting money aside so that she could take the child to a private doctor. The child was quite intelligent, but knew she was forbidden to talk about her family situation. I was able to offer some services, including a local pediatrician who was willing to see the child without charging. I also put the mother in touch with local churches who could be of assistance. I took this opportunity to train my social work supervisees about illegal immigration and ways to help. The case was closed.

and emergency medical care are unavailable to the undocumented. Support services will need to be secured from informal and nontraditional sources, as suggested in the case above. Fearfulness and reluctance to share information with professionals are normal protective behaviors in such circumstances and should not be interpreted as pathological. Social workers need to take care not to be perceived as taking actions that put the client's status in jeopardy, or they may contribute to decisions that worsen the client's well-being, such as precipitous moves. The first step to effective service is awareness of immigration status and sensitivity to the possibility that the family being served may be undocumented.

Refugees are a special group of immigrants, defined as persons who are persecuted on the basis of race, religion, nationality, social group, or political opinion (Drachman, 1995). Those accepted into a country as refugees are usually given at least time-limited eligibility for special resettlement services. In Denmark, for example, priority is put on language training and family reunification. Families are supported by public assistance while adults are given intensive Danish lessons in order to facilitate their integration into the new society. Resettlement assistance in the United States has become more focused on employment. Length of eligibility for resettlement benefits has been reduced and language training, while offered, is secondary to preparation for employment and self-sufficiency.

It is easy to underestimate the difficulties refugees face in resettlement and adaptation. Almost all face what one Vietnamese scholar called "seven main agonies" of resettlement: culture shock; a language barrier; collapse of their support systems, including family; loss of status, loneliness, and cultural disorientation; lifestyle differences and value differences; unemployment or underemployment; and often, resulting emotional and mental health problems (Thuy, 1986, p. 7). Social workers encountering refugees during resettlement or in the years following the official resettlement period will need to assist them in coping with these multiple cultural and emotional challenges, as well as their needs for help with housing, job searching, and other basics.

Welfare reform in the 1990s has created special problems for legal refugees and immigrants in the United States. In one state, a particularly stringent set of regulations sanctions clients who fail to conform with job preparation and job search requirements, reducing their benefits with each sanction and permanently banning benefits to any family with three sanctions. The rules are implemented with little regard for language competence or cultural barriers to work and service, as the following Cases 9.2 and 9.3 illustrate.

In Case 9.2, 5 years after arrival, the Tran family is unprepared for self-sufficiency or employment. The many problems of resettlement, including language barriers, limited support system, unemployment, and disorientation have been complicated by the husband's illness and death and by welfare regulations that do not consider these to be reasons for continued support.

CASE 9.2: RESETTLEMENT AND SELF-SUFFICIENCY
Vichhyka Ngy, Asian Family Services

Mrs. Tran (not her real name), a Vietnamese mother of three teenagers, was referred to Asian Family Services after receiving a sanction from the TANF (Temporary Assistance to Needy Families) program. She had not attended a required job-training session being held at a community agency. Mrs. Tran and her family had been receiving benefits for the past 2 years after her husband died of cancer. The family had come from Vietnam about 3 years prior to his death during the Orderly Departure Program. The family had suffered considerable trauma prior to departure, as the husband had been an official in the South Vietnamese government and was imprisoned and tortured after the war. The father was diagnosed with cancer soon after arriving in the United States, and his wife devoted herself to caring for him. Mrs. Tran spoke and understood almost no English, had no working experience in the United States, and no vocational skills. The social worker at Asian Family Services explained to her that she had to attend the training course or she could lose her welfare benefits. After sitting through several all-day sessions entirely in English, she understood nothing and dropped out. She was given her second sanction by the welfare department. Asian Family Services had obtained a small grant for day-care training, delivered in the Asian languages. The social worker was able to intervene with the welfare department and enroll Mrs. Tran in the training. She completed the course and received a positive evaluation. However, her English ability was so limited that she was not able to get a job. Her welfare benefits were terminated, leaving the family without income. Subsequently, repeated calls to her home went unanswered, and the social worker from Asian Family Services has not been able to contact Mrs. Tran. A neighbor reported that the family moved to another state to be with relatives.

Cultural Knowledge

Lack of knowledge of culture can easily lead to misdiagnosis and labeling of clients as resistant. The following case was referred by the welfare department after a Vietnamese family was sanctioned when the mother failed to comply with a directive to attend a job readiness program. The Asian Family Services agency was asked to intervene to work on the family's resistance.

It is clear that social workers in the mainstream welfare departments and child welfare agencies are unable to effectively serve the population of Southeast Asians if they communicate in English-language directives, order clients to attend trainings they cannot comprehend, and apply unrealistic job expectations. Failure to communicate with clients and to understand family dynamics and cultural expectations exacerbate negative case results, as in missing or ignoring family violence.

CASE 9.3: RESISTANCE OR ABUSE: MISDIAGNOSIS
Vichhyka Ngy, Asian Family Services

At the request of the welfare department, the social worker from Asian Family Services went to the home to explain the job readiness requirements to the Nguyen family (not their real name), comprised of a husband, his wife, and three adolescent children. The husband had come to the United States from Vietnam first, later sponsoring his wife and children. When the social worker explained the requirements of the welfare department that Mrs. Nguyen attend a job readiness program, the family agreed to comply. The social worker arranged to pick the client up and drive her to the training. On the arranged day, however, the client was not waiting and no one answered the door. Several days later, Mrs. Nguyen appeared at the Asian Family Services office in great distress and very fearful that her husband would find out that she had come for help. The story she told to the worker was that she had not answered the door or complied with the welfare department regulations because her husband would not let her leave the house. He was extremely controlling and abusive. He destroys everything she enjoys to punish her; he chopped off the plants she was growing, destroyed the fish tank she enjoyed, and threw away the radio that her children had bought for her. He threatens her with deportation. Tensions in the home continued to escalate, and one of the children shared some of this with the school psychologist, resulting in a referral to the child welfare agency. Mr. Nguyen responded by moving to an adjacent town. His wife was forced to join him after the welfare department cut off all benefits for her noncompliance with the job readiness requirements. The loss of benefits has escalated family violence and increased Mrs. Nguyen's dependence on her abusive husband.

Cultural knowledge is necessary for competent social work. Workers should refrain from quick judgments or labeling of families until cultural practices are understood. For example, in many cultures, it is usual for parents and very young children to share bedrooms or even beds. In the West, this may be considered abnormal. Certain traditional healing practices, such as coining or cupping, may leave marks that can be confused with marks of child abuse. Many, if not most immigrants, no matter how limited their incomes, send money to family members in the home country. In other circumstances, they may pass up important opportunities for self-advancement to help a family member in a small business or to care for relatives. Understanding the importance of the extended family and the extent and intensity of family obligations is needed for social workers to properly interpret client behavior. Because "family" has different definitions in different cultures, social work methods must be adapted. A Canadian social worker told of her difficulties in working with a woman around placement of her child, as the woman was receiving intense pressure from relatives about the proper course of action and felt compelled to follow their advice (Legault, 1996). In other cases, the family that comes to meet with the social worker may include parents, children, grandparents, and an uncle. Clashes between the worker's and client's concepts of family may make case progress difficult. Gender roles are another common area of misunderstanding and culture clash between social workers and immigrant families. If a woman is passive and submissive during a family interview, she may be acting in a culturally appropriate manner, not exhibiting low self-esteem. To resolve problems, it is important that the social worker understand who makes family decisions and who listens to whom within the family if interventions are to be successful. Social workers in such cases may struggle to find new and more subtle ways of satisfying the goal of self-determination.

In Asian cultures, it is not typical to discuss relationship problems outside the family or to identify problems as emotional or mental in nature. Thus a client may present with a physical complaint or with a financial problem. If the social worker refers the case too quickly, the underlying relationship and/or emotional problems will be missed. In such cases, the worker must first work on concrete needs to build trust. Many immigrants also experience huge barriers in accessing normal social and health services, especially problems of transportation and language. Advising a client to "have your family take you to the clinic" will not be effective if the family fears going to the clinic or if the only family members who can drive are in factory jobs in which they cannot get time off. Social work with immigrants may require the worker to do more for the client in the beginning to prepare the client for the long term by teaching them how to be more independent. Thus instead of telling a client to take the bus to the health clinic, the worker may need to give detailed instructions about how to take the bus or find an escort for the first trip, and to write out the English request to the clinic staff for the client to present on arrival.

Immigrants may expect the social worker to be directive and often will not respond well to "talk therapy" or to facilitative approaches that work to get the client to arrive at the solution to the problem. An educational approach to treatment is often useful. Educational efforts should be attempted in child neglect and abuse cases if the child is not in imminent danger of serious harm. It is usual in West Indian, African, and Southeast Asian families to use physical punishment. Indeed, West Indian families may assert that spanking or beating children is necessary if children are to grow up to be disciplined and responsible. These families may exhibit no other characteristics of dysfunctional families; rather, they may be loving and strongly dedicated to their children's education and future. Precipitous child removal in such cases will likely cause more harm to the children than leaving them in the family home. An approach of education and partnership with the parents should be attempted. The child welfare worker can support the parents' desire to raise well-disciplined children and acknowledge the parents' wish to be seen as responsible and law-abiding residents of their current community. Thus careful explanation of legal requirements combined with teaching of alternative means of child discipline may prove successful and should be attempted unless the child is at serious risk of injury.

It is also important not to apply cultural information rigidly and to all members of a group without individualization. Cultural knowledge applied indiscriminantly is as damaging as no cultural information. Utilization of the stage-of-migration framework on a case by case basis will help ensure that social workers do not assume that all Afghan refugees or immigrants from Guyana had a similar experience.

Working Through Interpreters

Ideally, interventions are provided by professionally trained personnel who speak the same language as the person being served. In many cases, this is not possible, especially in areas with diverse populations but without large concentrations of any single linguistic group. Social workers therefore need to learn to work through interpreters to provide adequate service. The first imperative is to secure an interpreter. In several of the cases presented above, agencies attempted to interact in English with families who spoke no English. It is also important to use a professional interpreter, not a family member. In many instances, family members will not translate correctly because they will want to protect each other or safeguard certain information. They may also be unable to interpret accurately due to lack of familiarity with the concepts, terminology, or laws being discussed by the social worker. The potential for miscommunication is considerable. It is especially important not to use children to interpret for their parents, as this exacerbates already problematic generational conflicts in role and respect. Child welfare agencies have sometimes made the mistake of using a child as interpreter during investigation of his or her own case. In one case, a refugee mother was being investigated for child neglect after neighbors reported that she was leaving her 10-year-old daughter home alone to care for younger siblings. The child welfare worker used the 10-year-old child to tell the mother that she must never put a child as young as 10 in charge as it was against the law. The mother must have found the message very confusing, because the social worker had just put the child in charge by using her as the mother's translator (Barbour & Buch, 1986).

Whenever feasible, the agency should employ translators. This permits adequate training and supervision and can minimize problems of translation. Unless the translator fully understands the purpose of the interviewing process and has both linguistic skill and appropriate empathy, he or she may translate verbatim even when this masks the meaning of the communication. Baker (1981) cites a case in which verbatim translation of a judge's question about agency custody led three unaccompanied minors to believe they were being put into slavery. Even more problematic is when a translator takes such liberties that he or she provides "independent intervention," usually without the social worker's knowledge, by telling the worker what he or she thinks is the correct case decision rather than repeating the client's expressed wishes.

Social workers and other mental health professionals rely on subtle cues of body language, and the way the client expresses his or her concerns, not just on words. This is the most difficult challenge to overcome in the use of translators as only the best trained and empathetic will be able to interpret these cues and feed them back to the professional without intervening. It should be emphasized that without cultural knowledge of the meanings of gestures or postures in the culture of the client, it is dangerous for a therapist or other professional to interpret these. Those who work with immigrants who cannot communicate in the professional's language need to secure training in working with interpreters so that difficulties can be minimized. They will also have to advocate to ensure that adequate translation services are provided. Social work administrators have the responsibility to ensure that translation services are adequately and fairly arranged, which will be discussed further below.

A final point in this overview of practice challenges with international populations is use of cultural consultation. In working with clients from a different culture, the worker will encounter "gray" areas in assessment in which there is uncertainty as to whether a behavior is culturally appropriate or is pathological. Before proceeding to attach labels to the behavior or to design an intervention, it is wise to seek consultation from someone with the specific knowledge of the culture.

INTERNATIONAL ADOPTION

Worldwide, there are more than 20,000 adoptions per year in which people from one country, usually an industrialized country, adopt children from another, usually developing, country (Bartholet, 1993). In the United States, the number of international adoptions was in the range of 7,000–10,000 per year from 1986 through 1995, accounting for 10% to 15% of all adoptions. Beginning in 1996, the number grew, reaching 15,774 in 1998 (Joint Council on International Children's Services, 1999). Among other countries with significant international adoptions are France with 3,777 in 1998, Canada with 2,222, and Germany with 1,567, about 25% of all German adoptions (Joint Council on International Children's Services, 1999). In Norway, Denmark, Holland, and Israel, there are so few native infants available for adoption that most adoptions are international (Simon, Altstein, & Melli, 1994).

Interest in international adoption has roots in humanitarian concerns about war orphans after World War II and the abandoned children, including those fathered by foreign servicemen, of the Korean War. The practice has expanded as the availability of infants for in-country adoption has decreased dramatically in Western Europe and North America as a result of birth control, abortion, and lifestyle changes that have made single motherhood more acceptable. More infants are without homes in countries with high rates of poverty, high birth rates, and the enduring stigma for bearing an out-of-wedlock child. Countries may also become sources for adoption due to special circumstances. Romania had large numbers of young children abandoned in institutions as a result of the policies of the Ceausescu regime. After the fall of that regime, revelation of conditions in the institutions fueled concern and considerable interest in adopting Romanian children; in the period from January 1990 to April 1991, for example, Canada admitted more than 1,000 Romanian adoptees (Marcovitch, Cesaroni, Roberts, & Swanson, 1995). China's one-child policy coupled with traditional preferences for male children has led to availability of Chinese baby girls for adoption.

At the policy level, international adoption is controversial. The debates center around two issues. The first is whether it is good for a child to be raised by parents of a different culture, and often a different race, and therefore to lose their cultural identity. Children adopted by people from a foreign country leads to "the separation of children not only from their birth parents, but from their racial, cultural and national communities as well" (Bartholet, 1993, p. 90). The second is a macro-level critique that views adoption as another case in which poor countries are asked to provide resources (children) to wealthier countries, a practice some believe ultimately exploits women and children (Herrmann & Kasper, 1992). Complicating these debates are cases of baby-selling and of agents who place children for adoption against the wishes of their birth parents. Although all experts agree that the procedures for good adoption must include adequate prerelease counseling and a freely chosen decision to relinquish a child, not pressured by either coercion or the offer of money, the complexities of international adoption have allowed some unscrupulous practices to occur. Opinions in developing countries are influenced by rumors that children are adopted by foreigners for use as slaves, for sexual abuse, or even for sale of vital organs. Debates over what is best for the child and the macro-level symbolism of international adoption remain active.

Overview of the Basic Facts

"International adoption is a three way intersection between social work, law, and international relations" (Kendrick, 1998). All three dimensions are important to its practice, and social work professionals involved in international adoption must have knowledge of the law and knowledge of and skill in international relations to fortify their social work expertise. Through a complex process and the efforts of social workers or other professionals in at least two countries, "a child without parents in one country is united with parents in another country" (Kendrick, 1998).

International adoption practice first requires sound adoption practices. Families applying to adopt need to be carefully screened; home studies are required to ensure that the family is willing and capable of providing a good home and parenting for an adopted child. Second, children approved for international placement must be legally free for adoption, with informed and uncoerced consent of their parent or parents. Once these two conditions have been met, the third element of good adoption practice usually requires a period of supervision before the adoption is legally finalized. All steps of the process take on new complexities in international adoption in which laws and regulations of two countries must be satisfied.

Some countries forbid international adoption while others heavily regulate the practice. Countries allowing children to be placed for out-of-country adoption may set standards for approval of adoptive parents. Some do not allow single-parent adoptions; others have minimum or maximum age restrictions. Social agencies working with adoptions in these countries must comply with these guidelines in addition to applying their own criteria for acceptable families.

International adoption is often an expensive process. In addition to the fees paid to adoption agencies to cover the cost of the process, a number of countries require that the parents travel to the country for the adoption placement. At times, lengthy and uncertain stays are required. A family expecting a 3-week stay in Bolivia may be required to stay for 6 or more weeks before a placement is approved. Costs in travel, living expenses, and lost wages can be considerable; social workers need to provide families with accurate information about fees and travel requirements while also preparing them for the need to remain flexible to on-site changes. During the time of the country visit, families must also live with uncertainty about the outcome of their efforts. Although agencies try to protect families from unscrupulous agents and highly unstable local conditions, some families have paid large fees to reputable agencies and traveled to distant sites only to have to return without the promised child. Increased international policy setting and regulation are needed to prevent these unfortunate occurrences.

Many of the children placed for foreign adoptions are cared for in institutions prior to their placement. The quality of caregiving varies, but often staff-children ratios are high, resources are limited, and children suffer various types of physical and emotional deprivation. Adoptees from institutions, especially if the stay was prolonged, will be more likely to have developmental delays and disabilities (Groza, 1997). Parents who travel to the child's country may see firsthand the institutional conditions and have an idea of what the child has experienced. Others may have very limited information about the child's preplacement experience or background. Adoption practice now emphasizes providing parents with detailed information on the child's background and heritage. This is not always possible in international adoption.

Adoption finalization can become a multistage process. The adoption may have been finalized in the child's country of origin; in other cases, finalization is done in the adopters home country. Because this is not automatically granted, U.S. citizens must apply for citizenship for their adopted child. Proposed legislation would rectify this and grant citizenship when adoptions are final. The citizenship step cannot be overlooked. In 1999, the

United States deported its first international adoptee, using provisions of a 1996 law requiring deportation of any noncitizen convicted of a felony. In this case, a 26-year-old man, adopted by a U.S. family when he was 4, was deported to Thailand—a country in which he has no ties (Joint Council on International Children's Services, 1999).

Follow-up studies of international adoptees have generally shown positive adoption and adjustment outcomes. While initially many children, especially those adopted at an older age or from very deprived institutional settings, exhibit a number of physical, medical, and behavioral problems, these usually decrease over time. A recent report, however, suggests that adoptions of children from orphanages in Russia and Romania are disrupting at a much higher-than-normal rate, raising concerns over the impact of severe early deprivation (Holtan, 1999). However, long-range studies have shown that by young adulthood most foreign adoptees differ little on adjustment measures from their nonadopted peers, and most report positive relationships with their adoptive families.

In spite of positive findings, some researchers, especially in Europe, have concerns over international adoption. Simon et al. (1994) report on several such studies from Scandinavia. Although finding overall success, adopted adolescents in Norway exhibited traits that suggested they may become marginalized as adults in Norwegian society; and in Denmark, 90% of international adoptees surveyed "reported feeling 'mostly Danish' " (Simon et al., 1994, p. 65); however, about 20% had limited education and faced dim employment prospects. Acknowledging successful family integration in most cases, the researchers question whether the almost homogeneous societies of Scandinavia can provide suitable environments for foreign adoptees of different races. Overall, however, follow-up studies of adult and adolescent international adoptees discovered adjustment similar to in-country same-race adoptees and quite similar to nonadopted persons (Bartholet, 1993; Groza, 1997; Simon et al., 1994).

Social Work Roles in International Adoption

Although other professions are involved in international adoption work, social workers play the full range of roles in adoption practice: home study and preparation of families; cultural plans; follow-up services, interaction with foreign orphanages and agencies; and adoption policy influencing.

Home Study and Preparation of Families. Follow-up studies conducted with adopting families have shown that good preparation contributes to adoption success. Furthermore, most families indicate that they would have liked more preparation than what was received and expressed an interest in continuing support services. Groza (1997) recommends a thorough educational preparation for families.

Early in the preparation process, social workers guide families in examining their reasons for considering international adoption and exploring

IMPORTANT ELEMENTS IN EDUCATING FAMILIES ABOUT INTERNATIONAL ADOPTION:

- details on the legal and social process of adoption in both the United States and abroad
- issues of abandonment, separation, grief, loss and mourning for adoptees that are evident throughout the life cycle
- issues of separation, grief, loss and mourning for infertile couples that are evident throughout the life cycle
- the adoptive family's life cycle and unique issues in family formation
- individual and family identity development in adoption
- unique issues of attachment in adoption
- outcomes and risks in international adoptions

Groza, Encyclopedia of Social Work, 1997, p. 4

the ramifications of adopting a child from a different culture and race. Some couples may not have thought through these issues beyond early childhood. Or they may not have considered the support that will be given or withheld by extended family members. It is crucial that adopting couples recognize and accept that by adopting a foreign child, they are becoming a multicultural and usually multiracial family forever. The social worker plays an important role in facilitating this exploration.

Social workers also help families to consider the possibility that the child they adopt may have medical or developmental problems that are not evident in the initial medical screenings and to decide whether they can parent a child with disabilities. A Canadian study of parents of Romanian adoptees showed that more than 88% had considered the risks of such problems before adopting, suggesting good preparation (Marcovitch et al., 1995).

In assessing suitability for adoption, maturity and flexibility are important family characteristics. These will be tested early as the couple negotiates the often tortuous path to a finalized adoption, and tested often throughout parenting a child who may have developmental delays, medical problems, attachment difficulties, and adolescent identity concerns complicated by his or her status as a foreign-born adoptee. Care in the assessment phase is particularly important. After being helped by social workers to explore motivation, implications, and their own readiness, some families will decide not to proceed.

Assisting With a Cultural Plan. One of the objections to international adoption is that it deprives a child of his or her culture. It is therefore important that the adoptive family "have positive feelings about the child's country, racial and cultural heritage" and that they take purposeful steps to maintain the heritage in some ways (Kendrick, 1998). Groza (1997) recommends that social workers help each adopting family to develop a "cultural plan that will help the child build an identity as a cultural and ethnic person" (p. 4). He suggests adapting the life book idea (a type of scrapbook to help children placed in out-of-home care to remember their earlier life) to prepare a cultural life book. The period of in-country time required for child placement and approval can be productively used by the parents to familiarize themselves with the culture and begin a collection of photographs and other items. One mother told of purchasing a small emerald in Bogata that she planned to present to her Colombian adopted daughter when she was old enough to appreciate not only the gem but its origins. Another family has made an album documenting the entire adoption process, with ample photographs of the child's town of origin in Bolivia. The initial journey should be only a foundation for continued efforts to ensure that the child has opportunities to learn about his or her culture and country of origin.

Social workers also need to prepare families for legal hurdles and for complications that can arise in negotiating between two legal systems. A thorough knowledge of laws and procedures in all "sending" countries, as well as of U.S. adoption and adoption-related immigration laws, is essential.

Follow-up Services. After the finalization of an adoption, some families will need continuing services for special medical problems or for emotional problems of their children. Many families welcome continued or intermittent support in coping with the "normal" issues of parenting a child from another culture. Holtan (1999) recommends "ongoing post-finalization services as needed over time over the life of the family" in order to address special needs of international adopting families (p. 4). For those families who need mental health intervention, adoption agencies should be ready to make appropriate referrals. Other families seek only support and some may take a role in developing their own services. Adoptive parents in some locales have developed groups; some of the more successful ones hold periodic cultural events, support group meetings, and events for the adoptees, including teen activities and support groups. Social workers can assist families by suggesting involvement in such activities or by organizing a group in areas where none exist.

Relationships With Source Country Agencies. In some agencies, social workers travel periodically to the sending (birth) countries and help build and maintain positive and trusting relationships between adoption agencies, orphanages, and local legal authorities. Their practices may also have positive effects on child welfare practices in the source countries. One agency, for example, uses videotapes of children in orphanages to introduce them to prospective parents. The orphanage staff in Russia was shown how to take a video that would show a child's gross motor skills and whether the child follows voices. Through this activity, the importance of attention from adults and the importance of developmental activities were communicated; in small ways, this subtle education may improve institutional practices. Other contributions by adoption social workers have been more direct. Adoption social workers helped develop a foster care system in Romania and developed a training curriculum on child development for institutions in Bulgaria. Some direct financial assistance to improve care for children remaining in their countries has also been provided (E. Kendrick, personal communication, July 15, 1999). With additional attention to these roles, international adoption might be one "spur" to improve services to children worldwide.

Social Work's Influence on International Adoption Policy. In spite of the research showing positive outcomes for children, international adoption remains controversial. The Convention on the Rights of the Child clearly states a preference for in-country placement, but does approve of intercountry placement when that is not feasible: "Recognize that inter-country adoption may be considered as an alternative means of child's care, if the child cannot be placed in a foster or an adoptive family or cannot in any suitable manner be cared for in the child's country of origin" (United Nations, 1989, article 21(b)). The reporting requirements under the convention underscore this hierarchy of options by asking countries allowing international adoptions to report on the extent to which "due regard is paid to the desirability of continuity in the child's upbringing and to the child's ethnic, religious, cultural and linguistic background" in considering alternative placements (Rios-Kohn, 1998, p. 22). Article 21 of the convention further calls for safeguards to ensure that intercountry adoptions maintain good standards, are carried out by competent authorities, are not done for financial gain, and are contingent on informed consent following counseling of parents, relatives, and guardians.

The Hague Convention on Protection of Children and Cooperation in Respect of Intercountry Adoption, approved in 1993, reflects a more favorable view of international adoption, indicating it is a legitimate option for children who cannot be raised by their own parents and probably better for the child than in-country foster care or institutionalization (Groza, 1997; Rios-Kohn, 1998). The conference that drafted the convention also developed standards for adoption that could improve the process and reduce child trafficking if implemented by a majority of countries. The convention became effective in 1995 in ratifying countries. To date, it has been signed but not ratified in the U.S. Congress.

Social workers in both sending and receiving countries can contribute to informed discussions on the topic. They can assure that agency practices are ethical, taking care that payment of fees is not allowed to influence judgments about adoption suitability, and can advocate for adequate preparation, screening and, follow-up services. Social workers in sending countries can also be vigilant about not allowing fee payments to influence practice. They can also work to assure that informed consent is secured and that birth parents have access to counseling. Dialogue between social workers from sending and receiving countries would be useful in resolving challenging issues—such as what happens to the child when an overseas adoption fails—and in cultural maintenance for adopted children.

INTERCOUNTRY CASEWORK

"Intercountry casework is a method of extending individualized social services to persons whose problems require study or action in another country [and] a method of interagency co-operation designed to bring together on behalf of a client social services in more than one country" (cited in Cox, 1984, p. 44). In certain respects, both refugee resettlement and international adoption require elements of intercountry casework. As migration and other forms of international contact have increased, there are many additional situations that require intercountry work. Among these are cross-national marriages and divorces, child abductions, repatriation or return migration, claims for retirement or disability benefits earned in another country, medical crises that occur in another country, crimes committed by noncitizens, and a host of other family relationship problems when family members live in different countries (Cox, 1986). Indeed, resolving even simple client requests may present overwhelming difficulties to the untrained social worker.

Marriage, Divorce, and Child Custody

Marriages between partners from different countries can pose special challenges. Marriage does not bring the partner rights of citizenship, and procedures must be followed to gain proper visas and entry permits. Children born in mixed-country marriages often have automatic dual nationality. This grants the children a number of rights and privileges, but it may also in-

---

CASE 9.4: SIMPLE INTERCOUNTRY CASEWORK CAN BE COMPLEX

As one social worker related:

> Although I did not identify it as such at the time, I tried to engage in intercountry casework on one occasion and experienced tremendous obstacles. I advocated for a client's spouse, who was trying to obtain a copy of his birth certificate from his country of origin, Guatemala. My client's spouse was from a small village and informed me that he was not familiar with the larger institutions of the country. The obstacles I faced included: not knowing where to begin, not being able to get any guidance from my co-workers or supervisors who were equally uninformed, not knowing Guatemala's political structure or government institutions, not knowing the Guatemalan culture or customs, and not knowing Spanish. Needless to say, I proved to be an ineffective advocate in this case. (Carroll, 1997)

volve unforseen duties. Boys, for example, may be subject to military service requirements in both countries. And whichever country the child is physically in will treat the child as their own national, not as a foreign citizen. This has important implications in cases of parental child abduction, which will be discussed next. Social workers may be most likely to encounter the partners of these mixed marriages when they experience marital discord; the special challenges of cross-cultural marriage often contributes to the couple's difficulties. In other cases, social workers will be called on to assist with intercountry work to resolve problems of child support, custody, and visitation, especially in families in which the parents are divorced.

International Child Abduction

In working with divorced or separated families in which parents are from different countries, social workers should be aware of the possibility of international child abduction. This is not a common phenomenon, however, between 1973 and 1986, at least 2,700 children were kidnapped by one of their parents and taken from the United States to another country (Hegar & Greif, 1991). Recovering a child taken to another part of one's own country can be difficult, but recovering a child taken out of the country is much more complicated, especially in those countries that have not signed the Hague Convention on International Child Abduction.

In many international marriages, stresses arise due to cultural differences. These also exist during separation and after divorce. Hegar and Greif (1991) suggest that abduction may occur due to the stress on the noncustodial parent in seeing their children brought up largely outside of their culture. Custody guidelines may also highlight cultural conflict. Whereas custody decisions in the United States have tended to favor mothers, Islamic law favors fathers in custody disputes. In other countries, such as Kenya, the children traditionally belong to the father, although young children are customarily left in the mother's care. Older children, however, will usually be given to the father or even to the father's relatives over the claims of the mother. These differences in traditional expectations will exacerbate emotional stress during initial custody procedures and, if an abduction occurs, will make recovery of the child less likely.

Hegar and Greif (1991) suggest preventative steps in working with parents whose international marriages are breaking up. In addition to the usual efforts to work out custody and visitation arrangements, workers may advise parents to learn about requirements for exiting the country and to see if they can block having a passport issued for a child. Other precautions such as frequent photographs and fingerprinting may also be advised. Social workers also need to learn about the risks of international abduction and familiarize themselves with the custody expectations of the cultures represented in their caseload. Cases may pose practice and ethical dilemmas. For example, how should the social worker advise a divorced mother as to whether to allow her ex-husband to take or send the children to visit grandparents in Africa? How can the value of extended family contact and cultural maintenance be weighed against the risk of the children's not returning from the visit? These are not easily resolved issues. What is clear is that the social worker should not give any advice without adequate legal and cultural knowledge.

The Hague Convention may offer some protection, yet additional work on international standards and agreements appears necessary. A study by the International Social Service (ISS) (1979) found that even involvement of social workers in investigating the best interests of the child often did not resolve the situation. Rather, they found that social workers tended to "identify with the parent of his own nationality and language" (p. 114). Nonetheless, their recommendation at the time was that professional investigation by internationally experienced social workers be used to determine the best course of action. Cooperation between nations in honoring such judgments should also be required by international law. Until that time, the experience of International Social Service suggests that successful return is most often accomplished when the parents are helped to come to an agreement on which country is best for raising the child (Cox, 1984).

Family Reunion

Work with international populations often involves assisting with attempts at family reunion. Immigrants and refugees, once established in their new environment, often wish to bring additional members of their immediate or extended family to join them and may turn to social workers for assistance. Depending on the national policies and the relationship of the parties, the ease with which families reunite will differ. In other cases, the immigrant may be considering return to his or her own country and may need assistance in making plans for the return. This is frequently contemplated at the time of retirement.

Social Security and Other Benefits Casework

In an example cited earlier in the chapter, a social worker related how difficult it was to attempt to obtain a birth certificate from another country. Securing entitlements earned in another country for clients is another challenge of international casework. Adults who have worked in various countries may have earned pensions, accident coverage, or family allowances in a country other than the one of their current residence. Returning migrants often can claim pensions earned in the country in which they spent their adult lives. Liaison work with the appropriate offices in the other country is often needed. Benefit eligibility should not be neglected even if the social worker's primary role with the family is to assist with the emotional impact of a death or accident. Workers should explore with international families whether they may be eligible for benefits from either or both countries of parents' origin and current residence (or perhaps even additional countries in which part of their work life was spent).

Deportation

Other types of cases may include work with persons who commit crimes in a country other than the country of their nationality and potential deportation cases. These require professionals to be knowledgeable about criminal or civil law where the crime was committed plus relevant immigration law. New regulations in the United States, for example, make persons subject to deportation for even relatively minor criminal convictions that occurred years earlier. Recent cases include a Jamaican deported at age 40 when he applied for citizenship because of a conviction for jumping over a subway turnstile when he was 19. Or, a 12-year U.S. Army veteran from Jamaica who was jailed and threatened with deportation for involvement in a minor skirmish during his military service in Japan more than 15 years earlier. The incident was judged so minor by the army that he had still received an honorable discharge (Caribnet, personal communication, February 17, 1998). Unless well informed about the laws and regulations, social workers may take such threats too lightly and misadvise clients on necessary actions.

SOCIAL WORK IN BORDER AREAS

A special case of intercountry work involves work in border areas. In these regions, social workers will encounter some families who are actively transnational in that they move back and forth over borders, legally or illegally. Sometimes, a move is precipitated by a social welfare investigation, such as suspected child abuse; in other instances, it may be involuntary, as when a juvenile offender is sent back to Mexico by authorities in Texas. In child welfare, there are many cases with overlapping jurisdiction: American children with relatives in Mexico, Mexican children in Mexico with relatives in the United States, Mexican children in the United States with relatives in Mexico, and so on (Daigle, 1994). In all cases, continuity of service is compromised. An important strategy for service improvement is the development of interagency collaboration agreements between agencies on both sides of the border. These are enhanced when social workers in both locales exchange information and develop personal working relationships.

Padilla and Daigle have discussed international social work collaboration at the U.S.-Mexico border in several articles. Their research shows the importance of international work because problems of child welfare, health care, and youth services deteriorate unless flexible and coordinated service can be developed on both sides of the border. They cite a case example of effective collaboration in which a child under protective custody of the state of Texas was placed in a relative's home in Mexico; there the placement was assisted by a Mexican social worker who conducted home visits for the Texas agency (Padilla & Daigle, 1998). The Los Angeles Department of Children Services has set up an international placement office as an extension of provisions of the Interstate Compact. The caseload is sizable; estimates are that 50 to 70 cases involving overlapping jurisdiction with Mexico or Asian countries are usually open and that three to four children per month are placed from Los Angeles into Mexico (Daigle, 1994).

Cooperation between agencies in different countries usually begins with informal contacts, often one social worker to another, and is later formalized in agreements. Agreements call for such activities as assisting each other in obtaining key documents, conducting home studies or other investigations, assisting with information and referral to service resources in each community, exchanging literature and information, and other activities necessary to ensure that child protection is not compromised by the border location (Padilla and Daigle, 1998, citing an agreement between agencies in El Paso and Juárez). The researchers found that immigration status—whether or not clients were legal or illegal—was seldom a focus in the agencies' collaborative activities. This is facilitated by the local nature of the agreements for cooperation. The authors fear, however, that mandatory reporting requirements, if enforced in the future, could jeopardize many current arrangements.

Effective international border practice requires the following elements: "forming working relationships, structuring formal agreements, ensuring reciprocity, and establishing effective systems of information exchange" (Padilla & Daigle, 1998, p. 66). Ability to communicate is key, of course, and some collaborations have been disrupted by the loss of bilingual workers. Thus careful attention to bilingual communication is needed on both sides of the border. The model used in one agency was to appoint bilingual social workers to official positions as international liaisons. Formal agreements are important to ensure that collaboration continues when personal relationships are disrupted by personnel changes.

Effective collaboration builds on an understanding of the differences between social welfare systems and philosophies of social work in both countries. As explained in Chapter 4, social work roles and priorities may vary by country and these differences need to be understood for coordinated practice. Daigle (1994) found that cooperative efforts had to recognize that definitions of child abuse and philosophies about caring for children differed between Mexican and U.S. social workers. These differences had to be accommodated in working agreements. Regular communication was helpful in addressing these differences; one Texas agency held joint staff meetings with Mexico's Desarrollo Integral de la Familia every few months (Daigle, 1994).

Padilla and Daigle (1998) found that working agreements are most feasible if done at the local and the agency level rather than systemwide or national. These are, therefore, agreements that can be developed through the efforts of individual social workers and social work administrators. Achieving agreement at higher levels of government involves complications with laws and international relations. Daigle (1994) recommends that states as well as cities develop policies on areas of overlapping jurisdiction in child welfare, for example, policies that would detail legal procedures and set "case philosophy" (p. 42). Ultimately, it is important that national governments recognize the binational nature of child protection and set appropriate guidelines. Binational issues are not confined to border areas. Many immigrants settle far from borders, in areas less able to handle relationships with home countries. Nappa County, California, for example, has a large foreign-born population, but no social work contacts in Mexico. Therefore, a number of undocumented children are in long-term foster care, even children who have relatives in Mexico willing and able to provide care (Daigle, 1994).

As movement of people and sensitivity to internationalization of social problems increase, efforts to manage services in border regions and in binational cases are likely to grow and improve.

INTERNATIONAL PRACTICE ISSUES FOR SOCIAL WORK PLANNERS, ADMINISTRATORS, AND COMMUNITY ORGANIZERS

Social work planners, administrators, and community organizers also face challenges of internationally related practice in their daily functions. For example:

- A community organizer is upset that so few of the black parents in the school district turned out to vote on the school funding referendum. She is unaware that the majority of them are West Indian immigrants and few are citizens; therefore, although they pay property taxes, they are not eligible to vote.
- The administrator of a mental health clinic serving a diverse clientele, including Asians, is interviewing a Vietnamese man for a position as program director. The man is very quiet during the interview, looks down frequently, and downplays many of the accomplishments his reference letters extolled. The administrator is puzzled and does not know how to assess the man's competence for the position.
- The program planner for a community youth center notices that the number of teenage girls utilizing the drop-in center has declined gradually. The neighborhood has experienced an influx of immigrant families from Colombia.
- Staff relations at a health clinic serving a diverse community have deteriorated. The receptionist has resigned, and the only Khmer-speaking clinician has indicated that she is unhappy. Both have frequently been asked to serve as interpreters, which is outside of their job descriptions and duties.

- The campaign director for the local United Way is preparing her approach to a corporation that historically has been a major donor. Within the past year, the corporation has been acquired by a Japanese corporation and this will be the first campaign approach to the new team.

- An executive director must guide a board of directors through a contentious decision to divest the agency portfolio of investments in companies using child labor in Asia.

In carrying out interventions to address these six scenarios and others like them, social work planners, administrators, and organizers will need both their macropractice skills and knowledge about cross-cultural communication and international policy.

As community demographics change and international populations grow, social agencies need to change in several areas. First, they must reexamine their services to ensure they are needed by area residents. New services may be needed, or current ones may need to be redesigned. The agency may also need to revise its marketing strategies to reach new residents, who will not respond to traditional means of marketing such as flyers or radio advertising. Staff composition and staff cultural competence will also need to be addressed; these issues are part of the broader issue of service accessibility, which includes cultural relevance, language, and service design.

Good social service planning requires good data, beginning with basic demographic data. This may be difficult to obtain. Racial and linguistic group statistics may not reveal nationality or immigrant status. Thus West Indian immigrants may be counted as African Americans and Colombian immigrants as Hispanics. In areas of changing demographics, agencies may need to conduct their own population surveys—ideally in collaboration with other agencies and organizations.

Client groups are more likely to use services or to participate in organizations whose staff and leadership include members of their group. An important administrative role is recruitment and maintenance of a diverse staff, which is as representative as possible of the service area. This will require new types of outreach and employment advertising to attract candidates from a wider pool. Administrators will need skill in cross-cultural interviewing to accurately assess potential candidates from diverse ethnic backgrounds (Thiederman, 1988). In interviewing a Vietnamese candidate, for example, the culturally competent administrator would not expect a lot of eye contact; to elicit information about how the candidate might perform on the job, the administrator would frame questions more as discussions of problem-solving methods than as invitations for the candidate to boast about past accomplishments.

Similar types of cultural knowledge will also assist in designing services and marketing. A mixed-gender teen drop-in center that was freely used by African-American girls may not be used by immigrant girls from South America, as their families may not allow them the freedom of attending activities in the evening unescorted by family chaperones. Service planners could redesign the service, or personal outreach—to families in their homes and through the local churches attended by the families—to explain the services and reassure the families of their safety may be needed. Thus culture and tradition must be considered in designing and marketing social services just as it is used in one-to-one delivery of service.

Providing translators and interpreters is crucial to adequate social services for non-English-speaking clients. The optimal solution is to hire multilingual staff; however, this is difficult, especially when there are many linguistic groups in one service area. Typically, social workers or other professionals are "borrowed" from their normal work to serve as translators or paraprofessionals and clerical staff are asked to take on translation tasks. These strategies often create job dissatisfaction. Staff asked to take on extra duties may become overburdened, and professionals may resent being used in what they consider paraprofessional tasks. Social work administrators must address staff workload fairness issues while working to ensure adequate interpreter services. Potential solutions include providing extra pay for translation services by professionals and paraprofessionals or creating a new classification of support staff, such as combining usual clerical or aide duties with translation responsibilities, possibly at better pay and, at least, with a specific title. Plans should be made with consent and participation of all staff involved (Healy, 1996).

Lack of knowledge can cause serious errors in service judgment in internationally related matters. The following case illustrates an administrative decision made without adequate knowledge of relevant law and agency responsibility.

Knowledge gaps and fear of the unknown interfere with rational approaches to decision making. Sound administrative practice requires clear

CASE 9.5: KNOWING LEGAL AND ETHICAL RESPONSIBILITIES

The administrator of a nonprofit shelter for battered women received a request from a shelter in a neighboring state to accept a transfer client. The woman's husband had discovered the location of the shelter, and it was believed that her life was at risk. Agency policy permitted accepting clients from other shelters in such circumstances; in fact, the agency's mission identifies ensuring safety for women without regard to their race, religion, national origin, sexual orientation, or political beliefs as its number one priority. The woman in question, however, was an undocumented immigrant from Central America; she spoke only Spanish and had no relatives in the United States. The shelter had Spanish-speaking staff. However, the director feared that accepting such a client might break a law or violate funding arrangements. The administrator refused the request.

Anonymous personal communication

definition of problems and the gathering—sometimes very quickly—of enough information for action. The director in this case needed basic information on the legal rights and obligations of nonprofit agencies and their staffs under immigration laws. Optimally, a discussion of this issue among leadership staff and members of the board of directors would have occurred prior to a crisis, and as in the direct service case (Case 9.1), the director would have trained the staff in identifying and utilizing alternative support sources to assist the undocumented client in making plans for the future.

Policy Issues and Agency Boards

Some social service agencies, through their boards of directors, have a public policy component through which they speak out directly on issues or participate in coalition efforts. Administrators need to be sure that relevant internationally related policies in areas such as immigration, adoption, and family reunification are included in agency's policies. In addition, agencies may express their policy agenda in other ways, such as through socially responsible investment of the agency's assets. The area of investing has led agencies into some limited discussion of international issues and has often exposed gaps in board knowledge. The following case tells the story of a board of directors and an executive wrestling with divestiture during the antiapartheid movement.

The process of educational strategies and utilization of worldwide networks in human services can be used by administrators to resolve similar policy-level dilemmas. Expansion of the international component of pub-

CASE 9.6: HELPING A BOARD
GAIN INTERNATIONAL KNOWLEDGE

In 1987, the board of directors of a large YWCA spent almost a year to reach a decision whether to divest its $10 million portfolio from companies doing business in apartheid South Africa. Anti-racism had been identified as the agency's most important goal: "to eliminate racism wherever it is found and by any means necessary." Thus the decision initially seemed clear-cut. The group soon discovered that there were areas of conflict—What about the financial stewardship responsibilities of the board? Were some board members more concerned with racism in South Africa than at home? Members also discovered gaps in their knowledge—would divesting truly aid in eliminating apartheid? With the executive director's guidance, the board began an educational process: experts from nearby universities were invited in to talk with the board, written materials were collected for board use, and input was solicited from the YWCA of South Africa. Eventually, the board resolved its conflicts and voted to divest the portfolio of South African holdings.

lic policy work is important for agencies who are active in the domestic-international interface of social work. Additional information about the policy role of the profession, including its agencies, will be covered in Chapter 10.

CONCLUSION

This chapter has briefly discussed the many areas of practice that may involve social workers in international work. It is hard to imagine a social work career in the 21st century that will not bring the practitioner into periodic contact with situations that require knowledge beyond the borders of one's own country. Even if migration were to end today, the current numbers of binational and even multinational families would generate a substantial caseload of internationally related practice problems. Undoubtedly, migration will continue and the demand for international knowledge and intercultural sensitivity will grow. In addition to internationally related practice, social work will be asked to respond to the challenges of global policy. This will be examined in the next chapter.

REFERENCES

Baker, N.G. (1981). Social work through an interpreter, *Social Work 26*(5), 291–297.

Barbour, J., & Buch, T. (1986). Child welfare. In Healy, L.M. (Ed.), *Toward improving service to Southeast Asian refugees*. West Hartford, CT: University of Connecticut School of Social Work.

Bartholet, E. (1993). International adoption: Current status and future prospects, *The Future of Children: Adoption 3*(1), 89–103.

Carroll, S. (1997). Unpublished student paper, University of Connecticut School of Social Work, West Hartford, CT.

Cox, D. (Ed.). (1984). *Intercountry casework: Some reflections on sixty years experience of international social service, 1924–1984.* Geneva: International Social Service.

Cox, D. (1986). Intercountry casework, *International Social Work, 29,* 247–256.

Daigle, L. (1994). *Child welfare services along the U.S.-Mexico border: Efforts in Bi-National Cooperation.* (Working Paper No. 74.) University of Texas at Austin.

Drachman, D. (1992). A stage-of-migration framework for service to immigrant populations. *Social Work, 37*(1), 68–72.

Drachman, D. (1995). Immigration statuses and their influence on service provision, access, and use. *Social Work, 40*(2), 188–197.

Groza, V. (1997). Adoption: International. In R.L. Edwards (Ed.), *Encyclopedia of Social Work* (19th ed.) (1997 suppl.) 1–14. Washington, DC: NASW Press.

Healy, L.M. (1996). International dimensions of diversity: Issues for the social agency workplace. *Journal of Multicultural Social Work, 4*(4), 97–116.

Hegar, R.L., & Greif, G.L. (1991). Parental kidnapping across international borders. *International Social Work, 34,* 353–363.

Herrmann, Kenneth J., Jr., & Kasper, B., (1992). International adoption: The exploitation of women and children. *Affilia, 7*(1), 45–58.

Holtan, B. (1999), "From the Director . . . Barb Holtan," *Tressler Family Connections.* March/April; 2–4.

International Social Service (1979). International child abduction. In David R. Cox, (Ed.), *Intercountry casework: Some reflections on sixty years experience of international social service 1924–1984* (pp. 113–115). Geneva, Switzerland: Author.

Joint Council on International Children's Services (1999). Deportation update, ⟨http://www.jcics.org/deportation.html⟩ (accessed 11/17/99).

Joint Council on International Children's Services (1999), website, www.jcics.org.

Kendrick, E. (1998). *International adoptions.* Paper prepared for the Lutheran Social Services, New England. (Rocky Hill, CT office).

Legault, G. (1996). Social work practice in situations of intercultural misunderstandings. *Journal of Multicultural Social Work, 4*(4), 49–66.

Marcovitch, S., Cesaroni, L., Roberts, W., & Swanson, C. (1995). Romanian adoption: Parents' dreams, nightmares, and realities, *Child Welfare, 74*(5): 993–1017.

Matthews, L. (1994). *Social workers' knowledge of client-culture and its use in mental health care of English-speaking Caribbean immigrants.* Unpublished doctoral dissertation, Hunter College of the City University of New York.

Padilla, Y.C., & Daigle, L.E. (1998). Inter-agency collaboration in an international setting. *Administration in Social Work, 22*(1), 65–81.

Rios-Kohn, R. (1998). Intercountry adoption: An international perspective on the practice and standards. *Adoption Quarterly, 1*(4), 3–32.

Simon, R.J., Altstein, H., & Melli, M.S. (1994). *The case for transracial adoption.* Washington, DC: The American University Press.

Thiederman, S. (1988). Overcoming cultural and language barriers. *Personnel Journal, 67*(12), 34–40.

Thuy, V. (1986). The psychosocial needs of Southeast Asian refugees: Principles for understanding. In L. M. Healy (Ed.), *Toward improving service to Southeast Asian refugees.* West Hartford, CT: University of Connecticut School of Social Work.

United Nations (1989). *Convention on the Rights of the Child.* Available at www. unhchr.ch. Accessed August 23, 2000.

CHAPTER 10

UNDERSTANDING AND INFLUENCING GLOBAL POLICY

There are numerous, often untapped, opportunities for social workers to influence global social policy. These range from local or national lobbying and educational campaigns to collaborative ventures on a global scale. Three dimensions of international social work action, as defined in Chapter 1, relate to global social policy. The first is the capacity of social workers to develop and promulgate positions on social aspects of their own country's foreign policy and other policies that affect people in other countries. The second is social work's competence to work as a worldwide movement to develop positions on important global social issues, to contribute to the resolution of global problems related to the profession's sphere of expertise, and to influence global social policies of world bodies. Comparative policy analysis, undertaken to gain a better understanding of social policy or to identify potential innovations that can be borrowed from other systems, is the third aspect of international social work action. It will be discussed briefly in this chapter and more fully in Chapter 12.

This chapter emphasizes the what, why, when, and how of policy action in the international social work arena. Following a brief definition of social policy and social welfare, the focus will be on international policy and the emerging field of global policy. A rationale for social work action will be discussed, including consideration of policy content and values. The stages of international/global policy processes will be described in the context of opportunities for influence. Influence strategies will be briefly outlined before turning to case examples that illustrate the policy arenas, stages, and strategies discussed.

INTERNATIONAL AND GLOBAL SOCIAL POLICY DEFINED

Social policy shapes the context for social work interventions and for clients' well-being. Social policy usually refers to "those principles, procedures, and courses of action established in statute, administrative code and agency regulation that affect people's social well-being" (Dear, 1995, p. 2227). The scope is potentially broad, including social services, health, education, housing, and the social impacts of economic and environmental policies. The goal of social policy is enhanced social welfare, defined by Midgley (1997) as "a condition of human well-being that exists when social problems are managed, when human needs are met, and when social opportunities are maximised" (p. 5). Midgley's broad definition is useful in examining global social policies because the concept of maximizing social opportunities fits with the human rights emphasis of many such policies.

Although an earlier emphasis in international social work was on comparative social policy analysis, an action-oriented policy-influencing approach is more in keeping with the definition of international social work used in this book. This approach also fits with general trends in the field of social policy:

> The social policy context of social work practice is being transformed from strictly descriptive, historical and conceptual orientations that exclude practice realities to a prescriptive, problem-solving, action- and practice-oriented interventive method for social policy reform. Helping people by formulating and implementing social policy is the core of this development. (Iatridis, 1995, pp. 1855–1856)

Types of Policy or Policy Arenas

In Chapter 1, the increasing impact that the policies of one nation are having on the people and policies of other nations was described as a facet of global interdependence. Each country has social welfare policies that identify social entitlements, benefits, and social protections and address social rights and their limits. These are usually labeled domestic policy; however, in the global perspective, policies are rarely purely domestic in impact. The policies of one nation may influence the development and content of policies of other nations, discussed in Chapter 5 as social policy emulation. Some policy actions at the national level have a direct cross-national impact and affect people from other countries or the general state of well-being in other countries. Immigration laws stand out as particularly cogent examples. It is also at the national level that social aspects of foreign policy should be considered, including foreign assistance programs and issues dealing with social questions at the UN and other intergovernmental bodies. Although international in impact, the targets of influence for such policies are individual national governments; therefore, they may be referred to as international aspects of national policy.

For social workers in the industrialized countries, influencing internationally related national policies is a particularly important role. This was underscored at a 1986 gathering of African NGOs; these organizations issued a declaration calling on "Northern NGOs to 'reorient their activities' towards development education, advocacy and information flows, and in particular to attack 'policies of their governments, corporations and multilateral institutions . . . which adversely affect the quality of life and political and economic independence of African countries' " (Clark, 1992, p. 195).

European educators who were asked to suggest international roles for American social workers expressed the same sentiment, indicating that an important international role for social workers is to monitor the international actions of their own governments and to seek to influence these toward social justice (Healy, 1985).

Other policies are more truly global in content and impact and by nature of the processes through which they are adopted. Global social policies are those formulated by international intergovernmental bodies either with or without the force of sanctions to encourage compliance. The targets for influence efforts are therefore international organizations.

Deacon and co-authors (1997) argue that globalization will transform traditional social policy analysis and lead to more emphasis on global social policy. They predict the increasing "supranationalization or globalization of social policy instruments, policy and provision" (p. 2). The three essential purposes of social policy—regulation, redistribution, and social provision—are at least weakly present in some global policies. Current evidence of these, although somewhat minimal to date, exists most clearly in the European Union (EU), but there are also examples from the UN and World Bank. There are already some international organizations that raise money from nations and spend it on the basis of social needs, thus engaging in redistribution. UNICEF, UNDP, and the World Food Program are all examples of this. The World Bank raises money from member states and lends it to others at non-market terms, also a form of redistribution. Recent pressure on the IMF and the World Bank to soften loan conditions and preserve a broader social safety net in developing countries is the result of a global social reformist effort aimed at redistribution of resources.

These international bodies—the UN, World Bank, IMF, the Organization for Economic Cooperation and Development (OECD), the International Labor Organization (ILO), and the EU—also have the "capacity to influence national social policy" (Deacon, Hulse, & Stubbs, 1997, p. 24). The role of the IMF in regulating the policies of debtor nations was explained in Chapter 5. The UN human rights conventions, such as on women and on children, include compliance provisions that require changes in national policy in many nations. Thus there is considerable regulation in the human rights area. Whereas direct provision by international organizations is less frequent, Deacon et al. cite the UN High Commission for Refugees as an example of an agency involved in considerable international social provision. Using Midgley's (1997) definition of social welfare, expansion and guarantees of human rights are also social provisions. Therefore, "global standards and agenda setting play roles in the rapid expansion of programs of some states" (Deacon et al., 1997, p. 6). In addition, there are a growing number of instances in which supranational agencies are undertaking efforts "to secure poverty programmes, to secure human and political rights, and to protect minorities" (Deacon et al., 1997, p. 26).

Each of the areas discussed above is a potential arena for social work policy practice and action.

RATIONALE FOR SOCIAL WORK INVOLVEMENT: POLICY AGENDA AND PROFESSIONAL VALUES

Strong arguments for the necessity of social work involvement in global policy are the nature of the policy agenda and the ethical commitments of the profession.

Policy Agenda

Global policy agenda is dominated by issues that are within the expertise and concern of professional social work. As discussed in an earlier chapter, most of these fall within the two overarching themes of development and human rights. In the discussion of global interdependence in Chapter 5, the following issues were presented: migration, HIV/AIDS, poverty, the status of women, and street children. Each is part of the policy agenda at both the national and global level. And there are many more issues on the global agenda that are of concern to social work, including drug abuse and other addictions; aging; interethnic violence and conflict; child labor, child abuse and neglect, and other child welfare issues; mental health; and the rights of minority groups and indigenous peoples. All of these are appropriately within the domain of social work expertise, which supports the claim that the profession has a role in policy formulation and implementation. The cases later in this chapter will focus on immigration, violence against women, and child welfare as policy issues.

Values and Ethical Commitments

Social workers are bound by ethical codes at the international level and the national level, as explained in Chapter 7. Many of these codes define all social workers' responsibilities as including social reform or social change, in addition to their everyday practice duties. As stated in the IFSW Code of Ethics (1994), social workers should "contribute professional expertise to the development of policies and programs which improve the quality of life in society" (Section 3.2.6). In addition, social workers should "identify and interpret social needs" (Section 3.2.7) and "identify and interpret the basis and nature of individual, group, community, national and international social problems" (Section 3.2.8). Many national codes express similar values. There are a number of points addressing social responsibility in the NASW Code of Ethics, but one provision explicitly states: "The social worker should advocate changes in policy and legislation to improve social conditions and to promote social justice" (National Association of Social Workers, 1996, VI.F.6).

The involvement of the social work profession in social policy varies from country to country. In the United Kingdom, social policy is defined as a separate profession, and in the U.S. tradition, both areas are part of social work. In spite of this difference, the IFSW Code of Ethics suggests that social workers must accept the responsibility for social change in the interdependent world.

SOCIAL POLICY ACTIONS IN PRACTICE

Comparative and Global Policy Analysis

Policy analysis is an important skill for international policy action because social workers must know how to analyze domestic policies for their international impact and global policies in order to determine appropriate action. Einbinder (1995) describes policy analysis as "a set of technical skills used to describe, assess and influence social policies and a perspective about what government should do that is based on an assessment of the circumstances and potential for interventions to make things better" (p. 1850). Comparative social policy involves analysis of other countries' social welfare policies in order to learn different ways of addressing social problems and to gain a better understanding of the policies of nations in relation to each other. Cross-national analysis "is concerned with understanding why services and benefits are provided in a certain prescribed way at a specific point in history given all possible alternatives and options. It is a focus on the reasons that explain policy and program service delivery choices that differentiates analysis from description" (Tracy, 1992). These areas will be discussed further in Chapter 12.

There are considerable methodological challenges involved in comparative policy analysis. Among the most common problems are accuracy and comparability of data across nations; variations in definitions of terms and concepts; and the need to explore cultural differences in policy environment, content, and process in order to make appropriate interpretations (Midgley, 1997).

In keeping with their assessment of policy as increasingly global, Deacon and colleagues advocate a shift in the locus of analysis from comparative to global. They recommend a process for global policy analysis that includes an analysis of pressures for globalization versus national sovereignty in the policy being considered and recasting such traditional analytical concepts as social justice, rights and entitlements, universality and diversity, and public versus private provision as global phenomena. The analyst would also examine global goals, obstacles, and strategies for policy improvement (Deacon et al., 1997). An understanding of comparative policy and the skill of analysis at the comparative and global level are important foundations for global policy influencing efforts.

Stages of the Policy-Making Process: When to Influence Policy

The making of policy is a continuous process that begins with agenda setting and continues throughout the implementation of a regulation or program. Thus policy can be influenced during three stages of this process: agenda setting, policy formulation, and implementation (Willetts, 1996).

Agenda Setting. Agenda setting is a critical stage of the policy-making process. It is during this phase that what will be discussed or worked on is decided. According to DiNitto and Dye (1983), "Deciding what is to be decided is the most important stage of the policy-making process. . . . Societal conditions not defined as problems never become policy issues" (p. 14).

Through data gathering, educational campaigns, and other public activities, new social problems are defined and recognized and become part of the policy agenda. The example of violence against women demonstrates the emergence of a new social problem. Thirty years ago, in almost every country in the world, domestic violence was regarded as a private issue. Today, it is widely recognized as a social problem requiring intervention. As a result of information and publicity campaigns, the problem of violence against women was placed prominently on the agenda of the 1993 World Conference on Human Rights in Vienna; the Vienna Declaration and Programme of Action (1993) specifically called for establishing a Special Rapporteur on Violence Against Women. Two years later, the Beijing Platform for Action (1995), emanating from the Women's Conference, identified violence against women as one of 12 areas of critical concern. Case 10.2 will demonstrate the use of international machinery to influence a national policy agenda on violence against women.

Policy Formulation. The policy formulation phase is, of course, the core phase when policy intent and content are specified and agreement is secured. The target for influence at this stage is a national legislature, a national delegation to the UN, a UN committee, the UN General Assembly, or, perhaps, a world conference. To influence this phase, social workers and the NGOs through which they work need to have a vision of desired policy directions; these become the ingredients for efforts to influence policy makers to include particular elements in a policy. Sharing research and documentation with policy makers can be useful at this stage, especially if the authors have credibility. Case 10.3 demonstrates social work involvement in a global policy formulation effort.

Policy Implementation. During the implementation phase, policy can become operational, be neglected, or as often happens, redefined. Influencing implementation is essential to reshape policy, to ensure that directives are carried out, and to influence interpretations and regulations (Willetts, 1996). In the past, social workers (and others) often assumed that the need for influencing was complete when a policy was adopted or a law was passed. Implementation analysis has shown that there is a continuing need for oversight and advocacy by interested parties to ensure that policies are implemented as designed, with appropriate resources and attention to policy intent. This requires focus on new targets of influence, usually multiple ones, including funders, administrative bodies, and sometimes, courts and the original legislative body.

Strategies: How to Influence Policy

There are many strategies available to social workers for influencing international and global policy. As explained above, many policies with international impact are made at the national level. In large part, skills used by social workers to influence local or national policy can also be adapted to the global policy arena. It is important, however, that social workers understand how policy is developed at the global level in order to identify differences in the process; these include the nature of representation and special provisions—reporting requirements, complaint procedures, rapporteurs—that create opportunities for influencing policy making and implementation. In the process of policy influencing, social workers may take on roles as researchers, community educators, lobbyists, coalition builders, advocates, and even diplomats. Radda Barnen, the Save the Children organization in Sweden, identified these roles for NGO action on human rights policy, as illustrated in the box below.

These multiple roles are appropriate for social work action in the global policy arena. Each will be discussed briefly.

Social workers have opportunities through their practice to collect data on social problems. These data can make important contributions to shaping the policy agenda and to policy formulation, especially because social workers have access to information about how people experience social conditions. Quantitative data are enlivened by selective use of case examples from social work practice; such cases certainly capture public attention but are also effective in helping legislators and diplomats understand the human face of social problems. Thus gathering data, developing case studies, and other research on social conditions are useful influence strategies.

Lobbying is well understood as a strategy for policy influence. Letter writing and calling legislators to support or oppose policy initiatives or to suggest new laws or revisions to proposed laws are important actions when the target for influence is a national legislature. Offering to share data and technical expertise with legislators who are drafting or supporting legislation may be useful. Lobbying is more effective if coordinated through professional organizations or other NGOs in order to mobilize many con-

ROLES FOR NGOS IN POLICY INFLUENCING

- monitoring and fact finding in their own or other countries;
- investigating and reporting on violations;
- informing and educating about human rights matters and the work of international organisations;
- mobilising interest groups and lobbying national governments and international bodies;
- advising on or directly contributing to the implementation of human rights standards.

Radda Barnen, 1993, quoted in Longford, 1996, pp. 234–235

stituents to contact legislators on the same issues. Ensuring that policies with international social impact are added to the legislative action agendas of such organizations is an important step. Thus an important role is to influence the lobbying agenda of social work professional groups. Direct lobbying of representatives at intergovernmental bodies is less often used. Instead, influencing is done by lobbying at the national level to affect the votes of country representatives or by using consultative status through NGOs to influence policy development. These will be illustrated in Case 10.3 later in the chapter.

Electronic lobbying is an important supplement to traditional letter writing, telephoning, and radio or television advertising. The power of international communications technologies was demonstrated in 1989 when student activists and their supporters were able to use fax machines to notify the world of the democratization movement in China and of the crushing of student dissent in Tien An Men Square. Electronic mail—email—is now used to share information, issue calls for action, generate and circulate petitions around the globe, and directly lobby policy makers. Dedicated websites can be developed; they are useful in educating the public on policy issues. Fitzgerald and McNutt (1999) argue that electronic advocacy, "the use of technologically intensive media to influence stakeholders to effect policy change," is replacing older techniques that have been rendered less effective by changes in the policy environment (p. 334). On a similar note, Ife predicted that more widespread use of the Internet would "allow links to be developed between people working on a social justice agenda in different countries, so that they can learn from each others' experiences and develop common action strategies" (quoted in Johnson, 1999, p. 378).

Public education is particularly important in shaping international policy. Effective public education campaigns require skill in developing educational messages and in use of the media to get wide distribution of information. Public opinion is an important element in global policy. Olsen (1996) suggests that the public is more internationally minded than official government representatives and may be an important force for global humanitarianism in the future. Public opinion, shaped by media attention, has been important in mobilizing action on a number of global issues. When a severe famine occurred in Ethiopia in the 1980s, extensive television coverage resulted in both unprecedented private giving and demands for government action. The successful action campaign against marketing baby formula to poor countries—also in the 1980s—was due in part to public outcry, stimulated by an effective media public education campaign. These cases and many others demonstrate the effectiveness of educational campaigns and media attention in influencing action on global problems. Public education, then, is likely to grow in importance as a strategy for global social change.

Education combined with community organization can be useful in empowering affected communities to advocate for themselves. Direct work with the poor, usually through NGOs, leads to raised consciousness and concerted action (Clark, 1992). In this way, social work contributes to the building of small and large social movements that will have an impact on policy. Grassroots movements have been important in formulation of environmental and development policies, drawing on the direct experience of those affected.

To make an impact in the global arena, interdisciplinary efforts are almost always necessary. Development and human rights, the major policy foci, are both multidisciplinary fields. Social workers must form coalitions with persons from law, agriculture, public health, education, child development, and other fields in order to influence the interdisciplinary bureaucracies of the UN. Links to economists may be useful in pressuring the World Bank about policy issues. Although important in domestic work, interdisciplinary efforts are essential internationally. Readers will recall that in Chapter 3 lack of skill and effort in interdisciplinary work were suggested as causes of social work's diminished influence in the UN system as development became the focus.

Diplomacy, including an understanding of the politics of compromise, is also essential in most policy work, especially in the international arena. When they approach country representatives, policy influencers must be sensitive to cultural differences in communication and to the impact of national interests and international politics. As Case 10.3 will illustrate, knowing how and when to compromise is an essential part of international diplomacy. In the case of the Convention on the Rights of the Child, the right to freedom of religion and the issue of abortion were left vague in order to secure agreement to the treaty as a whole. At times, to press for specificity could unravel months of hard work.

The international policy-making and implementation processes have special provisions that create opportunities for influence. For the social rights protected by human rights treaties, advocates can utilize the international complaint-recourse procedures and complaint-information procedures provided under the treaties to draw attention to policy implementation problems and violations (Byrnes, 1993). The treaties also require reporting by states parties on their compliance with treaty provisions. The UN committees designated to deal with human rights reports accept input from NGOs and use such information as part of the review of a country's progress. Social workers can work through NGOs to submit relevant data on policy noncompliance or implementation problems in areas such as children's services, rights of women, and treatment of minorities. If the UN body finds areas of concern, this criticism becomes pressure for policy change if it is publicized widely. Social workers and NGOs can utilize these as opportunities for effecting change.

Shaming may be an unusual term for social work practice, but shaming can be another tool for policy influence by using the global standards in conventions to cajole or embarrass countries into policy improvements or better implementation of international agreements. Byrnes (1993) refers to this strategy as "bringing the international back home" to influence the national context (p. 58). Another way of expressing this role is that social workers will act as what Sankey (1996) referred to as "the conscience of the world" (p. 273), a label he gave to human rights NGOs.

TYPES OF POLICIES AND STRATEGIES FOR INFLUENCE

Three cases have been selected to illustrate aspects of international and global policy. Case 10.1 discusses a domestic policy that is having significant impact on international populations and on other countries—an example of internationally related domestic policy. Case 10.2 is an example of utilization of international human rights machinery to influence national policy development, and Case 10.3 demonstrates a long-term policy formulation effort in global social policy. Each of the cases will illustrate use of various influence strategies and aspects of the phases of the policy process.

The laws presented in Case 10.1 are examples of domestic policies that are having an impact on international populations and on the countries from which they come—policies at the domestic-international interface. The targets for change efforts in such cases are at the national level; in this case, both legislative changes and court challenges are being pursued.

Social work involvement has included legislative lobbying, public education, coalition building, and public policy development. To lobby for legislative change, social workers had to determine what policy is desirable yet achievable and what elements are negotiable—policy formulation. Efforts are strengthened by coalition building, especially collaboration with immigrant groups and human rights advocacy groups. Participation in public education with other like-minded groups is an important function for social workers working to create the climate for policy change; it has particular urgency in this case. Already, some of the welfare reform provisions that denied benefits such as food stamps to long-term permanent residents have been revised due to public outcry. Deportation is less well understood, and on the face of it, the public is likely to support the deportation of criminals. Social workers can contribute real-life stories from their case experiences that can engender public sympathy and build support for at least a restoration of an appeal procedure in deportation cases. Thus appropriate social work policy actions would include education both of the public and members of the profession, legislative lobbying, and coalition building. Policy development would be guided by the values of "social justice, equality, democratic processes and empowerment of disadvantaged and powerless people" (Iatridis, 1995, p. 1856).

Deportations create the need for policy actions by social workers in the receiving countries to ensure that deportees are assisted in resettlement or, in the case of dangerous offenders, that mechanisms are developed for follow-up monitoring. Together, social workers and migration advocates might join to initiate cross-national discussions on new migration issues.

Of course, the laws outlined in Case 10.1 have also heightened the need for social work knowledge. Misinformed advice to a client could result in

CASE 10.1: DOMESTIC POLICY WITH INTERNATIONAL IMPACT

Three laws passed by the U.S. Congress in 1996 affected long-term immigrant residents: Illegal Immigration Reform and Immigrant Responsibility Act, Anti-terrorism and Effective Death Penalty Act, and Personal Responsibility and Work Opportunity Reconciliation Act (welfare reform). As the bills were being considered, immigration advocates warned Congress of the potential negative effects of the legislation, but there was relatively little opposition mounted. Instead, the bills were swept into passage by politicians taking advantage of a wave of anti-immigrant sentiment that was part of larger concerns about "undeserving populations" unfairly taxing the American working family.

By 1998, the impacts on families in the United States and in source countries were being felt. Deportation clauses have proved particularly onerous and have posed special challenges for social workers. Among the effects of the bills:

- It is now more difficult to reunite families of immigrants, as income requirements for sponsorship have been raised.
- The appeals process for deportation cases has been totally eliminated; deportations have increased, leading to separation of partners and separation of parents from children. Because those deported are permanently barred from the United States, these are permanent separations unless the U.S. citizen children move to the country to which their parent has been deported.
- Many more offenses are now deportable offenses, including relatively minor crimes; family violence offenses are included.
- Resident immigrants can be deported for offenses committed 20 or more years ago, even if when committed the act would not have qualified as a felony.
- The increased number of deportees is having a negative effect on the receiving countries. Deportees fall into two major groups—those convicted of serious offenses, including drugs and violence, who are sent home with no warning to officials in their home countries and those who have committed minor offenses, who may have come to the U.S. when they were very young and have no current ties to their homeland. Both groups are creating a destablizing effect on the countries to which they return. (Ward, 1999)

Although somewhat late to recognize the potential harm in the legislation, social workers in various states have organized to lobby for changes. In Connecticut, for example, a social worker is heading up a voluntary organization of West Indian immigrants, which has mobilized a campaign

(continued)

on the issue. Their actions have included holding a series of educational fora for immigrants on the impact of the law; holding legislative fora for candidates for Congress to ask them to comment on the law and commit to working for change; linking to a national Caribbean coalition on the same issue; and conducting individual lobbying activities of letter writing and calling. An important part of the effort has been to unite immigrant groups into the Connecticut Legal Immigrant and Refugee Advocacy Coalition to work on the issue. There have also been efforts to urge social work organizations to make immigration reform a legislative action priority (Joyce Hamilton, personal communications, October 14, 1999).

deportation and permanent barring from the United States. For example, a community organizer may encourage long-term resident immigrants to apply for citizenship in order to strengthen their political clout; however, it was during citizenship applications that many of the deportees were "uncovered" as prior offenders and deported. Thus any social worker working with immigrants should be informed of the risks. Another practice challenge is the interaction of the immigration provisions with domestic violence laws and guidelines for "good practice." Should a social worker encourage a battered woman to call the police on her immigrant partner and father of her children if the result may be his deportation and therefore loss of all support? What impact might these provisions have on child protective services practice? The NASW (2000) policy statement on immigrants and refugees opposes laws that make domestic violence crimes by immigrants deportable offenses. The current reality, however, is that deportation may result from convictions for family assault. And although it would seem clear that social work confidentiality ethics would prevent social workers from complying with any mandatory reporting of illegal immigrants to authorities, clearer guidelines may be needed. At a minimum, social workers have an obligation to learn all that they can about reporting requirements in immigration cases and the ethical implication of compliance. In these areas, social work policy development is needed to guide professional action.

Among the useful policy influence strategies are using international human rights machinery to promote change and bringing international standards into domestic policy discussions to encourage change at home. Case 10.2 demonstrates these with emphasis on the successful efforts of a research and action group in Japan in using international human rights hearings and conferences to promote change in Japanese government policy.

Case 10.2 demonstrates the effective use of international human rights machinery to lobby for policy changes at the national level. Although this strategy may not work in all countries, many nations are influenced either by the "pull" of participating in international movements or by the "push" of negative international publicity showing them to be out of compliance with world standards. Sometimes, merely using international standards to

CASE 10.2: USING INTERNATIONAL MACHINERY TO INFLUENCE DOMESTIC POLICY

Movements to address violence against women began in Japan in the 1980s. Perhaps the greatest obstacle was the prevailing official attitude in Japan that domestic violence is "a personal, private and infrequent problem, as opposed to a prevalent, serious social problem" (Yoshihama, 1996, p. 1). Groups conducted research studies, documenting considerable incidence of violence against women and showing that a serious problem existed. Still, the national government was slow to acknowledge the issue.

A working group, the Domestic Violence Action and Research Group (DVARG), decided to take their advocacy efforts to the international level. The group was comprised of social workers and colleagues from other disciplines, including law and education. In 1993, DVARG participated in the NGO forum at the UN World Conference on Human Rights in Vienna. Through a workshop on Violence Against Asian Pacific Women and distribution of results of the research conducted in Japan to conference participants, delegates from other governments, and UN staff, the group was able to "let the rest of the world know of the virtual lack of responses by the Japanese government to the problem of domestic violence" (Yoshihama, 1996, p. 3). The group continued with the international strategy, presenting workshops at an ECOSOC-sponsored Asian Pacific Symposium on Women in Development in Manila in late 1993 and at the World Conference on Women in Beijing in 1995. The Japanese study results were included in several global reports on domestic violence, including the final report of the Special Rapporteur on Violence Against Women appointed by the UN.

Through these activities and the global publicity that accompanied them, the DVARG succeeded in getting the attention of the Japanese government. Responding to this combination of internal and external pressure, the Japanese government proposed creation of a UN fund to combat violence against women in 1995. At home, a plan to develop antiviolence legislation was announced in 1996.

Case developed from Yoshihama, 1996, 1998.

encourage change at home will be effective; this strategy can be enhanced by research on programs and policy changes that have been enacted elsewhere (Byrnes, 1993). In other cases, such as the Japanese example above, "shaming" is needed through drawing international attention to lack of compliance with standards. Thus as one observer noted, human rights treaties are both "a tool and a stick to use in lobbying government" (cited in van der Straeten, 1990, p. 31).

As noted earlier, a number of international mechanisms exist through which human rights–related policies can be influenced. In Jamaica, the NGO Jamaica Coalition on the Rights of the Child filed an alternative NGO report that supplemented and challenged the official report by the Jamaican government on compliance with the Convention on the Rights of the Child (CRC). The information provided was used by a UN committee in its recommendations to the government for needed changes in policy and services for children. This example also demonstrates successful influencing of the implementation phase of policy. The CRC, in particular, includes basic standards for certain social services. The process that led to the convention is discussed in Case 10.3.

The 10-year period of the drafting of the CRC provided numerous opportunities for social work participation in the shaping of global policy. An excellent example of global social policy, the Convention recognizes a wide array of children's rights. "To recognize in a legally binding document that children are members of the international community and have specific rights as individuals, separate from the government, separate from the family, is remarkable—and I think revolutionary is a fair word to use for that" (cited in vander Straeten, 1990, p. 27). First proposed in February 1978 by the government of Poland, the CRC was unanimously adopted by the UN General Assembly in 1989 and has been ratified by all but two UN member nations as of 1999.

Case 10.3 illustrates that social workers can have an important influence on the formulation of global policy. Through activities that have followed the adoption and ratification of the CRC, social workers have also influenced the implementation process in many countries. The importance of this role is underscored by the fact that the convention is the only human rights treaty that gives NGOs a role in monitoring compliance (Longford, 1996). In this case, social workers were able to capitalize on an opportunity to work on an issue raised by UN delegates.

CASE 10.3: SHAPING GLOBAL POLICY: THE CONVENTION ON THE RIGHTS OF THE CHILD

Social work involvement in the convention's drafting process was channeled through various NGOs with consultative status to the UN, including the International Council on Social Welfare (ICSW) and Defense for Children International (DCI). The CRC was drafted by a working group comprised of member states of the Commission on Human Rights but open to all governments and to NGOs with consultative status. More than 40 NGOs participated. "There seems to be general recognition within the

(continued)

UN, among governments, and in the NGO community itself, that their impact on the Convention on the Rights of the Child was both quite unprecedented in degree and particularly useful and constructive" (Longford, 1996, p. 222). Although the outcome is an important international policy affecting social work, the process is instructive to those who wish to influence policy on the global level in the future.

NGO influence did not get off to a good start. As described by Longford, who represented Britain on the working group, "The NGO contribution at the 1983 meeting was not particularly impressive. . . . Some of the NGO speakers were inexperienced and put forward in an unconvincing way points of view that were either irrelevant or impracticable" (1996, p. 221). Nigel Cantwell, from the lead NGO, Defense for Children International (DCI), put it this way:

> There was a feeling of great frustration among NGO representatives, however; they knew that they had a potentially major contribution to make and that they—and children—were somehow losing out because of an inability to "get the message" over in the right way and at the right time. Very few had had previous experience of working within this kind of context. Individual NGOs were certainly given the floor almost every time they requested it, but all too often they wasted these valuable opportunities by labouring a viewpoint that was clearly not viable or even arguing a point among themselves, rather than putting a reasoned proposal to the government delegates. (cited in Longford, 1996, p. 223)

The NGOs took action and reorganized themselves to improve their impact. They formed a group to address two major problems, lack of preparedness and the need to develop a more unified NGO position. Over the next 5 years, about 20 NGOs cooperated through the group, with DCI assuming the role of secretariat. The group met regularly and developed cogent proposals for submission to the working group. Patience and willingness to stick with the process over many years were important to a successful strategy. Cairnes, a representative of the UN Office of the Presbyterian Church, described the efforts of the core group who monitored the ways issues were being shaped during the drafting process: "If there were concerns about certain elements, they might publicize that and say 'we need to get a rush on and put some heat on governments to see if we can get this turned around.' It's that kind of back and forth—revision, revision, revision—process until you get to the point where you've got the best available" (cited in vander Straeten, 1990, p. 11).

The NGOs also developed strategies for formal and informal influence of working group members, holding annual "briefings" for country delegates prior to the official meetings and taking advantage of opportunities to interact informally with the country representatives:

(continued)

As the NGO representatives became more familiar with the procedures within the U.N., they became more skilled negotiators, and they organised themselves to become an effective lobby. . . . Members of the NGO group made the most of the opportunities provided by social events to develop informal contacts with governmental delegates and the Working Group Chairman. The friendships which built up during our weeks in Geneva were certainly an important ingredient in the teamwork which developed in the whole Working Group as drafting progressed. (Longford, 1996, pp. 224–225).

At the end of the process, the NGO group believed it had had substantial influence on the substance of about 15 of the articles, had some impact on almost that many, and had, in fact, proposed the language adopted for 2 (Longford, 1996). This impact was achieved by adding organization and coordination to the already substantial NGO advantage of expertise in children's issues. In addition, increased knowledge of UN procedures and sensitivity to the demands of international policy formulation and adoption proved critical. International policy making, especially in declarations and conventions, is a process of working for achievable concensus, not securing a majority of votes. "NGO delegates showed great wisdom in not pressing too hard for the inclusion of overambitious provisions which could have created problems for many countries" (Longford, 1996, p. 227).

CONCLUSION

The cases and other examples discussed in this chapter demonstrate that social work has considerable potential to influence international and global policy and has had some modest success in past efforts. The agenda is large, perhaps daunting. Deacon et al. (1997) argue that the major challenge in global policy in the future will be to determine how to balance human needs with global capitalism. Lorenz (1997) argues that the social work profession should make this its priority in global policy; because of the extensive contact social workers have with those who "lose" in the global economy, the profession is well positioned to call attention to the negative effects of market principles dominating the social domain. Thus he calls for social work to play a role in educating the public on "the distinction between what the market can achieve and what it cannot achieve" (p. 9).

Such a macro-level agenda will seem beyond the reach of many social workers, but there are opportunities for much more modest action. The greatest barrier to international or global action, however, is failure to consider global responsibilities as part of professional commitment. Educational efforts to help social workers remove "borders" from their thinking about social policy and action are needed. The impact of global interdependence on professional roles and responsibilities needs much greater attention.

As suggested in Chapter 7, attention to values will assist in this redefinition of role. It is useful to draw on the values that Iatridis (1995) suggests for policy practice because they are highly relevant in developing policy positions at the global level; global policy practice should be shaped by commitments to "social justice, equality, democratic processes, and empowerment of disadvantaged and powerless people" (p. 1856). These values provide a link to social work's mission, and they can be useful to individual social workers, to NGOs, and to organized professional bodies in selecting a policy agenda and in guiding policy content and strategy formulation.

Nonetheless, the challenge to address global capitalism and to engage in policy analysis and influence at the global level will seem overwhelming to many social workers. There are shorter-term policy actions that may help social workers who wonder where to start. Examples of realistic shorter-term actions are:

1. Encourage and develop cross-border agreements on social service practice, such as those discussed in Chapter 9.

2. Encourage the signing and ratification of global treaties related to social work, such as the Hague Convention on Intercountry Adoption. Social workers in the U.S. can lobby and conduct public education campaigns to urge ratification of the CRC and CEDAW while those in countries that have registered official reservations to provisions in CEDAW can work to overcome these.

3. Engage in public education campaigns, especially on human rights issues and treaty obligations. This will require increased knowledge of the global treaties and their potential to influence national policies and services.

4. Learn as much as possible about how immigration policy affects families in countries with significant levels of immigration or emigration, and work to influence policies to keep immigration processes as "family friendly" as possible. Included in this is the responsibility to be fully informed of reporting requirements and their legal and ethical ramifications.

Social agencies have a role in international policy. Beyond specific services offered, agencies express their commitments through public policy activities and through use of agency resources. Agency public policy agendas should include related international issues, especially immigration policies that affect agencies' clients. Agencies can also include international issues within their sphere of interest—for example, a family-planning agency might advocate world population assistance, a YWCA could lobby on global women's issues, and international adoption agencies could address child welfare improvements for children in other countries. Some international advocacy can be done at very local levels by bringing case experience to policy makers.

Public policy can also be influenced using agency resources. Socially responsible investing is one such strategy for influencing international policy. Widespread in the 1980s around the issue of apartheid in South Africa, more recent programs of socially responsible investing have avoided investments in companies involved in gun sales, in sales of products produced with exploitive child labor, or in companies engaged in environmental degradation.

Finally, the international professional organizations could expand their efforts in policy influencing. The process would be more dynamic and involve more social workers if part of the agendas of international social work meetings were devoted to policy and issue discussions. The purposes of such discussions would include member education but would emphasize development of a policy agenda and action plans. Issues for international attention could be identified and priorities agreed on. The meetings could facilitate the formation of international coalitions to work on social work's positions on issues, with lobbying conducted electronically between meetings. Some of this is currently done by IFSW, but it could be expanded within that organization and in the IASSW and in regional groups. A strong global policy presence will be essential for the profession to maintain its viability in the 21st century.

REFERENCES

Byrnes, A. (1993). Some strategies for using international human rights law and procedures to advance women's human rights. In M. Schuler (Ed.), *Claiming our place: Working the human rights system to women's advantage* (pp. 51–64). Washington, DC: Institute for Women, Law and Development.

Clark, J. (1992). Policy influence, lobbying and advocacy. In M. Edwards & D. Hulme (Eds.), *Making a difference: NGOs and development in a changing world* (pp. 191–202). London: Earthscan Publications.

Deacon, B., Hulse, M., & Stubbs, P. (1997). *Global social policy: International organizations and the future of welfare.* London: Sage.

Dear, R. (1995). Social welfare policy. In R. Edwards (Ed.), *Encyclopedia of Social Work* (19th ed., pp. 2226–2237). Washington, DC: NASW Press.

DiNitto, D.M., & Dye, T.R. (1983). *Social welfare politics and public policy.* Englewood Cliffs, NJ: Prentice Hall.

Einbinder, S.D. (1995). Policy analysis. In R. Edwards (Ed.), *Encyclopedia of social work* (19th ed., pp. 1849–1855). Washington, DC: NASW Press.

Fitzgerald, E., & McNutt, J. (1999). Electronic advocacy in policy practice: A framework for teaching technologically based practice. *Journal of Social Work Education, 35*(3), 331–341.

Healy, L.M. (1985). *The role of the international dimension in graduate social work education in the United States.* Unpublished doctoral dissertation, Rutgers University, New Brunswick, NJ.

Iatridis, Demetrius (1995). Policy practice. In R. Edwards (Ed.), *Encyclopedia of social work* (19th ed., pp. 1855–1866). Washington, DC: NASW Press.

International Federation of Social Workers (1994). *International code of ethics for the professional social worker.* Oslo, Norway: Author.

Johnson, A. (1999). "Globalization from below: Using the internet to internationalize social work education. *Journal of Social Work Education, 35*(3), 377–393.

Longford, M. (1996). NGOs and the rights of the child. In P. Willetts (Ed.), *The conscience of the world* (pp. 214–240). Washington, DC: Brookings Institution.

Lorenz, W. (1997, August 24). *Social work in a changing Europe.* Paper presented to the Joint European Regional Seminar of IFSW and EASSW on Culture and Identity, Dublin, Ireland.

Midgley, J. (1997). *Social welfare in global context.* Thousand Oaks, CA: Sage.

National Association of Social Workers (1996). *Code of ethics.* Washington, DC: Author.

National Association of Social Workers (2000). Immigrants and refugees. In *Social Work Speaks National Association of Social Workers Policy Statements 2000–2003* (5th ed., pp. 170–177). Washington, DC: Author.

Olsen, G.R. (1996). Public opinion, international civil society, and North-South policy since the cold war. In O. Stokke (Ed.), *Foreign aid towards the year 2000: Experience and challenges.* London: Frank Cass & Co.

Sankey, J. (1996). Conclusions. In P. Willetts (Ed.), *The conscience of the world.* Washington, DC: Brookings Institution.

Tracy, M. (1992). "Cross-national social welfare policy analysis in the graduate curriculum: A comparative process model. *Journal of Social Work Education 28*(3), 341–352.

United Nations (1995). *Platform for action and the Beijing Declaration.* New York: Author.

United Nations (1993). *The Vienna Declaration and Programme of Action.* New York: Author.

vander Straeten, S. (1990). The United Nations Convention on the Rights of the Child: An interviewing and oral history project of social work in the international community. [Interview with Jim Cairnes]. Unpublished transcript. Warren Wilson College. Asheville, NC.

Ward, C.A. (1999). *Consequences of United States immigration policy: A Caribbean perspective.* Washington, DC: National Coalition on Caribbean Affairs.

Willetts, P. (1996). *Consultative status for NGOs at the United Nations. In P. Willetts (Ed.),* The conscience of the world (pp. 31–62). Washington, DC: Brookings Institution.

Yoshihama, M. (1996, November). Anti-domestic violence movements in Japan: A nationwide action-oriented research project and advocacy through international mechanisms. Paper presented at the International Social Work Conference, School of Social Work, University of Michigan, Ann Arbor, MI.

Yoshihama, M. (1998). Domestic violence in Japan: Research, program developments, and emerging movements. In A.R. Roberts (Ed.), *Battered women and their families* (2nd ed.). New York: Springer.

CHAPTER 11

EDUCATION FOR INTERNATIONAL PROFESSIONAL ACTION

Current Realities, Future Challenges

The preceding chapters support the argument that social workers need knowledge of international issues in order to practice competently in the 21st century. In this chapter, curriculum policy and content and other educational activities that support international learning in various parts of the world will be reviewed. Trends in related areas in higher education will be discussed, such as global, multicultural, and development education. The chapter will conclude with recommendations for developing educational programs to enhance international social work competence.

CURRENT PATTERNS: EDUCATION FOR INTERNATIONAL SOCIAL WORK

In many ways, social work education reflects the current state of development of international social work. Many, but not all, educational programs include some international content, but very few offer comprehensive curriculum in this area. In addition to course content, some programs offer a variety of internationally related activities such as faculty exchange, international field placements, study trips, and recruitment of international students.

In examining international education, the primary focus is placed on content—what students are taught about international topics. International curriculum content can be structured in various ways. The most common are to organize specialized courses on international topics or to infuse international content in parts of the general curriculum. Either approach can be adopted minimally or comprehensively, as shown in Table 11.1. Thus a program using the specialized, or focus, approach may offer a single course on international social welfare or social work or may develop a sequence of courses leading to specialization. Infusion may be relatively minimal—perhaps inclusion of a few modules or units in one or two courses—or comprehensive. The comprehensive approach to infusion is referred to as internationalization of the curriculum. In this approach, the concept of bor-

TABLE 11.1 Models for International Social Work Curricula

Target Group	Degree of Comprehensiveness	
	Minimum Essentials	Comprehensive
All students	Infusion of one or several modules	Internationalization of total curriculum
Self-selected group	Elective course	International concentration

ders is removed, and all subjects are examined in an international context. To date, internationalization remains more a goal than a reality.

In most schools of social work throughout the world, attention to international topics is minimal and is not sufficient to prepare students for the international responsibilities of practice or policy. Although no current comprehensive data are available, many studies have been done over the past decade that contribute to understanding the state of international curriculum. These will be summarized briefly below.

Global Overview of International Curriculum

A global study of international aspects of social work education was carried out in the late 1980s. All member schools of the International Association of Schools of Social Work (IASSW), 444, were surveyed, and 214 usable responses were received, or nearly 50% (Healy, 1990). The survey was conducted in four languages, English, French, Spanish, and Japanese. Responding schools represented the broad range of IASSW members, from postsecondary programs to schools offering graduate degrees, and 43 countries from all the world's regions: Africa, 20 responses; Asia, 70 responses; Europe, 68 responses; North America, 48 responses; and Latin America, 8 responses.

Nearly three quarters of the responding schools reported that some international content was included in their curricula; of these, more than half offered one or more courses specifically focused on international social work or social welfare (89 schools, or 42% of the total respondents). Estimates of the percentage of students' coursework devoted to international content ranged from a high of almost 19% in Africa to a low of just under 6% in North America. European programs reported the second lowest percentage at about 7% of coursework. A range of content areas were emphasized in these curricula. In just over half the responding programs, most or all students receive content on social and economic development. Three other subject areas were covered by at least one third of the schools: regional social policy issues (46%), cross-cultural content (42%), and global policy issues (34%). At the time of the study, global interdependence was reported as a topic by only 23% of programs. Other topics addressed by relatively few schools were the functions of social work in other countries (19%) and the functions of international social work organizations (13%). Schools in North

America were least likely to address issues related to the international profession; in fact, only three programs responded that students received information about these topics.

Other important regional differences were reported. Notably, all responding Latin American schools reported inclusion of content on social and economic development and on policy issues of interest to the region. This is consistent with the emphasis on political study discussed in the section on Argentina in Chapter 4. Cross-cultural content is covered by more than 70% of programs in North America, far higher than in any other region. In social work curriculum, the United States and Canada may well be leaders in this area. The study of comparative social welfare policy was also considerably higher in North America than in any other region. At the time of the survey, more African schools addressed global interdependence than did schools in other regions. The extent to which Africa has suffered from external controls and structural adjustment is a likely explanation, as illustrated in earlier discussions in this text.

Given the relatively underdeveloped state of international curriculum, it is encouraging that very few social work schools (7%) judged their international content fully adequate, and only 38% rated coverage as minimally adequate. Globally, almost 9 out of 10 respondents said that international content should be required for all students and recommended that 10% to 20% of students' coursework be devoted to international topics. Thus curriculum reform and increased globalization were widely supported by respondents to the survey. Some of their specific ideas for reform will be reported later in this chapter.

Although these data are still useful, there are limitations. The study predated most of the efforts to establish social work education in Russia and Eastern Europe and therefore does not shed light on the coverage of international topics in emerging programs. It would be useful to know if increased globalism and the extensive international consultation received by these programs have influenced the development of new curricula to include international perspectives. In the decade since the survey, other changes could also be expected, due to increased sensitivity to global interdependence in Asia and North America. Changes in Europe should be even more profound, as European Union (EU) policies on reciprocity in credentials and grants to encourage exchanges have intensified. Recent studies by Lyons (1996) and by Nagy and Falk (1996), however, suggest that such changes have been modest. Current information on the United States, Europe, and Japan follows.

International Content in the United States. Social work curriculum in the United States is regulated by the Council on Social Work Education (CSWE) through periodically issued curriculum policy statements. These statements identify essential components of curriculum that must be offered if a program is to be accredited. At the time of this writing, no international content was required. Individual social work programs decide whether to include international content, and if so, what content should be offered and how it should be structured. The Curriculum Policy Statement (CPS) adopted in 1992 does include the following statement as a "premise underlying social work education": "Effective social work programs recognize the interdependence of nations and the importance of worldwide professional cooperation" (Council on Social Work Education [CSWE], 1994, p. 134). The new statement on interdependence, however, is included in a portion of the policy statement that is not used to evaluate programs for accreditation. Thus, in reality, it states an emerging philosophy, not a true policy. Nonetheless, some programs have initiated internationalization efforts in response to the statement. (Historical note: The 1962 CSWE CPS contained several references to international social work, stating that students should gain knowledge of the profession in other countries and knowledge of other social welfare systems. The statement adopted in 1984 contained no reference to international or comparative content. For more information, see Healy [1999].)

The inclusion of international content in U.S. social work programs varies widely in terms of coverage, content, and curriculum approaches used. The high degree of variation is due in part to the lack of accreditation standards in this area; it also reflects an area in the process of development. A typical approach in Master's programs is to begin the international curriculum process by developing a specialized course on international social welfare or a topic within that area. The number of courses focusing on international topics is increasing; although it is more difficult to document, it is likely that there is a parallel increase in infused content.

A recent survey requesting international course materials yielded 69 course outlines on international topics from master's (MSW) and baccalaureate (BSW) programs; the majority were from MSW programs (Healy & Asamoah, 1997). Although this is not the total number being offered, comparison to earlier studies indicates substantial growth. A study of MSW programs, published in 1986, reported 39 courses offered by 27 programs (Healy, 1986), and a study published in 1980 found only 12 MSW courses on international topics (Boehm, 1980). It is more difficult to assess the number of programs that are infusing international content into mainstream courses. Most programs report some inclusion of international content; in many instances, however, the inclusion is anecdotal and haphazard, not an organized part of a curriculum plan. Thus examination of written course materials may show no evidence of international content.

There has been a recent shift in the emphasis of many of the specialized courses, indicating maturation in the field. Comparative social policy, usually limited to the Western welfare states, had been the dominant model for single courses on international social welfare. The comparative approach provided interesting knowledge, but it was not particularly effective in engaging students in defining a practice or other professional role related to the knowledge. Therefore, students could seldom see the applicability of the knowledge to their own futures. The new course emphases on global social problems, social development processes, special populations such as immigrants and displaced persons, and human rights are more appropriate preparation for international professional action.

> The largest number of courses now seem to emphasize the struggle for development in poorer nations and apply the development paradigm to global problems in developing and developed countries. Social policy is still the dominant area of focus, but an increasing number of courses also include practice content, and assignments increasingly encourage students to link international learning to their responsibilities as professional social workers. (Healy & Asamoah, 1997, p. v)

Sample course titles of these focus courses are International Social Work: Global Dimensions in Policy Analysis and Social Development Practice; Global Problems and Social Work Responsibility; Social Work and Displaced Populations: Refugees, Immigrants, and International Migrants; Social Development Practice; Human Rights; and Experiencing Community Among the Poor of Mexico. The latter is an example of travel study, an option used by programs to combine academic work with an experiential/cross-cultural component.

Although few programs have comprehensively infused international perspectives in their curricula, more are beginning the process of introducing international content. There is also growing recognition that international content need not be confined to social policy courses and that curriculum areas such as practice, human behavior/social environment, and ethics are enhanced by international content.

Several initiatives to encourage and assist curriculum development have been sponsored by the International Commission of the CSWE. The council's strategic plan calls for further work in this area; perhaps the next curriculum policy statement will lead rather than follow the field.

International Content in Europe. Within the EU, provisions for professional mobility allow social workers educated in one member country to freely travel to other member nations to work as social workers, as long as the training received meets agreed-upon EU standards. The EU has sponsored a number of initiatives to provide funding for professional exchanges in order to facilitate mobility and to encourage development of European perspectives. Under the ERASMUS program, in effect from 1987 to 1997, social work exchanges among EU countries grew. ERASMUS provided funds for curriculum development, faculty exchange, and multicountry seminars, as well as for student exchange programs, in an effort to facilitate "Europeanization at social as well as economic levels," and "development of a European consciousness and identity" (Lyons & Ramanathan, 1999, p. 177). Additional exchanges with former Eastern bloc nations were funded through another EU initiative, TEMPUS. From these funding schemes, several intensive exchange programs in European social work have emerged. Lyons (1996) describes two: a collaborative program between Britain and Denmark and a Cooperative European Social Studies program in the Netherlands. In the former, 12 Danish and 12 U.K. students study together for one term in Copenhagen and another in Portsmouth, England. Between the academic semesters, students complete a field internship in the country other than their own (Horncastle, 1994; Lyons, 1996). In 1994, a master's degree in Comparative European Social Studies was established at the school of social work in Maastricht, with an emphasis on comparative European welfare; drawing students from various European countries, a potential outcome is development of a European social welfare perspective (Lyons, 1996).

Lyons (1996) criticized the developments to date for focusing too narrowly on European comparative social policy, stating that this approach ignores larger global issues and fails to provide "opportunities for students to participate and give meaning to their own aspirations to work cross-culturally and internationally" (p. 190). Nagy and Falk (1996), who surveyed international curriculum efforts in Europe as well as in Australia, Canada, and the United States, also found international content in European schools to be Eurocentric; only 24 of 60 European schools responding to their survey offered a course focused on international issues, while 19 offered cross-cultural content. The authors' assessment was that the content showed little interest in issues of developing countries; where multiculturalism was emphasized, the focus was on domestic populations.

International Content in Japan. Interest in international issues has increased in Japan as the country's role in world affairs has become more prominent. In 1996, a survey showed that 29 out of 51 responding schools of social work offered courses on international social welfare (Mori, 1996). Whereas comparative social welfare was the most frequently covered topic in these courses, there was a wide variety of focal topics, including Asian sociology, war and peace, and human life and death. Multicultural issues were covered in a few of the courses, but was not a major theme. "Until recently, Japan was a homogeneous society and there has been little concern for or development of social work practice dealing with multicultural issues" (Mori, 1996, p. 219).

Coverage of international social work content in Japan increased considerably between 1988 and 1996. Twenty-nine special courses in international social welfare were identified in 1996 compared with 14 (out of 39 respondents) in 1992 and only 11 (out of 48 respondents) in 1988 (Kojima, 1988, 1992). In the 1988 study, Kojima found that the major purposes of international courses in Japan were to understand comparative social welfare, to understand the position of Japanese social welfare in the context of international trends, and to give students an international perspective. Among the Japanese programs that included international content in other areas of the curriculum, the most frequently covered topics were comparative social welfare policy, functions of social workers in other countries, and basic concepts of social or economic development (Kojima, 1988). Japanese educators demonstrate interests in particular social issues, including some not highly ranked in importance in other parts of the world. The issues they consider most important for the curriculum are human rights, peace, status of children worldwide, problems of the aged, and problems of the disabled (Kojima, 1988). In areas of peace, the aged, and the disabled, Japan leads other countries in level of interest.

In commenting on the wide variation in international content offered, Mori (1996) said that it may suggest a positive plurality of ideas, but more likely, she concludes, "it is . . . due to international social welfare being still a fragmented and not established mainstream course of study" (p. 219).

Field Placements and Educational Exchanges

International learning in social work can be facilitated through practicum opportunities. Many schools of social work have arranged international field placements for students. Surprisingly, 44% of responding schools in the global survey reported having had students complete field placements in other countries; Europe accounted for nearly half of these (Healy, 1990). Although 44% of schools is an impressive total, closer examination reveals that most of these schools have placed relatively few students in such placements and that international placements are handled on an episodic basis rather than as planned components of regular programs.

There are some examples of organized approaches to international field placement. One is the program described earlier between Denmark and Great Britain in which students complete their practicum in the country other than their own. For several years during the 1980s, Fordham University in New York City had a fieldwork unit in a refugee camp in Thailand, funded by Catholic Relief Services. An instructor from Fordham traveled with the students and assisted them in integrating their practical experience in Thailand with the rest of their education. And as mentioned earlier in the book, the Social Welfare Training course in Jamaica had an established program for Jamaican participants to complete an internship in Puerto Rico, and those from other Caribbean islands did internships in Jamaica. Each of these organized programs was undergirded by a philosophy of the value of cross-national experiential learning. The special challenges presented by international placements, which have impeded their use, and the opportunities for improvements will be discussed later in the chapter.

The Contribution of Other Learning Experiences

International perspectives are introduced through a number of other programs and strategies in addition to course content and practicums. Schools may informally enrich international learning by recruiting internationally diverse faculties and/or student bodies. Students exposed to instructors and peers from other countries will gain from informal interchanges and from classroom dialogue. An increasing number of schools are engaged in exchange or linkage projects with schools in other countries. Most of these agreements include faculty exchanges; some extend to student exchanges.

Studies suggest that about one third of U.S. schools have linkage arrangements with foreign schools (Healy, 1986, 1997); participation in such arrangements is greater in Europe, due to the many supports available under EU programs. Perhaps the most frequently reported international activities in the educational sector are the research and professional activities of faculty members. In a survey of U.S. schools of social work, for example, 85% reported that members of the faculty were engaged in international study, teaching, or research or were active with international social work organizations (Healy, 1986). The majority of schools had faculty members who present papers at international conferences. These instructors undoubtedly bring their international experiences into the classroom and may be responsible for a significant amount of anecdotal infusion of international perspectives. Planned curriculum and field experiences are essential for international education; however, there is untapped potential for improving ways to mine the experiences of international students and the international experiences of program faculty.

TRENDS IN BROADER EDUCATIONAL MOVEMENTS

The degree of internationalism within social work education is influenced by trends within higher education in general, including philosophical trends and the availability of funding and other support. In the United States, for example, support for international education has gone through cycles of expansion and decline. In 1966, Congress passed the International Education Act to improve U.S. capabilities in international relations and foreign language. In a speech to the annual meeting of the CSWE, the assistant secretary for education at the Department of Health, Education and Welfare (since dissolved and reconstituted as the Department of Health and Human Services and the Department of Education) predicted that the act would provide new funds for the education of graduate-level specialists in international studies in a range of professional schools including social work (Miller, 1968). In fact, funding for the act was never appropriated, and instead, international education entered a period of significant decline. Funding plummeted from both governmental and foundation sources—federal expenditures for research in foreign affairs fell from more than $20 million in 1969 to just $8.5 million in 1979, while Ford Foundation funds for international affairs training fell from $27 million annually in the mid-1960s to less than $3 million in 1978 (Healy, 1985, citing National Council on Foreign Language and International Studies brochure). The impact of decline—fewer specialists in strategically important language and area studies such as Asia and Latin America—led to another cycle of expansion. A presidential commission, the President's Commission on Foreign Language and International Studies, was established, and it issued a report in 1979 calling for increased attention to international education and foreign language (President's Commission on Foreign Language and International Studies, 1979). The late 1980's brought both promotion of the importance of global interdependence among business and intellectual leaders and attacks on global education as "un-American" by right-wing groups (Tye, 1999). Similar patterns of swings from neo-isolationism to interest in international affairs have followed in governmental programs and at many universities, in other countries as well as the United States. In his study of worldwide global education, Tye (1999) reported that extensive in-service global education training programs for teachers in Canada were cut back after the Canadian International Development Agency (CIDA) withdrew its funding. Social work is certainly influenced by such trends.

Philosophical and intellectual trends are also important. As social work education works toward internationalization, it can draw on developments in related fields in higher education. One source are other professions, many of which are more advanced in the internationalization process. Business schools have developed an array of courses and specializations focusing on the global aspects of their field; public health and the law have also taken steps to address international perspectives.

In general undergraduate education, there are a number of interdisciplinary curriculum movements that aim to introduce an international or global perspective. These movements are related to social work interests and may offer ideas for educational reform in the profession. Hughes-Wiener (1988) defined four domains that contribute to education for an international perspective: global education, contemporary cultures education, curriculum on intercultural relations, and development studies. Elements of these are addressed in various ways in levels of education from preschool through university. Tye (1999) identified peace and conflict studies, development education, intercultural education, human rights studies, and environmental studies as educational movements related to the broader global education field. "While each of these movements was seen as having its own goals, content, and constituencies, in the final analysis they were all seen as inextricably intertwined with global education and its goals" (Tye, 1999, p. 5).

In a work now considered a classic (see Hanvey [1979]), Hanvey described the outcome of global education as consisting of the following five elements: "perspective consciousness, 'state of the planet' awareness, cross-cultural awareness, knowledge of global dynamics, and awareness of human choices" (cited in Hughes-Wiener, 1988, p. 140). More recently, Tye (1999) described global education as

> learning about those problems and issues which cut across national boundaries and about the interconnectedness of systems—cultural, ecological, economic, political and technological. Global education also involves learning to understand and appreciate our neighbors who have different cultural backgrounds from ours; to see the world through the eyes and minds of others; and to realize that other people of the world need and want much the same things.

The emphases on cross-cultural understanding, human needs and choices, and interconnectedness of systems should resonate with social work educators.

Specialties Within Global Education

Peace Studies. Peace and conflict studies encompass the exploration of mechanisms for resolving and avoiding conflict and the search for the conditions that ensure peace such as economic and social justice. It should be underscored that peace studies are not only the study of methods of avoiding war but also the study of the pursuit of global justice (Wrightson & Ackermann, 1994). This emphasis increases its relevance for social work education.

Global Environmental Studies. Environmental studies have gained increased recognition as an important element of global education, cutting across science, ethics, politics, and other disciplines. Environmental studies include the examination of environmental problems—including deforestation, desertification, pollution, water shortages, and global warming—the study of ethical paradigms of resource use and personal responsibility, and the study of global and institutional politics in addressing environmental issues. The emphases on sustainability and on the need for an "ecological paradigm which stresses the harmoniousness of human interaction with the natural world" suggest that social work can borrow from environmental studies (Jancar, 1994, p. 307).

Human Rights Education. Human rights education is often included with other key topics in international education. Dimensions of values, international and national law, development, and domestic and global politics are addressed in teaching human rights, already emphasized as an critical aspect of international social work. Closer collaboration with interdisciplinary movements in human rights education could enhance social work education.

Multicultural Education. Multicultural or diversity education combine the two elements labeled contemporary cultures education and intercultural relations education by Hughes-Wiener (1988); the purposes of multicultural education are to teach both about various cultures in order to promote understanding and to teach about intercultural interactions to improve the capacity for effective work. Multicultural education is a required component of social work education in the United States, Canada, Great Britain, and probably elsewhere. Social work education has done a commendable job in recognizing the importance of cultural competence and in putting emphasis on it in the education of professionals. Attention to international aspects of cultural competence have lagged behind.

There has been very little interchange between general intercultural or multicultural education and social work education. More surprisingly, within higher education in general and within social work, there has been almost no interchange between ethnic studies or domestic multicultural education and international studies. A study conducted for the 1979 President's Commission on Foreign Language and International Studies declared that

DEVELOPMENT EDUCATION: DESIRED KNOWLEDGE GOALS

Development education builds relevant knowledge by:

- disseminating analysis of impediments to genuine development, particularly conditions of poverty and hunger in the Third World and their relationship to First World affluence
- reporting on people and nations struggling for a better life and the social political and economic context within which development efforts are being made
- presenting the facts that document the reality of global interdependence, mutual interest and common threats and concerns and the inextricable link between local and global problems and their solutions
- familiarizing the public with transnational inequities and conflicts that inhibit people's capacity to achieve their own goals for a decent quality of life
- making known the wide variety of structures and models through which development, in all its diversity, occurs

Quoted from Joint Working Group on Development Education, 1984, pp. 3–4.

scholars in ethnic studies and international studies were so resistant to collaboration that there was truly a "psychological distance" between the fields (Hawkins, 1979). The situation in social work is much the same. In curriculum work for the future, ties with colleagues in multicultural studies would enhance international social work education.

Development Education. The development education movement is another particularly relevant field for social work. Development education aims to create a "committed constituency for development" through education about world poverty, social justice, and possibilities and responsibilities for action (Joint Working Group on Development Education, 1984). Development education efforts can be found in universities and in NGO-sponsored public or specialized educational efforts. It is particularly congruent with international social work. The values and attitude outcomes for development education are discussed in Chapter 7. The knowledge and skills components of development education are also highly relevant for consideration by social work education.

In spite of the obvious links to needed social work knowledge and values, development education is not well known within social work education; efforts are needed to increase cooperation between the fields.

OBSTACLES TO INCREASING INTERNATIONAL EDUCATION

There are many real and perceived barriers, or obstacles, that have impeded the development of global education in social work and in higher education in general. In the late 1980s international survey cited earlier, respondents identified the following as significant obstacles, in descending order: lack of time in a full curriculum, lack of financial resources, not seen as relevant to graduates' jobs, rigid curriculum requirements, faculty unprepared to teach international content, and lack of curriculum materials (Healy, 1990). The obstacles were not equally experienced in all regions, but lack of time in a full curriculum was ranked first among obstacles to international curriculum in all five regions. Lack of financial resources was a frequent concern in Africa and Latin America. One third of respondents from North America cited rigid curriculum requirements as a barrier, the highest of any region, while more than one third of Asian respondents indicated that the faculty did not have the levels of competence and training necessary to teach international content. Only in North America did as many as 21% cite lack of student interest. The highest for any other region was 6%. In Tye's (1999) 52-country study of general global education, the most frequently mentioned obstacle was lack of adequate teacher training in global issues. This was followed by lack of "legitimacy" (my word) in the curriculum, in that global education is not an established curriculum area but must fit into existing areas. Lack of resources was also important in some areas, as were national or religious politics that favored cultural isolationism.

As a nonrequired area of social work education, particular problems that have faced international course content are lack of institutionalization and legitimacy. Offerings have often been dependent on a single faculty member, or only a few in each program; sustainability has been jeopardized when there are no institutional policies or structures to ensure that international content continues to be taught.

PLANS FOR IMPROVED INTERNATIONAL EDUCATION

Plans for improving international, or global, education for social workers should focus on the goal of preparation for international professional action. Improvements must build on current realities and should consider obstacles and opportunities, including learning from and linking to other areas in higher education. In the absence of standards for this area of education, each program has the responsibility to design its own international dimension. Education for international professional action encompasses a vast arena of potential areas of study. Planning and selectivity are key because sound curriculum requires careful design. "The social work curriculum is optimally viewed as an integrated system, with each component contributing to overall expected educational outcomes" (Ewalt, 1983). Currently, international curriculum suffers from lack of clear design and organization and, in many social work programs, fits haphazardly, if at all, with overall program educational goals.

Optimal curriculum design begins with defining a program mission and overall program goals. Learning outcomes for students and outcomes for other program activities are then delineated. As components of the educational program are developed, they should be designed to contribute to meeting overall educational goals and student outcomes. Therefore, in selecting international content and structure, educators need to consider how international learning will contribute to the overall mission of their school. One or more overall goals for international learning should be developed, tailored to each program. More than 30 years ago, Konopka (1969) proposed two broad goals for international learning that are still applicable today and could be adopted or adapted: (a) to improve the practice of social work in one's own country through knowledge of practices elsewhere; and (b) "to prepare for intelligent international cooperation in social work practice, theory and research" (pp. 1–3).

International Educational Outcomes

More specific educational outcomes flow from the overall goals for international learning specified by the program. There are three widely accepted categories of educational outcomes: changed attitudes, knowledge, and skills. Thus educators must identify the outcomes desired in order to select the most appropriate areas for inclusion in their educational program.

Attitude. In the global study discussed earlier (Healy, 1990), educators were asked to consider the value of five attitude outcomes. In order of importance, these are: sensitivity to cultural difference, concern for the problems of poor nations, a general worldview, an appreciation of global interdependence, and professional commitment to address global problems. Most respondents rated all outcomes as important; for purposes of curriculum design, therefore, they may all be considered potentially valuable attitude outcomes for social work students. With the exception of the lowest ranked outcome, these are similar to the five outcomes for global education defined by Hanvey (1979). Shaping attitudes is a particularly important consideration in designing international curriculum. A worldview and some understanding of the implications of global interdependence for one's professional role and identity are prerequisites for international professional action. Sensitivity to cultural difference is almost universally accepted as a component of social work, although the international dimensions of this responsibility are less well understood and need additional emphasis. Combining concern for global poverty with a professional commitment for action is a precondition for international solutions to the most pressing problems in the social work domain of expertise.

Knowledge. Content selected to give students knowledge can be chosen to support skill outcomes and to give students a base of minimum essentials in international social work. Categories of essential international knowledge for social work are: (a) cross-cultural knowledge, (b) understanding of major global social issues and the efforts to address them, (c) the international profession, and (d) resources for future learning. These can be expanded to the learning objectives listed in the box that follows.

Optimally, programs should include some content to support each knowledge area. Selection must be done with careful attention to the outcomes desired.

ESSENTIAL INTERNATIONAL KNOWLEDGE FOR SOCIAL WORK

a. Cross-cultural knowledge
   1. Knowledge of the role of culture in understanding human behavior
   2. Knowledge of cultures other than one's own and the principles for learning about cultures
   3. Understanding of the process and impact of voluntary and involuntary migration
   4. Knowledge of cross-cultural practice principles
   5. Knowledge of the major forces of human oppression internationally

b. Understanding of major global social issues and the efforts to address them
   1. Knowledge of selected world social problems
   2. Knowledge of the social welfare activities of major world organizations, including the UN
   3. Knowledge of basic concepts of social development
   4. Knowledge of major instruments of human rights
   5. Understanding of the social impacts of global interdependence

c. The international profession
   1. Knowledge of the profession in international context, including familiarity with the functions of social work in some other countries
   2. Knowledge of the roles of the international social work organizations

d. Resources for future learning
   1. Knowledge of some of the major sources of global and cross-national social welfare data
   2. Familiarity with social work scholarship in one or more other countries or regions, especially in one's area of professional interest and expertise

Skill. Desired skill outcomes are those that flow from the definition of international social work used in Chapter 1. Students should learn to practice effectively with international populations and to handle practice situations that require international knowledge. They should be able to contribute to domestic practice and policy through their knowledge of alternative social welfare systems and innovations in other countries. In fulfilling the policy and social change responsibilities of professionals, social workers should be able to identify, analyze, and influence aspects of public policy that affect social well-being in other countries and those that have an impact on international populations. Each of these skill outcomes moves beyond the capacity to act as an informed citizen in the global era, which is a fundamental expectation for all educated persons. It is also important for schools of social work to train specialists. Some social workers should gain adequate skill to become international practitioners in order to contribute directly to development work. Others need sufficient knowledge of policies and systems to work in coalitions with others from different nations and disciplines to monitor and influence global social policy, as defined in Chapter 10. For this to occur systematically, some schools of social work should develop skill-focused specializations in international social work, combining training in planning, community development, TOT, and program and fiscal management with international internships, content on international social welfare, and opportunities for language training.

Delivery and Resources for International Education: Possibilities Created by Technology

Increased use of communications technology is offering numerous enhancements to international education in social work. At the simplest level, resources available on the World Wide Web increase the accessibility of international information to students and faculty. Especially useful are websites maintained by the UN, government websites or those developed by university research centers that contain extensive country data, and the websites of social work organizations in many countries. In some cases, primary source data can be easily obtained. On the website of the UN High Commission for Human Rights, for example, full texts of country reports on compliance with the Convention on the Rights of the Child or the Convention on the Elimination of all Forms of Discrimination Against Women can be found along with commission hearing commentaries. Such information is valuable for teaching and research. In discussing use of the Internet in teaching a course on human diversity, Miller-Cribbs and Chadiha (1999) note the increase in "access to international/global perspectives thus allowing [students] to make cross-cultural comparisons" (p. 102).

Various models of distance education may enhance international learning. Used in a number of countries to bring education to students in rural or underserved areas or to bring education into the workplace, distance education can also be international. Ramapo College of New Jersey, in the United States, for example, received a significant technology grant in the late

1980s to strengthen its global and multicultural curriculum. Through purchase and use of satellite dishes, video production equipment, and a video-teleconference facility, the college could link students and professors with counterparts in other parts of the world for live interactions and shared class sessions (Mitchell Kahn, personal communication, May 4, 2000). Whereas video technology offers the most satisfying and exciting linkages, audio technology is far less expensive. An example of successful use of audio distance education is the University of the West Indies system through which training is delivered throughout the English-speaking Caribbean network of 14 countries.

Web-based courses have expanded the options in distance education. Some merely make course information, lectures, and tests available by computer. Others are interactive, involving students in computer-assisted discussion and dialogue with the instructor, often with video. Potentially, web-based courses remove geographic barriers to education. For the courses transmitting information without video or interactivity, such courses can be offered to a worldwide audience. Although worldwide interactive courses are potentially feasible, the need for faster machines and real-time transmission complicates delivery. Nonetheless, the possibilities are exciting; Rafferty (1998) mentions experiments with the "global university" in institutions with Internet-based distance learning (p. 108). Other experiments are offering degrees that are totally web-based.

Johnson reports about the successful E-mail Partnership Project, which linked students from a U.S. school with Romanian students via email. Students were required to communicate at least twice a week with partners in the other country to discuss social problems or issues and to use what they learned in a class assignment. Labeled "globalization from below," the project achieved success as students "established common bonds, recognized cultural diversity, and prepared individually and professionally, for cross-cultural collaboration" (Johnson, 1999, p. 392). Students called it "the next best thing to being there."

The main advantage of using the Internet for education is accessibility; vast amounts of information and links to global data sources are made available to those who have access to computers with Internet capability. The disadvantages are information overload and difficulties in verifying the accuracy of some website information. Cost of hardware and software, reliance on telephone lines and electric power, and the English-language dominance in most websites create additional disadvantages for developing countries.

Curriculum Structure

At the beginning of the chapter, the two major approaches to structuring curriculum content—special, or focus, courses and infusion—were defined. The primary advantage of the focus approach is depth. In a specialized course or sequence, international content can be explored more fully and students can be given the opportunity to research global problems or aspects of international social work as their main assignment. However, there are two important advantages to the infusion approach that make it preferable for a program that has to choose one methodology. Infusion in required elements of the curriculum means that all students are reached by international learning, not just those who select it as a special interest. In addition, infusion can move students and the field as a whole closer to the ideal of removing the concept of borders as a rigid barrier to learning in social work. Infusion is challenging and poses many implementation difficulties because most, if not all, instructors must gain sufficient knowledge to teach in the area. The approaches can be blended to offer a knowledge base for all students, with opportunities for specialization for those who plan to pursue international practice or research and for those who would like to explore the global dimensions of their own areas of expertise, such as child welfare or aging.

Field Placements

An international practicum is a potentially powerful tool for international learning in social work and is particularly important preparation for international practice. Through such placements, students become immersed in a cross-cultural learning experience and must confront different views of human behavior and perspectives about how things should operate. They learn within different systems of social welfare and address problems that may exist in their home communities but that are viewed and remedied in very different ways. In addition to the learning, completing an international field placement can prepare interested students for future international work by providing them with the valuable prerequisite of previous overseas experience. Students often return from international placements and report that these were life-altering experiences.

There are many difficulties in arranging such experiences, and these difficulties have prevented full development of international placements as usual or accepted parts of social work education. The educational barriers can be inferred from earlier chapters. For example, social work is defined differently in different countries. Educational standards and content vary considerably. Thus a student placed in a country in which the education for social work is at the baccalaureate level or outside the university often will not be supervised by a master's-level social worker—a requirement of programs in the United States. Because the functions of social workers vary, the tasks expected of practicum students will not always fit perfectly with those expected by the sending educational program. For example, Danish students who completed a practicum in the United States resisted working with children because the major work with children in Denmark is done by social pedagogues; the U.S. agencies that were most eager to accept the Danish students were agencies that provided children's services. Arrangements for appropriate experiences and supervision require considerable preparatory work and must be built on relationships between sending and host programs or between faculty in those programs. Programs subject to strict accreditation standards have to worry about comparability issues. And all educators are concerned that students' experiences are applicable to their future careers and consistent with the goals of the schools.

Good international field programs also require a sound philosophy and adequate preparation and debriefing of participants. Unless the educational program and the student place a high value on cross-cultural learning, international placements should not be attempted. Students are most likely to find field experiences at home that fit school requirements. An international field placement, however, can provide a professional development experience that is profound in its impact. Students—and their supporting faculty members—must be prepared for difference. They must be prepared to tolerate ambiguity and struggle to learn cultural meanings throughout their experience. A student who returned to the United States from a 4-month internship in India related that he found it difficult to know whether he was performing well in the eyes of his supervisor. At times, he was asked to take on tasks that made no sense to him, for example, to attend a meeting conducted entirely in Hindi, although he understood no Hindi. Yet his field instructor wrote very glowing evaluations and requested that the student return to India to assist the agency further. It took several months after his return to fully integrate the experience; eventually the student realized the value and usefulness of his experiences and he returned to India for another short placement. The processes of adaptation and learning can be assisted by offering preplacement preparation seminars and ensuring that there are opportunities to discuss and integrate the experiences upon return.

Exceptions to standards should be made in instances where it is more reasonable to make exceptions than to honor the standard. For example, it may be possible to arrange for a master's-level supervisor for a student by using an expatriate. This, however, would undermine the essential reason for the international placement—cross-cultural and comparative learning. A more reasonable approximation of the standard would be to secure supervision from a professionally trained social worker, using the host country's definition of professional training. Communications technology makes contact between the programs much easier. In most places, students can keep in regular e-mail contact with faculty in their home program; voice or video contact may also be possible, allowing for supplementary advising and support.

Lyons and Ramanathan (1999) offer a classification of models for international placement assignments that may help programs clarify their expectations. The first model is observational/educational; within this model, a student's primary assignments would be to make a variety of field visits or to "shadow" one or more local practitioners. This may be combined with attending classes or seminars. Students would record their observations and impressions for discussion during the placement and upon return to their home institution. The second model, at the other end of the continuum, are placements aimed at professional skill development in the student's area of

social work specialty, such as administration, casework, community organization, medical social work, or child and family. Assignments would emphasize actual practice while also including cross-national and cross-cultural
analyses.

A third model, perhaps used the least often, includes some practice opportunities but would emphasize "the students' ability to organize themselves and to adapt and learn effectively, under probably very different
circumstances" (Lyons and Ramanthan, 1999, p. 185). A fourth model, which
can either stand alone or be used in combination with one of the others, is
described as a project approach. The student plans and carries out a study
on an area or topic of interest, permitting comparative analysis with work
they have done in their home country.

Discussion of these alternative models and agreement among the student, the home institution, and the host institution and agency as to which
model will best fit the placement would avoid problems of conflicting and
often unstated expectations. The process may also assist the student and participating institutions to identify the important components of the international placement to ensure appropriate learning. International placements
for master's level students have usually used the second model—skill development. This is the most demanding to arrange and complete in terms
of language and cultural competence. Replacing or blending this with the
third model may offer more realistic and useful learning opportunities.

STRATEGIES FOR REFORM

In designing curriculum for the future, the question should not be whether
to include international perspectives in social work education; rather, one
should ask how educators could conceive of teaching only a nation-specific
curriculum. Why has the concept of borders prevented social work educators from adopting a holistic and global approach to the profession?

Reform efforts must consider the barriers to strengthening international
education that educators perceive, as well as recommendations for optimal
content and related experiences. There are alternative strategies to address
the concerns over rigid and crowded curriculum. Global or international
content could be added to the list of required areas for study by revising the
curriculum policy statement in the United States and elsewhere; this action
would ensure its inclusion, but could further crowd and complicate the curriculum. An alternative strategy would be to seek to relax and simplify accreditation and other curriculum requirements, allowing programs more
flexibility in designing programs. Educational organizations, including the
IASSW, CSWE, the Canadian Association of Schools of Social Work
(CASSW), and other national bodies, could propose guidelines or "best practices" recommendations for international curriculum rather than mandating
inclusion. Approaches to global education that are parsimonious, by fitting
into existing curriculum areas, would be most likely to be well received, regardless of accreditation standards.

Faculty development and training are important in ensuring the success of internationalizing social work education. Many current educators received their training in programs with little or no international content; they may therefore lack the knowledge or confidence to teach international material. As with multicultural content, faculty development efforts can be helpful.

Issues of relevance and sustainability must be addressed. The recommendations that will be offered below address these by linking international education to program and institutional mission. Although the issues of adequate finances and other resources cannot be minimized, these seem to be less serious barriers to internationalization than the structural areas identified in various surveys.

Toward a Sustainable International Educational Program

A sound international educational program in social work is one that enhances the overall educational program of the school, reaches most, if not all, students, and contributes to students' professional development in ways that lead to international professional action, and it is one that can be sustained. The following steps are suggested to move toward this ideal.

A social work program's international goals should be linked to the mission of the university, or other educational institution, where relevant. Because an increasing number of colleges and universities identify globalization as part of their missions, internationalizing social work is now a strategy that can enhance the credibility of the profession within the larger academy. International goals should then be built into the social work program's mission statement to provide a framework for program coherence.

Programs should seek ways to increase community relevance in developing an international focus and goals. An example would be to identify concentrations of immigrant groups in the school's service area or to focus on social problems of both local and global concern. It is also important to underscore that internationalization and indigenization are not mutually exclusive concepts. In the 21st century, both are necessary for the advancement of social work education, and programs can simultaneously work on both processes.

It is important to institutionalize the international program and curriculum. Strategies include ensuring that a critical mass of teaching staff are involved in the international program; creating a structure, such as a committee or center, with responsibility for the international program; and ensuring that there are no institutional disincentives for international involvement. When international activities are viewed as peripheral, they may be undervalued in considering faculty workload, tenure, and promotion, or other evaluative criteria, and in evaluation of student work.

As the faculty designs the international aspects of the curriculum, clear outcomes for international learning that are appropriate for the level of education and related to the mission of the program must be developed; at least some of these outcomes should address professional responsibility and action. Educators should carefully select content capable of meeting the defined outcomes and select the model for presenting content (infusion, focus course(s), or specialization) that is most appropriate. For example, specialization would be the ideal model for preparing international development practitioners, whereas infusion would be more likely to result in a worldview for all students. Ways to reduce the traditional and rigid dichotomies between what is domestic and what is international should be sought as curriculum is developed. And faculty development opportunities need to be planned and offered to ensure that the program can move forward.

Additional challenges to the educational sector will be to assume the lead in addressing the following issues: to expand meaningful opportunities for mutual exchange in the field of social work and to develop theoretical and practice concepts that are widely—if not universally—relevant to social work discourse. These will be discussed in next chapter.

REFERENCES

Boehm, W.W. (1980). Teaching and learning international social welfare, *International Social Work, 23*(2), 17–24.

Council on Social Work Education (CSWE). (1994). Curriculum Policy Statement for Master's Degree Programs in Social Work Education. In *Handbook for accreditation standards and procedures* (pp. 134–144). Alexandria, VA: Author.

Ewalt, P. (1983). *Curriculum design and development for graduate social work education.* New York: Council on Social Work Education.

Hanvey, R. (1979). *An attainable global perspective.* New York: Global Perspectives in Education.

Hawkins, J.N. (1979). Ethnic studies and international studies: Interrelationships. In *President's Commission on Foreign Language and International Studies, Background Papers and Studies* (pp. 23–29). Washington, DC: U.S. Department of Health, Education and Welfare.

Healy, L.M. (1985). *The role of the international dimension in graduate social work education in the United States.* Unpublished doctoral dissertation, Rutgers University, New Brunswick, NJ.

Healy, L.M. (1986). The international dimension in social work education: Current efforts, future challenges. *International Social Work, 29*(2), 135–147.

Healy, L.M. (1990). [International content in social work educational programs worldwide]. Unpublished raw data.

Healy, L.M. (1997, April). Baccalaureate survey reveals growing internationalization. *InterEd—Newsletter of the CSWE International Commission.* (Available from the CSWE, Alexandria, VA.)

Healy, L.M. (1999). International social work curriculum in historical perspective. In C. Ramanathan & R. Link (Eds.), *All our futures: Principles and resources for social work practice in a global era* (pp. 14–29). Belmont, CA: Brooks/Cole.

Healy, L.M., & Asamoah, Y.W. (Eds.). (1997). *Global perspectives in social work education: A collection of course outlines on international aspects of social work.* Alexandria, VA: Council on Social Work Education.

Horncastle, J. (1994). Training for international social work: initial experiences. *International Social Work, 37*(4), 309–318.

Hughes-Wiener, G. (1988). An overview of international education in the schools. *Education and Urban Society, 20*(2), 139–158.

Jancar, B. (1994). The environment, population growth and resource scarcity. In M. Klare (Ed.), *Peace and world security studies: A curriculum guide* (pp. 304–324). Boulder, CO: Lynne Rienner Publishers.

Johnson, A.K. (1999). Globalization from below: Using the Internet to internationalize social work education. *Journal of Social Work Education 35*(3), 377–393.

Joint Working Group on Development Education (1984). *A framework for development education in the United States*. New York: InterAction.

Kojima, Y. (1988). Japan's national report on international content in social work curricula. In *Year Book of Social Work Education* (pp. 57–79) (vol. 9). Tokyo: Japan Association of Schools of Social Work.

Kojima, Y. (1992). Recent trends of international social work education in Japan and Asia. In *Year Book of Social Work Education* (vol. 13, pp. 49–59). Tokyo: Japan Association of Schools of Social Work.

Konopka, G. (1969). Introduction to workshop on teaching of comparative social welfare. In K. Kendall (Ed.), *Teaching of comparative social welfare: A workshop report*. New York: Council on Social Work Education.

Lyons, K. (1996). Education for international social work. In K. Yeung, C. Yeung, & A. Dave (Eds.), *Proceedings: Joint World Congress of the International Federation of Social Workers and the International Association of Schools of Social Work, July 24–27, 1996* (pp. 189–191). Hong Kong: IFSW, IASSW, and HKSWA.

Lyons, K., & Ramanathan, C.S. (1999). Models of field practice in global settings. In C. Ramanathan & R. Link (Eds.), *All our futures: Principles and resources for social work practice in a global era.* (pp. 175–192). Belmont, CA: Brooks/Cole.

Miller, P. (1968). Social work education and the International Education Act. *Social Work Education Reporter, 16*(2), 34–37.

Miller-Cribbs, J.E., & Chadiha, L.A. (1998). Integrating the Internet in a human diversity course. *Computers in Human Services, 15*(2/3), 97–108.

Mori, K. (1996). "Changes in international social welfare in Japan. In K. Yeung, C. Yeung, & A. Dave (Eds.), *Proceedings: Joint World Congress of the International Federation of Social Workers and the International Association of Schools of Social Work, July 24–27, 1996* (pp. 217–219). Hong Kong: IFSW, IASSW, and HKSWA.

Nagy, G., & Falk, D. (1996). Teaching international and cross-cultural social work. Paper presented at the Joint World Congress of the International Federation of Social Workers and the International Association of Schools of Social Work, Hong Kong.

President's Commission on Foreign Language and International Studies (1979). *Strength through wisdom: A critique of U.S. capability*. Washington, DC: U.S. Department of Health, Education and Welfare.

Rafferty, J. (1998). Changing to learn: Learning to change. *Computers in Human Services, 15*(2/3), 159–169.

Tye, K.A. (1999). Global education: A worldwide movement. *Issues in Global Education. Newsletter of the American Forum for Global Education,* issue 150. Available at http://www.globaled.org/issues/150/a.html.

Wrightson, P.S., & Ackermann, A. (1994). The nexus between peace studies and international security studies in the post-cold war era. In M. Klare (Ed.), *Peace and world order studies: A curriculum guide.* (pp. 55–65). Boulder, CO: Lynne Rienner.

CHAPTER 12

SOCIAL WORK AS A FORCE
FOR HUMANE GLOBAL CHANGE
AND DEVELOPMENT

As the world enters the 21st century and social work its second, major global challenges abound. The need for development is as great as ever, especially in the face of a widening global rich-poor gap; social exclusion, exacerbated by the globalization of the economy, is widening the gap between those who do and do not benefit from social and economic progress within nations as well as between nations. The concept of security, long a centerpiece of international relations, has taken on an added meaning as secure borders do little to bring security to families facing long-term unemployment, declining social welfare benefits, and risks of personal violence. Although progress in setting standards has been made, there has been failure in realizing the promises made in the 20th century in terms of guarantees of human rights for all. Peace and intergroup harmony remain elusive in the face of sustained or perhaps growing interethnic, racial, and religious conflict in many parts of the world. And resource shortages, especially resources devoted to human service needs, create an urgent need for sustainable, resource-efficient social interventions.

For its second century, social work can rightly claim to be a global profession. Attention can turn to efforts to strengthen the profession's role in international action as a force for humane global social change and development. In this concluding chapter, exchange as a mechanism for strengthening the global identity of the profession will be discussed. Globally relevant concepts for social work dialogue and theory development will be explored. The chapter and book will conclude with thoughts about the emergence of an international civil society and the growing acceptance of global responsibility as an element of global citizenship. These elements are likely to increase the relevance of social work as a global force.

INTERNATIONAL EXCHANGE

Revisiting Social Work as a Global Profession

As preparation for considering international exchanges and collaborative work, it is important to redefine social work as a worldwide or global profession rather than continuing to view it as a European and American profession that has spread to Africa, Asia, and Latin America. Although its origins in Europe and the United States are historical facts, this view is no longer a useful framework for defining the profession because it ties social work to old themes about export, borrowing, and cultural imposition. It is equally factual to assert that social work is a global profession—it currently exists in most countries and has been present in all regions of the world for more than 60 years.

Learning From Abroad: Comparative Policy Analysis and Technology Transfer

International social work encourages many forms of international learning and sharing, beginning with the traditional activity of comparative social policy analysis. There are two major benefits to be derived from comparative policy analysis in social work and social welfare. The first is enhanced knowledge of one's own system through assessment of its place in the global system. The other is technology transfer—the identification of innovations in other countries that can be adapted or adopted at home.

It is only possible to fully understand a social welfare system by comparing it with other systems and by assessing a system's place in the worldwide network. Such study may expose widely accepted truisms as mere opinions. Politicians and corporate leaders in the United States, for example, have resisted the idea of paid maternity and paternity leaves, claiming that to grant such leave would destroy American business competitiveness in the world economy. The argument sounds less convincing when compared to the policy and business practices of America's competitors in Western Europe, where almost all countries offer leave with pay not only to new parents but also to employees with ill family members. Thus the comparative view shows that to claim that such a policy is impossible is clearly invalid; more accurately, it can be asserted that parental leave is not a policy priority in the United States.

Through comparative study, policy analysts may discover programs or policies that have the potential to enhance domestic social welfare. The process of borrowing an innovation from abroad is called *technology transfer*. The adaptation of microloans and self-employment ventures described in Case 1.3 is one example of technology transfer, in this case from Bangladesh to the United States. The literature has sometimes labeled this *reverse technology transfer*, assuming that most transfer is from industrialized to developing nations. The process of international sharing, exchange, and borrowing, however, need not be tied to preconceived ideas of the origins of the donor or recipient.

Exchange as an Important Mechanism for Expansion of Global Perspective

International exchange projects and programs have been prominent in the development of social work as a global profession. As explained earlier, there was extensive exchange of ideas, information, and personnel in social work's early decades. The founders were strong advocates for international exchange and active participants in it. A paper at the First International Conference of Social Work called for "constant contact between social workers on an international intellectual basis" (Jebb, 1929, p. 651). The cross-fertilization and inspiration that resulted led to the founding of schools of social work throughout the world. Direct service programs were also initiated as social workers transplanted and adapted ideas they learned through foreign travel or through exchanges of ideas with colleagues at international meetings. The desire for sustained exchange led to the creation of the various international professional organizations, which through regular conferences, newsletters, an international journal, and other projects continue to encourage intercountry contact and sharing. Although exchange has continued, there have been some barriers, especially the reality and the legacy of what is called the *export model.*

Legacy of the Export Model. At times in the history of social work, inequality of opportunity and inequality in access to resources among the countries of the world have led to negative patterns in professional communication and exchange. In the export model, social welfare theories, practice models, and curricula have been inappropriately and uncritically exported or borrowed. Exchange relationships under these conditions were largely one-way relationships between an expert, or donor, and a recipient. Although the situation has improved, unequal exchange still occurs; some of the recent consultation projects to former Soviet bloc countries appear dangerously close to earlier models of large-scale transplantation of models of social work education or professional organization developed for industrialized countries with very different socioeconomic and cultural environments. It is questionable whether one-way or unequal exchange relationships deserve the label *exchange.* Models based on export and imposition do little to contribute to international social work, and may actually damage the programs.

Many authors have been harshly critical of these export efforts (see, e.g., Khinduka, 1971; Midgley, 1981). Wagner interprets the issue more gently, labeling the one-way transfer of benefits "gift-giving." Exchange is an economic concept; therefore, using market terminology to apply to ideas and information in the social work profession, exchange is likely to occur only when each party to the transaction has something of value to transmit to the other. Thus "it is unlikely that in an early phase of contact between unequal partners, transactions will be exchange-dominated" (Wagner, 1992, p. 125). Instead, one-way transfer of resources is likely to characterize the relationship between social workers in industrialized and developing nations, or between those in countries with long-established social work institutions and those exploring the field. Wagner (1992) suggests that social workers may feel particularly comfortable with this approach: "Social workers and social work educators probably have more affinity with the concept of unilateral transfer than with the concept of exchange, because it is based on altruism, rather than economic utility and self-interest" (p. 126). Unfortunately, this altruistic intent has led to transplantation of social welfare models ill-suited to some of their recipients and has impeded the development of local variety in social work. It may have also impeded the development of international social work by stalling true exchange relationships in the field. Some in the profession may avoid international exchange out of fear of entering into unequal or exploitive relationships.

Mutual Exchange in Social Work. In spite of past difficulties, international exchange must be embraced as a mechanism to move social work forward. International dialogue is essential for the growth and development of social work theory and methods and to foster collaborative work on the social problems that are discussed in previous chapters. The most important dimension of exchange is mutuality. True exchange implies mutuality. According to theories of exchange, exchange exists only when all partners benefit from a relationship or transaction. Optimally, the benefits received are equal or equally valued, although partners may receive different "commodities" from the exchange. Exchange is a broad concept and does not only apply to personnel. Exchange can involve physical resources—money, equipment, books—information, ideas, access, referrals, or even reputation/legitimation.

Exchanges in social work occur at many levels. Some are episodic in nature; these include the exchanges of information at professional conferences and relatively short-term dialogue between social workers by mail or computer, often to address a particular issue or research question. Organized programs or projects of exchange may develop between educational programs, between social work professional organizations, or between agencies. The EU efforts to encourage exchange through funded projects of ERASMUS, TEMPUS, and, more recently SOCRATES have been discussed earlier in the book. Schools of social work have set up bilateral exchange projects; some have been relatively short in duration, while others have extended over many years. The interorganizational efforts of child welfare agencies in Texas, California, and Mexico described in Chapter 9 provide examples of agency-based exchange programs.

The literature on exchange and interorganizational relations suggests that the following factors are related to success: goal interdependence—the identification of common interests; mutuality in resource exchange—each partner contributes resources valued by the receiving partner (Schmidt & Kochan, 1977); frequent contact and communication between the partners (Morris, 1962); and the attitudes and behaviors of the personnel involved. Participants in successful exchanges tend to have high levels of interpersonal trust, open-mindedness, a willingness to take risks and try new approaches, and sensitivity to organizational and cultural differences (Maxwell, 1994; Healy, Maxwell, & Pine, 1999).

Social workers will find exchange projects particularly useful if they focus on mutual problems or issues. Global migration patterns provide opportunities for links between source and receiving areas of migration. For example, a multiyear project was developed between the University of Connecticut in the United States and the University of the West Indies in Jamaica to work on issues related to large-scale Jamaican migration to the Hartford, Connecticut, area. Activities included training of service providers in Connecticut on West Indian family issues, joint faculty scholarly work on issues of migration, student exchange, and two-way curriculum consultation and exchanges of materials (Healy et al., 1999). Emphasis on a social issue or problem of mutual interest is another mechanism for fruitful exchange. The School of Social Work in Esbjerg, Denmark, is part of a multicountry linkage focused around issues of aging and social work. Activities include annual conferences, curriculum exchange, and development of materials for teaching (I. Hjerrild, personal communication, June 8, 1998).

Technology and Exchange. Advances in technology are making exchange far easier. It is interesting to note, however, that prior generations have observed the same. At the 1928 First International Conference of Social Work, a delegate from Budapest remarked in a speech:

> The world of today is smaller than it has ever been before. New methods of communication and transport facilities and the new techniques of production, link nations, classes together. Goods, thoughts, ideas and knowledge circulate through the countries and the masses in one continuous stream and prepare the minds of people for a broader and deeper understanding of life. (Rajniss, 1929, pp. 441–442)

A very optimistic statement for the era of steamships and telegraph! (And it should serve as a reminder that whatever is written here could be out-of-date by the time it is read.)

Jet travel, satellite television, international telephone and fax service, and especially the Internet, have significantly modified approaches to international exchange. Videoconferencing via dedicated services or web-based video may replace or supplement exchange programs involving travel. From email to online videoconferencing, technology has put international exchange within the reach of many.

Researchers can exchanges files, papers, and research results electronically, easing the process of cross-national research collaboration.

> In a matter of minutes, for example, scholars now can publish the results of completed analysis on the Internet. In doing so, they are able to make the results of their research instantly available to thousands of scholars scattered everywhere across the planet. (Estes, 1999, p. 124)

Estes reported that as of 1999, more than 2,000 scholarly journals were being published exclusively on the Internet. People in countries with slow and unreliable mail service may have increased access to information. International migrants can now keep up with their home countries by reading newspapers online.

Computer bulletin or message boards, listservs and chat rooms offer possibilities for global information sharing and dialogue. An important element that makes these electronic communications useful is the philosophy of the Internet: "If you know something, share it" (P. Petrella, personal communication, May 18, 2000). A problem or question posed on a message board or newsgroup is likely to generate helpful responses from all over the world. Questions may vary from "I am having trouble installing xyz software, can you help?" to "I am developing a peer-support and counseling program in Tanzania aimed at adolescents at risk of HIV—any ideas for what works?" The questioner is put in touch with "experts"—admittedly self-appointed ones—from around the world. Possibilities for technology transfer in the human services are considerable.

Another technology tool, a listserv (or mailing list), brings those with like interests and/or expertise together to share information and solve problems. The number of social work listservs is expanding.

The value of a listserv to social workers in various parts of the world is considerable. A social work educator in Malaysia wrote:

> When I first started teaching, I discovered the NISW [National Institute of Social Work, U.K.] listgroup and got answers to every question I sent out. I also used the NISW listserv to get comments and statements from social workers all over the world about what social work meant to them or what they did as a social worker in their country. These statements were then used as part of an exhibition to expose students to the breadth and depth of social work. (Chong, 1998, p. 179)

Writing from Malaysia, a country that had been relatively isolated from the early developments in social work, Chong concluded that "information technology and the borderless world provide students with a potential arena to discover the ethos of the profession" (Chong, 1998, p. 179). More importantly for international professional action, electronic communications can encourage mutuality in exchange relationships. Chong's observations about what he labels "telesocial work" have relevance for exchange among all countries. "The telesocial work concept can also be extended internationally so that trained social workers in Malaysia can access appropriate expertise outside the country, adapt the knowledge to the local context and, through the exchange of views, broaden the knowledge base of both parties" (Chong, 1998, p. 178).

In addition to the benefits and promises of technology, there are barriers to its use and dangers that the rich-poor gap will be exacerbated by the high costs of technology.

The high costs of constantly upgrading and changing of hardware and software are difficult for the poorer countries. However, they also benefit from the fact that the costs of testing are borne by the industrialized countries; developing countries are at the later stages of the technology chain, and they purchase the equipment after it has been tested and mass-produced at lower costs (P. Petrella, personal communication, May 18, 2000).

Computers and other telecommunications equipment rely on phone lines and electricity. Although advocating for increased use of information technology in Malaysia, Chong (1998) reports that only 17% of people in Malaysia have access to phone lines, and in Sarawak State, only 56% of schools have electricity. For many students, the Internet is likely to be available only in a university library or computer lab, with competition for usage. Practitioners, especially those in rural areas, may have little or no access. Yet, Internet access is common enough to cause the Peace Corps to worry about whether email will corrupt the tradition of volunteer immersion and relative isolation in their local placements.

Language presents an additional barrier. Software and Internet search engines are English-language-dominated. Although websites in other languages are increasing in number, the number is still small compared to sites in English.

On balance, the Internet is a significant resource and is a benefit to scholars in developing countries where books and professional journals are very scarce. Compared to other resource gaps, the Internet provides developing countries a window of access that is potentially very useful, especially if the philosophy of "if you know it, share it" flourishes. The impact of inequities should not be ignored, however.

Social work can mine these new tools to improve and expand exchange among colleagues around the world. A recent article noted the growth in strength of NGO coalitions that play major roles in political activism on the global scene. "New coalitions can be built online. . . . More important, the Internet allows new partnerships between groups in rich and poor countries" ("Non-Governmental Order, the" 1999, p. 21). Local activists collect data on local conditions and feed the data by e-mail to global NGOs; the information becomes a powerful tool to address issues such as debt reduction, world trade agreements, or exploitive labor practices. Through computer technologies and traditional means, exchange can assist social work to develop a global social movement capable of contributing to solutions to social problems and issues of the present and future.

GLOBALLY RELEVANT CONCEPTUAL FRAMEWORKS

Exchange will be enhanced as social work moves away from use of narrow nation-specific concepts and develops concepts of more universal relevance. These should be emphasized to facilitate global collaboration and further explication of the roles of social work. Universally relevant concepts can serve as what my co-authors and I labeled in an earlier article "conceptual channels" for global communication (Asamoah, Healy, & Mayadas, 1997).

Particularly salient concepts for global work are social development, human rights, multiculturalism/cultural competence, social exclusion/inclusion, security, and sustainability. These are salient because they are within social work's domain and because they may well be the cutting-edge concepts for international action in the early 21st century. Otunnu (1992) argues that what he calls the "emerging global agenda" will emphasize values and standards, with particular emphasis on human rights and democracy. Rosenau (1992) identifies a shift in the priorities of international policies in the post–cold war world; human rights, justice, and material progress are replacing national sovereignty as the dominant themes for diplomacy and global action. Rosenau also discusses the challenges of "sub-groupism" in multiethnic societies. If these authors are correct, social work knowledge should be increasingly relevant to the most important concerns in world affairs. It is perhaps, then, even more incumbent upon the profession to expand dialogue and increase its contribution in the key areas of social development, human rights, and multiculturalism.

Social Development

Development is optimally understood as a continuum without an endpoint. There is no point at which a country can be labeled *fully developed* nor one at which a country is *undeveloped.* In this view, all countries have areas in which progress is necessary and, therefore, all countries are developing. These ideas were well developed in Estes' (1984, 1997) work on an *index of social progress,* in which 45 indicators are used to measure a country's level of development. Through use of measures of welfare effort (the extent to which a nation provides social insurances), ethnic and cultural conflict, susceptibility to natural disasters, incidence of violence, and violations of civil liberties, in addition to the more usual indicators of GDP, literacy, and infant mortality, the index demonstrates the applicability of the development concept to all nations (Estes, 1995). Analysis of the index suggests a development agenda for each nation, no matter how economically privileged. On this index, as of 1995, Denmark earns the top ranking among 160 nations for its combination of sound welfare effort, good performance on indicators of social well-being, and low incidence of violence and conflict. The United States is tied for 27th due to poorer performance on these dimensions. A recent United Nations Development Program (UNDP, 1996) report concurred with Estes, listing the following as indicators of the need for development in the industrialized countries: 2 million people infected with HIV, women's wages at only two thirds of men's wage, more than 100 million people living below the official poverty level, more than 5 million homeless, unemployment over 8%, and more than 100,000 women raped each year.

These studies underscore the importance of social development—a concept that emphasizes equity and participation (see Chapter 8). Social development is defined as "a process of planned social change designed to promote the well-being of the population as a whole in conjunction with a dynamic process of economic development" (Midgley, 1995, p. 25). Important components of the definition are that it emphasizes process; prefers universal interventions that affect the total population, not just a segment or subgroup; and expresses the well-being goal as holistically defined, that is, linking economic and social well-being. The concept of development has suffered from considerable definitional problems; therefore, much of the social development literature within the field of social work focuses on definition (e.g., see Jones and Pandey, 1981; Omer, 1979; Paiva, 1977; Sanders, 1982). Comparatively less has been written about the actual practice strategies of social development.

Midgley (1999) recommends three sets of intervention strategies to operationalize the social development approach: human capital development, social capital development, and encouragement of self-employment or other productive employment projects. Although social workers sometimes reject the notions of human and social capital as dehumanizing, the terms are used in economics and development literature. Human capital development involves investments in people that increase productivity, including enhancements to education, health, and nutrition. Social capital is enhanced through capacity building in communities and other social units, often through mobilizing groups to engage in self-help and infrastructure-creating efforts. Social capital development embodies much of traditional community development techniques. Self-employment projects provide assistance, often in the form of microloans and technical assistance, to help individuals begin small business ventures. These three approaches are illustrated in case examples, for example, the emergency education program for young children in war-torn Bosnia described in Case 1.4 is an example of human capital development; the program used a development model for enhancing the capacity of the children to move forward after their traumatic war experiences. The community shelter clinics project implemented in Jamaica following Hurricane Gilbert (in Chapter 4) is an example of social capital development; the project met the dual goals of infrastructure development, in improved housing, and community capacity building, in its impact on strengthening or initiating community organizations. The Grameen bank microloan and microenterprise efforts in Case 1.3 illustrate the social development approach of productive employment and self-employment. The case also illustrates the relevance of social development concepts and strategies for the industrialized countries as well as the developing nations in which their use is more accepted. Properly applied, these strategies for social development demonstrate the importance of both economic and social development. The social development approach should emphasize the needs of people but not denigrate the importance of economic development. Conversely, economic development is important, but it should not be pursued in such a way that subordinates the needs of people to production or that funnels rewards only, or primarily, to the privileged (Korten & Klauss, 1984).

Whereas Midgley is correct in stating that there has been excessive focus on definitional issues, it is important not to lose sight of important characteristics discussed in the definitional literature. Particularly important and relevant to social work are the foci on participation, capacity building, and equity and inclusion. Interest in social development has intensified since the 1995 World Summit for Social Development. The summit's priorities on issues of concern to social work—poverty eradication, equality for women, and all aspects of social integration aimed at reversing the trends toward social exclusion—should continue to strengthen social work interest in social development. Given the still considerable definitional and strategic confusions, this concept is a particularly important one for international exchange and dialogue within the global social work community.

Human Rights

Human rights are addressed several times in this book, for example, as the recent focus of the work of the IFSW (Chapter 3), as an important accomplishment of the UN (Chapter 6), as interrelated with issues of professional values and ethics (Chapter 7), and as an aspect of global policy responsibilities and prospects for social workers (Chapter 10). As mentioned in Chapter 3, the IFSW has asserted that social work is a human rights profession. Indeed, human rights can serve as a statement of social work values, a source of policy guidelines, and a framework for professional practice. As such, it becomes a core concept for global dialogue and strategy development in social work.

It is the comprehensive definition of human rights spelled out in the Universal Declaration of Human Rights, the Covenant on Civil and Political Rights, and the Covenant on Social and Economic Rights that provides the rationale for defining social work as a human rights profession. In existing human rights "law," there are four categories of rights. The first two are recognition of human dignity and respect for civil and political rights, such as freedom of assembly, thought, and religion and right to protections of laws. In the United States, these personal and political freedoms are officially regarded as the totality of the human rights field, leaving the elements most applicable to social work aside. The third set of human rights, referred to as *second-generation rights,* includes economic rights, such as the right to food, health care, education, and social security, and the right to good working conditions ("Human Rights Law Survey," 1998). The final group of rights, known as *third-generation* or *solidarity rights,* includes the right to peace, to a clean environment, and to international distributive justice. These rights can be achieved only through international cooperation (Wronka, 1995). Taken together, the rights spelled out in the universal declaration and subsequent conventions and declarations encompass a significant part of the profession's agenda of working for economic security and social participation for all and for equality for special populations, including women, children, migrants, and racial and ethnic minorities.

The practice dimension of social work as human rights work is particularly interesting. Direct social work practice with individuals and groups as well as community and policy work can be defined as human rights practice. The human rights orientation helps social workers focus on social justice rather than individual pathology. "Their [social workers] work puts them in a particularly sensitive position in society, where their way of intervening in situations deemed 'problematic' can either reduce these problems to the level of individual pathology or help to articulate them as issues of social injustice" (Lorenz, 1994, p. 167). Lorenz urges social workers to base their practice on the promotion of rights. Using a human rights model in work with a woman abused by her spouse, for example, the social worker considers the woman to be a victim of human rights violations. This definition expands the role of case documentation, as information about human rights violations are used not only to assist the victim through individual interventions but also to publicly document such violations for use in working to end domestic violence. In some settings, defining a client as a victim is seen in a negative light. In human rights work, however, the impact of this label is different, and both the client and the social worker are empowered by seeing themselves as part of a broad struggle for global human rights. The human rights model bridges the gulf between individual interventions and advocacy/social change; through assessment, service, and case documentation, both purposes are served. The social worker—quite possibly with the client—uses the documentation to influence legislatures, funders, and/or public opinion. An example of the power of this approach is that in several cases in Canada, women have been given refugee status based on their history and continuing fear of domestic violence.

Nations have different records on human rights; however, no nation is without problems in first- and second-generation rights. Within the United States, for example, a country that prides itself on its human rights record in civil and political rights, there have been significant retreats from international criminal justice standards, especially in juvenile law. A number of states permit treatment of young offenders as adults, with no protections for their immaturity. The United States, Iran, Saudi Arabia, Pakistan, and Nigeria are the only nations that permit the execution of offenders for crimes committed when they were minors—a practice that violates the Convention on Civil and Political Rights (Weinstein, 2000). It should be noted that this is one of the few international human rights treaties that the United States has ratified. Thus even without venturing into the complex arena of second- or third-generation rights, human rights is a relevant concept for international dialogue and collaboration in social work.

Two particular areas in which social work values and human rights policies intersect are in the guarantees of equality and nondiscrimination, as discussed in Chapter 7, and in economic and social rights, as detailed in the Universal Declaration of Human Rights, the Covenant on Economic and Social Rights, and in the European Social Charter. The fact that broad global protections of civil, political, social, and economic rights may not extend automatically to special populations is suggested by the specialized conventions adopted to protect women and children and to protect against racial discrimination. A remaining challenge is to secure global recognition of human rights for sexual minorities and protection against discrimination based on sexual orientation. Many countries have laws prohibiting homosexuality; some have severe penalties for the practice. Violence against gay men

THE EUROPEAN SOCIAL CHARTER

The European Social Charter was issued by the Council of Europe in 1961; its aim is to achieve maintenance and further realization of human rights and fundamental freedoms in the member states. It proposes that social and economic rights should be secured without discrimination "on grounds of race, colour, sex, religion, political opinion, national extraction or social origin" (Council of Europe, 1961, p. 1). The Charter was revised in 1996 in order to preserve gains made and to "give it fresh impetus" (Council of Europe, 1996, p. 1). The 1996 version attempts to address the social changes that have occurred since the charter's original adoption. The original charter laid out as its goal the attainment of basic rights and principles, including the rights of workers, women, children, and the disabled. The 1996 version has expanded these principles, particularly in the area of workers' rights. In addition, it emphasizes rights to social welfare services, medical assistance, housing, protection against poverty and social exclusion, and social protection of the elderly.

and lesbians is common and is often overlooked by police and courts (Dorf and Perez, 1995). With social work's special knowledge of human behavior and ethical codes requiring antidiscrimination, the profession can provide leadership in overcoming this important human rights hurdle.

Multiculturalism and Cultural Competence

Two trends are giving added importance to social work's emphasis on cultural competence and multiculturalism. The first trend is the continuation of large migrations that turn formerly homogeneous populations into diverse ones therefore increasing the cultural, racial, and ethnic diversity of most nations. Migration and its impacts are discussed in several of the preceding chapters. The second trend is the growing incidence of ethnic conflicts. Some of the conflicts are instigated by direct appeals to racism or by politicians who use ethnicity to mobilize discontent or, if in power, who overtly pursue policies that favor their own ethnic group. Too often, "the escalation from ethnic superiority to 'ethnic cleansing' and then subsequently to genocide can become an irresistible process" (Mehta, 1997, p. 96). The horrific violence of Serbs against Muslims in Bosnia, of Hutu against Tutsi and moderate Hutu in Rwanda, and the conflict between ethnic Albanians and Serbs in Kosovo are recent examples of severe ethnic conflict. Added to these are many more minor or less-publicized conflicts and the long-term struggles such as those between Catholics and Protestants in Northern Ireland and between Palestinians and Israelis in the Middle East.

The profession has long recognized the importance of culture and social environment on human behavior, and social workers are probably ahead of many other professions in their knowledge and competence in this area.

Much more, however, remains to be done, both in reexamining and refining the utility of relevant concepts and in improving knowledge and skills for conflict avoidance and resolution.

Approaches to study, practice, and policy in the area of cultural diversity are varied. The assimilationist model has been for the most part discarded, although it still has adherents. As discussed in Chapter 7, the immigrant resettlement policies in Denmark emphasize assimilation into Danish culture. The two dominant approaches to diversity (although there is far from terminological agreement on these labels) are cultural pluralism and multiculturalism, both of which reject a Eurocentric view of the world. As defined by Manning (1995), cultural pluralism "emphasizes the unique attributes/experiences of 'distinct' social groups in isolation of each other," with the aim of creating mutual understanding among groups, contrasted to multiculturalism, which "explicitly recognizes the interrelationships between various racial/ethnic/national and cultural groups along the multiple dimensions that define social life" (p. 150). Multiculturalism as so defined examines issues of structural inequality and power relationships, while cultural pluralism focuses on learning about others in order to improve intergroup understanding.

These divergent approaches pose challenges for social work, because these terms have been more ambiguous within the profession than the definitions given above. Within what is labeled *multicultural practice,* the emphasis may be on ethnic sensitivity and cultural competence, or it may be on oppression of diverse populations (Gutierrez, Fredricksen, & Soifer, 1999). The goal of preparation for cultural competence is to improve the capacity of social workers to serve diverse cultures through learning about cultures and cultural differences; when the emphasis is on racism, sexism, and other oppressions, the goal is to prepare social workers to work for social justice and empowerment of oppressed groups (Gutierrez et al., 1999).

Professional debates have taken place as to whether antiracist practice should supplant culturally competent practice. The historic dual commitment of the social work profession mandates attention to both approaches to cultural diversity. Learning about cultures in order to improve services and to address intergroup conflict is essential, but not sufficient. The social justice mission of the profession requires an antioppression framework and action agenda. Thus both cultural competence and antiracist practice are important, and the profession's attention to further development of these ideas should intensify. Multicultural social work must maintain a delicate balance in respecting culture without treating it as sacrosanct when human rights are being violated, thus promoting both human rights and cultural pluralism (Ayton-Shenker, 1995). (See discussion in Chapter 7 also.)

Within these areas, there is a need for increased attention to the process and impact of migration. Here, too, knowledge about the cultures of international populations within nations along with knowledge of the oppressive forces that force migrants to flee and that continue to impede justice in their places of resettlement are important. Through linkages and exchanges or through the international organizations, social workers could be more effectively engaged in working at the systems level to address migration and multicultural issues.

The profession also needs to work on conflict avoidance and conflict resolution strategies that can be applied at micro and macro levels. Social work has developed some expertise in this on micro levels, but it needs to work collaboratively across nations and with other disciplines to develop and apply macro-level strategies for encouraging ethnic harmony and ethnic justice. The scale of the challenge and urgency ranges from the everyday social relations in a highly diverse society such as Mauritius to the reconstructive efforts needed to build human relations in places such as Bosnia and Rwanda that have seen ethnic tension turn to widespread ethnic slaughter among former neighbors. Mehta (1997) encourages the social work profession to become involved in preventive diplomacy, that is, efforts to "discourage . . . hostilities, reduce tensions, address differences, create channels for resolution and alleviate insecurities and material conditions that tempt violence" (p. 101). Reconciliation and reconstruction are also important; these phases of intervention involve "monitoring violations of human rights; mediating; fostering interethnic dialogue; institution building; strengthening government infrastructure; national capacity building in all spheres; and promoting education for peace and nonviolent conflict resolution" (Mehta, 1997, p. 103).

Social Exclusion/Inclusion

Led by social thinkers in Europe, including social workers, social exclusion has become an important theme in social planning, policy analysis, and practice. Definitions of social exclusion range from relatively narrow ones focusing on economics to broad "inclusive" definitions. One simple definition is offered by the Commission of the European Communities: "[exclusion of] part of the population from economic and social life and from their share of the general prosperity" (as quoted in Rodgers, Gore, & Figueiredo, 1995, p. 43). The term *social exclusion* originated in France in the 1970s and was originally applied to disadvantaged or marginalized social groups, such as the mentally ill, substance abusers, or families with multiple problems. It was in the 1980s that the term evolved to refer to "the nature of the 'new poverty' associated with technological change and economic restructuring [and characterized by] a progressive rupture of the relationship between the individual and society" (Gore, 1995, pp. 1–2). Important elements of the concept are French ideas about citizenship and social integration; social exclusion expresses the loss of social solidarity as part of the population no longer participates in significant opportunities available in the society (Gore, 1995).

As a method, the concept provides "a way of analysing how and why individuals and groups fail to have access to or benefit from the possibilities offered by societies and economies" (Rodgers, 1995, p. 44). Many groups can be covered by this concept, including refugees, street children, ex-offenders, the long-term unemployed, the never employed, the minimally educated, and those with mental or physical disabilities. The relevance of the concept to social work should be evident. As Lorenz (1994) explained

> Social workers deal with people who potentially do not belong: homeless people, people excluded from mainstream life because of their poverty, their physical or mental difficulties in coping with social demands, people who have become victims of power inequalities within the family. (p. 136)

Poverty is a major factor and/or outcome of social exclusion and social workers may be particularly interested in the way that poverty is defined within social exclusion. Poverty is defined in social terms and as relative deprivation, rather than as falling below a particular income level or lacking a set of commodities or expenditures. Instead of using "the Anglo-Saxon notion of poverty as distributional, social exclusion focuses on relational issues—inadequate social participation" (Gore, 1995, p. 9).

Social exclusion can be applied nationally or globally. The growing gap in wealth between the richest and poorest nations and between the richest and poorest segments of the population within nations is a major indicator of social exclusion. Refugees, migrants, and the displaced are often excluded from all benefits of citizenship—sometimes for their lifetimes and even the lifetimes of their children. Within the globalization of economies and institutions, social exclusion can be applied to analysis of trade, aid, migration, and debt policies, and so on. The concept also links to other critical concepts; for example, the socially excluded include those who are excluded from human rights and those who are excluded from security. An example of the latter will be given in the next section.

The social work profession needs to work cross-nationally to determine if the concept of social exclusion adds important insight to existing concepts, such as poverty and marginality, and to further specify its social work applications. The concept needs additional work to move beyond its Eurocentric focus. As an applied profession, social work will be particularly interested in development of effective strategies for social inclusion. Research indicates that expanding the rights of disadvantaged ethnic, racial, caste groups, and women will be important goals because these have surfaced as factors in exclusion in countries at all levels of development (Rodgers, et al., 1995). Participatory strategies are also key, as social and civic participation are forms of inclusion.

Security

Security has not been a significant concept in social work, but it may increase in relevance due to new global understandings of the term. No longer confined to security from crime or war, although these certainly remain major issues, security now refers to prospects for a peaceful existence without threats of violence, present or future hunger, or lack of income. Insecurity has increased in the industrialized nations as fewer can count on long-term employment and as the benefits of the welfare state are reduced or restricted to those who are "socially included." Low-skilled workers are most at risk, and globalization has perhaps worsened their plight. "Globalization thus simultaneously increases the demand for social insurance while decreasing the capacity to provide it" (Sutherland, 1998). In the United States, insecurity has increased considerably due to job instability, layoffs, and cutbacks; decreases in the proportion of jobs that provide healthcare and retirement benefits; and abolition of the government's obligation to provide public assistance to those without income (under the label of welfare reform).

Refugees and other immigrants experience lack of security in many aspects of their lives. The threats to security are obvious in the transit and refugee camp stages of migration. However, insecurity continues in places where immigrants may face expulsion or unexpected deportation. Gore (1995) cites the example of migrant workers from Yeman who were working in the Gulf States until they were expelled after the outbreak of the Persian Gulf War in 1991. Insecurity in the Gulf region resulted following the invasion of Kuwait by Iraq and the subsequent U.S. and allied military response; one result was disruption in production and reduced need for guest workers. One million workers were returned to Yemen; two thirds of them had not lived in Yeman for more than 10 years, and an even higher number had no housing or land in Yemen. The changes to U.S. welfare and immigration laws described in Chapter 10 illustrate the insecurity faced by even long-term legal immigrants in the United States; they are denied provisions for security in the face of old age and illness that are provided to citizens and may be denied security of residence if found to have committed offenses in the distant past. These are just two examples of the large numbers of people around the world who live without security. The links among the concepts of security, social exclusion, and human rights should be apparent. The challenge for social work is to design interventions and policies that improve client security.

Sustainability

The importance of sustainability in interventions is one of the lessons learned from development experience, as discussed in Chapter 8; its importance has been heightened by increased awareness of environmental limits and resource scarcity. The concept fits well with the ecological perspective in social work, as sustainability requires practice that is sensitive to the interactions among ecosystems, economies, and social and human factors and an approach to progress that preserves future capacity. Defined by the Sustainability Education Center (1999) as an "evolving paradigm for planning and decision making," sustainability is a useful concept in social work practice at both macro and micro levels (p. 1).

At the micro level of practice, for example, with individuals and families, attention might focus on ways to ensure that social work interventions can be sustained by the client in terms of the client's capacity to make continuing use of lessons learned through treatment. In family preservation and interventions to improve parenting, for example, the social worker needs to examine whether skills taught are likely to be sustained in terms of their demands on the parent's time, energy, literacy, and cultural acceptability. A program for teen mothers in May Pen, Jamaica, teaches the mothers how to use educational toys with their children and how to make the toys from scraps, for example, blocks made from milk cartons decorated with cutouts from old magazines; these homemade and resource-efficient toys are used in the program, even though its grant allows buying of expensive developmental toys from abroad. Through this simple strategy, the likelihood of sustainability is increased. Some of the child survival strategies initially favored by development agencies were found to be unsustainable because of the demands on the time of already greatly overworked and undernourished women in Africa. Interventions must match clients' resources—including their literacy, energy, and available time. This is as true in Boston, Massachusetts, and Esbjerg, Denmark, as in Kingston, Jamaica, or Port Louis, Mauritius.

In planning and administering social programs, social workers can also use the concept of sustainability to assess program dependence on material and human resources, including available leadership talent and human energy. Many programs do not survive past the term of their grants because they fail to consider availability of ongoing resources. Sustainability, therefore, is an additional concept that is universal in social work and likely to grow in significance in the face of dwindling funding for human services.

There are indications that the six concepts introduced above will be particularly relevant in linking social work to global action in the 21st century. Reasons for this optimism will be explained below.

CONCLUSION: TOWARD HUMANE SOCIAL CHANGE IN THE INTERNATIONAL CIVIL SOCIETY

In the literature on the post–cold war world, the concept of global responsibility is gaining increased attention. Global responsibility is connected to the growing importance of international civil society—the activities of nongovernmental bodies and of the citizenry of the world independent of their governments. International civil society is defined as: "All the complex relationships and political processes that lie outside national territory and the control of national states" (Olsen, 1996, p. 335). The concept of global responsibility is at the core of international civil society (Olsen, 1996). In an international civil society, citizenship takes on new meaning and has global dimensions.

Lorenz (1994) applies the term *committed citizenship* to the role that social workers can play globally in integrating rights and humanitarian obligations through action. This is related to *humane internationalism,* another useful concept in recent literature. Pratt (1989) defined humane internationalism as "an acceptance by the citizens of the industrialized states that they have ethical obligations towards those beyond their borders and that these in turn impose obligations upon their governments" (quoted in Olsen, 1996, p. 336). What these ideas suggest is growing strength of public opinion and nongovernmental forces in international policy and action. This, in turn, suggests increased avenues for social workers' impact—first, as citizens, but more importantly, as professionals acting through NGOs to channel this humane internationalism into action on world problems.

Humane internationalism influences how social workers think about a broad range of policies, from immigration policies and intercountry adoption to larger issues of trade and aid relationships. An important focus for international social work action is to bear witness to the failures of the market and to work to improve the well-being and inclusion of those who are at risk of being left behind by globalization. Since the early 1990s, UNDP reports have underscored that global interdependence demands action to address equity issues, and the reports have warned of overemphasis on global economic efficiency (see discussion in Olsen, 1996). Increased roles for NGOs and citizens may serve as an important counterweight to the forces of global capitalism; social workers can assist by encouraging political and economic behaviors that are sensitive to the global village.

International Social Work Revisited

What, then, is international social work? The components of international professional action are explored in considerable depth in Chapters 1 through 11, along with examinations of the rather overwhelming agenda of global problems and issues of concern to social work. In this final chapter, universal concepts for international social work have been briefly explored. If we return to the vexing question posed in Chapter 1—whether a practice is considered international if done by a social worker from the United States in Japan but domestic practice if done by a Japanese social worker—we realize that the answer is: It depends. It is possible that the practice is simply social work practice in Japan. The practice is international social work if it concerns itself with bilateral, multilateral, or global relationships, social policies, or problems. By the same token, social work done in Japan by a Japanese social worker can also be international social work if it focuses on internationally related issues. And in the case of our fictitious social worker from the United States, his or her practice may take on international dimensions after the fact if, on returning home, he or she introduces innovations learned during the stay in Japan.

International social work certainly includes what Jane Addams called "a growing world consciousness" (see Chapter 1) and new notions of citizenship and of a profession that embrace global responsibility. But the core of international social work is international professional action along the lines suggested by Lorenz:

Internationalising social work means critically questioning the conventional boundaries of solidarity, questioning the ideological assumptions, dressed up as economic arguments, behind measures of exclusion, pushing out the boundaries of solidarity [beyond the European] to a global perspective and ultimately contributing to a shift from the welfare discourse to one on human rights. (Lorenz, 1994, pp. 167–168)

Within the next decade or two, international social work may finally be regarded as just social work as the rigid dichotomies that borders have put into thinking about the profession and social workers' responsibilities as professionals fade or disappear. Until then, progress will depend upon purposeful and vigorous pursuit of opportunities for international professional action in a highly interdependent world.

REFERENCES

Asamoah, Y., Healy, L.M., & Mayadas, N. (1997). Ending the international-domestic dichotomy: New approaches to a global curriculum for the millennium. *Journal of Social Work Education, 33*(2), 389–401.

Ayton-Shenker, D. (1995). The challenge of human rights and cultural diversity. *Human Rights: United Nations Background Note.* New York: United Nations Department of Public Information.

Chong, G. (1998). Information technology and social work education in Malaysia: Challenges and prospects. *Computers in human services, 15*(2/3), 171–184.

Council of Europe (1961). European Social Charter. *European Treaties* ETS No. 35, Turin, 18.x.1961. Available at www.coe.fr/eng/legaltxt/35e.htm. Accessed January 25, 2000.

Council of Europe (1996). Revised Social Charter. *European Treaties,* ETS No. 163, Strasbourg, 3.v.1996. Available at www.coe.fr/eng/legaltxt/35e.htm. Accessed January 25, 2000.

Dorf, J., & Perez, G.C. (1995). Discrimination and the tolerance of difference: International lesbian human rights. In J. Peters & A. Wolper (Eds.), *Women's rights, human rights.* New York: Routledge.

Estes, R. (1984). *The social progress of nations.* New York: Praeger.

Estes, R. (1995). Indicators of social progress, ISP95. ⟨http://caster.ssw.upenn.edu/~restes/praxisindica95.htm⟩ (accessed 1/19/00).

Estes, R. (1997). The world social situation. 1970–1995: Professional challenges for a new century. ⟨http://caster.ssw.upenn.edu/~restes/jak2.html⟩ (accessed 1/19/00).

Estes, R. (1999). Informational tools for social workers: Research in the global age. In C. Ramanathan & R. Link. *All our futures. Principles & Resources for Social Work Practice in a Global Era* (pp. 121–137). Belmont, CA: Brooks-Cole.

Gore, C. (1995). Introduction: Markets, citizenship and social exclusion. In G. Rodgers, C. Gore, & J.B. Figueiredo, *Social exclusion: Rhetoric, reality, responses* (pp. 1–40). Geneva: International Labour Organization/International Institute for Labour Studies.

Gutierrez, L., Fredricksen, K., & Soifer, S. (1999). Perspectives of social work faculty on diversity and societal oppression content: Results from a national survey. *Journal of Social Work Education, 35,*(3), 409–419.

Healy, L.M., Maxwell, J.A., & Pine, B.A. (1999). *Exchanges that work: Mutuality and sustainability in a Caribbean/USA academic partnership. Social Development Issues, 21*(3), 14–21.

Human rights law survey. (1998, December 5). [Special survey.] *The Economist,* 1–16.

Jebb, E. (1929). International social service. In *International Conference of Social Work* [Proceedings] (Vol. I, pp. 637–655). First Conference, July 8–13, 1928, Paris.

Jones, J., & Pandey, R. (Eds.) (1981). *Social development: Conceptual, methodological and policy issues.* New York: St. Martin's Press.

Khinduka, S. (1971). Social Work in the Third World. *Social Service Review, 45*(1), 62–73.

Korten, D.C., & Klauss, R. (1984). *People-centered development: Contributions toward theory and planning frameworks.* West Hartford, CT: Kumarian Press.

Lorenz, W. (1994). *Social work in a changing Europe.* London: Routledge.

Manning, R.D. (1995). Multiculturalism in the United States: Clashing concepts, changing demographics and competing cultures. *International Journal of Group Tensions, 25*(2), 117–168.

Maxwell, J.A. (1994, July). *Educating social workers for interorganizational coordination.* Paper presented at the 27th Congress of the International Association of Social Workers, Amsterdam, The Netherlands.

Mehta, V. (1997). Ethnic conflict and violence in the modern world: Social work's role in building peace. In M.C. Hokenstad & J. Midgley (Eds.), *Issues in international social work* (pp. 92–109). Washington, DC: NASW Press.

Midgley, J. (1981). *Professional imperialism: Social work in the third world.* London: Heinemann.

Midgley, J. (1995). *Social Development.* London: Sage Publications.

Midgley, J. (1999). Social development in social work: Learning from global dialogue. In C.S. Ramanathan & R.J. Link (Eds.), *All our futures: Principles & resources for social work practice in a global era* (pp. 193–205). Belmont, CA: Brooks-Cole.

Morris, R. (1962). New concepts in community organization. In *National Conference on Social Welfare: The Social Welfare Reform* (pp. 238–245). New York: Columbia University Press.

The non-governmental order. (1999, December 11). *The Economist,* 20–21.

Olsen, G.R. (1996). Public opinion, international civil society, and North-South policy since the Cold War. In O. Stokke (Ed.), *Foreign aid towards the year 2000: Experience and challenges* (pp. 333–354). London: Frank Cass Co.

Omer, S. (1979). Social development. *International Social Work, 22*(3), 11–26.

Otunnu, O. (1992). Emerging trends in the new world situation. *The Round Table, 324,* 401–409.

Paiva, F.J.X. (1977). A conception of social development. *Social Service Review, 51*(2), 327–336.

Rajniss, F.F. (1929). The contribution of social casework to other fields of social endeavor. In *International Conference of Social Work* [Proceedings] (Vol. II, pp. 441–461). First Conference, July 8–13, 1928, Paris.

Rodgers, G. (1995). What is special about a social exclusion approach? In G. Rodgers, C. Gore, & J.B. Figueiredo, *Social exclusion: Rhetoric, reality, responses* (pp. 43–55). Geneva: International Labour Organization/International Institute for Labour Studies.

Rodgers, G., Gore, C., & Figueiredo, J.B. (1995). *Social exclusion: Rhetoric, reality, responses.* Geneva: International Labour Organization/International Institute for Labor Studies.

Rosenau, J.N. (1992). Normative challenges in a turbulent world. *Ethics and International Affairs, 6,* 1–19.

Sanders, D. (Ed.) (1982). *The developmental perspective in social work.* Manoa, HI: University of Hawaii Press.

Schmidt, S.M., & Kochan, T.A. (1977). "Interorganizational relationships: Patterns and motivations. *Administrative Science Quarterly, 22,* 220–234.

Sustainability Education Center. (1999). The SEC goals. New York: American Forum for Global Education, ⟨www.globaled.org/sustain/sustain.html⟩ (accessed 1/7/00).

Sutherland, P.D. (1998). Answering globalization's challenges. Overseas Development Council Commentary. ⟨http://www.odc.org/commentarypdsview.html⟩ (accessed 1/6/00).

United Nations Development Program (1996). *Human development report 1996.* New York: Oxford University Press.

Wagner, A. (1992). Social work education in an integrated Europe: Plea for a global perspective. *Journal of Teaching in Social Work, 6*(2), 115–130.

Weinstein, H. (2000, January 21). Pope asks Bush to halt pending execution. *The Hartford Courant,* p. A9.

Wronka, J. (1995). Human rights. In R. Edwards (Ed.), *Encyclopedia of social work* (19th Ed., pp. 1405–1418). Washington, DC: NASW Press.

International Federation of Social Workers Ethics of Social Work— Principles and Standards

1. BACKGROUND

Ethical awareness is a necessary part of the professional practice of any social worker. His or her ability to act ethically is an essential aspect of the quality of the service offered to clients.

The purpose of IFSW's work on ethics is to promote ethical debate and reflection in the member associations and among the providers of social work in member countries.

The basis for the further development of IFSW's work on ethics is to be found in *"Ethics of Social Work-Principles and Standards," which consists of two documents, "International Declaration of Ethical Principles of Social Work" and "International Ethical Standards for Social Workers."* These documents present the basic ethical principles of the social work profession, recommend procedure when the work presents ethical dilemmas, and deal with the profession's and the individual social worker's relation to clients, colleagues, and others in the field. The documents are components in a continuing process of use, review and revision.

2. INTERNATIONAL DECLARATION OF ETHICAL PRINCIPLES OF SOCIAL WORK

2.1 Introduction

The IFSW recognizes the need for a declaration of ethical principles for guidance in dealing with ethical problems in social work.

The purposes of the International Declaration of Ethical Principles are:
1. to formulate a set of basic principles for social work, which can be adapted to cultural and social settings,
2. to identify ethical problem areas in the practice of social work (below referred to as "problem areas"), and
3. to provide guidance as to the choice of methods for dealing with ethical issues/problems (below referred to as "methods for addressing ethical issues/problems").

Compliance

The International Declaration of Ethical Principles assumes that both member associations of the IFSW and their constituent members adhere to the principles formulated therein. The IFSW expects each member association to assist its members in identifying and dealing with ethical issues/problems in the practice of their profession.

Member associations of the IFSW and individual members of these can report any member association to the Executive Committee of the IFSW should it neglect to adhere to these principles. National Associations who experience difficulties adopting these principles should notify the Executive Committee of IFSW. The Executive Committee may impose the stipulations and intentions of the Declaration of Ethical Principles on an association which neglects to comply. Should this not be sufficient the Executive Committee can, as a following measure, suggest suspension or exclusion of the association.

The *International Declaration of Ethical Principles* should be made publicly known. This would enable clients, employers, professionals from other disciplines, and the general public to have expectations in accordance with the ethical foundations of social work.

We acknowledge that a detailed set of ethical standards for the member associations would be unrealistic due to legal, cultural and government differences among the member countries.

2.2 The Principles

Social workers serve the development of human beings through adherence to the following basic principles:

2.2.1   Every human being has a unique value, which justifies moral consideration for that person.

2.2.2   Each individual has the right to self-fulfilment to the extent that is does not encroach upon the same right of others, and has an obligation to contribute to the well-being of society.

2.2.3   Each society, regardless of its form, should function to provide the maximum benefits for all of its members.

2.2.4   Social workers have a commitment to principles of social justice.

2.2.5   Social workers have the responsibility to devote objective and disciplined knowledge and skill to aide individuals, groups, communities, and societies in their development and resolution of personal-societal conflicts and their consequences.

2.2.6   Social workers are expected to provide the best possible assistance to anybody seeking their help and advice, without unfair discrimination on the basis of gender, age, disability, colour, social class, race, religion, language, political beliefs, or sexual orientation.

2.2.7   Social workers respect the basic human rights of individuals and groups as expressed in the *United Nations Universal Declaration of Human Rights* and other international conventions derived from that Declaration.

2.2.8   Social workers pay regard to the principles of privacy, confidentiality, and responsible use of information in their professional work. Social workers respect justified confidentiality even when their country's legislation is in conflict with this demand.

2.2.9   Social workers are expected to work in full collaboration with their clients, working for the best interests of the clients but paying due regard to the interests of others involved. Clients are encouraged to participate as much as possible, and should be informed of risks and likely benefits of proposed courses of action.

2.2.10   Social workers generally expect clients to take responsibility in collaboration with them, for determining courses of action affecting their lives. Compulsion which might be necessary to solve one party's problems at the expense of the interests of others involved should only take place after careful explicit evaluation of the claims of the conflicting parties. Social workers should minimise the use of legal compulsion.

2.2.11   Social work is inconsistent with direct or indirect support of individuals, groups, political forces or power-structures suppressing their fellow human beings by employing terrorism, torture or similar brutal means.

2.2.12   Social workers make ethically justified decisions, and stand by them, paying due regard to the *IFSW International Declaration of Ethical Principles*, and to the *"International Ethical Standards for Social Workers"* adopted by their national professional association.

2.3 Problem Areas

2.3.1 The problem areas raising ethical issues directly are not necessarily universal due to cultural and governmental differences. Each national association is encouraged to promote discussion and clarification of important issues and problems particularly relevant to its country. The following problem areas are, however, widely recognized:

1. *when the loyalty of the social worker is in the middle of conflicting interests*

   - between those of the social worker's own and the client's
   - between conflicting interests of individual clients and other individuals
   - between the conflicting interests of groups of clients
   - between groups of clients and the rest of the population
   - between systems/institutions and groups of clients
   - between system/institution/employer and social workers
   - between different groups of professionals

2. *the fact that the social worker functions both as a helper and controller*
   The relation between these two opposite aspects of social work demands a clarification based on an explicit choice of values in order to avoid a mixing-up of motives or the lack of clarity in motives, actions and consequences of actions. When social workers are expected to play a role in the state control of citizens they are obliged to clarify the ethical implications of this role and to what extent this role is acceptable in relation to the basic ethical principles of social work.

3. *the duty of the social worker to protect the interests of the client will easily come into conflict with demands for efficiency and utility*

This problem is becoming important with the introduction and use of information technology within the fields of social work.

2.3.2 The principles declared in section 2.2 should always be at the base of any consideration given or choice made by social workers in dealing with issues/problems within these areas.

2.4 Methods for the Solution of Issues/Problems

2.4.1 The various national associations of social workers are obliged to treat matters in such a way that ethical issues/problems may be considered and tried to be solved in collective forums within the organization. Such forums should enable the individual social worker to discuss, analyse and consider ethical issues/problems in collaboration with colleagues, other expert groups and parties affected by the matter under discussion. In addition such forums should give the social worker opportunity to receive advice from colleagues and others. Ethical analysis and discussion should always seek to create possibilities and options.

2.4.2 The member associations are required to produce and/or adapt ethical standards for the different fields of work, especially for those fields where there are complicated ethical issues/problems as well as areas where the ethical principles of social work may come into conflict with the respective country's legal system or the policy of the authorities.

2.4.3 When ethical foundations are laid down as guidelines for actions within the practice of social work, it is the duty of the associations to aid the individual social worker in analysing and considering ethical issues/problems on the basis of:

1. The basic *principles* of the Declaration (section 2.2)

2. The ethical/moral and political *context* of the actions, i.e. an analysis of the values and forces constituting the framing conditions of the action.

3. The *motives* of the action, i.e. to advocate a higher level of consciousness of the aims and intentions the individual social worker might have regarding a course of action.

4. The *nature* of the action, i.e. help in providing an analysis of the moral content of the action, e.g. the use of compulsion as opposed to voluntary cooperation, guardianship vs participation, etc.

5. The *consequences* the action might have for different groups, i.e. an analysis of the consequences of different ways of action for all involved parties in both the short and long term.

2.4.4 The member associations are responsible for promoting debate, education and research regarding ethical questions.

3. INTERNATIONAL ETHICAL STANDARDS FOR SOCIAL WORKERS

(This section is based on the *"International Code of Ethics for the Professional Social Worker"* adopted by the IFSW in 1976, but does not include ethical principles since these are now contained in the new separate *International Declaration of Ethical Principles of Social Work* in section 2.2 of the present document.)

3.1 Preamble

Social work originates variously from humanitarian, religious and democratic ideals and philosophies and has universal application to meet human needs arising from personal-societal interactions and to develop human potential. Professional social workers are dedicated to service for the welfare and self-fulfilment of human beings; to the development and disciplined use of validated knowledge regarding human and societal behavior; to the development of resources to meet individual, group, national, and international needs and aspirations; and to the achievement of social justice. On the basis of the *International Declaration of Ethical Principles of Social Work,* the social worker is obliged to recognize these standards of ethical conduct.

3.2 General Standards of Ethical Conduct

3.2.1 Seek to understand each individual client and the client system, and the elements which affect behavior and the service required.

3.2.2 Uphold and advance the values, knowledge and methodology of the profession, refraining from any behavior which damages the functioning of the profession.

3.2.3 Recognise professional and personal limitations.

3.2.4 Encourage the utilisation of all relevant knowledge and skills.

3.2.5 Apply relevant methods in the development and validation of knowledge.

3.2.6 Contribute professional expertise to the development of policies and programs which improve the quality of life in society.

3.2.7 Identify and interpret social needs.

3.2.8 Identify and interpret the basis and nature of individual, group, community, national, and international social problems.

3.2.9 Identify and interpret the work of the social work profession.

3.2.10 Clarify whether public statements are made or actions performed on an individual basis or as representative of a professional association, agency or organization, or other group.

3.3 Social Work Standards Relative to Clients

3.3.1 Accept primary responsibility to identified clients, but within limitations set by the ethical claims of others.

3.3.2 Maintain the client's right to a relationship of trust, to privacy and confidentiality and to responsible use of information. The collection and sharing of information or data is related to the professional service function with the client informed as to its necessity and use. No information is released without prior knowledge and informed consent of the client, except where the client cannot be responsible or others may be seriously jeopardized. A client has access to social work records concerning them.

3.3.3 Recognise and respect the individual goals, responsibilities, and differences of clients. Within the scope of the agency and the client's social milieu, the professional service shall assist clients to take responsibility for personal actions and help all clients with equal willingness. Where the professional service cannot be provided under such conditions the clients shall be so informed in such as way as to leave the clients free to act.

3.3.4 Help the client-individual, group, community, or society-to achieve self-fulfilment and maximum potential within the limits of the respective rights of others. The service shall be based upon helping the client to understand and use the professional relationship, in furtherance of the client's legitimate desires and interests.

3.4 Social Work Standards Relative to Agencies and Organizations

3.4.1 Work and/or cooperate with those agencies and organizations whose policies, procedures, and operations are directed toward adequate service delivery and encouragement of professional practice consistent with the ethical principles of the IFSW.

3.4.2 Responsibly execute the stated aims and functions of the agency or organizations, contributing to the development of sound policies, procedures, and practice in order to obtain the best possible standards or practice.

3.4.3 Sustain ultimate responsibility to the client, initiating desirable alterations of policies, procedures, and practice, through appropriate agency and organization channels. If necessary remedies are not achieved after channels have been exhausted, initiate appropriate appeals to higher authorities or the wider community of interest.

3.4.4 Ensure professional accountability to client and community for efficiency and effectiveness through periodic review of the process of service provision.

3.4.5 Use all possible ethical means to bring unethical practice to an end when policies, procedures and practices are in direct conflict with the ethical principles of social work.

3.5 Social Work Standards Relative to Colleagues

3.5.1 Acknowledge the education, training and performance of social work colleagues and professionals from other disciplines, extending all necessary co-operation that will enhance effective services.

3.5.2 Recognise differences of opinion and practice of social work colleagues and other professionals, expressing criticism through channels in a responsible manner.

3.5.3 Promote and share opportunities for knowledge, experience, and ideas with all social work colleagues, professionals from other disciplines and volunteers for the purpose of mutual improvement.

3.5.4 Bring any violations of professional ethics and standards to the attention of the appropriate bodies inside and outside the profession, and ensure that relevant clients are properly involved.

3.5.5 Defend colleagues against unjust actions.

3.6 Standards Relative to the Profession

3.6.1 Maintain the values, ethical principles, knowledge and methodology of the profession and contribute to their clarification and improvement.

3.6.2 Uphold the professional standards of practice and work for their advancement.

3.6.3 Defend the profession against unjust criticism and work to increase confidence in the necessity for professional practice.

3.6.4 Present constructive criticism of the profession, its theories, methods and practices.

3.6.5 Encourage new approaches and methodologies needed to meet new and existing needs.

Adopted by the IFSW General Meeting, Colombo, Sri Lanka, July 6–8, 1994.

U.N. Summit for Social Development— Ten Commitments

1. We commit ourselves to creating an economic, political, social, cultural and legal environment that will enable people to achieve social development.

2. We commit ourselves to the goal of eradicating poverty in the world, through decisive national actions and international cooperation, as an ethical, social, political and economic imperative of humankind.

3. We commit ourselves to promoting the goal of full employment as a basic priority of our economic and social policies, and to enabling all men and women to attain secure and sustainable livelihoods through freely chosen productive employment and work.

4. We commit ourselves to promoting social integration by fostering societies that are stable, safe and just and that are based on the promotion and protection of all human rights, as well as on non-discrimination, tolerance, respect for diversity, equality of opportunity, solidarity, security and participation of all people, including disadvantaged and vulnerable groups and persons.

5. We commit ourselves to promoting full respect for human dignity and to achieving equality and equity between women and men, and to recognizing and enhancing the participation and leadership roles of women in political, civil, economic, social and cultural life and in development.

6. We commit ourselves to promoting and attaining the goals of universal and equitable access to quality education, the highest attainable standard of physical and mental health and the access of all to primary health care, making particular efforts to rectify inequalities relating to social conditions and without distinction as to race, national origin, gender, age or disability, respecting and promoting our common and particular cultures; striving to strengthen the role of culture in development; preserving the essential bases of people-centered sustainable development; and contributing to the full development of human resources and to social development. The purpose of these activities is to eradicate poverty, promote full and productive employment and foster social integration.

7. We commit ourselves to accelerating the economic, social and human resource development of Africa and the least developed countries.

United Nations, (1995). *The Copenhagen Declaration and Programme of Action.* World Summit for Social Development. 6–12 March 1995. New York: Author.

8. We commit ourselves to ensuring that when structural adjustment programmes are agreed to they include social development goals, in particular eradicating poverty, promoting full and productive employment and enhancing social integration.

9. We commit ourselves to increasing significantly and/or utilizing more efficiently the resources allocated to social development in order to achieve the goals of the Summit through national action and regional and international cooperation.

10. We commit ourselves to an improved and strengthened framework for international, regional and subregional cooperation for social development, in a spirit of partnership,through the United Nations and other multilateral institutions.

Milestones in the International History of Social Work Around the World

1856 European International Conference on Charity and Welfare initiated.

1861 International Red Cross founded in Switzerland.

1869 Charity Organization Society founded in London.

1873 Octavia Hill conducts first training programs for social workers in England.

1877 Charity Organization Society begins in Buffalo, New York.

1884 Toynbee Hall opens in London.

1889 Hull House opens in Chicago.

1895 First paid employed social worker, Mary Stewart, is hired by the Royal Free Hospital in London.

1898 A 6-week summer training course for social workers in held in New York.

1899 The first school of social work in the world is opened in Amsterdam. The Institute for Social Work Training offered a full 2-year course, including fieldwork.

   A training course for young women interested in social work is organized in Germany by Alice Salomon.

1903 The School of Sociology, a 2-year social work course, grows out of the London Charity Organization Society trainings.

1904 The New York School of Philanthropy is founded (later to become the Columbia University School of Social Work).

1908 First school of social work in Germany is founded by Alice Salomon.

1909 Social workers from several countries meet at the International Congress of Women in Canada.

1915 Jane Addams attends the Women's Peace Conference at The Hague and then travels to Berlin to meet with the german chancellor in an attempt to convince him to end World War I hostilities. Other delegates travel to other capitals involved in the war of nations.

1917 *Social Diagnosis* by Mary Richmond is published. The book has a significant impact on the professionalization of social work in Europe as well as the United States.

1919 Save the Children Fund is founded by Eglantyne Jebb in England.

   The International Labor Organization (ILO) is founded under the auspices of the League of Nations. It is the oldest of the UN specialized agencies.

1921   International Migration Service is founded with headquarters in Geneva and New York. It is later renamed International Social Service.

Ida Pruitt begins medical social work services in a hospital in Beijing, China.

1922   Social work training is started in a new sociology department at Yanjing University in Beijing, with the assistance of Princeton University.

1924   The Declaration on the Rights of the Child, authored by Eglantyne Jebb, is adopted by the League of Nations.

The first school of social work in Africa is opened at the University of Cape Town in South Africa.

1925   The first school of social work in Latin America is opened in Santiago, Chile.

The Training School for Social Work is founded at the Free University of Poland in Warsaw by Madame Helene Radlinska.

1926   Nagpada Neighborhood House, a settlement house, is opened in Bombay, India, by Dr. Clifford Manshardt.

1928   The First International Conference of Social Work is held in Paris.

The International Conference of Social Work (ICSW) and the International Permanent Secretariat of Social Workers, predecessor to the IFSW, are founded.

1929   The International Association of Schools of Social Work is formed with 46 member schools in 10 countries (although it originated through the 1928 conference).

1931   Jane Addams is awarded the Nobel Peace Prize.

1932   Alice Salomon is awarded the Silver Medal for Merit to the State by the Prussian Cabinet, and the School she founded is named the Alice Salomon School of Social Work.

1936   The Tata Institute of Social Sciences is founded in Bombay, the first school of social work in India.

Egypt opens its first school of social work in Cairo.

1937   The first International Survey of Social Work Education is published. The survey is conducted by Alice Salomon and funded by the Russell Sage Foundation.

Alice Salomon, stripped of all honors and her name removed from the school of social work, is expelled from Germany by the Gestapo and begins life in exile in New York.

1938   The Moyne Commission, set up as a result of unrest in Jamaica, leads to expansion of social welfare and community development in the then British West Indies.

1939   The first technical assistance program of the U.S. government brings social work educators from Latin America to the United States for training.

1939–46 All international meetings of social workers are suspended, including the 4th International Conference planned for 1940.

1941   The Jan H. Hofmeyr School of Social Work is established in South Africa, the first school of social work for South African nonwhites.

1943   United Nations Relief and Rehabilitation Administration (UNRRA) is founded by 44 nations to solve the relief needs of the 35 countries invaded by Axis powers in World War II.

1944–47 Many social workers contribute to relief efforts in Europe and China through the UNRRA.

1945   The United Nations is founded with 51 nations as members of the General Assembly.

The World Health Organization (WHO) is established at the request of Brazil at the founding convention of the UN.

1946   UNICEF is founded.

1948   The UN adopts the Universal Declaration of Human Rights.

1950   First United Nations Survey of Social Work Education is published, authored by Katherine Kendall.

1952   Social work and other social sciences are abolished as fields of study in the People's Republic of China.

1955   Second UN Survey of Social Work Education is published.

1958   *Training for Social Work: Third International Survey* is published by the UN. A landmark study, it explored the nature of social work and was authored by Eileen Younghusband.

1962   U.S. Council on Social Work Education adopts a curriculum policy statement requiring students to gain knowledge of international issues.

1963–68 U.S. Department of State appoints social welfare attachés to the U.S. embassies in Brazil (Mary Catherine Jennings) and India (Ruby Pernell).

1968   The United Nations International Conference of Ministers Responsible for Social Welfare is held.

1969   The UN adopts the Convention on the Elimination of All Forms of Racial Discrimination.

1971   The Fifth Survey of Social Work Education is published by the UN.

1976   The International Code of Ethics is adopted by the International Federation of Social Workers at its meeting in Puerto Rico.

1977–78 The Inter-University Consortium for International Social Development is founded (date uncertain).

1979   The UN adopts the Convention on the Elimination of All Forms of Discrimination Against Women.

1980s   Social Work reestablished in China and parts of Eastern Europe.

1987   The UN Interregional Consultation on Developmental Social Welfare Policy and Programmes is held in Vienna, Austria.

1988   IFSW publishes a set of policy papers for social work on global issues.

1989   The UN adopts the Convention on the Rights of the Child.

1994   *Human Rights and Social Work: A Manual for Schools of Social Work and the Social Work Profession* is published by the United Nations. It is the result of an IFSW/IASSW/UN project.

A Revised Code of Ethical Principles is adopted by IFSW at its meeting in Sri Lanka.

1995   The World Summit for Social Development is held in Copenhagen, Denmark.

1996   IFSW issues a policy statement on Human Rights.

2000   IFSW adopts a new definition of social work.

Glossary of Terms and Abbreviations

AASW American Association of Social Workers; one of the predecessor organizations to NASW

ACF Administration for Children and Families (within DHHS)

AFSC American Friends Service Committee

AID Agency for International Development; the foreign assistance agency of the US government

Bilateral aid aid given from a donor country directly to a recipient country

CARE Cooperative for American Relief Everywhere; a U.S.-based relief and development NGO, now known only by its acronym

CASW Canadian Association of Social Workers

CEDAW Convention on the Elimination of All Forms of Discrimination Against Women

CIDA Canadian International Development Agency; the foreign assistance agency of the Canadian government

CIP Council of International Programs

COS Charity Organization Society

CRC Convention on the Rights of the Child

CSWE Council on Social Work Education; professional association for social work education in the United States

DAWN Development Alternatives With Women for a New Era (based in Barbados)

DCF Department of Children and Families (an agency of the State of Connecticut, U.S.A.)

Debt service interest and principal due on a loan

Devaluation lowering the value of a country's currency relative to other world currencies

DHEW Department of Health, Education and Welfare; former agency of the U.S. government, it has been divided into DHHS and the Department of Education

DHHS Department of Health and Human Services, US government agency

DHR Division for Humanitarian Response (Save the Children's relief division)

ECOSOC Economic and Social Council (UN)

ERASMUS a program initiated by the EU in 1987 that funded faculty and student exchanges and other activities among educational institutions in the EU countries; the program was in effect for a decade and was intended to contribute to professional mobility and to development of a European perspective

EU European Union

FAO Food and Agriculture Organization (UN)

GDP gross domestic product

GGLS Group Guaranteed Lending and Savings

GNP gross national product

Grameen Bank an NGO based in Bangladesh well known for its microcredit programs

HDI Human Development Index (UNDP's index of progress on human well-being)

IASSW International Association of Schools of Social Work

IBRD International Bank for Reconstruction; part of the World Bank Group

ICSW International Council on Social Welfare

ICVA International Council of Voluntary Agencies

IDA International Development Association; part of the World Bank Group

IFSW International Federation of Social Workers

ILO International Labor Organization

IMF International Monetary Fund

Indigenization the process of adapting ideas, materials, or innovations to make them culturally relevant or of creating indigenous forms that address needs, resources, and culture of a specific country or people

Infant mortality rate annual number of deaths of infants under the age of 1 year per 1,000 live births

InterAction a coaliation of more than 150 U.S. based relief and development NGOs

ISS International Social Service

IUCISD Inter-University Consortium for International Social Development

Maternal mortality rate annual number of deaths due to pregnancy or child-birth per 100,000 live births

M&E monitoring and evaluation

Multilateral aid aid provided by contributions of multiple donor countries through an international organization to various recipient countries

NASW National Association of Social Workers; the largest professional association for social workers in the United States

NGO nongovernmental organization

NIC newly industrialized country

Nonaligned a term from the cold war era to refer to countries that were not strongly allied to either the United States, Britain, or their allies or to the Soviet bloc

North roughly geographical, but, more relevantly, a political term referring to industrialized or developed countries (see South)

ODA official development assistance

OECD Organization of Economic Cooperation and Development; comprised of the world's most industrialized/developed countries, its aim is to encourage economic cooperation

OPEC Organization of Petroleum Exporting Countries

ORR Office of Refugee Resettlement; part of DHHS

PLAN an NGO focusing on programs for children; formerly known as Foster Parents Plan International

PVO private voluntary organization; a term largely interchangeable with NGO

Rapporteur An official appointed to gather information on a specific topic, usually for a limited period of time. The Special Rapporteur on Violence Against Women, for example, was appointed by the UN Commission on Human Rights to report on cases of violence against women

Remittances funds sent by migrants back to family or others in their countries of origin

Repatriation sending refugees back to their countries of origin

SC Save the Children; an international NGO focusing on programs for children

SCI Sara Communication Initiative

SILIC Severely indebted low-income country

Social exclusion a condition of economic and social marginality

SOCRATES funding program of the EU that replaced ERASMUS in 1997; it also funds exchange but places more emphasis on institutional relationships and less on student mobility

South roughly geographical, but, more relevantly, a political term referring to developing countries (see North)

Structural adjustment a set of policies imposed as conditions of international loans that require a country to restructure its economy (Policies usually include privatization, lower government spending, reduction or elimination of subsidies, and, sometimes, currency devaluation.)

Sustainability the preservation of future capacity for development

TEMPUS similar to the ERASMUS program; TEMPUS funded exchanges between institutions in the EU and those in the countries of the former Soviet Union and Eastern Europe

TOT training of trainers

UN United Nations

UNAIDS joint UN program on HIV/AIDS; comprised of six UN agencies: UNICEF, UNDP, UNFPA, UNESCO, WHO and the World Bank Group

UNCTAD UN Conference on Trade and Development

UNDP UN Development Program

UNESCO UN Educational, Scientific and Cultural Organization

UNFPA UN Fund for Population Activities

UNHCR UN High Commission for Refugees

UNICEF UN Children's Fund

UNIFEM UN Development Fund for Women; has a relationship termed *autonomous association* with UNDP

UNRRA UN Relief and Rehabilitation Administration

USAID U.S. Agency for International Development—see AID

USIA U.S. Information Agency

WCI Woman/Child Impact

WHO World Health Organization

YMCA Young Men's Christian Association

YWCA Young Women's Christian Association

Index